THE GHOST FESTIVAL
IN MEDIEVAL CHINA

目連七月十五日。是眾僧解夏
之日。歡喜俱會一處。用救汝母
當生淨土目連即依佛勅。市買
楊業栢枝造得盂蘭盆齋得娘
離狗身。目連娘於佛前受五百
戒願娘捨邪心歸正道感得天
母。來迎接得娘生忉利天宮受
諸快樂當揚說法度脫眾生若

THE GHOST FESTIVAL
IN MEDIEVAL CHINA

BY

Stephen F. Teiser

PRINCETON

UNIVERSITY PRESS

Copyright © 1988 by Princeton University Press
Published by Princeton University Press, 41 William Street,
Princeton, New Jersey 08540
In the United Kingdom: Princeton University Press, Chichester, West Sussex

Library of Congress Cataloging-in-Publication Data
Teiser, Stephen F.
The ghost festival in China.
Bibliography: p.   Includes index.
1. Ullambana.   2. Memorial rites and ceremonies, Buddhist—China.   3. Yü lan p'en ching—
Criticism, interpretation, etc.   4. Moggallāna.   5. Pretas (Buddhism)   I. Title.

ISBN 0-691-05525-4
ISBN 0-691-02677-7 (pbk.)

This book has been composed in Linotron Bembo

Princeton University Press books are printed on acid-free paper and meet the guidelines
for permanence and durability of the Committee on Production Guidelines for Book
Longevity of the Council on Library Resources

Second printing, and first paperback printing, 1996

Printed in the United States of America
by Princeton Academic Press

1 3 5 7 9 10 8 6 4 2

Frontispiece: Mu-lien administering the precepts to his mother in front of the Buddha and the
assembly of monks. Section from a Japanese scroll dated 1346, thought to be based on a
thirteenth-century Chinese scripture. Photograph by permission of the Kyoto temple,
Konkōji, and courtesy of the Tokyo National Research Institute of Cultural Properties.

To S. A. T.
   C. J. R.
   G. S. R.

Contents

CONTENTS

CONTENTS

Preface

EVEN A BRIEF EXPERIENCE of the ghost festival leaves an impression of spirited diversity. My own encounter with the annual celebration began in Taiwan on September 5, 1979, when string after string of firecrackers punctuated an already fitful night of sleep. All month long hungry ghosts had been wandering the earth, released from their usual torments in the dark regions of hell to visit their families, who welcomed their own kin but warded off stranger ghosts with noisemakers and smoke. The festivities reached their peak the next day, the fifteenth (also the full moon) of the seventh lunar month. A former teacher took me on a visit to a small Buddhist temple called "The Linked Clouds Meditation Hall" (Lien-yün ch'an-yüan) in Taipei. The temple was staffed by a score of nuns, who had just the day before concluded their summer meditation retreat. People streamed in and out of the small chapel all morning. Some joined the nuns in reciting Buddhist scriptures (sūtras), some commissioned prayer slips dedicating merit to their ancestors, while others simply burned incense, offered a short prayer, and left.

Fixing the shape of the festival subsequently proved to be a curious task. In tracing the smoke of the ghost festival back to its hazy origins in early medieval China, I uncovered a surprising abundance of sources: canonical sūtras proclaiming the origins of the ghost festival; picture tales narrating the adventures of a fearless ascetic named Mu-lien, who rescued his mother from purgatory; poems and rhapsodies echoing a Taoist cosmology; other sources attesting to the roles played by monks and merchants, emperors and common folk in the celebration of the seventh moon. These documents left no doubt that the symbolism, rituals, and mythology of the ghost festival pervaded the entire social landscape of medieval China.

Yet I also discovered that the dispersion of the festival throughout Chinese society remained unexplored in modern scholarship and almost unmentioned in traditional historiography. Understanding the causes of this vacuum helped directly in overcoming it. The outstanding majority of sources for the history of Chinese religion were produced by people who shared an "institutional" bias, either as officials and would-be officials predisposed against the Buddhist church or as history-writing monks who emphasized the canonical beginnings and orderly teleology of the services held within temple walls. In either case the "diffused" nature of Chinese religion and of the ghost festival—its vitality in a broad range of social contexts that we would not usually identify as distinctively "religious"—was systematically denied.

As a complex symbolic event, the festival drew together every social class and expressed a challenging blend of values. The myths of the ghost festival were not defined in any single authoritative text or canon, nor were its ritual forms limited to a particular context. In light of this diversity, largely suppressed in previous studies, my analysis uses the festival as a focus of widely held values. It is only with such a focus that the multiple meanings that the festival assumed for a broad range of people in medieval China begin to appear.

The "theory" in this book will not be found apart from the narrative used to document, and to construct, the "facts." The concerns that gave rise to this study are located in the eclecticism that dominates poststructuralist inquiry in a host of fields (history, anthropology, literary theory) outside of Sinology and Buddhist studies. To define the many manifestations of the ghost festival I have drawn upon a number of disciplines. In addition to the standard Sinological and Buddhological tools, I have found anthropological concepts especially helpful for the light they cast on several topics that preoccupy the historian of religion: shamanism and monasticism, class and kinship, myth and ritual. My account attempts to wed some of these global considerations to the distinctive tonalities of the Chinese case.

The first part of this book is more narrowly concerned with the events that occurred annually on the fifteenth day of the seventh month in medieval China. Chapter Two examines the indigenous antecedents to the ghost festival, Indic models for the monastic meditation retreat, and the early history of Taoist-sponsored celebrations. Chapter Three, the longest chapter, is an episodic presentation of all evidence relevant to the ghost festival in medieval times. Chronologically arranged, it records the spread of the festival in all of its forms throughout Chinese society. It includes translations of a broad range of texts—canonical and apocryphal sūtras, commentaries and lecture texts, liturgies, diary entries, poetry and prose pieces, oral tales, historical accounts—and it describes in detail several of the better documented celebrations. Focusing on discrete events and specific texts, this chapter illustrates the many meanings that the ghost festival assumed for different segments of T'ang society.

A more synthetic and synchronic analysis is presented in Chapters Four through Seven, which explore the significance of the ghost festival against the background of Chinese religion and society. Each chapter addresses a particular aspect of medieval Chinese religion: mythology, shamanism, cosmology, and family religion. Each chapter may be seen as answering from a single perspective the question of how the ghost festival became so widespread in Chinese society. Taken together, the later chapters also offer the beginnings of an interpretive history of Chinese religion.

In translating from the Chinese, I have attempted to follow the medieval Chinese interpretation of the text in question, a task that is complicated by the large number of foreign words in medieval Chinese literature. In general, I have tried to make my English version appear to a modern English-speaking audience as the Chinese version appeared to a medieval Chinese audience. For the most part, words transliterated from the Sanskrit that sound foreign to the Chinese ear I have likewise rendered as foreign (Sanskrit) words in English translation. As for poetry, I regret that my attempts at translation never convey the rhyme and seldom reflect the meter of the original.

Acknowledgments

LIKE OTHER RITES of passage, authoring a book affirms one's place in a broader community. The labor of this particular study would not have been possible without the contributions of a number of people, and I would like to express my heartfelt thanks to some of them.

Even if this book were not about filial piety, I would still begin by registering my gratitude to my parents. Their loving support sustained me through the long course of training and casting about required before this particular project could begin. Likewise, Virginia Jackson has for several years been a source of inspiration and sustenance. Her own sacrifices allowed me several stretches of uninterrupted work, while her poet's eye made its gaze felt throughout the writing and rewriting of this book.

Portions of this work are based on my doctoral dissertation, submitted to the Departments of Religion and East Asian Studies at Princeton University, where many members of the faculty shared unstintingly their knowledge and expertise. Alan Sponberg's contributions as a Buddhologist and critical thinker have proven especially enriching. Denis Twitchett served as an invaluable guide to the complexity of medieval Chinese society as well as to the sources one uses to imagine that society. I would also like to thank the professional staff of Gest Oriental Library, especially Diane Perushek, Min-chih Chou, and Soowon Kim, who gave generously of their time and skills.

I was fortunate to receive the assistance of three eminent scholars of T'ang civilization who shared their wisdom at the beginning stages of this project. Raoul Birnbaum, Victor Mair, and John McRae read and commented upon early drafts of several chapters, and I am grateful for their criticisms and encouragement. Portions of this work were delivered in 1985 and 1986 as lectures at the University of California at Los Angeles, Harvard University, and Princeton University, where audiences provided helpful comments and questions. The responses of students enrolled in my courses at Middlebury College also helped in formulating some of the broader points made in these pages.

Producing this book has proven to be an uncommon pleasure, thanks to the readers of the original manuscript and above all to the skilled editorial hands of Margaret Case at Princeton University Press. Help provided by other friends and associates in the form of general criticisms, philological expertise, hospitality, and mirth I can only note

ACKNOWLEDGMENTS

in passing: Leslie Daniels, Lorraine Fuhrmann, Howard Goodman, Peter Gregory, Helen Hardacre, Hai-chün Huang, Donald Lopez, Jacob Meskin, Peter Patel, Willard Peterson, Alexander Steiner, Hai-t'ao T'ang, Kyoko Tokuno, and Timothy Tsu. The encouragement and corrections offered by these people and others too numerous to name have saved me from countless errors of fact and expression. I alone am responsible for whatever shortcomings remain.

Abbreviations

BEFEO	*Bulletin de l'Ecole Française d'Extrême-Orient*
CWTTT	*Chung-wen ta tz'u-tien*
HJAS	*Harvard Journal of Asiatic Studies*
HR	*History of Religions*
IBK	*Indogaku bukkyōgaku kenkyū*
JA	*Journal Asiatique*
JAOS	*Journal of the American Oriental Society*
JAS	*Journal of Asian Studies*
MBDJ	Mochizuki, *Bukkyō dai jiten*
MDKJ	Morohashi, *Dai kanwa jiten*
OBDJ	Oda, *Bukkyō dai jiten*
P.	Fonds manuscrit de Tun-houang Pelliot
Peking	Peking collection of Tun-huang manuscripts
PWYF	*P'ei-wen yün-fu*
S.	Stein collection of Tun-huang manuscripts
T.	*Taishō shinshū daizōkyō*
TFTT	Ting, *Fo-hsüeh ta tz'u-tien*
THPT	*Tun-huang pao-tsang*
THPWC	*Tun-huang pien-wen chi*
TP	*T'oung Pao*
TT.	*Tao-tsang*
Z.	*Dai nihon zoku zōkyō*
ZS.	*Dai nihon bukkyō zensho*

THE GHOST FESTIVAL

IN MEDIEVAL CHINA

ONE

Introduction

The Spread of the Ghost Festival

IN THE SEVENTH MONTH of 840, the Japanese pilgrim Ennin (793–864) made his way southwest from Mount Wu-t'ai (in present-day Shansi) toward the T'ang capital of Ch'ang-an. His journal entry for the fifteenth of the month describes a busy scene in the metropolitan prefecture of T'ai-yüan:

> Fifteenth day. On the invitation of the head of Ssu-chung ssu, we went with the mendicants to their temple for the forenoon feast. After the feast we entered Tu-t'o ssu and performed the yü-lan-p'en service and then went to the prefectural [headquarters] to see the Dragon Spring. Next we went to Ch'ung-fu ssu and paid reverence. In all of the Buddha halls, pavilions, and cloisters were arrayed displays; their radiant colors dazzled people, and their offerings were splendorous. Everyone in the city had come out to perform the ritual tour. At twilight [the monks] released themselves [in repentance].[1]

The residents of T'ai-yüan converged on Ch'ung-fu ssu to take part in the ghost festival, which in T'ang times was most frequently called by its Buddhist name of "yü-lan-p'en." The festival combined the interests of monks, householders, and ancestors in an annual celebration of renewal. Most residents of the city, laypeople with no exclusive religious affiliation, provided for the salvation of their ancestors by making offerings to the monastic community (the Sangha). By donating gifts to the Buddhist establishment donors produced a stock of merit that was dedicated to their forebears, who received the benefits in the form of a better rebirth and a more comfortable existence in the heavens or hells of the other world.

In fact, it is probably the tortuous conditions of life in purgatory that

[1] *Nittō guhō junrei gyōki*, in Ono Katsutoshi, *Nittō guhō junrei gyōki no kenkyū*, 4 vols. (Tokyo: Suzuki gakujutsu zaidan, 1964–69), 3:173, usually following Ono's translation and annotation, 3:173–76; cf. Edwin O. Reischauer, trans., *Ennin's Diary: The Record of a Pilgrimage to China in Search of the Law* (New York: Ronald Press Co., 1955), pp. 268–69.

3

give the festival its odd-sounding name of yü-lan-p'en (Middle Chinese "wuǎ lan bwən").[2] In Chinese the term fails to make literal sense, and for over a millennium most native speakers have assumed that the term derives from a foreign word transliterated into Chinese sounds. In the popular understanding, "yü-lan" is a foreign word describing the pitiable fate of those hanging upside-down in the subterranean prisons of hell, while "p'en" is the Chinese word indicating a bowl or tray in which offerings are placed. Thus, "yü-lan-p'en" is usually taken to mean the "bowl" in which are placed offerings to monks given with the intention of rescuing one's ancestors from the fate of "hanging upside-down" in hell.[3]

Offerings to monks were especially efficacious on the full moon of the seventh month, since this was the day on which the Sangha ended its three-month summer retreat. During this period monks abstained from contact with lay society and pursued an intensified regimen of meditation completed with the monastic ritual Ennin refers to as "releasing themselves," confession and repentance of their transgressions in front of fellow monks. Having accumulated ascetic energy in retreat, monks released it in communion with householders. Moreover, the festival was held just at the time of the autumn harvest. Thus the ghost festival not only marked the symbolic passage of monks and ancestors to new forms of existence, it also ushered in the completion of a cycle of plant life.

Coming at the juncture of the full moon, the new season, the fall harvest, the peak of monastic asceticism, the rebirth of ancestors, and the assembly of the local community, the ghost festival was celebrated on a broad scale by all classes of people throughout medieval Chinese society. Ennin reports great crowds of people, brightly colored decorations, and lavish offerings for north China in the year 840. The melding of the festival with traditional practices may be judged in Yin Yao-fan's (ca. 814) allusion to the age-old folk practice of divination. In a poem written on the occasion of the ghost festival he writes:

[2] I give Pulleyblank's reconstruction of the Early Middle Chinese; Edwin G. Pulleyblank, *Middle Chinese: A Study in Historical Phonology* (Vancouver: University of British Columbia Press, 1984). Karlgren's reconstruction in Ancient Chinese is "jiu lǎ b'uən," in Archaic Chinese, "*giwo glǎn b'wən"; Bernhard Karlgren, *Grammata Serica Recensa*, published in *Bulletin of the Museum of Far Eastern Antiquities* 29 (1957).

[3] The etymology of "yü-lan-p'en" is discussed at greater length below. The two earliest surviving commentaries on *The Yü-lan-p'en Sūtra* both follow the popular understanding; see *Yü-lan-p'en ching tsan-shu (Hui-ching Commentary)*, T. no. 2781, 85:540a; and *Yü-lan-p'en ching shu (Tsung-mi Commentary)*, T. no. 1792, 39:506c–7a.

Sweep off the altar and heaven and earth stand stern,
Toss the slips and ghosts and spirits jump startled.[4]

For south China, Tsung Lin's (ca. 498–561) account of yearly observances in the countryside describes the festive, even raucous atmosphere
of the celebration:

On the fifteenth day of the seventh month monks, nuns, religious,
and lay alike furnish bowls for offerings at the various temples and
monasteries. *The Yü-lan-p'en Sūtra* says that [these offerings] bring
merit covering seven generations, and the practice of sending
them with banners and flowers, singing and drumming, and food
probably derives from this. . . . later generations [of our time]
have expanded the ornamentation, pushing their skillful artistry to
the point of [offering] cut wood, carved bamboo, and pretty cuttings [of paper] patterned after flowers and leaves.[5]

Had the ghost festival been limited to a local cult phenomenon, it
would hardly be known to later history. Its ritual and material connections with the monastic community secured its place in Buddhist historiography, while its vital function in the ancestral cult and the local
community insured its survival into modern times. A further index of
the spread of the festival in China is supplied by the involvement of the
emperor and the state. For as many years as not during the T'ang dynasty, seventh-month offerings to both Buddhist and Taoist monks at
officially sanctioned temples in the capital cities and in the provinces
were supplied out of state coffers, with the benefits dedicated to everyone's ancestors. The most illustrious ancestors in the whole empire,
however, were honored and aided in the rituals performed privately by
the Son of Heaven. The ancestral tablets of previous emperors, kept in
the Imperial Ancestral Temple, were brought out, and offerings were
made to them in bowls decorated with golden kingfisher feathers. In
most years, after completing the ritual obligations to his ancestors, the
emperor then joined in the festivities at the larger temples of the city.
Te-tsung's (r. 779–805) reference to Chang-ching ssu as the "meditation bureau" in a poem of 791 illustrates well the integral place of religion, ritual, and politics in the imperial celebration of the ghost festival:

[4] Translation from Yin Yao-fan's poem, "On Watching Taoist Masters Pace the Void
on Chung-yüan," contained in *Ch'üan t'ang shih*, ed. P'eng Ting-ch'iu (1645–1719), 12
vols. (Taipei: Ching-wei shu-chü, 1965), p. 5566. On Yin see *T'ang ts'ai-tzu chuan*, Hsin
Wen-fang (ca. 1304) (Shanghai: Ku-tien wen-hsüeh ch'u-pan-she, 1957), pp. 97–98.
[5] See below, Chapter Three, for references and a full translation.

5

People from all over crowd the imperial city,
Lining the roads, forming many walls.

For the Dharma-feast meeting in early fall,
We drive out to visit the meditation bureau.[6]

The pervasiveness of the ghost festival in medieval Chinese society
went well beyond the multifaceted ritual of renewal celebrated
throughout the empire by emperors and the common folk. Myths connected with the festival gripped the imagination of medieval China,
finding expression in genres ranging from oral tales to canonical sūtras
written in the literary language.

Most people learned the story of the festival through the prosimetric
"transformation tales" (pien-wen) told by professional storytellers. Yü-
lan-p'en is the subject of the most famous of such popular entertainments in the T'ang, entitled The Transformation Text on Mu-lien Saving
His Mother from the Dark Regions. The transformation text follows a disciple of the Buddha named Mu-[chien-]lien (Sanskrit: Maudgalyāyana)
as he searches for his deceased parents. Mu-lien, the disciple of the
Buddha most adept at supernatural powers, uses his skills to try to find
his parents, first in the heavens and then in the hells. Having found his
father leading a comfortable life in Brahmā's Heaven, Mu-lien passes
through the gates of the Yellow Springs and proceeds into the underworld. Mu-lien is drawn deeper and deeper into the infernal regions in
search of his mother, named Ch'ing-t'i. The bureaucrat-gods whom he
encounters along the way treat him most courteously in recognition of
his prowess in mystical flight, but none of them know where his
mother has been reborn.

In style and substance The Transformation Text on Mu-lien Saving His
Mother draws a gruesomely entertaining and edifying picture of the underworld. The audience knows from the start that Ch'ing-t'i has been
reborn in the deepest of all hells, Avīci Hell, where she suffers retribution for her evil deeds in a previous life. The focus of the drama,
however, is on Mu-lien's journey, in the course of which the purgatorial hells of popular Chinese religion are described in terrifying detail.
Mu-lien meets the great King Yama, Ti-tsang (Skt.: Kṣitigarbha) Bodhisattva, the General of the Five Paths, messengers of the Magistrate of
Mount T'ai, and their numerous underlings. He shudders at the sight
of ox-headed gaolers forcing sinners across the great river running
through the underworld, and the prospect of people being forced to
embrace hot copper pillars that burn away their chests induces even

---

[6] See below, Chapter Three, for references and a translation of the entire poem.

greater trembling and trepidation. The tale is nearly at an end by the time Mu-lien locates Ch'ing-t'i in Avīci Hell, her body nailed down with forty-nine long metal spikes. At this point the Buddha intervenes, smashing down prison walls and releasing the denizens of hell to a higher rebirth.

It is also in the last few scenes of the tale that yü-lan-p'en enters explicitly into the story. Ch'ing-t'i has been reborn as a hungry ghost endowed with a ravenous appetite that she can never satisfy due to her needle-thin neck. In fact, Mu-lien tries to send her a food offering through the normal vehicle of the ancestral altar, but the food bursts into flame just as it reaches her mouth. To rescue her from this fate, the Buddha institutes the yü-lan-p'en festival: he instructs Mu-lien to provide a grand feast of "yü-lan bowls" on the fifteenth day of the seventh month, just as monks emerge from their summer retreat. The Buddha prescribes this same method of ancestral salvation for other filial sons to follow in future generations, and the story ends with Ch'ing-t'i's ascension to the heavens.

The myth related in other forms of medieval literature differs considerably from the popular tale. The tortures and torments, even the basic structure of hell, are absent in two sūtras accepted into the Chinese Buddhist canon, *The Sūtra on Offering Bowls to Repay Kindness* and *The Yü-lan-p'en Sūtra*. These sources make no mention of Mu-lien's shamanic flight or of Ch'ing-t'i's biography, focusing instead on the story of the founding of the festival by the historical Buddha. The Buddha's instructions for carrying out the ritual are given in great detail, with special emphasis on the role of monks as intermediaries between descendants and ancestors. The sūtras reflect the interests of a monastic and self-consciously Buddhist audience, legitimizing the offerings given in the seventh month by tracing them back to the authority of the Buddha.

The Yü-lan-p'en Sūtra was also a popular subject in the temple lectures that monks gave to interested lay people during the T'ang. Surviving portions of *The Lecture Text on the Yü-lan-p'en Sūtra* (ca. 850) expound at length upon the topic of filiality. The duties of sons toward their parents and the kindnesses bestowed by senior generations (especially mothers) upon juniors are also discussed in commentaries on *The Yü-lan-p'en Sūtra*, at least six of which were written prior to the eleventh century. Some commentators adopted a refined literary style to provide a close exegesis of the text, while others (notably Tsung-mi [780–841]) drew on the full range of traditional Chinese literature to demonstrate how the ghost festival fulfilled the basic ideals of Chinese religion.

7

Given the power with which the myth of Mu-lien and the ritual established after his example affected the shape of medieval Chinese religion, it is hardly surprising to find myths and rituals of the ghost festival persisting in other times and other places. The livelier versions of
the myth related in T'ang transformation texts became the subject of
numerous plays, morality books, and precious scrolls, all of which
supplied new genres for popular entertainment in early modern China.
By the time that sources allow a close look at local history it is clear that
the festival itself, long held in conjunction with services honoring the
"Middle Primordial" (chung-yüan) of the Taoist pantheon, had taken
on a great deal of local color. An early eighteenth-century compendium notes the diversity of names given to the seventh-moon festival:
"The Yü-lan Assembly" (yü-lan hui), "The Ghost Festival" (kuei-
chieh), "The Day [Honoring] the Middle Primordial" (chung-yüan jih),
"Releasing [Hungry Ghosts with] Burning Mouths" (fang yen-k'ou),
"The Universal Passage [of Hungry Ghosts Out of Hell]" (p'u-tu),
"Gathering Orphaned Souls" (ch'iang-ku), "Sending Grains" (sung ma-
ku), and "The Melon Festival" (kua-chieh). In some regions rituals were
performed in Buddhist and Taoist temples, in other regions at grave-
side, in clan halls, and inside or outside the home. In addition to the
gifts given to the Sangha, offerings included grain, melons, and other
first fruits of the harvest, cakes, rice, wine, incense, sheep, and mock
sheep made from flour. In some places paper money and paper horses
were sent by fire to the ancestors, while in other places (especially south
China) lanterns were set adrift in boats.[7] In modern times the festival
may be found in some form or another in every area of Chinese influence, from the sembahjang hantu ritual in Java to the p'u-tu rite in Hawaii.[8]

Mu-lien's legacy is also evident in greater East Asia, whence the
ghost festival traveled from China in medieval times. The legend of
Mu-lien emerges at the very beginning of Korean prose literature in the
fifteenth-century collection Wŏrin sŏkpo.[9] Records of seasonal observances in Korea from the late eighteenth century report two kinds of cel-

[7] See the collation of notices from local gazetteers in (Ch'in-ting) Ku-chin t'u-shu chi-
ch'eng (completed 1725), ed. Ch'en Meng-lei et al., 100 vols. (Taipei: Wen-hsing shu-
tien, 1964), 3:692–94.

[8] For Java, see Claudine Lombard-Salmon, "Survivance d'un rite bouddhique à Java:
la cérémonie du pu-du (avalambana)," BEFEO 62 (1975):457–86. For Hawaii, see Duane
Pang, "The P'u-tu Ritual," in Buddhist and Taoist Studies I, ed. Michael Saso and David
W. Chappell, Asian Studies at Hawaii, No. 18 (Honolulu: University Press of Hawaii,
1977), pp. 95–122.

[9] See Minn Yong-gyu, "Wŏrin sŏkpo che isip-sam chan'gwŏn," Tongbang hakchi 6 (June
1963):1–18.

ebration held on the fifteenth day of the seventh month: one called *paek-chong il* ("The Day on Which One Hundred Kinds [of Food Are Offered to the Buddha]"), and one called *mang-hon il* ("Lost Souls' Day"), in which people offer fruit, wine, and other foods to the souls of their deceased relatives.[10]

Further to the east, yü-lan-p'en (as *urabon, obon,* or *bon*) had become a part of court Buddhism in Japan as early as 606, and on the fifteenth day of the seventh month of 659 historical records relate that, "By a decree to the ministers, the Empress had *The Yü-lan-p'en Sūtra* expounded in all the temples of the capital to repay [the kindness bestowed by] seven generations of ancestors."[11] Temple records preserved in the Imperial Repository (Shōsōin) at Nara provide tantalizing glimpses of the actual administration of urabon. An inventory from Daianji dated 747 itemizes the money in different accounts: out of a total amount of 6,473,832 cash belonging to the temple, the holdings of the urabon account came to 17,510 cash.[12] Other documents establish that the seventh month was indeed a busy time for scribes in the temples of the Japanese capital in the eighth century, with the worst rush coming between the twelfth and sixteenth of the month, when fresh copies of *The Yü-lan-p'en Sūtra* and *The Sūtra on Offering Bowls to Repay Kindness* were in heavy demand.[13] In Japanese literature the story of Mu-lien's experiences in hell went through numerous transformations in a variety of genres, including the collection of Indian, Chinese, and Japanese tales compiled in 1407 by the monk Gentō, *Sangoku denki (Recorded Tales from Three Countries).*[14] At the local level, the festival flourishes in contemporary Japan, where everything comes to a halt in the seventh month so that people can return home in time to perform the

[10] See the eighteenth-century chronicle *Tongguk sesigi* by Hong Sŏng-mo, translated in Kan Jie'on [Kang Chae-ŏn], *Chōsen saijiki,* Tōyō bunko, Vol. 193 (Tokyo: Heibonsha, 1971), pp. 123–24.

[11] In the year 606, feasts were held on 4/8 (the traditional observance of the Buddha's birthday) and on 7/15; see *Nihon shoki,* Nihon koten bungaku taikei, Vols. 67–68 (Tokyo: Iwanami shoten, 1967, 1965), 2:187. The notice for the year 659 is translated from *Nihon shoki,* 2:341; following William G. Aston, trans., *Nihongi: Chronicles of Japan from the Earliest Times to A.D. 697,* 2 vols. (Rutland: Charles E. Tuttle Co., 1972), 2:263.

[12] "Daianji shizai chō," reproduced in Ishida Mosaku, *Shakyō yori mitaru nara-chō bukkyō no kenkyū,* Tōyō bunko ronsō, Vol. 11 (Tokyo: Tōyō bunko, 1930), pp. 64–65.

[13] See documents dated 743 and 763, respectively, in *Dai nihon komonjo, hennen monjo,* ed. Tokyo teikoku daigaku shiryō hensanjo (Tokyo: Tokyo teikoku daigaku, 1901–40), 8:190–91 and 5:451–52.

[14] See *Sangoku denki,* Gentō (ca. 1407), 2 vols., ed. Ikegami Jun'ichi (Tokyo: Miyai shoten, 1976–82), 1:122–29. For a survey of Japanese legends of Mu-lien, see Iwamoto Yutaka, *Bukkyō setsuwa kenkyū,* Vol. 4, *Jigoku meguri no bungaku* (Tokyo: Kaimei shoten, 1979), pp. 50–170.

"Dance of Bon" (*bon odori*). One observer reports from a village not far
from Tokyo:

> Then, the counterpart of the mid-winter New Year's holiday, one
> of the two yearly Settlement Days when one paid off debts and
> gave servants their wages, there was the mid-summer Bon holi-
> day, the All Souls festival at the August full moon when for two
> or three nights running there would be dancing; the outside circle
> this way, the inner one that, round and round the frantic drum-
> mers, Kanejirō's buxom widow blooming in the atmosphere of
> sexual excitement and everyone conscious of the electric charges
> between Sanetoshi's eldest and Kentarō's girl every time the cir-
> cles brought them together—and the young men jumping into the
> drummers' circle to take their show-off turn at singing, each
> vying to outdo the last in voice-power and intricate tremolos. [15]

THE SIGNIFICANCE OF THE GHOST FESTIVAL

Setting aside for the moment its legacy in East Asian religion, a strong
case can be made for the importance of the ghost festival merely on the
basis of its diffusion through the entire fabric of medieval Chinese society. Its pervasiveness during a period in which relatively little is
known about Chinese life—the social life of the vast majority of people
left largely unrecorded in the surviving corpus of historical sources
compiled by scholar-bureaucrats—makes it an important area of study
in the first place simply as a story yet untold. The French historian
Jacques Gernet describes the tremendous gap in current knowledge of
medieval Chinese religion:

> Devotional activities pose a basic and wide-ranging problem, that
> of the assimilation of Buddhism by the Chinese world's forms of
> religious life. Neither the philosophical and doctrinal borrowings
> nor even the half-fearful veneration of the semi-barbarian mon-
> archs of North China for wonder-working monks suffice to ex-
> plain the general impulse of intense fervour felt by the Chinese
> world from the end of the fifth century onwards. In short they do
> not explain how Buddhism became in China a great *religion*. There
> took place at the level of local cults and communities a subterra-
> nean activity about which very little is known. The results alone
> were to emerge into the light when Buddhism had become a

[15] Ronald P. Dore, *Shinohata: A Portrait of a Japanese Village* (New York: Pantheon
Books, 1978), pp. 223–24.

Chinese religion with its priesthood, its faithful, and its places of worship.[16]

The story of the "subterranean activity" of the ghost festival told here is limited mostly to the medieval period, typically thought to commence in the third century and to merge indistinctly into "early modern" China in the ninth or tenth. While social historians are still far from agreement over the nature of the social, economic, and political changes that occurred toward the end of the period,[17] there is a consensus that from the third to the eighth centuries Chinese society was composed largely of two classes: peasants bound to the land they worked and members of endogamous aristocracies from whose ranks government officials invariably came. Agriculture and landholding were organized around a manorial system; theoretically the government distributed land to each family of the empire, but in practice land came to be concentrated in estates belonging to powerful clans and to the Buddhist church. Beginning in the ninth and tenth centuries, this structure began to change. A money economy came into existence, and with it there developed a mercantile class based in the cities. In the countryside, different forms of land tenancy also evolved which, together with the emergence of an urban middle class, contributed to the dissolution of the medieval family system. Social mobility also increased with the democratization of examinations for government service, the development of printing, and a broadening of the system of public education.

The study of the ghost festival undertaken here focuses especially on the T'ang dynasty (618–907). Most of the documents I have been able to unearth on the early ghost festival date from this dynasty, and the

[16] Jacques Gernet, *A History of Chinese Civilization*, trans. J. R. Foster (Cambridge: Cambridge University Press, 1982), p. 215.

[17] Among a mountain of studies, see especially: Patricia Buckley Ebrey, *The Aristocratic Families of Early Imperial China: A Case Study of the Po-ling Ts'ui Family* (Cambridge: Cambridge University Press, 1978); Mark Elvin, *The Pattern of the Chinese Past* (Stanford: Stanford University Press, 1973); David Johnson, *The Medieval Chinese Oligarchy* (Boulder: Westview Press, 1977); Joseph P. McDermott, "Charting Blank Spaces and Disputed Regions: The Problem of Sung Land Tenure," JAS 44:1 (November 1984):13–41; Edwin G. Pulleyblank, *The Background of the Rebellion of An Lu-shan* (Oxford: Oxford University Press, 1955); Michio Tanigawa, *Medieval Chinese Society and the Local "Community,"* trans. Joshua A. Fogel (Berkeley: University of California Press, 1985); Denis C. Twitchett, "The Composition of the T'ang Ruling Class: New Evidence from Tun-huang," in *Perspectives on the T'ang*, ed. Arthur F. Wright and Denis C. Twitchett (New Haven: Yale University Press, 1973); and idem, "Introduction," in *The Cambridge History of China*, Vol. 3, Part 1, *Sui and T'ang China, 589–906*, ed. Denis C. Twitchett (Cambridge: Cambridge University Press, 1979), esp. pp. 8–31.

T'ang provides the most obvious examples of the celebration of the festival on the part of the emperor and the Buddhist church. The T'ang is probably the most critical period in the assimilation of Indic and Central Asian culture from the west, its major capital city of Ch'ang-an serving as a cosmopolitan hub to merchants and monks, travelers and traders from all directions. The pantheons, philosophies, legends, and rituals "imported" into China at the start of the medieval period became in the T'ang more fully accepted into the traditional patterns of Chinese religion, which were themselves transformed in the process. Many of the basic forms of later folk religion had surfaced by the late T'ang: a Buddho-Taoist pantheon staffed by bureaucratic divinities; a systematized picture of the afterlife in heavens and hells; the involvement of Buddhist and Taoist monks as ritual specialists at critical junctures in the life of the individual and the community; and a comprehensive worldview in terms of which fate and retribution could be figured and the divinatory arts could be practiced.

Confining the seventh-month festival to the recesses of Chinese social history, however, would be rather poor history. The myth of Mu-lien and the ritual established at his request occupy a telling place in the history of Chinese religion and in the comparative study of religion and society.

The two major figures in the yü-lan-p'en myth are a monk and a mother, neither of whom would appear to be very highly valued in a culture where the most pervasive social and religious institution is based on the principles of procreation and male descent. Even in its canonical versions, the story concerns Mu-lien saving his mother and not his father; rather than producing male descendants, Mu-lien attends to the salvation of his female ascendant. The myth of Mu-lien is quite exceptional in its preoccupation with the state of the mother after death, suggesting a course of action alternative to but not necessarily inimical to the ancestral patriliny.[18]

If the ghost festival fostered the acceptance of traditionally marginal roles, it also affirmed the motivating ideal of mainstream Chinese life, filial devotion. Mu-lien spares naught in bringing aid to his mother. In Avīci Hell he even offers to trade places and suffer the tortures that she alone deserves. The audience is shown that no matter how self-sacrificing, children can never fully repay the kindnesses bestowed on them by parents. Commentators from medieval times to the present have iden-

[18] See Stephen F. Teiser, "Mother, Son, and Hungry Ghost: Gender and Salvation in the Mythology of Mu-lien," paper presented at the Annual Meeting of the American Academy of Religion in Atlanta, November, 1986.

tified filial devotion as the essential teaching of the ghost festival. Filiality or "politeness to the dead" is also the moral of the story in Juliet
Bredon's empathetic chronicle of Chinese customs in the 1920s. She
writes:

> People who are far from their ancestral tombs—too far to make a
> personal visit—prepare paper bags filled with mock-money. On
> each bag, a strip of red paper with the name and date of death of
> the person for whom it is intended is written. These are laid on an
> improvised altar and, while the priests chant *Sutras*, members of
> the family in turn make deep *k'o t'ous* to the spirits of their forefa-
> thers—even the little children who can not understand the mean-
> ing of their filial obeisance. They find it so hard to be serious
> when, after the mass is over, the bags are taken into the courtyard
> and set alight. "Oh, the pretty bonfire!" a small boy exclaims.
> "Hush! Little Dragon," whispers his mother, drawing him aside
> into the shadows to tell him the reason for this beautiful and
> touching custom. "To-day," she says softly, "all the dead leave
> their tombs and come back to us. The sky is thronged with an in-
> visible procession."
>
> "Why do they come back, mother?" he murmurs.
>
> "Because, my treasure, they love us and expect us to love and
> serve them. Therefore, irreverence is very wrong and cruel." Un-
> wise too, since naughty spirits are also abroad these days, ready to
> harm little boys and girls who, for this reason, are forbidden to go
> out after nightfall during this festival.
>
> "Little Dragon," throughly sobered now, bobs his head in a
> jerky *k'o t'ou*. It is his attempt at an apology to spirits, bad and
> good. Thus, very tenderly, children in China are given their first
> lesson in politeness to the dead.[19]

The involvement of the dead also means that the ghost festival
speaks to issues and problems in fields less exotic and less bound to
texts than Buddhology or the history of Chinese religions. As a rite of
passage, the early autumn festival marks a shift in agricultural work
and it signifies the end of the monastic retreat. In addition, it helps to
effect the passage of the dead from the status of a recently deceased,
threatening ghost to that of a stable, pure, and venerated ancestor. Although it is observed on a yearly schedule not synchronized with the
death of any single person, the ghost festival marks an important tran-

---

[19] Juliet Bredon and Igor Mitrophanow, *The Moon Year: A Record of Chinese Customs
and Festivals* (Shanghai: Kelly and Walsh, 1927), pp. 380–81.

sition in the life of the family, which is composed of members both living and dead. Like mortuary rituals performed in many other cultures, the festival subsumes the potentially shattering consequences of the death of individuals under the perpetually regenerating forces of the community and the cosmos.

The ghost festival also illustrates the Chinese answer to a problem posed in all societies that institutionalize, for some of their members, an ascetic way of life. The relationship between monk and householder varied throughout the Buddhist-influenced cultures of Asia. Most Asian societies incorporated monasticism by recourse to a circuit of exchange in which lay people provided material support for the Sangha while monks bestowed religious benefits on lay people. The Chinese solution not only accepted monasticism, it placed the renouncer at the very center of secular life: in the ghost festival the participation of monks is deemed essential for the salvation of ancestors.

Another issue raised in the transmission of Buddhism eastward from India was the relation between the Indian cosmology assumed in Buddhist thought and practice and the gods and concepts of the afterlife assumed in indigenous cultures. Certainly *kamis, nagas, nats,* and immortals all learned to live with the Buddhist view of things, and vice versa, but infinite variations were always possible. The underworld through which Mu-lien travels in the popular versions of the ghost festival myth reflects an important stage in the evolving cosmology of Chinese religion. Some deities of foreign origin, like King Yama, had assumed a place under the administration of the age-old Magistrate of Mount T'ai, while others (like Ti-tsang Bodhisattva) dispensed aid to hell dwellers and argued on behalf of inmates for exceptions to the harsh laws of retribution. By T'ang times, deities of Chinese and Indian origin had joined forces in administering a single karmic law that extended from the woeful states in which most ancestors were reborn to the blissful, less populated abodes of heaven. As Joseph Edkins, describing the ghost festival in nineteenth-century Peking, writes:

> The belief in metempsychosis among the Hindoos connected itself with the Chinese sacrifices to the ancestors. The two things combined formed an engine of great power for affecting the public mind.[20]

The public mind was also captured by the figure of Mu-lien, who united in one person the attributes of an austere, far-seeing monk and those of a demon queller roving through the dark regions. These two

[20] Joseph Edkins, *Chinese Buddhism: A Volume of Sketches, Historical, Descriptive, and Critical* (London: Trübner and Co., 1880), p. 268.

sets of attributes tended to appeal to two different audiences: monks and state authorities on the one hand, who admired his ability to travel through different cosmic realms in staid postures and circumscribed settings; and on the other hand the vast majority of Chinese people, for whom Mu-lien played the role of spirit medium, sending his spirit to do battle in worlds above and below the earth. Like shamans in other parts of the world, the Mu-lien portrayed in ghost festival tales satisfied simultaneously elite and folk conceptions of sacred power.

THE FORMS OF RELIGION IN CHINESE SOCIETY

To claim that the ghost festival in its mythic and ritual forms suffused all classes of medieval Chinese society is to make a further chain of as-sertions concerning the very nature of Chinese religion. Unlike the modalities of religion found in modern industrial countries and in some tribal societies, religion in China functioned in the first place *within* such institutions as the family, the community, and the state, and only secondarily as an institution distinct from all other social groupings. In China the most recognizable forms of religious activity—recognizable to *us*, i.e., those for whom either Church, Faith, or God describes the limits of the sacred—were derivative and far less numerous than feasts held in the community, or banquets given to honor the ancestors, or rites of passage conducted in clan halls. Moreover, religion in China— "religion" meaning the family of activities in which myth and ritual, symbol and cosmology figure prominently—more often than not af-firmed the immanence of sacrality and allowed for the realization of a transcendent Way within the bounds of the profane. These facts require some elaboration, since they have important implications for the shape that the ghost festival took in traditional Chinese society and for the critical methods best suited to discern that shape.

In an introductory work composed largely on a train commuting be-tween Paris and Tonnerre in 1922, Marcel Granet writes:

> If religion were defined by the more or less explicit adherence by individuals to a dogma, and their more or less great respect for a clergy, it would be equally as false to say that the Chinese practise two or three religions as that they practise one. Indeed, in China there exist as almost definite beliefs only those about Ancestors, and if anyone deserves the title of priest, it is a layman: the pater-familias.[21]

[21] Marcel Granet, *The Religion of the Chinese People*, trans. Maurice Freedman (New York: Harper and Row, 1977), p. 146.

15

To a general French audience in 1922, as to any audience in this century, one of the first prejudices to be put to rest in the study of Chinese religion is the predilection to sort religions and to define the general phenomenon in terms of a specific set of credos which preclude the believer from giving allegiance to any other authority. The point, echoed frequently by historians and anthropologists far removed from the oversight of Durkheim and Chavannes, is not that the Chinese lack "religion," but that religion in China is not a differentiated function of social life.[22]

The most systematic elaboration of this viewpoint may be found in C. K. Yang's work, *Religion in Chinese Society* (1961). Yang distinguishes two basic forms of religion, institutional and diffused. Institutional religion, says Yang, possesses:

(1) an independent theology or cosmic interpretation of the universe and human events, (2) an independent form of worship consisting of symbols (gods, spirits, and their images) and rituals, and (3) an independent organization of personnel to facilitate the interpretation of theological views and to pursue cultic worship. With separate concept, ritual, and structure, religion assumes the nature of a separate social institution, and hence its designation as an institutional religion. On the other hand, diffused religion is conceived of as a religion having its theology, cultus, and personnel so intimately diffused into one or more secular social institutions that they become part of the concept, rituals, and structure of the latter, thus having no significant independent existence.

To this Yang adds the equally important point that diffused religion in traditional China was the primary form of religion:

the religious element was diffused into all major social institutions and into the organized life of every community in China. *It was in its diffused form that people made their most intimate contact with religion.*[23]

[22] In *La Pensée chinoise* (Paris: Albin Michel, 1968), p. 476, Granet writes further: "It is often said that the Chinese have no religion, and sometimes taught that their mythology might as well be said to be non-existent. The truth is that in China *religion* is not, any more than *law*, a *differentiated function* of social activity. . . ." For similar statements, see Jacques Gernet, *Les Aspects économiques du bouddhisme dans la société chinoise du Ve au Xe siècle* (Saigon: Ecole Française d'Extrême-Orient, 1956), p. xiii; and Sawada Mizuho, *Jigoku hen: chūgoku no meikai setsu* (Kyoto: Hōzōkan, 1968), preface.

[23] C. K. Yang, *Religion in Chinese Society: A Study of Contemporary Social Functions of Religion and Some of Their Historical Factors* (Berkeley: University of California Press, 1961), pp. 294–95, 296; emphasis added in the last quotation.

The relevance of Yang's analysis to the subject of this study is that it makes of the ghost festival not something "exotic," "cultic," "devotional," "folk," or in any way marginal to Chinese religion, but rather something quite central to the fabric of daily life of the vast majority of people in medieval China. While it did mark an important event in the yearly cycle of life for monks, yü-lan-p'en was even more firmly anchored in the dominant social institution in China, the family. Its rituals became part of the system of observances that united living and ancestral members of the family, reinforcing their reciprocal obligations and harmonizing the rhythms of family and monastic life with the agricultural schedule. The mythology of the ghost festival gave voice to the basic worldview of medieval Chinese religion, a cosmology not argued systematically in treatises, but rather, assumed in the practice of ritual.

While the ghost festival was rooted in the primary form of religious life, "diffused religion," it also reached into most areas of "institutional religion" as well. Indeed, if Yang's analysis of institutional and diffused religion in China is to be faulted, that is only because it tends to create too wide a gulf between the two poles. Given the way in which the seventh-moon festival brought the Sangha into the midst of family life, and the way in which state religion and the emperor's own ancestral cult actively sponsored offerings on that day, perhaps it is best to view the ghost festival as spanning the entire spectrum between diffused and institutional religion.

Translated into the perhaps more familiar terms of class analysis, the ideology and activities of the ghost festival were shared by both elite and folk, the scholar-producing gentry class and peasant farmers. While the versions of the Mu-lien myth and the styles of its celebration were different for these two groups, the commonalities are no less striking. The evidence supplied by this study of the ghost festival attests to the largely hospitable interplay between folk and elite levels of culture, a trait which has been attributed far more frequently to medieval and especially early modern China than to corresponding periods of European history.[24]

A serious consideration of the social contexts of the ghost festival in medieval China also dictates that special attention be paid to the nature of the primary texts used in this study. It is an irrefutable but insufficiently appreciated fact that the major sources on medieval China were

[24] See, for example, David Johnson, Andrew Nathan, and Evelyn Rawski, eds., *Popular Culture in Late Imperial China* (Berkeley: University of California Press, 1985); and Peter Burke, *Popular Culture in Early Modern Europe* (London: Temple Smith, 1978).

written by members of the elite: monks or scholar-bureaucrats. In either case the authors of almost all texts surviving from this time viewed the world from the perspective of institutional religion: from within the monastery or through the eyes of the government. To use these sources without radical criticism, or even to begin our study with these texts, is to limit our field of vision to that of the monk or the state official; it is to insure from the start that the place of the ghost festival in the most pervasive form of Chinese religion will remain obscured.

A tremendous amount of detail about the ghost festival—how long the celebrations lasted, how many temples the average family visited, what pictures were used to illustrate Mu-lien's adventures, what prayers were said in receiving offerings, the clothes people wore to festivities—is simply unrecoverable. Most of the minutiae in which modern historians take such interest will never be known. By virtue of their literacy, recordkeepers in traditional China had already lifted themselves into a social class that deemed the everyday life of "the people" to be unworthy of historical note. As Derk Bodde notes, in imperial China:

> it was inevitable that writing, although of course used for multiple purposes, should have functioned above all as an adjunct of government. Essays, poetry, history, philosophy, and later on drama and fiction: all of these as well as other types of written expression were for the most part produced by men who, if not bureaucrats themselves, were at least would-be bureaucrats, retired bureaucrats, or the friends, relatives, or hangers-on of bureaucrats. This fact severely limits our view of premodern China. For it means that we have to see it through the eyes of men who, with rare exceptions, tended to idealize, to treat with superior condescension, or simply to ignore many aspects—especially the more seamy aspects—of everyday life essential to the great population mass known as "the people."[25]

Literati took as little interest in folk observances as they did in folk literature, which "was seldom written down and less often preserved. Popular literature was, quite simply, beneath the dignity of the fully literate."[26]

How to sift and how to construe the literature on the ghost festival that does exist remains an important issue. Many sources relevant to

[25] Derk Bodde, *Festivals in Classical China: New Year and Other Annual Observances during the Han Dynasty, 206 B.C.–A.D. 220* (Princeton: Princeton University Press, 1975), p. 2.
[26] Victor H. Mair, "Lay Students and the Making of Written Vernacular Narrative: An Inventory of Tun-huang Manuscripts," *Chinoperl Papers* No. 10 (1981):92.

the festival are contained in the Chinese Buddhist canon: sūtras, commentaries, and histories. My interpretation of this important set of texts is pursued in light of the recognition that, whatever else they may be—repositories of wisdom, literary exemplars, defining marks of a high tradition—canons are social institutions. The Chinese Buddhist canon was not merely a "useful organizing concept for pedagogy" or a set of texts grouped together for reasons purely soteriological, literary, or philosophical. A canon is also, as Henry L. Gates remarks, "a mechanism for political control."[27]

The canon in China was defined at the request of the state by highly placed members of the Buddhist establishment. The making of the Buddhist canon was a process of disavowal as much as it was an enterprise of creation: authority was established by selecting which existing texts were to be allowed "into the canon" (ju-tsang).[28] Prior to the large-scale use of woodblock printing in later times, only a fraction of texts judged noncanonical survived very long.

This is not to suggest that the apocryphal versions of the Mu-lien myth threatened political subversion or advocated making prostrations to animals, as did some writings, later banned from the canon, of the Teaching of the Three Stages (san-chieh chiao) in the sixth and seventh centuries. But the yü-lan-p'en sūtras that were accepted into the Chinese canon did differ from noncanonical sources in their conformity to a monastic view of orthopraxis, and they showed little interest in the purgatorial chambers of the underworld. Mu-lien's unruly side is kept under control, subordinated to the Buddha's superior powers, and only in the commentaries on the canonical sūtras is there any interest, furtively displayed, in Mu-lien's mother's previous life.

To escape the constraints of a singularistic perspective, I construct my picture of the ghost festival beginning not with canonical texts but with texts deriving from the milieu of diffused religion. I attempt to retrieve these popular texts out of the jungle of "cult" and "local religion," and to reestablish their position on home ground. My goal in this respect is to place the ghost festival against the background of a to-

[27] Henry L. Gates, Jr., "Criticism in the Jungle," in *Black Literature and Literary Theory*, ed. Henry L. Gates, Jr. (New York: Methuen, 1984), p. 2.

[28] On the definition of the Chinese Buddhist canon and a study of several important noncanonical works, see Makita Tairyō, *Gikyō kenkyū* (Kyoto: Kyoto daigaku jinbun kagaku kenkyūjo, 1976), esp. pp. 1–124. On the formation of the Pāli, Chinese, and Tibetan Buddhist canons, see Louis Renou and Jean Filliozat, *L'Inde classique: manuel des études indiennes*, 2 vols. (Paris: Payot, 1947 and Paris: Imprimerie Nationale, 1953), Sections 1947–74, 2107–62, and 2033–44.

tal social landscape, to view it not just from the position of the literati, but from as many different social situations as possible.

The cache of manuscripts uncovered at Tun-huang in northwest China in the first decade of this century makes this goal a realistic one. Among the roughly 42,000 pieces of writing are to be found several written records of the picture tale told to the masses by storytellers, *The Transformation Text on Mu-lien Saving His Mother*; a sūtra on yü-lan-p'en explicitly excluded from the canon of Chinese Buddhism; and a transcription of an exegetical lecture on *The Yü-lan-p'en Sūtra*. These and other sources provide important clues as to what common people in medieval times found significant and entertaining about the ghost festival.

Another way to avoid the limitations of traditional historiography is to comb through those sources more tangential to the official task of history writing. For medieval China, this avenue leads through poetry, occasional prose pieces, diaries, encyclopedias, and liturgical texts. The results of this sifting do not prove inconsequential: the first certain reference to the celebration of the festival in the countryside of south China in 561; diary entries portraying discontent with the government suppression of offerings at Buddhist temples in 844; and several pieces—including one striking rhapsody by Yang Chiung (650–ca. 694) and one notably unimpressive poem by Emperor Te-tsung (r. 779–805)—written on the occasion of the ghost festival.

THE PLACE OF BUDDHISM IN CHINESE SOCIETY

Although the ghost festival is found only in East Asia in medieval times, many of its ritual and mythological components derive from lands to the west of China: not only India, but the many kingdoms and trading centers of Central Asia so crucial in the dissemination of Indic and Aryan culture to the east. Indian Buddhist literature preserves a rich store of tales about Maudgalyāyana (Chinese: Mu-lien) who, together with his best friend, Śāriputra, joined the ranks of the Buddha's followers and quickly demonstrated their prowess in superhuman powers and in wisdom, respectively. In collections of legends detailing the previous lives of the Buddha's disciples (*avadānas*), Mu-lien often plays the role of seer, divulging to hungry ghosts and hell dwellers the atrocities committed in previous lives for which they now suffer the consequences. Yü-lan-p'en literature preserves and embellishes these aspects of Mu-lien's character. Likewise, the Chinese celebration of the ghost festival was based partly on the monastic rain retreat, which in India and Central Asia was held often, but not always, between the fourth and seventh months. Other nonspecifically Buddhist aspects of Indian culture found in the ghost festival include a world-disk cosmograph with vertically arranged planes of existence, a system of rebirth governed by karma, and a reciprocal relationship between householders and renouncers. The list could go on.

By the time that it appears in the historical record (the sixth and seventh centuries), the ghost festival was thoroughly integrated into the traditional patterns of Chinese social life. It did, however, preserve a trace of the exotic: its odd-sounding Buddhist name. To the Chinese eye, "yü-lan-p'en" in its written form *looks* foreign. Passages from *The Yü-lan-p'en Sūtra* make it clear that "yü-lan-p'en" is a kind of "p'en" ("bowl") in which offerings are placed, but in the sūtra the meaning of "yü-lan" remains obscure (literally, "cup iris"). Unlike other foreign-sounding words in Chinese literature, the mystery cannot be solved by reference to the original Sanskrit or Central Asian versions of the text, since none now exist, if indeed they ever did.

This single etymological mystery has dominated all previous scholarship on the ghost festival. The vast majority of books, articles, and research notes published on yü-lan-p'en is devoted largely, if not wholly, to ascertaining the problematic origins of the Chinese word "yü-lan-p'en." It is hardly an exaggeration to claim that most scholars have been obsessed with the search for the primal word event in Sanskritic and Indo-European languages that lies behind the Chinese disguise of "yü-lan-p'en." The findings as well as the assumptions of this search, pursued by American, Chinese, Dutch, English, French, German, and Japanese scholars, bear further discussion here.[29]

[29] An incomplete listing of studies dealing with the etymology of "yü-lan-p'en," which I summarize in the next three paragraphs, would include: Ashikaga Enshō, "Notes on Urabon (Yü Lan P'en, Ullambana)," JAOS 71:1 (January–March 1951):71–75; Bredon, *The Moon Year*, p. 384; Kenneth K. S. Ch'en, *The Chinese Transformation of Buddhism* (Princeton: Princeton University Press, 1973), pp. 61–64; J.J.L. Duyvendak, "The Buddhistic Festival of All-Souls in China and Japan," *Acta Orientalia* 5:1 (1926):39–40, 44; Ernest J. Eitel, *Handbook of Chinese Buddhism*, second ed. (1904; reprint ed., Peking: Wen-tien-ko, 1939), p. 154b; *Fan-i ming-i chi*, Fa-yün (1088–1158), T. no. 2131, 54:1112c; Wilhelm Grube, "Zur pekinger Volkskunde," *Veröffentlichungen aus dem Königlichen Museum für Völkerkunde* 7:4 (1901):78–79; Honda Gi'ei, "Urabon kyō to jōdo urabon kyō," in *Butten no naisō to gaisō* (Tokyo: Kōbundō, 1967); *I-ch'ieh-ching yin-i*, Hsüan-ying (737–820), T. no. 2128, 54:535b; Ikeda Chōtatsu, "Urabon kyō ni tsuite," *Shūkyō kenkyū* N.S. 3:1 (January 1926):59–64; Iwamoto Yutaka, *Bukkyō setsuwa kenkyū*, Vol. 2, *Bukkyō setsuwa no genryū to tenkai* (Tokyo: Kaimei shoten, 1978), pp. 373–93 and Vol. 4, *Jigoku meguri no bungaku* (Tokyo: Kaimei shoten, 1979), passim; Victor H. Mair, *Tun-huang Popular Narratives* (Cambridge: Cambridge University Press, 1983), p. 224, n. to line 11; MBDJ, pp. 243c–44b; Murase Yukihiro, *Geien nisshō*, in Nihon zuihitsu zenshū, Vol. 1 (Tokyo: Kokumin tosho kabushiki kaisha, 1927), p. 555; Bunyiu Nanjio, A

Three basic kinds of explanation for the etymology of "yü-lan-p'en" have been offered. The first kind postulates Indo-European origins for "yü-lan-p'en." According to these theories, the original word represented phonetically by the Chinese was: the Sanskrit "*avalambana*" (Buddhist Hybrid Sanskrit: "*ullambana*"), meaning "hanging down, depending on"; the Pāli "*ullampana*," meaning "salvation, rescue, full of mercy"; or the Iranian "*urvan*" (carried to China in Sogdian form: "*rw'n*" or " *'rw'n*"), meaning "soul."

A second explanation follows the standard Chinese understanding of "p'en" as the Chinese word for "bowl" and of "yü-lan" as a transliteration of a foreign term for "upside down." On this basis, "yü-lan-p'en" may refer to the bowl into which offerings are placed to save ancestors from the fate of hanging upside down in purgatory or to the manner in which offerings are sometimes made, by inverting the bowl of offerings intended for wandering spirits. Other interpreters accept "bowl" as the meaning of "p'en," but suggest that the Chinese term is the shortened form of a Chinese transliteration (*p'en-tso-na*) of the Sanskrit word "*bhājana*," meaning "vessel."

A third theory explains the meaning of "yü-lan-p'en" by reference to spoken Chinese. Some scholars have suggested that the *sound* "yü-lan-p'en" represents a word different from the commonly accepted orthography, namely "yü-lan-p'en[b]," meaning "tray-shaped bamboo basket." Others suggest that the shortened sound "yü-lan" represents either "yü-lan[b]," meaning "fish basket," or "yü-lan[c]," referring to a cup of nectar and a basket of doughnuts. The shortened sound "lan-p'en" has also been interpreted as "magnolia bowl." My own survey of popular usage in liturgy, lecture texts, and regional names for the festival merely affirms that the more melodious shortened forms of "yü-lan" and "lan-p'en" are indeed quite common.[30] It is as if the spo-

---

Catalogue of the Chinese Translation of the Buddhist Tripitaka (1883; reprint ed., San Francisco: Chinese Materials Center, 1975), p. 78; Paul Pelliot, Review of Schlegel, "Les Termes bouddhiques Yu-lan-p'en et Yu-lan-p'o," BEFEO 1 (1901):277–78; Jean Przyluski, "Les Rites d'Avalambana," *Mélanges chinois et bouddhiques* 1 (1931–32):221–25; Sawada Mizuho, *Jigoku hen: chūgoku no meikai setsu* (Kyoto: Hōzōkan, 1968), pp. 131–33; Marinus Willem de Visser, *Ancient Buddhism in Japan*, 2 vols. (Leiden: E. J. Brill, 1935), 1:59–68; *Yü-lan-p'en ching shu (Tsung-mi Commentary)*, Tsung-mi (780–841), T. no. 1792, 39:506c–7a; *Yü-lan-p'en ching shu hsiao-heng ch'ao*, Yü-jung (Sung), Z. 1, 94:4, p. 375ra-b; and *Yü-lan-p'en ching tsan-shu (Hui-ching Commentary)*, Hui-ching (578–ca. 645), T. no. 2781, 85:540a.

[30] The popular handbook of common knowledge, *Tsa-ch'ao*, refers to "Yü-lan Buddha bowls" *(yü-lan fo-p'en); Tsa-ch'ao*, P. no. 2721, reproduced in Naba Toshisada, "Tō shōbon zashō kō," (1942), reprinted in *Tōdai shakai bunka shi kenkyū* (Tokyo: Sōbunsha, 1974), p. 227. *The Lecture Text on the Yü-lan-p'en Sūtra makes reference to "The Sūtra on*

22

ken language reclaimed a philological disaster by domesticating the foreign word.

In view of the lack of any hard facts on its Indic origins, the results of etymology ("discourse about the true sense") must remain hypothetical. My own analysis is of a different order, intended not to replace but to supplement the standard Buddhological treatments. I have chosen to explore the most immediate context of the ghost festival, the medieval Chinese society in which it was practiced. In fact, Chinese sources promise to yield a far greater wealth of information on all aspects of the ghost festival than do the farther reaches of Indo-European philology.

How to construe the Buddhist elements in the ghost festival remains—or should remain—an open question. Which versions of Maudgalyāyana's biography are relevant to the Chinese figure of Mu-lien? Did the ghost festival have particular affinities with one Buddhist "sect" more than any others? How was the law of karma combined with a bureaucratic administration of the cosmos? Which elements prevail in the ghost festival, Indic or Chinese ones?

Answers to these questions have varied widely, but most of them share the unspoken assumption that Indic origins logically entail non-Chineseness, that what is Indian is and always has been different from what is Chinese. If concern with the salvation of one's mother is found in Buddhist mythology, then it could not have been truly Chinese. Or if the goal of long life and happiness in heaven expressed in yü-lan-p'en liturgy was originally a Chinese concern, then it conflicted with the normative claims of Buddhism.

Even the most careful scholars and the most persuasive studies appear to assume an *essential* difference between Indian religion and Chinese religion.[31] My own analysis adopts instead a more fluid defi-

---

the Purity of Yü-lan" (Yü-lan ch'ing-ching ching), see Tun-huang chüan-tzu, 6 vols. (Taipei: Shih-men t'u-shu, 1976), 2:1. "Yü-lan Assembly" (yü-lan hui) is a frequent name for the ghost festival in later regional usage, see Ku-chin t'u-shu chi-ch'eng, 3:692–94. See my bibliography of primary sources for liturgical texts and commentaries on "Lan-p'en."

[31] The most important Western-language study of the place of filiality in Chinese Buddhism begins with the statement, "Buddhism started in India as a religion advocating abandonment of family, but it ended in China praising the virtue of filial piety." The same study concludes with the statement, "The accommodation by the Buddhists to Chinese ethics is probably one of the chief reasons why the foreign religion was so readily accepted by the Chinese despite many features that were opposed to Chinese culture." See Kenneth K. S. Ch'en, "Filial Piety in Chinese Buddhism," HJAS 28 (1968):81, 97. Scholars ranging from anthropologists to epigraphers have begun to question the traditional stereotype of Indian Buddhism as asocial. See, for example, Louis Dumont, "World Renunciation in Indian Religions," Contributions to Indian Sociology 4 (1960), re-

nition of Buddhism and a less historically rigid understanding of Chinese religion. To assume that Indian Buddhism was a self-existing whole that could change into another entity (Chinese Buddhism) only by a radical alteration of its basic core is to preclude from the beginning any comprehensive understanding of the ghost festival, in which elements originally deriving from India and from China were synthesized in a complex and coherent whole.

The un-Nāgārjunian view of "Iranian," "Indian," or "Chinese" essences results in a schizophrenic reading of the ghost festival and, more generally, of postclassical Chinese religion; it makes impossible a reading of "Chinese Buddhism" as a coherent, sense-making system of religion. For some authors the festival remains an unconvincing mixture of the Buddhist notion of universal salvation with Chinese practicality and this-worldliness.[32] For others, the presumed origin of the festival in the monastic retreat of the Dharmagupta sect in India of the fourth and fifth centuries marks its essential foreignness.[33] Iwamoto Yutaka states most strongly the non-Chinese origins of the ghost festival, reaching back beyond Buddhism to ancient Iranian religions. For him, not only is the name of the festival itself derived from the Iranian term for soul (imported by Sogdians into China), but the very notion of salvation expounded in T'ang transformation tales is an essentially Iranian idea. Iwamoto argues that the soteriological themes found in the canonical sūtras derive from the monotheistic and dualistic religions of western Asia (Zoroastrianism, Christianity, and Manichaeism), which were carried by Greeks, Shakas, Parthians, and Kushans from Iran to northwest India beginning in the second century A.D. Moreover, Iwamoto suggests that the mytheme of a son saving his mother from hell in ghost festival mythology derives from the Greek myth of Dionysus descending to hell to rescue his mother, Semele, a myth transmitted to China through the Dionysian cults popular in northern Asia.[34]

A consideration of diffused religion in medieval times, however, appears to contradict the presumption that Buddhism remained foreign to China. Whatever their origin, all of the components of the ghost fes-

---

printed in *Homo Hierarchicus: The Caste System and Its Implications*, revised ed., trans. Mark Sainsbury et al. (Chicago: University of Chicago Press, 1980), pp. 267–86; and Gregory Schopen, "Filial Piety and the Monk in the Practice of Indian Buddhism: A Question of Sinicization Viewed from the Other Side," TP 70:1–3 (1984):110–26.

[32] See, for example, Tsuda Sōkichi, *Shina bukkyō no kenkyū* (Tokyo: Iwanami shoten, 1957), pp. 235–62.

[33] See Ogawa Kan'ichi, *Bukkyō bunka shi kenkyū* (Kyoto: Nagata bunshōdō, 1973), pp. 159–71.

[34] Iwamoto, *Jigoku meguri no bungaku*, pp. 184–99.

tival had become a seamless part of Chinese religion by the early T'ang, if not earlier. To demonstrate this assertion, as I attempt to do in this study, is to allow for interplay between "Indian" and "Chinese" aspects in the religion of medieval China; it is to understand medieval Chinese Buddhism not as an uneasy layering of essentially different strata, but as a complex and comprehensive whole.

TWO

The Prehistory
of the Ghost Festival

AT ITS PEAK in T'ang times the ghost festival was celebrated on a grand scale by people from all walks of life. The spread of the festival in medieval times (to be described in detail in Chapter Three) may be attributed to a number of factors. Later chapters discuss the place of the Mulien myth in Chinese Buddhist mythology and the Buddhist and Chinese understandings of the figure of the shaman, a role which Mulien appears to have mastered. Other chapters explore the cosmology of the ghost festival and show how ghost festival rituals were incorporated into the basic patterns of Chinese life, providing a more efficient means of communicating with the ancestors.

This chapter provides another kind of historical explanation for the popularity of the ghost festival in medieval times. It examines the precedents for holding celebrations on the fifteenth day of the seventh month and discusses the character of these earlier festivals. Not surprisingly, in China this day had long been an occasion of renewal, with emperors presenting their ancestors with the first fruits of harvest and common people marking the conjunction of death and rebirth. The themes evident in these early celebrations, characteristic of Chinese festivals in general, were to emerge as an important part of the ghost festival in later times.

Other precedents for the ghost festival originated outside of China. The schedule followed by Chinese monks, deriving largely from Indian sources, also included special celebrations on the fifteenth day of the seventh month. For the Sangha, this was a day of culmination and release. Their summer retreat having come to an end, monks confessed their transgressions of the Vinaya and donned new robes. For world renouncers, the day brought a relaxation of ascetic practice and the beginning of a new year. These monastic customs also constituted an important factor in the spread and development of the ghost festival.

Buddhism was not the only institutional religion in China. The Taoist church, at about the same time as the Buddhist church, began sponsoring celebrations on the fifteenth day of the seventh month. This was a day of judgment, during which gods of the celestial hierarchy descended to earth to tally up people's good and bad actions and to mete out judgment accordingly. Celebrants made confessions and presented offerings to Taoist masters at Taoist temples. This chapter explores the history and symbolism of these rituals, since they were an important ingredient in the medieval celebration of the ghost festival.

ANTECEDENTS IN INDIGENOUS CHINESE RELIGION

The ghost festival was held on the fifteenth day of the seventh lunar month, a day that carried numerous significations in traditional China. It must be remembered that the Chinese calendar was (until the founding of the Republic) partly based on lunar phases and partly synchronized with the solar year. Derk Bodde writes:

> The traditional Chinese calendar . . . consists of twelve months referred to by number, each beginning with the new moon and reaching its midpoint with the full moon. These twelve lunations total 354 days, which means that individual lunations have a length of either twenty-nine or thirty days. Like the lunations themselves, the days included in them do not bear names but are consecutively numbered.
>
> In China, as elsewhere, the major problem in calendar-making has been to reconcile as far as possible the in fact incommensurate movements of the sun and moon. . . . The Chinese solution has been to insert an intercalary month, usually at three-year but sometimes at two-year intervals, in such a way that seven intercalations occur every nineteen years. . . . The Chinese intercalary month does not come at the end of the lunar year. Rather it may be inserted between any two months (except the first, eleventh, and twelfth) in such a way as to insure that the Winter Solstice always falls in the eleventh month, the Spring Equinox in the second, the Summer Solstice in the fifth, and the Autumn Equinox in the eighth. The net result is a calendar whose lunar New Year (first day of the first lunar month) fluctuates from year to year anywhere between January 21 and February 20.[1]

Thus, while the fifteenth day of the seventh lunar month (7/15) always marked a full moon, it varied considerably within the solar and agricultural year. The fifteenth day of the seventh month always fell between the Summer Solstice and the Autumn Equinox, and it was always associated with ripening, darkening, and decay, but its

[1] Derk Bodde, *Festivals in Classical China* (Princeton: Princeton University Press, 1975), pp. 26–27. See also Joseph Needham, with the assistance of Wang Ling et al., *Science and Civilization in China*, 7 vols. (Cambridge: Cambridge University Press, 1954–), 3:390–408.

coordination with the progress of the sun was inexact. The precise correspondence of 7/15 with agricultural rhythms was further attenuated by regional variation: in north China, early autumn marks the beginning of harvest, while in south China, a second planting of rice is often made at this time.

The agricultural processes and governmental operations appropriate to each month are described at length in the *Yüeh ling* ("Monthly Ordinances"), which forms a section of the early Han ritual book, the *Li-chi (Book of Rites)*. The "Monthly Ordinances" presents an idealized picture of the actions undertaken by the Chou ruler, whose ritual observances were thought to link the Way of heaven and the Way of man.[2] The "Monthly Ordinances" were quite influential in the formation of Han ritual, and they provide a detailed and dependable picture of the rhythms of the seventh month prior to the development of Buddhist and Taoist services.

The seventh month marks the beginning of cooling winds and frozen morning dew. As the "Monthly Ordinances" notes, "Cool winds come; the white dew descends; the cicada of the cold chirps. [Young] hawks at this time sacrifice birds, as the first step they take to killing [and eating] them."[3]

Not only animal life, but plant life too begins the turn toward ripening and decay. The "Monthly Ordinances" describes the imperial celebration of the inauguration of autumn:

In this month there takes place the inauguration of autumn. Three days before the ceremony, the Grand Recorder informs the Son of Heaven, saying, "On such-and-such a day is the inauguration of autumn. The character of the season is fully seen in metal." On this the Son of Heaven devotes himself to self-adjustment; and on the day he leads in person the three ducal ministers, the nine high ministers, the princes of states [at court], and his great officers, to meet the autumn in the western suburb, and on their return he rewards the General-in-Chief, and the military officers in the court.[4]

---

[2] The "Monthly Ordinances" are also imbued with the schema of the "five phases" (*wu-hsing*), a system of thought that became popular only in the late Chou and early Han dynasties, which thus belies an earlier provenance for the book. For introductions to the theory of the five phases, see Fung Yu-lan, *A History of Chinese Philosophy*, 2 vols., second ed., trans. Derk Bodde (Princeton: Princeton University Press, 1952–53), 2:11–16, 19–32; and Needham, *Science and Civilization in China*, 2:216–345.

[3] *Li-chi cheng-i* (Taipei: Kuang-wen shu-chü, 1971), p. 143b; translation from James Legge, trans., *Li Chi: Book of Rites*, 2 vols., ed. Ch'u and Winberg Chai (reprint ed., New York: University Books, 1967), 1:283–84.

[4] *Li-chi cheng-i*, p. 143b; translation from Legge, *Li Chi*, 1:284. In five phases theory,

The same source also portrays the "tasting" (ch'ang) of the first fruits of harvest by the emperor and his ancestors in a ritual that joins the themes of agricultural fertility with the concerns of the ancestral cult: "In this month the farmers present their grain. The Son of Heaven tastes it, while still new, first offering some in the apartment at the back of the ancestral temple."[5]

Other celebrations held during the seventh month used methods of purification and the joining of the sexes to bring about world renewal. The "Lustration" (hsi[b]) festival, for instance, was held on the fourteenth day of the seventh month. On this day in the Han dynasty large numbers of people—apparently drawn from all classes of society—converged on riverbanks under gaily colored canopies to indulge in food, drink, and poetry.[6]

Eight days before the full moon was the date of the meeting of the two ill-fated constellation lovers, the Cowherd and the Weaving Maiden, which, at least by the end of the second century A.D., was marked by popular celebrations.[7] Having been banished to opposite sides of the Milky Way, the Cowherd (Ch'ien-niu) and Weaving Maiden (Chih-nü) were allowed to meet only one night per year. Medieval sources note a variety of practices on this day. People gathered outside to watch for bright lights and colors in the night sky, they set out feasts of wine and seasonal foods, and they sought divine assistance in the form of riches and the birth of sons.[8]

---

autumn corresponds to the element metal and to the West. Other sources describe the ch'u-liu sacrifice, held after the inauguration of autumn, in which the emperor kills game and then offers the meat to his ancestors; see Bodde, Festivals in Classical China, pp. 327–39.

[5] Li-chi cheng-i, p. 143c; translation mostly following Legge, trans., Li Chi, 1:285. The Chou-li mentions the ch'ang as one of the four seasonal offerings to the royal ancestors; see Chou-li cheng-i (Taipei: Kuang-wen shu-chü, 1972), p. 122c; and Edouard Biot, trans., Le Tcheou-li ou Rites des Tcheou, 3 vols. (Paris: Imprimerie Nationale, 1851), 1:422. For other Han references to the ch'ang ritual, see CWTTT, 4238:7.

[6] The "Lustration" festival of the seventh month was linked to the festival of "Purgation" (fu-ch'u) held in the third month of the year. On these two festivals, see Lao Kan, "Shang-ssu k'ao," Chung-yang yen-chiu-yüan li-shih yü-yen yen-chiu-so chi-k'an 29:1 (1970):243–62; Bodde, Festivals in Classical China, pp. 273–88; Marcel Granet, Festivals and Songs of Ancient China, trans. E. D. Edwards (London: Routledge, 1932), pp. 147–66; and Wolfram Eberhard, The Local Cultures of South and East China, trans. Alide Eberhard (Leiden: E. J. Brill, 1968), pp. 33–43.

[7] See Kominami Ichirō, Chūgoku no shinwa to monogatari: ko shōsetsu shi no tenkai (Tokyo: Iwanami shoten, 1984), pp. 13–94, esp. pp. 14–25.

[8] See Ching-ch'u sui-shih chi, Tsung Lin (ca. 498–561), in Moriya Mitsuo, Chūgoku ko saijiki no kenkyū (Tokyo: Teikoku shoin, 1963), pp. 356–59; Chin-ku-yüan chi, Li Yung (d. 746), in Moriya, Chūgoku ko saijiki no kenkyū, p. 443; and Kominami, Chūgoku no shinwa to monogatari, pp. 14–25.

All of these festivals held during the seventh month exhibit a blending of polarities that we will see surface later, in a variety of forms, in the ghost festival. Communication between generations is evident in the offerings presented by the preeminent descendant, the emperor, to his exalted ancestors, just as the ghost festival joins the senior and junior members of the family through the exchange of gifts. The seventh month brings the Weaving Maiden her only chance to cross the celestial stream that separates her from the Cowherd, just as the ghost festival brings into being the bridge that allows the ghostly inhabitants of the *yin* world to return to their loved ones in the *yang* world.

The ghost festival developed on the basis of these indigenous practices, and the widespread nature of ghost festival celebrations in medieval times is to be explained, in part, by these observances. The great span of time separating them should not lead us a priori to assume discontinuities between earlier and later celebrations. In fact what is most striking are the continuities, the shared themes and polarities in the Han festivals and the later festivals of Buddhist and Taoist coloring. They all share the character of the feasts described by Mikhail Bakhtin:

> The feast (every feast) is an important primary form of human culture. It cannot be explained merely by the practical conditions of the community's work, and it would be even more superficial to attribute it to the physiological demand for periodic rest. The feast had always an essential, meaningful philosophical content. No rest period or breathing spell can be rendered festive per se. . . . They must be sanctioned not by the world of practical conditions but by the highest aims of human existence, that is, by the world of ideals. Without this sanction there can be no festivity.
>
> The feast is always essentially related to time, either to the recurrence of an event in the natural (cosmic) cycle, or to biological or historic timeliness. Moreover, through all the stages of historic development feasts were linked to moments of crisis, of breaking points in the cycle of nature or in the life of society and man. Moments of death and revival, of change and renewal always led to a festive perception of the world. These moments, expressed in concrete form, created the peculiar character of the feasts.[9]

The similarities between pre-Buddhist and post-Buddhist feasts extend well beyond the trait of concern for the dead, which de Groot singles out as the principal and enduring indigenous contribution to the

---

[9] Mikhail Bakhtin, *Rabelais and His World*, trans. Helene Iswolsky (Bloomington: Indiana University Press, 1984), pp. 8–9.

ghost festival. After an examination of Han dynasty observances in the seventh month, de Groot writes:

> It follows from the above that if in fact Buddhist masses for the dead were celebrated throughout China in the seventh month, and if then all the inhabitants of the Middle Kingdom vied to celebrate the festival of offerings in honor of their deceased ancestors, then these ceremonies, however Buddhistic they may have become in ritual, already existed in China for many centuries before Buddhism penetrated there. The priests of the doctrine of Shakyamuni, when they began to invade China in the first two centuries of our era, erected an exotic edifice upon this base, which was provided them by the religion of a people who always showed extreme concern for the destiny of the dead.[10]

There are other continuities aside from an extreme concern for the destiny of the dead—which is surely no less "Buddhistic" or "Indian" than it is "Chinese." Foremost among them may well be the conjunction of the themes of decay and regeneration. The seasons themselves provide a model for this conjunction, as autumn inaugurates a turn toward darkness and the beginning of cold, at the same time that it marks the ripening of plant life and the expansiveness of the harvest. The seventh month combines impending decay and death with a celebration dedicated to the ancestors, progenitors and providers of life. Male and female mingle, in the heavens and on the ground, as do householders and those who have renounced the life of family and reproduction. The celebrations held in the middle of the seventh month are marked by such unions both before and after the development of the ghost festival.

THE MONASTIC SCHEDULE

The monastic rituals associated with the ghost festival in China are based partly on Indian models. In India the Buddhist Sangha ended its summer rain retreat with a ceremony of confession and the donning of new robes by monks. In India, as in China, the end of the summer retreat was an important juncture in the monastic schedule, with special celebrations marking this seasonal event. But there is little evidence linking the event in India with the salvation of the ancestors, and in China the role of lay people in this celebration was considerably greater than in India. Moreover, Indian and Central Asian Sanghas observed

---

[10] Jan J.M. de Groot, *Les Fêtes annuellement célebrées à Emoui*, 2 vols., trans. C. G. Chavannes, Annales du Musée Guimet, No. 12 (Paris: Ernest Leroux, 1886), pp. 405–6.

the retreat at varying times, while the Chinese Sangha appears to have followed an unchanging schedule.

The observance of a rainy season retreat (Skt.: *varṣā*, Ch.: *an-chü*) was a common practice among many groups of wandering ascetics in India in the fourth century B.C.[11] Vinaya sources show that the early Buddhist Sangha adopted the tradition of non-Buddhist sects in observing a three-month retreat during which monks undertook more strenuous religious practice and reduced their contacts with lay society.[12] These Vinaya accounts describe how the Buddha instituted the retreat, allowing monks to choose during which three months out of the four-month rainy season they wished to observe the retreat. The Buddha instructed his disciples to remain in one place, to follow a more intensive course of meditation and study, and to restrict as much as possible their intercourse with lay society. Isolation and asceticism were not, however, to be pursued to excess; most of the Vinaya accounts are filled with exceptions and extenuating circumstances. Monks were allowed to leave their place of retreat if they restricted their travels to less than seven days; if they were called by lay people to receive gifts and preach the Dharma; if they ministered to a monk, nun, or lay follower who was sick; if the settlement of a monastic schism demanded their presence elsewhere; or if a novice desired ordination. The Buddha also allowed his followers to break their isolation if they were attacked by beasts or robbers, if they were afflicted by fire or flood, or if they ran out of food.

Having spent ninety days in near-silent practice, cheek-by-jowl with other practitioners, monks in India (and China) concluded the session by airing any grievances and grudges they may have harbored during the period. The settling of accounts on the last day of retreat was formalized in the ceremony of "invitation" (Skt.: *pravāraṇa*, Ch.: *tzu-tzu*, or "releasing oneself" or "following one's bent"). In this ritual, mentioned in the earliest strata of the Buddhist canon, each monk "invites"

---

[11] See Sukumar Dutt, *Buddhist Monks and Monasteries of India: Their History and Their Contribution to Indian Culture* (London: George Allen and Unwin, 1962), pp. 52–55; and Etienne Lamotte, *L'Histoire du bouddhisme indien des origines à l'ère Śaka*, Publications de l'Institut Orientaliste de Louvain (1958; reprint ed., Louvain-la-Neuve: Institut Orientaliste, 1976), p. 66.

[12] For Vinaya accounts, all of them very similar, see Isaline B. Horner, trans., *The Book of the Discipline (Vinaya-Pitaka)*, 6 vols., Sacred Books of the Buddhists, Vols. 10, 11, 13, 14, 20, 25 (London: Luzac and Co., 1949–66), 4:183–207; *Shih-sung lü (Sarvāstivādavinaya)*, trans. Kumārajīva (350–409), T. no. 1435, 23:173b–78a; *Ssu-fen lü (Dharmaguptavinaya)*, trans. Buddhayaśas (ca. 408–412), T. no. 1428, 22:830b–35c; *Mi-sha-sai-pu ho-hsi wu-fen lü (Mahīśāsakavinaya)*, trans. Buddhajīva (ca. 423–24), T. no. 1421, 22:129a–30c; and *Ken-pen-shuo i-ch'ieh-yu-pu p'i-nai-yeh an-chü shih (Mūlasarvāstivādavinayavarṣāvastu)*, trans. I-ching (635–713), T. no. 1445, 23:1041a–44c.

other monks to report anything in his word or deed that they may have found contrary to the rules of discipline.[13] Having offered himself up for criticism, each monk then publicly repents any offenses.

Having purged themselves of wrongdoing and the suspicion of wrongdoing, monks inaugurate the new season by donning fresh robes. The distribution of robes (Skt.: *kaṭhina*, Ch.: *chia-ch'ih-na*) is described at length in most Vinaya texts.[14] These accounts provide extensive details on how a monk is chosen to distribute cloth to his fellow monks, who is eligible to receive new cloth, and how to make a suitable robe from the cloth. Interestingly, these accounts barely even mention the lay people who donate the new cloth. The early Indian rite thus stands in contrast to the *kaṭhina* rite celebrated in contemporary Southeast Asia[15] and to ghost festival celebrations in China, both of which highlight the coming together of lay and monastic communities at the end of the summer retreat.

Chinese monks in many ways followed the model provided by their Western contemporaries in Central Asia and India as recorded in the rules and examples of the Vinayapiṭaka. Both the Indian and Chinese monastic orders observed a summer retreat and held rituals of renewal

[13] Versions of the *Pravāraṇa sūtra* are preserved in the *Nikāyas* and the *Āgamas*; see Caroline A.F. Rhys Davids and F. L. Woodward, trans., *The Book of Kindred Sayings (Sanyutta-Nikaya) or Grouped Sayings*, 5 vols., Pali Text Society Translation Series, Nos. 7, 10, 13, 14, 16 (London: Oxford University Press, 1917–30), 1:242–44; *Shou hsin-sui ching (Pravāraṇasūtra)*, Dharmarakṣa (ca. 265–313), T. no. 61; *Hsin-sui ching (Pravāraṇasūtra)*, Chu T'an-wu-lan (ca. 381–395), T. no. 62; *Chung a-han ching (Madhyamāgama)*, Gautama Saṃghadeva (ca. 383–398), T. no. 26, 1:610a–c; *Tsa a-han ching (Saṃyuktāgama)*, Guṇabhadra (394–468), T. no. 99, 2:330a–c; *Pieh-i tsa a-han ching (Saṃyuktāgama)*, Anonymous (ca. 350–431), T. no. 100, 2:457a–c; and *Tseng-i a-han ching (Ekottarāgama)*, Gautama Saṃghadeva (ca. 383–398), T. no. 125, 2:676b–77b. The *Hsin-sui ching* is the longest and most developed of these texts, in which the Buddha and Śāriputra lead the Sangha in the ceremony of *pravāraṇa*. The ceremony is also described in Vinaya sources; see Horner, trans., *The Book of the Discipline*, 4:208–35; T. no. 1435, 23:165a–73a; T. no. 1428, 22:835c–43b; T. no. 1421, 22:130c–33c; and *Ken-pen-shuo i-ch'ieh-yu-pu p'i-nai-yeh sui-i shih (Mūlasarvāstivādavinayapravāraṇavastu)*, trans. I-ching (653–713), T. no. 1446. See also *Nan-hai chi-kuei nei-fa chuan*, I-ching (635–713), T. no. 2125, 54:217b–18a.

[14] Dutt, *Buddhist Monks and Monasteries*, p. 55; Lamotte, *Histoire*, p. 66. For a study of this festival in Vinaya sources, see Chang Kun, *A Comparative Study of the Kaṭhinavastu*, Indo-European Monographs, No. 1 (Gravenhage: Mouton, 1957).

[15] On the *kahteing* ritual in Burma, see Melford E. Spiro, *Buddhism and Society: A Great Tradition and Its Burmese Vicissitudes*, second ed. (Berkeley: University of California Press, 1982), pp. 226–28. On similar Khmer rituals, see Eveline Porée-Maspero, *Etudes sur les rites agraires des cambodgiens*, 3 vols., Le Monde d'outre-mer passé et present, Series 1, Vol. 14 (Paris: Mouton, 1962–69), 3:598–607. For the Thai ritual of *kathin*, see Howard K. Kaufman, *Bangkhaud: A Community Study in Thailand* (Locust Valley: J. J. Augustin, 1960), pp. 185–89.

at the end of it. World renouncers prepared for the passing of the new year—the Buddhist New Year (*fa-la*), beginning the first day after the summer retreat—by increasing their austerities and multiplying their ascetic energies. As the new year dawned, they released themselves: they broke loose from the stringent rules of summer, they unleashed the purified forces accumulated during retreat, they opened themselves up to criticism from fellow monks, they made a clean break from their past şins, they put on fresh garb. The end of retreat was a time of renewal.

But the Chinese Sangha far surpassed Indian and Central Asian monastic establishments in accentuating the themes of renewal latent in the ending of the summer retreat. The involvement of lay people and the emphasis on agricultural fertility are important hallmarks of Chinese practice to be discussed in later chapters. Here it may merely be noted that the timing of *pravāraṇa*, which varied considerably in the lands west of China, was made uniform throughout the Middle Kingdom. In the Vinaya sources, the Buddha is reported to have given individual monks the choice of three out of four months in which to make their retreat, and medieval Chinese writers note that their contemporaries in the West held the three-month retreat at various times, some beginning in the fourth, fifth, or sixth month, some in the twelfth.[16] The retreat in China, which had its own quite sizable climatic variations, seems to have been held consistently beginning in the middle of the fourth month and ending in the middle of the seventh month, as noted in pre-T'ang sources.[17]

The timing of the retreat in China is hardly insignificant. In the first place, the monastic schedule was calibrated on the basis of the indigenous luni-solar calendar so that the release of world renouncers always

[16] See *Kao-seng fa-hsien chuan*, Fa-hsien (ca. 399–416), T. no. 2085, 51:859b–c; James Legge, trans., *A Record of Buddhistic Kingdoms* (1886; reprint ed., San Francisco: Chinese Materials Center, 1975), pp. 44–47; *Ta-t'ang hsi-yü chi*, Hsüan-tsang (602–644), T. no. 2087, 51:872a, 875c–76a; Samuel Beal, trans., *Si-yu-ki: The Buddhist Records of the Western World*, 2 vols. (reprint ed., San Francisco: Chinese Materials Center, 1976), 1:38, 71–73; *Nan-hai chi-kuei nei-fa chuan*, I-ching (635–713), T. no. 2125, 54:217a–b; *Yü-lan-p'en ching shu hsin-chi (Yüan-chao Commentary)*, Z. 1, 35:2, p. 121rb; and *Yü-lan-p'en ching shu hsiao-heng ch'ao (Yü-jung Commentary)*, Z. 1, 94:4, pp. 406vb–7ra.

[17] See *Fan-wang ching*, attributed to Kumārajīva but probably written ca. 431–481, T. no. 1484, 24:1008a. See also Ishida Mizumaro, trans., *Bommō kyō*, Butten kōza, Vol. 14 (Tokyo: Daizō shuppansha, 1971), pp. 221–24; Jan J.M. de Groot, *Le Code du Mahāyāna en Chine: son influence sur la vie monacale et sur le monde laïque*, Verhandelingen der Koninklijke Akademie van Wetenschappen te Amsterdam: Afdeeling Letterkunde N.S., 1:2 (Amsterdam: Johannes Müller, 1893), pp. 69–71, 169; and *Ching-ch'u sui-shih chi*, Tsung Lin (ca. 498–561), in Moriya, *Chūgoku ko saijiki no kenkyū*, pp. 349–50.

fell on the full moon of the seventh month, a day which, in China, had always seen the celebration of rebirth and renewal. Buddhist monks in China welcomed the new year at a time when the whole world around them passed through a special time of regeneration. Second, the monastic schedule in China mirrored precisely the festival year of lay people: the monastic New Year fell exactly six months after the popular celebration of the secular New Year, held on the fifteenth day of the first month. By configuring its annual round of festivals as a perfect opposite to the secular calendar, the Chinese Sangha marked its difference from the secular world as well as it inability to extricate itself from the formal patterns of mainstream society.

Taoist Parallels

The Buddhist church was not the only organized religion to sponsor a festival of ancestral offerings on the first full moon of autumn. Taoists also held a festival on this day, called "*chung-yüan*," the day on which the "Middle Primordial" descended to earth to judge people's actions. Although some scholars assert that the Taoist festival originated prior to the Buddhist festival (which would make it an authentic episode in the "prehistory" of the ghost festival), it is more likely the case that the development of the Taoist festival was most strongly influenced by Buddhism. At any rate, by the T'ang dynasty there existed a scriptural basis for the festival, and in at least a few instances, celebrations involving sacrifices for the imperial ancestors and prohibitions of butchering were sponsored by the state.[18] Buddhist and Taoist elements were freely mixed during the occasion, as were the terms "chung-yüan" and "yü-lan-p'en," used as generic appellations for the fifteenth day of the seventh month. More importantly, for most people, making offerings at a Taoist temple in no way precluded making offerings at a Buddhist temple; both were deemed efficacious in bringing aid to the ancestors.

Very few sources record the actual observance of chung-yüan.[19] Ou-

[18] For state sponsorship of *san-yüan* (including chung-yüan) in 734 and 739, which prohibited the slaughter of animals and called for offerings at Taoist temples, see Ryū Shiman [Liu Chih-wan], *Chūgoku dōkyō no matsuri to shinkō*, Vol. 1 (Tokyo: Ōfūsha, 1983), pp. 439–40; and T. H. Barrett, "Taoism under the T'ang," draft chapter for *The Cambridge History of China*, Vol. 3, Part 2, ed. Denis C. Twitchett (Cambridge: Cambridge University Press, forthcoming), MS pp. 43–44.

[19] The paucity of references to the actual observance of chung-yüan probably reflects the scarcity of historical sources on Taoism as much as it does the actual incidence of chung-yüan celebrations in medieval times. For studies of chung-yüan, see Yoshioka Yoshitoyo, *Dōkyō to bukkyō*, Vol. 1 (Tokyo: Nihon gakujutsu shinkōkai, 1959), pp. 369–411, Vol. 2 (Tokyo: Toshima shobō, 1970), pp. 229–85; Akizuki Kan'ei, "Dōkyō no san-

yang Hsün's (557–641) encyclopedia, *I-wen lei-chü (The Classified Collection of Arts and Letters)*, reproduces an account of celebrations held at Buddhist temples written a century earlier and then quotes a Taoist source on chung-yüan:

> A Taoist scripture says, "The fifteenth day of the seventh month is the day of the Middle Primordial [chung-yüan]. The Officer of Earth checks his figures, searching through the human world to distinguish good from evil. All of the gods and assembled sages arrive together at the palace to decide upon the length [of people's lives]. Ghosts from the human world summon the records, and hungry ghosts and prisoners all converge at once. On this day grand dark-metropolis offerings should be made to the Jade Capital Mountain: select myriad flowers and fruits, precious gems and rare items, banners and jeweled vessels, delicacies and food, and offer them to all of the assembled sages. All day and all night Taoist masters should preach and chant this scripture, and great sages of the ten directions together should sing from its numinous pages. All of the prisoners and hungry ghosts can eat their fill, completely escape from suffering, and come back among humans.[20]

The Officer of Earth (the Middle Primordial) is an important member of the bureaucracy that administers heaven and hell. As one of the Three Primordials (san-yüan; the other two are the Upper Primordial and the Lower Primordial), he is responsible for adjudicating the records of everyone's actions and adjusting their life spans accordingly.

---

gen shisō ni tsuite," *Shūkyō kenkyū* 34:3 (January 1961):1; idem, "Sangen shisō no keisei ni tsuite," *Tōhō gaku* No. 22 (1961):27–40. For broader studies of medieval Taoist festivals including chung-yüan, see Ryū, *Chūgoku dōkyō no matsuri to shinkō*, 1:387–486; and Rolf A. Stein, "Religious Taoism and Popular Religion from the Second to the Twelfth Centuries," in *Facets of Taoism*, eds. Holmes Welch and Anna Seidel (New Haven: Yale University Press, 1979), pp. 53–82.

[20] Translation from *I-wen lei-chü*, Ou-yang Hsün (557–641), 2 vols. (Shanghai: Chung-hua shu-chü, 1965), p. 80. In the paragraph before the one translated here, Ou-yang cites the account in *Ching-ch'u sui-shih chi*, by Tsung Lin (ca. 498–561), which describes celebrations in Buddhist temples and gives a summary of *The Yü-lan-p'en Sūtra*. This passage is translated in Chapter Three, below. The account in *I-wen lei-chü* is repeated, with minor variations and some additions, in later encyclopedias: see *Ch'u-hsüeh chi*, Hsü Chien (659–729) (Peking: Chung-hua shu-chü, 1965), p. 79; *Po-shih liu-t'ieh shih-lei-chi*, Po Chü-i (772–846), 2 vols. (Taipei: Hsin-hsing shu-chü, 1969), pp. 71–72 (heavily abbreviated); and *T'ai-p'ing yü-lan* (completed 983), Li Fang, 12 vols. (Taipei: Hsin-hsing shu-chü, 1959), p. 272a.

He is assisted in the job by a host of underlings who serve as record-keepers, messengers, and jailers of the many spirits in hell.

The Three Primordials have a long and varied history in Taoism. The "Three Primordials" designate the primordial forces of heaven, earth, and man; the three supreme gods of the body; as well as the regions where these gods dwell in the body.[21] In the case of festivals dedicated to the san-yüan, the "Three Primordials" are the personified forces of the cosmos who govern its various spheres. A tripartite system of cosmic government—with thirty-six bureaus administered by the Upper Primordial, Officer of Heaven; forty-two bureaus administered by the Middle Primordial, Officer of Earth; and forty-two bureaus administered by the Lower Primordial, Officer of Water—is described at length in a fifth-century text. This scripture, *T'ai-shang tung-hsüan ling-pao san-yüan p'in-chieh kung-te ch'ing-chung ching (The Scripture of the Exalted One of the Sacred Jewel of Penetrating Mystery on the Prohibitions and Judgment of Merit of the Three Primordials)*, also contains a long list of the sins prohibited by the Three Primordials, ranging from criticizing the scripture and not observing fasts to lying, adultery, and murder.[22] The concept of trinitarian rule (and of offerings to the Three Officers [san-kuan], which preceded the development of the Three Primordials) probably goes back to the beginnings of organized Taoism in the second century A.D., when festivals were held on the fifth day of the seventh month.[23]

The description of chung-yüan in *The Classified Collection of Arts and Letters* draws attention to the judgment of human actions by the bureaucrat-gods of the celestial and infernal administration. Other sources from the seventh century highlight the repentance rituals that were part of the festivals of the Three Primordials: "During the feasts of the Three Primordials people confess their transgression of codes

[21] See Poul Andersen, *The Method of Holding the Three Ones: A Taoist Manual of Meditation of the Fourth Century A.D.*, Scandinavian Institute of Asian Studies, Studies on Asian Topics, No. 1 (London and Malmö: Curzon Press, 1979); the fourth-century text *Chin-ch'üeh ti-chün san-yüan chen-i ching*, TT. no. 253; and Isabelle Robinet, *Les Commentaires du Tao tö king jusqu'au VIIe siècle*, Mémoires de l'Institut des Hautes Etudes Chinoises, Vol. 5 (Paris: Presses Universitaires de France, 1977), pp. 149–203.

[22] *T'ai-shang tung-hsüan ling-pao san-yüan p'in-chieh kung-te ch'ing-chung ching*, TT. no. 456. Tu Kuang-t'ing's (850–933) collection of liturgies, *T'ai-shang huang-lu chai i*, contains a liturgy for san-yüan celebrations, TT. no. 507, chs. 32–34.

[23] See Henri Maspero, *Taoism and Chinese Religion*, trans. Frank A. Kierman, Jr. (Amherst: University of Massachusetts Press, 1981), pp. 34, 82; and *Wu-shang pi-yao* (completed 583), TT. no. 1130, chs. 44, 52, 56.

and prohibitions."[24] Thus, the chung-yüan festival involved not only offerings to gods and ancestors, but also rites of confession, which had long been an essential part of Taoist services.

Along with Taoist rituals held on chung-yüan there also developed a set of legends that justified and explained the celebration. As seen in such sixth-century texts as *T'ai-shang tung-hsüan ling-pao san-yüan yü-ching hsüan-tu ta-hsien ching* (*The Scripture of the Exalted One of the Sacred Jewel of Penetrating Mystery on Great Offerings to the Three Primordials of Jade Capital Mountain in the Dark Metropolis*), the Taoist legends drew extensively on the Buddhist mythology of the ghost festival. The Taoist scripture includes a parallel cast of characters as well as phrases employing the same locutions as *The Yü-lan-p'en Sūtra*. In *The Scripture on Great Offerings*, the Original Celestial Venerable (Yüan-shih t'ien-tsun), like the Buddha, emits rays of light illuminating the dark regions of the underworld. Evoking Mu-lien's request, the disciple of the Celestial Venerable, the Exalted Master of the Way (T'ai-shang tao-chün), asks what sins the many hell dwellers have committed to deserve their painful recompense. The Celestial Venerable proceeds to catalogue their previous offenses, and his disciple interviews the gods of the various realms. The Celestial Venerable concludes by pointing the way to salvation. The only way to liberate the denizens of hell from their torments is to present gifts to Taoist monks. Just as the Buddha tells Mu-lien, "It is not within your power as a single individual to do anything about it," so too does the Celestial Venerable inform his disciple that sinners in hell can only be released by collective offerings: "It is not within the power of a single individual to liberate them."[25]

Chung-yüan marked a breach in the normal structure of the cosmos when gods and goblins, ancestors and ghosts, immortals and hell dwellers all had a chance to visit the earthly realm of humans for a day. It was a time when offerings to the ancestors—the mainstay of Chinese family religion—were particularly efficacious. *The Scripture on Great Offerings* stipulates that food, fruit, cloth, banners, jewels, and other items be offered to various sages and Taoist priests on chung-yüan. As a result of these offerings one's ancestors, who suffer as inmates of hell and as hungry ghosts, "will obtain liberation and be fully fed; they will escape from all suffering and return to the human world."[26] A short

[24] *Chai-chieh lu* (late seventh century), TT. no. 464, p. 3v.

[25] Translation from *Yü-lan-p'en ching* (*The Yü-lan-p'en Sūtra*), T. no. 685, 16:779b; and from *T'ai-shang tung-hsüan ling-pao san-yüan yü-ching hsüan-tu ta-hsien ching*, TT. no. 370, p. 12. Yoshioka discusses a Tun-huang MS. of this source, S. no. 3061, in *Dōkyō to Bukkyō*, 2:231–49.

[26] *T'ai-shang tung-hsüan ling-pao san-yüan yü-ching hsüan-tu ta-hsien ching*, p. 12r.

poem written by Ling-hu Ch'u (765–837) gives voice to the privilege occasioned by chung-yüan:

"Presented to Honored Master Chang on Chung-yüan"

By luck the human world holds chung-yüan;
Without offerings to the dark metropolis, we would be forever
    separate.

Silent, quiet—incense burns in the immortals' temple;
The learned master bows to Jade Capital Mountain from afar.[27]

    The rupture and linkage afforded by chung-yüan worked both ways: gods and ancestors visited the human realm, and humans (at any rate the more ethereal among them) could visit the starry realms. One T'ang poet, Lu Kung (ca. 770–845), expresses his wish for the wings that would allow him to return to the jade palace along with the offerings sent there via the altar of a Taoist temple. In "Observing Buddhist Services on Chung-yüan," he writes:

Seasons change at the start of autumn;
The Three Primordials flow on course.

Clouds pad the sky-blue paces;
A memorial sent to the Jade Emperor's Palace.

Altar dotted with locust blooms,
Incense whirls, cypress-seed wind.

Feathered garb rising through the mist,
Jade hub cutting through space.

I long for a cloud-fed guest,
I pity the poor bugs raised on joint-weed.

Were I to receive the green satchel,
I could visit the vaporous expanse.[28]

Lu Kung envies the divine messenger who ascends to the higher heavens in the trappings of immortality wearing a dress of feathers and driving a jade-wheeled chariot. As a simple mortal, he feels left behind, an unwilling companion to the joint-weed bugs, creatures who see nei-

[27] Translation from *Ch'üan t'ang shih*, 12 vols. (Peking: Chung-hua shu-chü, 1960), p. 3751. Ling-hu Ch'u was from Hua province (present-day Kiangsu) and held a number of different posts both in the capital and in the provinces; see *Chiu t'ang shu*, Liu Hsü (887–946) (Peking: Chung-hua shu-chü, 1975), pp. 4459–65.

[28] Translation from *Ch'üan t'ang shih*, p. 5268. According to the brief biography in *Ch'üan t'ang shih*, Lu was a contemporary of Po Chü-i (772–846).

ther change nor the hope of transcendence.[29] Without proper authorization from the heavenly emperor (the green satchel for carrying edicts on official business), Lu Kung must content himself with a merely earthly existence.

CONCLUSIONS

Lu Kung and other literati drew on a largely Taoist vocabulary in their poems written on the occasion of chung-yüan, but in many respects the celebrations held on the full moon of the seventh month were nondenominational. Prior to the development of Buddhism and Taoism as organized religions in China, members of the ruling house had carried out ancestral sacrifices on this day. Moreover, the agricultural and cosmological rhythms of this time of year were self-consciously articulated and were well integrated into Chinese family religion.

While the growth of Buddhism and Taoism as institutionalized religions changed the setting (Buddhist/Taoist temples) and the medium (Buddhist/Taoist priests) of these ancestral offerings, the underlying social, religious, and cosmological structures of family religion remained strong. For the majority of Chinese people in the medieval period, the festival of yü-lan-p'en/chung-yüan marked the end of growth and the beginning of harvest, events in which the ancestors were implicated as both suppliers and recipients. Giving thanks and making offerings to the ancestors were the major activities of this important day. *Where* these activities were carried out—in the home or in a Taoist or Buddhist temple—was not an issue, for they could be carried out in any or all of these settings, without contradiction or diminution of their effects.

For the religious specialist the picture was somewhat different. Having developed rituals that complemented the preexisting base of family religion, both the Buddhist and Taoist churches sought to distinguish themselves from each other and to claim privileged (if not exclusive) access to the ancestors. This drive toward self-definition, to define the history and function of shared rituals in specifically Buddhist or Taoist terms, accelerated during the T'ang dynasty. T'ang rulers took advantage of the legitimizing symbolism of both Buddhism and Taoism and, at the same time, pitted these two churches against each other in order to check the power of their monastic orders and the size of their temples and estates. Hence it is not surprising to find Buddhist historians in the early seventh century disputing the authenticity and origin of the

[29] See PWYF, p. 4249a.

Middle Primordial and the offerings made in his name at Taoist temples.[30]

The apologetic efforts of Buddhist and Taoist historians need not blind us to the contours of the broader picture: for most people the distinction between "Buddhist" and "Taoist" aspects of the festival was irrelevant. Even in the case of later forms of Taoist meditation based on chung-yüan, Taoist adepts insisted upon the unity underlying chung-yüan and yü-lan-p'en. A twelfth-century meditation text, for example, provides instructions to the Taoist practitioner on the visualization of the gods and spirits dwelling in his body. By calling on the appropriate gods residing in his body, the initiate uses this form of meditation to refine his spirit and liberate it from its own internal prisons.[31] The esoteric ritual employs the paradigm of "refining" (lien) to describe the salvation of the meditator's spirit or soul, while the exoteric rituals performed in temples tend to picture the spirits being saved as ghosts or ancestors. But as Cheng Ssu-hsiao (1239–1316) points out, although they utilize different techniques, the two rituals have a common goal:

> From Taoism one studies the immortals' art of salvation by refining. From Buddhism one studies Ānanda's art of giving food [to lost souls]. Since they both involve a caring heart, we need not ask whether they derive from Buddhism or from Taoism. Their common measure is salvation from the dark regions.[32]

Contrary to the claims of traditional historiography, it must be recognized that Buddhist and Taoist versions of the seventh-moon festival grew out of a common structure, as the peaks of two pyramids sharing the same base. At one level, for a small number of people, offerings could be intended only for Buddhist or for Taoist priests and not both. At another level, where common people availed themselves of whichever temples and altars were closest-to-hand, offerings were carried out in a form in which Buddhist and Taoist elements were not distin-

---

[30] See Fa-lin's (572–640) criticisms in *Pien-cheng lun*, T. no. 2110, 52:548b; and the account by Hsüan-i (ca. 690–705), who had earlier served in the ranks of the Taoist hierarchy, in *Chien-cheng lun*, T. no. 2122, 52:567a–b.

[31] See *Ling-pao ta-lien nei-chih hsing-ch'ih chi-yao* (thirteenth century), TT. no. 407; and Judith M. Boltz, "Opening the Gates of Purgatory: A Twelfth-Century Taoist Meditation Technique for the Salvation of Lost Souls," in *Tantric and Taoist Studies in Honour of R. A. Stein*, Vol. 2, *Mélanges chinois et bouddhiques*, Vol. 21 (Brussels: Institut Belge des Hautes Etudes Chinoises, 1983), pp. 487–511.

[32] *T'ai-chi chi-lien nei-fa i-lüeh*, Cheng Ssu-hsiao (1239–1316), TT. no. 548, ch. 3, p. 40v.

guished.[33] It is precisely this synthesis of different traditions—indigenous ancestral and agricultural patterns, the monastic rituals of Indian Buddhism, the descent of Taoist gods—that accounts for the spread of the ghost festival (or "yü-lan-p'en," "chung-yüan," or whatever prejudice historians use to label it) throughout medieval Chinese society.

[33] Even Yoshioka, who insists on the "this-worldly" and Taoist origins of the ghost festival, writes: "Of course, among the folk, offerings were made in a form in which the teachings of both Buddhism and Taoism were thoroughly mixed," *Dōkyō to bukkyō*, 2:247. Erik Zürcher suggests the metaphor of two pyramids sharing the same base in "Buddhist Influence on Early Taoism: A Survey of Scriptural Evidence," TP 66:1–3 (1980):146.

THREE

An Episodic History
of the Ghost Festival
in Medieval China

PEOPLE from all levels of Chinese society took part in the ghost festival in medieval times, while the myth of Mu-lien's tour through hell was known in every corner of the empire. It is the burden of this chapter to provide a detailed historical account in support of this assertion.

Very few materials on the practice of the ghost festival are available in Western languages, and previous studies in Chinese and Japanese have either been quite broad in their chronological coverage, or have focused on canonical materials at the expense of "popular" ones, or vice versa.[1] I have, therefore, found it necessary to provide an episodic history of the festival from the fifth through the tenth centuries, concentrating on the most thickly documented celebrations and on all versions of the Mu-lien myth current in medieval times. An episodic arrangement has its drawbacks as well as its advantages, but it is hoped that the latter outweigh the former. The lack of a continuous narrative voice in this chapter is intentional: by focusing on discrete events and specific texts, this approach illustrates the many different meanings that the ghost festival assumed for people throughout T'ang society. The documentary style of arrangement also demonstrates the extent to which the ghost festival was embedded in the familial, political, poetic, and recreational life of medieval China, and why it has remained re-

[1] Standard treatments of the ghost festival in medieval times include: Ch'en Fang-ying, *Mu-lien chiu-mu ku-shih chih yen-chin chi ch'i yu-kuan wen-hsüeh chih yen-chiu*, History and Literature Series, No. 65 (Taipei: Taiwan National University, 1983); Kenneth K.S. Ch'en, *Buddhism in China: A Historical Survey* (Princeton: Princeton University Press, 1964), pp. 282–83; Iwamoto Yutaka, *Bukkyō setsuwa kenkyū*, Vol. 4, *Jigoku meguri no bungaku* (Tokyo: Kaimei shoten, 1979); Michihata Ryōshū, "Chūgoku bukkyō no minshūka," in *Chūgoku bukkyō*, Kōza bukkyō, Vol. 4 (Tokyo: Daizō shuppan kabushiki kaisha, 1957), pp. 115–16; idem, *Chūgoku bukkyō shi*, second ed. (Kyoto: Hōzōkan, 1958), pp. 96–98; Ogawa Kan'ichi, *Bukkyō bunka shi kenkyū* (Kyoto: Nagata bunshōdō, 1973), pp. 183–86; Otani Kōshō, *Tōdai no bukkyō girei*, 2 vols. (Tokyo: Yūkōsha, 1937), 1:23–30; Sawada Mizuho, *Jigoku hen: chūgoku no meikai setsu* (Kyoto: Hōzōkan, 1968), pp. 128–35; and Marinus Willem de Visser, *Ancient Buddhism in Japan*, 2 vols. (Leiden: E. J. Brill, 1935), 1:75, 84.

sistant to analysis for so many centuries. A more synthetic and synchronic picture of the festival is presented in later chapters.

To make the documents more accessible to general readers, wherever possible I offer translations and descriptions of the historical context of the documents and of their authors. The texts and episodes discussed below are arranged in chronological order. The bedrock of historical sequence is somewhat misleading, though, because many of the documents are copies of texts or records of oral traditions that began much earlier. The manuscript of *The Transformation Text on Mu-lien Saving His Mother*, for instance, may be dated only to around the year 800, while the storytelling traditions preserved in it probably extend back at least a few centuries before that.

Since my narrative in this chapter sticks so closely to the texts, some generalizations about the dispersion of the ghost festival in medieval Chinese society are offered here by way of summary. (Unless otherwise noted, further details and bibliographical references may be found in later sections of this chapter.)

The locus in which the ghost festival touched the lives of most people in medieval China was the local Buddhist temple. In his sixth-century account of folk customs in south China, Tsung Lin portrays great crowds of people from all walks of life converging on Buddhist temples to make offerings for the benefit of their ancestors on the fifteenth day of the seventh month. The Japanese pilgrim-monk Ennin describes a similar scene in the local temples of T'ai-yüan (present-day Shansi) in 840.[2] In the T'ang metropolitan areas poems written by courtiers and emperors make frequent reference to the crowded streets of Ch'ang-an and Lo-yang, as city dwellers joined the bustle of processions that visited the temples of the two capital cities. Commoners brought their own offerings, government officials carried offerings supplied by the state, and the emperor himself came out frequently to view the festivities. Musicians and popular entertainers were also part of the stir of medieval celebrations, which united a mood of festivity and diversion with themes more abstractly serious and religious.

The offerings supplied by common people, intended ultimately for their ancestors via the agency of the Sangha, included a wide range of brightly colored natural materials: paper flowers, carvings from wood and bamboo, and seasonal delicacies. The state often used the occasion to send gifts to the officially sponsored temples throughout the empire. Such gifts were supplied by the Central Office of the Imperial Workshop, while the merit resulting from the donation accrued to every-

[2] See Ennin's diary entry for 7/15/840, translated in Chapter One.

one's ancestors. In some years the offerings were sent to Taoist temples rather than Buddhist ones, but in either case people's ancestors reaped the soteriological benefits. Donations of large sums of money by rich lay donors were used to dress up the halls of the temples and to provide a vegetarian banquet for all visitors. Most of these donations were given directly to the Sangha or transferred to the Sangha account at the close of festivities, since it was the act of bestowing gifts on the Sangha (not the Buddha or the Dharma) that produced merit to aid the donor's ancestors.

The ritual of offering was a small but very important part of a broader celebration. The actual act of offering was accompanied by hymns praising the Buddha, the Dharma, and especially the Sangha. Judging from an early Sung liturgical text, in temples lay people called upon Mu-lien and other members of the Sangha to help release their ancestors from the torments of purgatory. Prayers accompanying the offering often singled out the deceased individuals to whom merit was to be transferred. A eulogy dating from the late T'ang, for instance, re-fers to two "princes" who gave their lives on the western borders, pre-sumably in the service of the state:

> on the fine festival of chung-yüan, an auspicious morning at the beginning of autumn, a sanctuary for the practice of yü-lan is es-tablished. In setting out a feast for their salvation, it is my earnest desire, as Great Guardian, Chief of Prefectural Headquarters, to make merit on behalf of the two princes.[3]

The fifteenth day of the seventh lunar month marked a time of re-generation for people from all walks of life. The seventh-moon festival occurred right around the late-summer or early-autumn harvest. Vi-tality and rebirth also characterized the experience of monks at this time of year. Members of the Sangha ended their three-month period of increased asceticism and isolation by confessing their transgressions to each other and then resuming contact with the lay world. The join-ing of worlds kept separate, which Mu-lien achieves by traveling to hell, was also echoed in T'ang poetry. Poems written on the seventh moon allude frequently to ethereal visitors from the mysterious moun-tains west of China and to sages and adepts ascending to heaven.

The version of the ghost festival myth with which most people in medieval China were familiar was the story of Mu-lien's fabulous tour

---

[3] *Tun-huang chüan-tzu* (Taipei: Shih-men t'u-shu, 1976), Vol. 6, No. 135, p. 1. This eulogy is not mentioned in other studies of the ghost festival. The identities of the two princes and the donor are unclear, nor am I certain of the donor's official post.

of hell contained in *The Transformation Text on Mu-lien Saving His Mother.* The average person knew little of the Mu-lien presented in the sūtras of the Buddhist canon. People learned about Mu-lien, not through the lectures or commentaries of Buddhist monks, but from popular storytellers who used picture scrolls to illustrate the scenes they described in their prosimetric tales. One such tale, *The Transformation Text on Mu-lien Saving His Mother*, was quite popular in T'ang times. The drama enacted in this transformation text concerns Mu-lien's search for his mother. Mu-lien appears decidedly unmonkish: he battles the demons and deities of the various hells, sweating profusely, weeping grievously, and pummelling himself into unconsciousness when he is defeated. The protagonist of the text is clearly Mu-lien, not the Buddha. Furthermore, the ghost festival itself fades into the background, superseded by the ogres and ox-headed soldiers who guard the many chambers of hell.

The myth contained in the sūtras directed toward a monastic and literate audience is somewhat different from the popular tale. *The Yü-lan-p'en Sūtra* and *The Sūtra on Offering Bowls to Repay Kindness*, two sūtras probably dating from the fourth or fifth century, were accepted as part of the Chinese Buddhist canon beginning in the sixth century. In these two brief texts the story of the ghost festival is a story about the founding of yü-lan-p'en by the historical Buddha, Śākyamuni, who teaches his fellow monks their ritual duties toward lay people in the seventh-month festival. The sūtras evince no interest at all in the previous lives of Mu-lien or of his mother, nor do they address the subject of the underworld. The canonical sūtras supply a legitimating myth for the festival by returning to the authority of the historical Buddha as creator of the festival. It is not accidental that the story is cast in the genre of a "sūtra" which claims to represent the word of the Buddha. In the eyes of the Chinese Buddhist establishment, the authenticity of yü-lan-p'en depended on its connection with the historical Buddha.

Further indications of the importance of the ghost festival to the monastic community may be gained from a consideration of the commentaries written on *The Yü-lan-p'en Sūtra.* Between the sixth and tenth centuries six commentaries are attributed to Chinese monks: Chi-tsang (549–623), Buddhātrata (ca. 618–626), Hui-ching (578–ca. 645), Hui-chao (d. 714), Tsung-mi (780–841), and Chih-lang (871–947).[4] Only

---

[4] On Chi-tsang, see *Hsü kao-seng chuan*, Tao-hsüan (596–667), T. no. 2060, 50:513c–15a; MBDJ, p. 530b; and *Bussho kaisetsu dai jiten*, ed. Ono Gemmyō (Tokyo: Daitō shuppansha, 1933–36), 1:216c. On Buddhātrata (or Chüeh-chiu), see *Sung kao-seng chuan*, Tsan-ning (919–1001), T. no. 2061, 50:717c; and *Bussho kaisetsu dai jiten*, 1:216c. On Hui-chao, see *Sung kao-seng chuan*, T. 50:728c; MBDJ, p. 280a–b; and *Bussho kaisetsu dai jiten*,

those by Hui-ching and Tsung-mi survive. Hui-ching's commentary may easily be judged a refined literary creation in its own right. In subject matter it sticks closely to the text, and the sources it cites derive from the most erudite levels of the Buddhist tradition. By contrast, Tsung-mi's commentary is an openly apologetic work, placing the ghost festival at the very center of Chinese society. It is addressed to a much broader audience than is Hui-ching's commentary, explaining and justifying the celebration of yü-lan-p'en in terms acceptable to lay and monk alike. Tsung-mi draws on some of the more popular elements of the yü-lan-p'en myth not contained in the canonical sūtras (e.g., the previous lives of Mu-lien and his mother). For Tsung-mi, the festival is the ultimate expression of filial devotion, a concept that he explains by reference to both Buddhist examples and to the classical texts of indigenous Chinese religion.

Buddhist lay people also took a special interest in the ghost festival. This social group was more involved in specifically Buddhist activities than were common people. In addition to making offerings on the fifteenth day of the seventh month, they also attended lectures given by Buddhist monks on various sūtras. Hence, their level of involvement in identifiably Buddhist activities was greater than that of other householders. In lectures given to such audiences on *The Yü-lan-p'en Sūtra*, filiality and charity were the major topics of discussion.

Information concerning the emperor's celebration of the ghost festival is also available in medieval sources. Many emperors appear to have participated in the festival in a style similar to that of the common people: imperial visits to temples in the capitals to view the festivities are reported for the reigns of Empress Wu (r. 690–705), Emperor Tai-tsung (r. 762–769), and Emperor Te-tsung (r. 779–805). Furthermore, most emperors probably made visits not recorded in surviving sources.

The historical record also permits a fairly detailed reconstruction of how the festival was observed in the imperial ancestral cult. The spirit tablets representing preceding generations of emperors in the T'ang line were taken from their niches in the Imperial Ancestral Temple and moved into the Palace Chapel. Here the emperor made offerings, probably similar to the lavish donations given by kings and queens portrayed in apocryphal yü-lan-p'en literature, for the benefit of the imperial patriliny. Some emperors—the case of Tai-tsung in the year 768 being a noticeable example—also used the occasion to make pro-

---

1:216c. On Chih-lang, see *Sung kao-seng chuan*, T. 50:884c–85a; and *Bussho kaisetsu dai jiten*, 1:215d. The commentaries by Hui-ching and Tsung-mi are discussed at length in this chapter.

visions for their mothers' salvation by sponsoring ceremonies at temples outside of the official ancestral cult.

Surviving sources do not permit the writing of a year-by-year chronicle of imperial participation or support provided for the ghost festival by the government, which depended largely on the official attitude, always fluctuating, toward the Buddhist church. In some years the emperor attended services as an observer, he made offerings for his own ancestors, and he saw to it that the state supplied offerings on everyone's behalf. In other years the public celebration of the ghost festival was prohibited, and items donated illicitly were turned over to the Taoist church.

Details to support this picture of medieval Chinese religion may be found in the episodes and writings described below.

THE CANONICAL SOURCES: *The Yü-lan-p'en Sūtra*
AND *The Sūtra on Offering Bowls to Repay Kindness*
(CA. 400–500)

The canonical sūtras describing the founding of the ghost festival emerge out of a murky past. Beginning in the sixth century two texts are associated with the ghost festival: *The Yü-lan-p'en Sūtra* and *The Sūtra on Offering Bowls to Repay Kindness*. The origins of these two texts can be established with even less exactitude than the actual celebration of the festival, the first certain record of which dates from the year 561. Some scholars postulate Indian or Central Asian authorship around the year 400 and multiple translations into Chinese, while others suggest that the texts were put together in China in the early sixth century.[5]

[5] Ogawa Kan'ichi suggests that *The Yü-lan-p'en Sūtra* grew out of the Dharmagupta sect in northwest India ca. 400, *Bukkyō bunka shi kenkyū* (Kyoto: Nagata bunshōdō, 1973), pp. 159–71. Makita Tairyō opts for a later date and Chinese origins, *Gikyō kenkyū* (Kyoto: Kyoto daigaku jinbun kagaku kenkyūjo, 1976), pp. 49–50, 84. A selective list of important scholarship on the two canonical sources would also include: Ch'en, *Mu-lien chiu-mu ku-shih chih yen-chin*, pp. 7–23; Fujino Ryūnen, "Urabon kyō dokugo," *Ryūkoku daigaku ronshū* No. 353 (1956):340–45; Ikeda Chōtatsu, "Urabon kyō ni tsuite," *Shūkyō kenkyū* N.S. 3:1 (January 1926):59–64; Ishigami Zennō, "Mokuren setsuwa no keifu," *Taishō daigaku kenkyū kiyō* No. 54 (November 1968):1–24; Iwamoto Yutaka, *Bukkyō setsuwa kenkyū*, Vol. 4, *Jigoku meguri no bungaku* (Tokyo: Kaimei shoten, 1979), pp. 10–20; Okabe Kazuo, "Urabon kyōrui yakkyōshiteki kenkyū," *Shūkyō kenkyū* 37:3 (March 1964):60–76; Sawada Mizuho, *Jigoku hen: chūgoku no meikai setsu* (Kyoto: Hōzōkan, 1968), pp. 130–33; and de Visser, *Ancient Buddhism in Japan*, 1:68–75. Chavannes' early (1902) French translation of *The Yü-lan-p'en Sūtra* remains a good guide to some of the problems involved in translating this short text; it is contained in Edouard Chavannes, *Dix Inscriptions chinoises de l'Asie Centrale d'après les estampages de M. Ch.-E. Bonin* (Paris: Imprimerie Nationale, 1902), pp. 53–57. Karl Ludwig Reichelt provides an extensive

The two extant canonical texts most likely represent different recensions current in the mid-sixth century. Given the lack of independent evidence prior to the sixth century, theories regarding when and where these textual traditions began must remain inconclusive. I have chosen ca. 400–500 as a reasonable average of the scholarly opinions.

I translate the two texts below in parallel columns:

The Yü-lan-p'en Sūtra	*The Sūtra on Offering Bowls to Repay Kindness*
Thus have I heard. Once, the Buddha resided in the kingdom of Śrāvastī, among the Jetavana trees in the garden of Anāthapiṇḍika. The Great Mu-chien-lien began to obtain the six penetrations. Desiring to save his parents to repay the kindness they had shown in nursing and feeding him, he used his divine eye to observe the worlds. He saw his departed mother reborn among the hungry ghosts: she never saw food or drink, and her skin hung off her bones. Mu-lien took pity, filled his bowl with rice, and sent it to his mother as an offering. When his mother received the bowl of rice, she used her left hand to guard the bowl and her right hand to gather up the rice, but before the food entered her mouth it changed into flaming coals, so in the end she could not eat. Mu-lien cried out in grief and wept tears. He rushed back to tell the Buddha	Thus have I heard. Once, the Buddha resided in the kingdom of Śrāvastī, among the Jetavana trees in the garden of Anāthapiṇḍika. The Great Mu-chien-lien began to obtain the six penetrations. Desiring to save his parents to repay the kindness they had shown in nursing and feeding him, he used his divine eye to observe the world. He saw his departed mother reborn among the hungry ghosts: she never saw food or drink, and her skin hung off her bones. Mu-lien took pity, filled his bowl with rice, and sent it to his mother as an offering. When his mother received the bowl of rice, she used her left hand to guard the rice and her right hand to gather up the food, but before the food entered her mouth it changed into flaming coals, so in the end she could not eat. Mu-lien rushed back to tell the Buddha

summary of the contents of the sūtra, *Truth and Tradition in Chinese Buddhism: A Study of Chinese Mahayana Buddhism*, trans. Katharina Van Wagenen Bugge (Shanghai: Commercial Press, 1927), pp. 114–18. The closest study of the text, still quite helpful to the modern translator, is Tsung-mi's (780–841) commentary, *Yü-lan-p'en ching shu*, T. no. 1792.

and laid out everything as it had happened.

The Buddha said, "The roots of your mother's sins are deep and tenacious. It is not within your power as a single individual to do anything about it. Even though the fame of your filial devotion moves heaven and earth, still spirits of heaven and spirits of earth, harmful demons and masters of the outer paths, monks and the four spirit kings of heaven cannot do anything about it. You must rely on the mighty spiritual power of the assembled monks of the ten directions in order to obtain her deliverance. I shall now preach for you the method of salvation, so that all beings in trouble may leave sadness and suffering, and the impediments caused by sin be wiped away."

The Buddha told Mu-lien, "On the fifteenth day of the seventh month, when the assembled monks of the ten directions release themselves, for the sake of seven generations of ancestors, your current parents, and those in distress, you should gather food of the one hundred flavors and five kinds of fruit, basins for washing and rinsing, incense, oil lamps and candles, and mattresses and bedding; take the sweetest, prettiest things in the world and place them in a

and laid out everything as it had happened.

The Buddha said, "The roots of your mother's sins are deep and tenacious. It is not within your power as a single individual to do anything about it.

You must rely on the mighty spiritual power of the assembled monks

in order to obtain her deliverance. I shall now preach for you the method of salvation, so that all beings in trouble may leave sadness and suffering."

The Buddha told Mu-lien, "On the fifteenth day of the seventh month,

for the sake of seven generations of ancestors and those in distress, you should gather grains,

basins for washing and rinsing, incense, oil lamps and candles, and mattresses and bedding; take the sweetest, prettiest things in the world

50

bowl and offer it to the assembled monks, those of great virtue of the ten directions. On this day, the entire assembly of saints—those in the mountains practicing meditation and concentration; those who have attained the fruit of the four paths;[6] those who practice pacing under trees; those who use the six penetrations to be free; those who convert others, hear preaching, and awaken to causality; and the great men, those *bodhisattvas* of the ten stages who provisionally manifest the form of a *bhikṣu*—all of those who are part of the great assembly shall with one mind receive the *patra* [bowl] of rice. [A monk who] possesses fully the purity of the precepts and the Way of the assembly of saints —his virtue is vast indeed. When you make offerings to these kinds of monks as they release themselves, then your current parents, seven generations of ancestors, and six kinds of relatives will obtain release from suffering in the three evil paths of rebirth; at that moment they will be liberated and clothed and fed naturally. If one's parents are living, they will have one hundred years of joy and happiness. If they are deceased, then seven generations of

and offer them to the assembled monks.

On this day, the entire assembly of saints—those in the mountains practicing meditation and concentration; those who have attained the fruit of the four paths; those who practice pacing under trees; those who use the six penetrations to fly; those who convert others, hear preaching, and awaken to causality; and the great men, those *bodhisattvas* who provisionally manifest the form of a *bhikṣu*—all of those who are part of the great assembly shall gather with one mind to receive the *patra* [bowl] of rice. [A monk who] possesses fully the purity of the precepts and the Way of the assembly of saints —his virtue is vast indeed. When you make offerings to an assembly of this kind, then seven generations of ancestors and five kinds of relatives will obtain release from the three evil paths of rebirth; at that moment they will be liberated and clothed and fed naturally."

---

[6] The four paths are stream-winner, once-comer, nonreturner, and *arhat*.

ancestors will be reborn in the
heavens; born freely through
transformation, they will enter
into the light of heavenly flowers
and receive unlimited joy."

Then the Buddha decreed that
the assembled monks of the ten
directions should first chant
prayers on behalf of the family
of the donor for seven generations of ancestors, that they
should practice meditation and
concentrate their thoughts, and
that they should then receive
the food. In receiving the bowls,
they should first place them in
front of the Buddha's *stūpa*; when
the assembled monks have
finished chanting prayers, they
may then individually partake of
the food.

At this time the *bhikṣu* Mu-lien
and the assembly of great
bodhisattvas rejoiced. Mu-lien's
sorrowful tears ended and the
sound of his crying died out.
Then, on that very day, Mu-
lien's mother gained release from
a *kalpa* of suffering as a hungry
ghost.

Then Mu-lien told the
Buddha, "The parents who gave
birth to me, your disciple, are
able to receive the power of the
merit of the Three Jewels because
of the mighty spiritual power of
the assembly of monks. But all of
the future disciples of the Buddha
who practice filial devotion, may
they or may they not also present
yü-lan bowls as required to save

The Buddha decreed that
the assembled monks,

on behalf of the family
of the sponsor for seven generations of ancestors,
should practice meditation and
concentrate their thoughts and
then partake of the offering.

their parents as well as seven generations of ancestors?"

The Buddha said, "Excellent! This question pleases me very much. It is just what I would like to preach, so listen well! My good sons, if there are *bhikṣus, bhikṣuṇīs,* kings of states, princes, sons of kings, great ministers, counselors, dignitaries of the three ranks, any government officials, or the majority of common people who practice filial compassion, then on behalf of their current parents and the past seven generations of ancestors, on the fifteenth day of the seventh month, the day on which Buddhas rejoice, the day on which monks release themselves, they must all place food and drink of the one hundred flavors inside the yü-lan bowl and donate it to monks of the ten directions who are releasing themselves. When the prayers are finished, one's present parents will attain long life, passing one hundred years without sickness and without any of the torments of suffering, while seven generations of ancestors will leave the sufferings of hungry ghosthood, attaining rebirth among gods and humans and blessings without limit."

The Buddha told all of the good sons and good daughters, "Those disciples of the Buddha who practice filial devotion must in every moment of

53

consciousness maintain the
thought of their parents,
including seven generations of
ancestors. Each year on the
fifteenth day of the seventh
month, out of filial devotion and
compassionate consideration for
the parents who gave birth to
them and for seven generations
of ancestors, they should always
make a yü-lan bowl and donate it
to the Buddha and Sangha to
repay the kindness bestowed by
parents in nurturing and caring
for them. All disciples of the
Buddha must carry out this law."

Upon hearing what the Buddha
preached, the *bhikṣu* Mu-lien
and the four classes of
disciples[7] rejoiced and put it
into practice.

The *bhikṣu* Mu-lien
and the entire assembly
rejoiced and put it
into practice.[8]

The Sūtra on Offering Bowls to Repay Kindness is about half the length
of *The Yü-lan-p'en Sūtra*. The longer sūtra fills in some brief lacunae
and elaborates several passages in the shorter version. It also adds some
episodes not included in *The Sūtra on Offering Bowls to Repay Kindness*:
the Buddha's request that monks chant prayers; the salvation of Mu-
lien's mother; and the long, largely repetitive answer to Mu-lien's
question concerning the practice of yü-lan-p'en by future disciples of
the Buddha.

The first reference to *The Yü-lan-p'en Sūtra* occurs in the monk Seng-
yu's (445–518) *Ch'u san-tsang chi chi (Collected Records from the Three Baskets)*, which notes the existence of "*The Yü-lan Sūtra* in one *chüan*."[9]
The Yü-lan-p'en Sūtra and *The Sūtra on Offering Bowls to Repay Kindness*
had a broad circulation in the sixth century, since they are quoted in a
Buddhist encyclopedia dating from 516 and in compilations on seasonal observances dating from 561 and 581.[10] There were two lines of

[7] The four classes of disciples are monks, nuns, laymen, and laywomen.

[8] Translations from T. no. 685, 16:779a–c, and T. no. 686, 16:780a.

[9] *Ch'u san-tsang chi chi*, Seng-yu (445–518), T. no. 2145, 55:28c.

[10] *Ching-lü i-hsiang* (516), Pao-ch'ang, T. no. 2121, quotes an abbreviated version of
The Sūtra on Offering Bowls to Repay Kindness, calling it "*The Yü-lan Sūtra*." The essentials

thought concerning the authorship of the sūtras. Earlier sources state that the author-translator of the texts is unknown while later sources, beginning in 597 with Fei Ch'ang-fang's *Li-tai san-pao chi (Record of the Three Jewels through the Ages)*, place *The Yü-lan-p'en Sūtra* among the 210 works translated by Dharmarakṣa (ca. 265–313).[11]

The Yü-lan-p'en Sūtra and *The Sūtra on Offering Bowls to Repay Kindness* represent the sparest versions of the ghost festival myth. Mu-lien and his mother occupy a relatively insignificant place, merely filling the necessary roles of filial son and departed ancestor without greater elaboration. The narrative focuses instead on the Buddha's founding of the festival, his instructions on how to carry out the ritual, and the ceremonial responsibilities of monks. In fact more attention is paid to the ritual actions of the Sangha in this source than in later yü-lan-p'en literature, which amplifies the offerings required of lay people. The gruesome details of Mu-lien's mother's suffering, the severity of the laws of karma, the importance of filiality—subjects that become important in

---

of the story are all there: Mu-lien's mother in hell, his unsuccessful offering, and the institution of yü-lan-p'en by the Buddha, T. 53:73c–74a. Tsung Lin's (ca. 498–561) record of seasonal observances, *Ching-ch'u sui-shih chi* (edited by Tu Kung-chan [ca. 581–624]), contains an abridgement of *The Yü-lan-p'en Sūtra*, including portions not present in *The Sūtra on Offering Bowls to Repay Kindness*; see Moriya Mitsuo, *Chūgoku ko saijiki no kenkyū* (Tokyo: Teikoku shoin, 1963), pp. 359–61. The *Yü-chu pao-tien* (ca. 581), Tu T'ai-ch'ing, quotes from an abbreviated version of *The Yü-lan-p'en Sūtra*, Pai-pu ts'ung-shu chi-ch'eng, No. 75 (Taipei: I-wen yin-shu-kuan, 1965), ch. 7, p. 14r–v. Tao-shih's *Fa-yüan chu-lin* (668), T. no. 2122, also quotes from *The Yü-lan-p'en Sūtra*, which it calls the *Hsiao-p'en pao-en ching (Sūtra on Repaying Kindness with Smaller Bowls)*, T. 53:751a.

[11] Fa-ching's catalogue of the Buddhist canon, *Chung-ching mu-lu* (ca. 594), T. no. 2146, links three sūtras as different translations of the same Sanskrit text: *The Yü-lan-p'en Sūtra, The Sūtra on Offering Bowls to Repay Kindness*, and the *Kuan-la ching*, translator unknown, T. 55:133b. The *Kuan-la ching* may have been the brief text now known under the title *Pan-ni-huan hou kuan-la ching (The Sūtra on Bathing [Statues on the Buddhist] New Year after the [Buddha's] Parinirvāna)*, T. no. 391, attributed to Dharmarakṣa, which mentions offerings to monks on the fifteenth day of the seventh month for the sake of the ancestors. Tsung-mi attributes authorship of the text to Fa-chü (ca. 290–306); see *Tsung-mi Commentary*, T. 39:506c. Fa-ching's assessment was one of the two standard views on the origins of the canonical texts. Other catalogues follow him in linking these three sūtras and admitting that the translator is unknown: Yen-tsung's *Chung-ching mu-lu* (completed 602), T. no. 2147, 55:160a; Ching-t'ai's *Chung-ching mu-lu* (completed 665), T. no. 2148, 55:194c; and Ming-ch'üan's *Ta-chou k'an-ting chung-ching mu-lu* (completed 695), T. no. 2153, 55:431c.

The other standard view, first formulated by Fei Ch'ang-fang in his *Li-tai san-pao chi* (completed 597), T. no. 2034, attributes authorship of *The Yü-lan-p'en Sūtra* to Dharmarakṣa, T. 49:64a. Catalogues that follow Fei's assessment include: Ching-yü's *Ku-chin i-ching t'u-chi* (completed 648), T. no. 2151, 55:354a; *Ta-t'ang nei-tien lu* (completed 664), Tao-hsüan, T. no. 2149, 55:235a; and *K'ai-yüan shih-chiao lu* (completed 730), Chih-sheng, T. no. 2154, 55:494c, 685a.

later versions of the myth—are mentioned only briefly in the two sūtras. In later sources Mu-lien's role is significantly developed to the
point that he, rather than the Buddha or Sangha, is the principal actor,
and Mu-lien's mother is provided with a biography interesting in its
own right. The canonical sources, probably like the actual performance
of the ritual they describe, thus provide a kernel for the later elaboration of the Mu-lien myth and the expansion of ghost festival practice.

Tsung Lin's Record of Seasonal Observances in Ching-ch'u
(ca. 561)

Buddhist histories do record imperial sponsorship of the ghost festival
for the years 483 and 538 A.D., but due to the lack of corroborating evidence, these accounts cannot be confirmed with any certainty.[12]

The earliest undisputable reference to the celebration of the ghost
festival occurs in Tsung Lin's (ca. 498–561) account of seasonal observances in south China, Ching-ch'u sui-shih chi (Record of Seasonal Observances in Ching-ch'u). He writes:

> On the fifteenth day of the seventh month, monks, nuns, reli-
> gious, and lay alike furnish bowls for offerings at the various tem-
> ples and monasteries. The Yü-lan-p'en Sūtra says that [these offer-
> ings] bring merit covering seven generations, and the practice of
> sending them with banners and flowers, singing and drumming,
> and food probably derives from this.
>
> The sūtra also says, "Mu-lien saw his departed mother reborn

[12] In his Pien-cheng lun, T. no. 2110, Fa-lin (572–640) reports that under the reign of
Emperor Kao (r. 479–483) of the Ch'i dynasty, "on the fifteenth day of the seventh
month, bowls were sent to all temples as offerings to three hundred famous monks," T.
52:503a.

The first mention of the sponsorship of the ghost festival at T'ung-t'ai ssu in 538 under
Emperor Wu (r. 502–550) of the Liang dynasty comes in Chih-p'an's thirteenth-century
history of Buddhism, Fo-tsu t'ung-chi, T. no. 2035, 49:450c, 351a. Emperor Wu was an
important patron of Buddhist institutions, and he sponsored many large feasts at T'ung-
t'ai ssu after its completion in 527, see Li-tai san-pao chi, T. no. 2035, 49:99c. Chih-p'an's
account remains suspect due to its late date and the lack of other evidence. If his account
does amount to the interpolation of a pious historian, it may have been based on the record of Emperor Wu having granted an empire-wide amnesty on the sixth day of the seventh month in the year 538. The History of the Liang Dynasty, written in the seventh century, reports that in the fourth year of Ta-t'ung (538), on the sixth day of the seventh
month, "an edict proclaimed a great act of grace throughout the empire on account of
the [Buddhist] disciple, Li Yin-chih of Tung-yeh [present-day Fukien] having discovered
an authentic śarīra [relic] of the Thus-Come One," Liang shu, Yao Ssu-lien (557–637), 2
vols. (Peking: Chung-hua shu-chü, 1973), p. 82.

among the hungry ghosts. He filled his bowl with rice and sent it to his mother as an offering, but before the food entered her mouth it changed into flaming coals, so in the end she could not eat. Mu-lien let out a great cry and rushed back to tell the Buddha. The Buddha said, 'Your mother's sins are grave; there is nothing that you as a single individual can do about it. You must rely on the mighty spiritual power of the assembled monks of the ten directions: for the sake of seven generations of ancestors and those in distress, you should gather [food] of the one hundred flavors and five kinds of fruit, place it in a bowl, and offer it to those of great virtue of the ten directions.' The Buddha decreed that the assembly of monks should chant prayers on behalf of seven generations of ancestors of the donor, that they should practice meditation and concentrate their thoughts, and that they should then receive the food. At this time Mu-lien's mother gained release from all of her sufferings as a hungry ghost. Mu-lien told the Buddha, 'Future disciples of the Buddha who practice filial devotion must also carry out the yü-lan-p'en offering.' The Buddha said, 'Wonderful.' "

Based on this, later generations [of our time] have expanded the ornamentation, pushing their skillful artistry to the point of [offering] cut wood, carved bamboo, and pretty cuttings [of paper] patterned after flowers and leaves.[13]

Tsung Lin's notice establishes quite clearly that celebrations flourished among the populace of south China in the mid-sixth century. Temples (and perhaps markets) were decorated, probably with banners

[13] Translation from the annotated text of Moriya, *Chūgoku ko saijiki no kenkyū*, pp. 359–61, following Moriya's translation in *Keiso saijiki*, Tōyō bunko, Vol. 324 (Tokyo: Heibonsha, 1978), pp. 196–97. Tsung Lin titled his work *Ching-ch'u chi*. Tu Kung-chan (ca. 581–624), a nephew of the author of the *Yü-chu pao-tien*, Tu T'ai-ch'ing, edited Tsung Lin's text and named it *Ching-ch'u sui-shih chi*. The work is extremely important in Chinese social history, as it represents the first real effort to describe the seasonal practices of common people in contrast to previous compendia of monthly ordinances, which described the idealized ritual and agricultural practices that were initiated by the ruler. See Moriya, *Chūgoku ko saijiki no kenkyū*, pp. 48–130, 263–65, for an excellent study of Tsung Lin's work.

Tsung Lin's account is quoted extensively in early encyclopedias. The *Yü-chu pao-tien*, Tu T'ai-ch'ing, quotes from it without identifying it as the source, ch. 7, pp. 12v–13v. See also *I-wen lei-chü*, Ou-yang Hsün, pp. 79–80; *Ch'u-hsüeh chi*, Hsü Chien (659–729) (Peking: Chung-hua shu-chü, 1962), p. 79; *Po-shih liu-t'ieh shih-lei-chi*, Po Chü-i (772–846), 2 vols. (Taipei: Hsin-hsing shu-chü, 1969), ch. 1, p. 72, which is a heavily abbreviated paraphrase; and *T'ai-p'ing yü-lan* (completed 983), Li Fang, 12 vols. (Taipei: Hsin-hsing shu-chü, 1959), p. 272a.

and flowers, and music and singing filled the air. Families collected delicacies to present to monks in the yü-lan bowls, offering lifelike flowers elaborately crafted from natural materials. As Tsung Lin does not mention government sponsorship, we may assume that such practices thrived outside the system of official temples and without the provision of offerings by the government.

The Yü-lan-p'en Sūtra was well known by this time, the story of Mu-lien and his mother providing justification for the ornate gifts offered during the festivities. Tsung Lin also mentions the notion of making merit for the ancestors, which was instrumental in synthesizing the rituals and symbols of Buddhism with ancestral religion.

The Pure Land Yü-lan-p'en Sūtra (CA. 600–650)

The Pure Land Yü-lan-p'en Sūtra, a sūtra-style work not included in the Chinese canon, represents a version of the Mu-lien myth that falls between the poles of folk and elite. It contains the same basic story as do the earlier canonical sūtras, but it also contains elements that the Buddhist establishment deemed unacceptable for inclusion in the canon: the story of Mu-lien's and his mother's actions in previous lives and the donation of lavish, even irresponsible, offerings by rulers of state. In its form and language it also tends toward the vernacular narratives and folk entertainments that were popular in later centuries. The first undisputable reference to the Pure Land sūtra comes in the year 664, and records dating from 730 show that it was quite popular among the common people despite its noncanonical status.

The Pure Land Yü-lan-p'en Sūtra[14] opens with the Buddha preaching to a large audience in the garden of Anāthapiṇḍika in the Jetavana trees in the Kingdom of Śrāvastī. From his lotus-gilded lion's throne, the World-Honored One emits rays of light from his mouth and then prefaces his teaching with a few short stanzas concerning "pure land conduct" (ching-t'u chih hsing), which state that the purity of the Pure Land as an objective state of being depends upon the purity of the "mind" or "thought" (hsin).[15]

The Pure Land sūtra then presents the basic story of the founding of

[14] Ching-t'u yü-lan-p'en ching, P. no. 2185, reproduced in the studies by Jaworski and Iwamoto (noted immediately below). Jan Jaworski, a student of Jean Przyluski, has written the best study and translation of the text, "L'Avalambana Sūtra de la terre pure," Monumenta Serica 1 (1935–36):82–107. Iwamoto Yutaka has also translated the text in Ji-goku meguri no bungaku, pp. 25–32.

[15] Jaworski and Iwamoto offer different interpretations of these lines; Jaworski, "L'A-valambana Sūtra de la terre pure," p. 94; Iwamoto, Jigoku meguri no bungaku, p. 25.

the ghost festival, paralleling the accounts in *The Yü-lan-p'en Sūtra* and *The Sūtra on Offering Bowls to Repay Kindness*. Mu-lien enters a state of meditation to search for his deceased mother, but to no avail. He returns to the Buddha for information on his mother's whereabouts. When the Buddha replies that Ch'ing-t'i has been reborn as a hungry ghost in hell, Mu-lien is overcome with grief; he sobs and rolls on the ground, unable even to pick himself up. Taking pity on his dedicated disciple, the Buddha teaches a method of making merit designed to free the ancestors from the torments of purgatory. Mu-lien performs the service as directed, presenting a bowl laden with food and other items to the Buddha and the Sangha as they emerge from their summer retreat. This act immediately bears fruit, and Mu-lien's mother is liberated from the realm of hungry ghosts and reborn among humans. Unlike the canonical and more literary sources, the Pure Land text describes Mu-lien's joy and amazement at being reunited with his mother:

> It was like searching for a golden grain of sand among all the sands of the Ganges and suddenly finding it. It was like a filial son hearing that his deceased mother had suddenly come back to life. It was like a man who is blind from birth suddenly having his eyes opened. It was like a person who has already died coming back to life. Such was Mu-lien's joy.[16]

Mu-lien is so happy, in fact, that his body gushes flames and rainwater, after which he settles down to hear the Buddha recapitulate his teaching on yü-lan-p'en to the audience.

The next section of the sūtra shows royalty and lay people performing the ritual of offering. Having witnessed the reunion of Mu-lien and his mother, which was secured by giving gifts to the Buddha and the Sangha, King Bimbisāra of Magadha orders his minister of the treasury to prepare an offering. In the Pure Land text the offerings are far more lavish than those described in the canonical texts: "five hundred bowls made of gold filled with a thousand kinds of flowers, five hundred silver bowls filled with a thousand kinds of red-gold incense, five hundred jade bowls filled with a thousand kinds of yellow lotus, five hundred agate bowls filled with a thousand kinds of red lotus flowers, five hundred coral bowls filled with a thousand kinds of greenwood incense, and five hundred amber bowls filled with a thousand kinds of

---

[16] *The Pure Land Yü-lan-p'en Sūtra*, lines ("line" and "lines" hereafter abbreviated "l." and "ll.," respectively) 28–31.

white lotus flowers."[17] King Bimbisāra and his treasure-bearing retinue pay their respects to the Buddha, present their offerings to him and to the Sangha, and then return home. The sūtra notes that seven generations of the king's ancestors were accordingly freed from seventy-two *kalpas* of suffering. Following King Bimbisāra's lead, Sudatta leads a large group of laymen and laywomen in making less extravagant offerings to the Buddha and the Sangha, followed by another round of royal offerings by King Prasenajit and Queen Mallikā.

The Pure Land Yü-lan-p'en Sūtra includes a long section on the past lives of Mu-lien and his mother in which the Buddha explains how their previous acts have led to their current situation. In a previous life Mu-lien was a pious boy named Lo-pu (Turnip), and his mother's name was Ch'ing-t'i. One day the boy set out on a journey, instructing his mother to make feasts for wandering almsmen during his absence. Ch'ing-t'i only pretended to provide the offerings, deceiving her own son about her stinginess. As a result of her greed she was reborn as a hungry ghost in hell, suffering the torments that the yü-lan-p'en offering is intended to relieve. The sūtra closes with the audience rejoicing, paying respects to the Buddha, and practicing the teaching.

The Pure Land Yü-lan-p'en Sūtra represents a significant elaboration of the version of the myth of Mu-lien contained in canonical sources. The story of the Buddha establishing the ghost festival after Mu-lien's unsuccessful attempt to succor his mother remains basically the same. The significant additions to the story concern the participation of rulers and the particulars of Mu-lien's previous life. The Pure Land sūtra describes the provision of gifts from the state treasury and the participation of state officials in yü-lan-p'en services; the description in the sūtra accords well with what is known of state-sponsored celebrations in the second half of the seventh century. The sūtra also shows that the benefits from state-sponsored offerings were believed to accrue to the emperor's ancestors for seven generations. While the details of state celebrations in China can be established in only a few well-documented cases, the theme of imperial patronage of the ghost festival as narrated in the Pure Land sūtra is clearly related to the use of Buddhist ritual apparatus in the Chinese imperial ancestral cult during the T'ang dynasty.

The offerings made by kings in the Pure Land sūtra are far more elaborate than those described in the canonical texts, and in the late seventh century we find the monk and encyclopedia writer Tao-shih (ca. 600–683) using this fact as scriptural license for lavish ghost festival of-

[17] *The Pure Land Yü-lan-p'en Sūtra*, ll. 46–50. Cf. Jaworski, "L'Avalambana Sūtra de la terre pure," p. 96.

ferings. He quotes from *The Pure Land Yü-lan-p'en Sūtra* to show that offerings of jewels and precious objects bring help for the ancestors, calling the sūtra *"The Pure Land Sūtra of the Larger Bowl" (Ta-p'en ching-t'u ching)* in contrast to the canonical text, *"The Sūtra on Repaying Kindness with the Smaller Bowl" (Hsiao-p'en pao-en ching)*.[18]

The Pure Land Yü-lan-p'en Sūtra also marks the first appearance in surviving Chinese literary sources of the story of Mu-lien and his mother in their previous lives. Stories of the previous lives of disciples and other important figures (a genre known as *"avadāna"*) generally betray a didactic purpose: they are compiled and told in order to illustrate the ineluctable workings of karmic retribution, and they often reflect the interests of an audience composed of lay people. The avadāna tale contained in the Pure Land text occupies an intermediate position among the different versions of the Mu-lien myth. The canonical sources make no mention of Mu-lien's previous life, the Pure Land sūtra includes it at the end of the text, while *The Transformation Text on Mu-lien Saving His Mother* includes it as an integral part of the narrative.

The literary form of *The Pure Land Yü-lan-p'en Sūtra* also represents an intermediary stage in the development of ghost festival mythology. It includes elements that probably derived from a milieu close to oral tradition: similes describing the reunion of mother and son, the colloquial expression "A-p'o" for "mother"; and a long section on the previous lives of mother and son. In other respects the Pure Land sūtra betrays a literary style and pretensions to canonical status: it opens ("Thus have I heard. . . .") and closes ("Then the immeasureable grand assembly rejoiced and practiced it.") in typical sūtra style, and the avadāna section remains an appendage to the main body of the story.

The sūtra may be dated to the period 600–650. It was never accepted as part of the official canon of Chinese Buddhism, but was quite in vogue during the T'ang. By chance a complete manuscript of the text was discovered at Tun-huang, and in 1936 Jan Jaworski published an important study and translation.[19]

The Pure Land text is first mentioned—with suspicion, as an apocryphal version of *The Yü-lan-p'en Sūtra*—in the year 664 in Tao-hsüan's

[18] *Fa-yüan chu-lin*, Tao-shih, T. no. 2122, 53:751a quotes loosely from ll. 40–46 of *The Pure Land Yü-lan-p'en Sūtra*; a second quotation, T. 53:751a-b, quotes from ll. 46–70.

[19] Jaworski, "L'Avalambana Sūtra de la terre pure," pp. 82–107. See also Iwamoto, *Jigoku meguri no bungaku*, pp. 25–32; Okabe Kazuo, "Urabon kyōrui no yakkyō shiteki kenkyū," *Shūkyō kenkyū* 37:3 (March 1964):70–72; Ogawa Kan'ichi, *Bukkyō bunka shi kenkyū* (Kyoto: Nagata bunshōdō, 1973), pp. 171–79; and Honda Gi'ei, "*Urabon kyō* to *Jōdo urabon kyō*," in *Butten no naisō to gaisō* (Tokyo: Kōbundō, 1967), pp. 557–77.

catalogue of the Buddhist canon.[20] By the early eighth century the sūtra had become so popular that most people considered it to be a true, canonical text. Chih-sheng, in his catalogue compiled in 730, also indicates that it may have been transmitted orally. In the section on "doubtful" (*i*) texts (apocryphal [*wei*ᵇ] as opposed to true or canonical [*chen*]) he writes:

> The Pure Land Yü-lan-p'en Sūtra in one *chüan* on five sheets. None of the records, old or new, register this sūtra. Having been transmitted popularly, it is now considered to be a true classic. On close investigation, its phrasing appears to touch people's feelings, but having examined the matter in detail, I have placed it in the record of doubtful texts.[21]

These comments from T'ang sources show clearly that the Pure Land sūtra was distributed broadly in Chinese society and that it appealed to the masses at large despite the aspersions cast on it by those who defined the Buddhist canon.[22] One of the leading clerics of the ninth century, Tsung-mi, quotes the Pure Land text in his commentary on the canonical yü-lan-p'en sūtra. He draws on the Pure Land sūtra's description of Mu-lien's mother's previous life, but *he does not name his source*, noting merely that, "A sūtra says. . . ."[23] Tsung-mi's tacit acceptance of the avadāna tale as part of the myth of Mu-lien suggests that by the early ninth century, learned members of the Buddhist establishment could no longer ignore the apocryphal versions of the myth. Tsung-mi not only signals its popularity and its noncanonical status, but also hints that other commentaries had been written on the Pure Land text. Unfortunately, these texts had been lost by the twelfth century.[24]

[20] Under his entry on *The Yü-lan-p'en Sūtra*, Tao-hsüan writes, "*The Yü-lan-p'en Sūtra*, on one sheet. There is another text of five sheets, entitled *The Pure Land Yü-lan-p'en Sūtra*. We do not know from which [Sanskrit text] it has been translated," *Ta-t'ang nei-tien lu*, T. no. 2149, 55:298b. The opinion is repeated in *Ta-chou k'an-ting chung-ching mu-lu*, T. no. 2153, 55:431c.

[21] *K'ai-yüan shih-chiao lu*, T. no. 2154, 55:671c–72a.

[22] *The Pure Land Yü-lan-p'en Sūtra* also circulated in eighth-century Japan. See the documents collected in *Dainihon komonjo, hennen monjo*, ed. Tokyo teikoku daigaku shiryō hensanjo (Tokyo: Tokyo teikoku daigaku, 1901–40), 5:451–52, 7:10, and 12:332.

[23] *Tsung-mi Commentary*, T. 39:509c.

[24] After a discussion of some of the details in the avadāna, Tsung-mi writes, "Other commentaries say otherwise, but none of them penetrate [the meaning]," T. 39:510a. Following Tsung-mi's comment, Yüan-chao writes, "There must have been other interpretations in older commentaries. These texts are now lost, so we cannot know what they say," *Yüan-chao Commentary*, Z. 1, 35:2, p. 120rb.

Hui-ching's *Commentary Praising the Yü-lan-p'en Sūtra* (CA. 636–639)

The earliest surviving commentary on *The Yü-lan-p'en Sūtra* was written by the eminent monk of Ch'ang-an, Hui-ching (578–ca. 645). In both style and content the *Yü-lan-p'en ching tsan-shu (Commentary Praising the Yü-lan-p'en Sūtra)* reflects the refined tastes and learned interests of its author. Hui-ching was well versed in the major trends of Buddhist thought of his day. He assisted in the translation of Sanskrit texts and he held important positions in the administration of the Sangha. His writings cover a broad range of topics.

Hui-ching's commentary follows closely the Mu-lien myth as it is presented in the earliest canonical sources. Mu-lien appears in the commentary as the ideal monk, one who combines the discipline required of the religious specialist with the devotion needed to sustain the ancestral cult. Mu-lien's previous life and his battles with demons are passed over in silence, as are his mother's biography and her tortures in hell. Hui-ching's monastic orientation is apparent in the commentary's sources, which derive from the "high" tradition of Chinese Buddhism rather than from the oral tradition or Chinese apocrypha.

Hui-ching was born into the Fang family in Ch'ang-shan (present-day Hopei) in the year 578.[25] At the age of fourteen he joined the monkhood, pursuing studies in Abhidharma and Mādhyamika philosophy. Between 589 and 601 he gave lectures in the capital, Ch'ang-an; these marked the beginning of a long career as a debater and public figure. In 628 he joined several prominent men of letters in assisting the Magadhan monk, Prabhāmitra (565–633), with a translation of the *Mahāyāna-sūtrālaṃkāra*, so impressing his co-workers that they referred to him as the "Bodhisattva of the East" (*tung-fang p'u-sa*).[26] Hui-ching authored over a dozen works, ranging from thirty-*chüan* commentaries on Yogācāra treatises to brief explanations of such lay-oriented texts as *The Yü-lan-p'en Sūtra*.[27]

---

[25] Hui-ching was sixty-eight years old in 645, according to his biography in *Hsü kao-seng chuan*, T. no. 2060, 50:446b. Biographical details in these two paragraphs are drawn from this source, T. 50:441c–46b; and from *Fo-tsu t'ung-chi*, T. no. 2035, 49:363b–65a; *Ta-t'ang nei-tien lu*, T. no. 2149, 55:281c; *Lung-hsing fo-chiao pien-nien t'ung-lun*, Tsu-hsiu (ca. 1164), Z. 2B, 3:3, pp. 259vb, and 267rb–va; and the documents collected in *Chung-kuo fo-chiao ssu-hsiang tzu-liao hsüan-pien*, ed. Shih Chün (Peking: Chung-hua shu-chü, 1983), Part 2, Vol. 4, pp. 405–6.

[26] The *Mahāyānasūtrālaṃkāra*, attributed to Asaṅga, is *Ta-sheng chuang-yen ching lun*, T. no. 1604.

[27] MBDJ, p. 280b–c lists thirteen works. To this list should be added the *Shih-i lun* in one *chüan*; it is noted in *Ta-t'ang nei-tien lu*, T. no. 2149, 55:281c. For a brief study and

Hui-ching was a powerful member of the Buddhist establishment in the Sui and early T'ang, counting among his friends such high-ranking officials as the Duke of Liang, Fang Hsüan-ling (578–648). Hui-ching was the abbot of Chi-kuo ssu, held an honorary position at P'u-kuang ssu, and was certainly well acquainted with the administration of large celebrations like the ghost festival. He often represented the Buddhist side in debates between proponents of the Three Teachings held during the T'ang. Among the opponents whom he met (and vanquished, according to the Buddhist historians) in such debates were K'ung Ying-ta (574–648) and the Taoist master Ts'ai Tzu-huang. In 645 he was called to take part in the translation of more scriptures (probably those brought back from the West in the same year by Hsüan-tsang [602–664]), but Hui-ching had to decline because of poor health.

Hui-ching's *Commentary Praising the Yü-lan-p'en Sūtra* was probably written between 636 and 639.[28] Because the commentary follows the sūtra so closely, I shall merely note some of its highlights here.

After explaining the meaning of the title ("yü-lan" refers to hungry ghosts hanging upside-down in hell, "p'en" means the basin in which offerings are placed) and discussing the organization of the sūtra,[29]

---

translation of Hui-ching's commentary on the *Wen-shih hsi-yü chung-seng ching*, trans. An Shih-kao (ca. 148–170), T. no. 701, see Ui Hakuju, *"Onshitsu gyōsho,"* in *Seiiki butten no kenkyū: Tonkō isho kanyaku* (Tokyo: Iwanami shoten, 1970), pp. 311–32. Hui-ching's commentary, *Wen-shih ching shu*, is S. no. 2497, printed as T. no. 2780. Hui-ching's works are very well represented in the Imperial Repository (Shōsōin) in Nara, according to catalogues and other documents mostly from the Tempyō era (729–749); see Ishida Mosaku, *Shakyō yori mitaru nara-chō bukkyō no kenkyū*, Tōyō bunko ronshu, No. 11 (Tokyo: Tōyō bunko, 1930), index nos. 1996, 2020, 2021, 2050, 2064, 2065, 2111, 2112, 2113, 2200, 2201, 2220, and 2500.

[28] My estimation of the date of authorship is based on Tao-hsüan's biography of Hui-ching. Tao-hsüan does not establish a specific date of composition, but his remark that Hui-ching's commentary on *The Yü-lan-p'en Sūtra* was popular comes in the middle of the biography, between events dated 636 and 639, T. 50:443a. Hui-ching's commentary is P. no. 2269, reproduced as T. no. 2781. The manuscript appears to be written with a quick hand, and corrections have been made with a thicker brush. The manuscript is almost completely intact, the major gaps falling at the beginning. Although the title at the end is merely *"P'en ching tsan-shu,"* the first several lines of the manuscript make clear that its full title was *"(Fo-shuo) yü-lan-p'en ching tsan-shu."* The commentary is written in a compact, elegant prose style containing many four-character sentences. It sticks closely to the text, using synonyms to gloss individual words and quoting short extracts from Buddhist sources to expand the glosses. Unlike Tsung-mi's commentary, it contains few lengthy digressions on such topics as filiality and merit. *The Yü-lan-p'en Sūtra* from which it quotes is very similar to the text now known under that title, although some of its wording follows the text of *The Sūtra on Offering Bowls to Repay Kindness*.

[29] Hui-ching divides the sūtra into three portions: "a portion on the origins of the teaching," "a portion on what the Sage [the Buddha] taught," and "a portion on carrying

Hui-ching begins a line-by-line commentary. Hui-ching gives special emphasis to Mu-lien's dual status as masterful meditator and filial son. He stresses the meditative context of Mu-lien's cosmic flight and shys away from the combat and gore that predominate in other renditions of Mu-lien's travels to the underworld. The hells receive virtually no elaboration in Hui-ching's account, which confines itself to restating Mu-lien's mother's lack of food and her frail physical condition. Nor is there any explanation of how her greedy actions led to her current state of woe. Compared to other versions of the story, Hui-ching's commentary betrays a more refined or monastic bent: Mu-lien is tamer and less adventuresome, while his mother lacks a history and even a name.

For Hui-ching, the story of Mu-lien is a story about filiality, which, as taught by the Buddha, consists of aiding the ancestors in whatever path of existence they inhabit. Hui-ching quotes from a sūtra, "Even if you collected a pile of precious gems reaching to the twenty-eighth heaven and gave them all away to people [as charity], the merit earned from this would not be one-tenth of the merit of making offerings to one's parents."[30] The unity of filiality with the highest ideals of Buddhism is an assumption common to all versions of the Mu-lien myth, be they canonical, commentarial, or theatrical. Where Hui-ching differs from other interpreters of the myth is in the sources he draws on to articulate this synthesis. Where later commentators (notably Tsung-mi) cite examples from the pre-Buddhist Chinese tradition—classics like the *Shih-ching (The Book of Songs)* and paragons of filiality like Tung Yung—Hui-ching draws almost exclusively on the Buddhist canon to explain the concept of filial devotion. The *Āgamas*, the *Nirvāṇa Sūtra*, and the *Mahāprajñāpāramitāśāstra* provide Hui-ching's points of reference. The framework he uses to synthesize monastic and lay ideals is defined by the erudite terms of Chinese Buddhist philosophy and by the officially approved stories of the Chinese Buddhist canon.

Hui-ching's *Commentary Praising the Yü-lan-p'en Sūtra* was apparently popular during his lifetime, and a copy of it had made its way to Japan by the middle of the eighth century, but it was not influential in later years.[31]

---

out the teaching." He also notes that the division of the sūtra according to the "old" exegetical style (later used in the *Tsung-mi Commentary* and in *The Lecture Text on the Yü-lan-p'en Sūtra*) amounts to the same thing, T. 85:540a.

[30] T. 85:541b. The passage quoted by Hui-ching expands upon the wording in the *Mo-lo wang ching (Sūtra on the King of Mallā)*, trans. Chü-ch'ü Ching-sheng (ca. 455–464), T. no. 517, 14:791b.

[31] On the popularity of the commentary during Hui-ching's lifetime, see *Hsü kao-seng*

CHAPTER 3

TAO-SHIH'S MEMORANDUM ON OFFERINGS TO THE BUDDHA
(CA. 668)

In his massive encyclopedia completed in 668, *Fa-yüan chu-lin (The Pearl Grove of the Dharma Garden)*, the scholar-monk Tao-shih tucked away a small document discussing the management and disposition of offerings at Buddhist temples. Although the piece is untitled and unattributed, it was most likely authored by Tao-shih himself sometime before 668. It provides a unique picture of how the ghost festival and other celebrations were administered by Sangha authorities in the official temples of Ch'ang-an.

Tao-shih's memorandum sheds significant light on the general character of state-sponsored celebrations in the late seventh century. In the first place it confirms that the celebration of the ghost festival at major temples in the capital was sponsored by the government for the well-being of the empire. Gifts were provided out of state coffers and were delivered to temple grounds by government officials. Services performed at these large temples included music, a communal banquet for all those who attended, and offerings and prayers in front of Buddha statues. Presents given to the Sangha at these temples were considered to be "national offerings" (*kuo-chia kung-yang*); apparently everyone's ancestors benefited from the exchange.

Tao-shih's account also reveals much about the philosophy and economy of T'ang festivals. In China the "Three Jewels" did not simply represent a formulaic refuge of faith. In China the "Three Jewels" also referred to the material objects that had value in the Buddhist religion: statues, halls, and reliquaries in temples constituted the Jewel of the Buddha; texts and divinatory instruments were Jewels of the Dharma; and temple lands, lodgings, and resident farmers constituted "permanent property of the Sangha" (*ch'ang-chu seng-wu*). Most temple property belonged to only one of the Three Jewels and could not be intermixed with property belonging to another of the Jewels. Only a small fraction of temple property, called "general temple funds and possessions" (*t'ung-yung chih wu*), could be used for any purpose without restriction.[32]

The need to maintain clear distinctions between the accounts of the Three Jewels had important implications for the mechanics and admin-

---

chuan, T. 50:443a. At least two copies of the commentary existed in the Imperial Repository in Nara during the Tempyō shōhō era (749–757); see the documents in *Dai nihon komonjo, hennen monjo*, 10:329 and 12:542.

[32] See Jacques Gernet, *Les Aspects économiques du bouddhisme dans la société chinoise du Ve au Xe siècle* (Saigon: Ecole Française d'Extrême-Orient, 1956), p. 63.

istration of the ghost festival. Offerings to the Sangha were the essence of the ghost festival. Offerings to the Buddha and to the Dharma were of course permissible during the festival, but gifts to monks were the only ones that brought merit to one's ancestors. Gifts to the Sangha were provided by private donors and by the state. Gifts to the Sangha could *not* be provided out of Sangha funds, since that could not properly be counted as an exchange between two different groups.

Making an offering to the Buddha was part of all Buddhist services, including the ghost festival, and Tao-shih discusses several ways of financing this offering. The offering may be supplied out of general temple funds; it may be supplied by a donor, in which case part of the offering is given to the Sangha after the service; or it may be supplied out of Sangha property, in which case the entire offering is returned to the Sangha account at the conclusion of the ritual.

During important festivals monks at large temples played host to hundreds and thousands of guests, including common people, government officials, entertainers, and emperors. Tao-shih's memorandum shows how seriously temple administrators viewed their ceremonial responsibilities to their guests. Monks did not simply make possible the transfer of benefits from living descendants to ancestors; they also fulfilled the responsibilities of a host at a large banquet. The Sangha catered the vegetarian feasts served to guests and often assumed the cost of the meal as well.

Tao-shih's document, placed in the part of *The Pearl Grove of the Dharma Garden* on "Offerings to the Buddha" (*hsien-fo*) in the section on "Sacrifices" (*chi-ssu*), is in the form of seven questions and answers.[33]

The first question asks about the source of the offerings made to the Buddha when crowds come for the festival on the fifteenth day of the seventh month. Tao-shih answers that when there is a large donor sponsoring the festival, offerings to the Buddha should be drawn from the common property of the temple. When there is no sponsor, Buddha offerings are to be provided out of the permanent property of the Sangha.

The second question asks:

[33] *Fa-yüan chu-lin*, T. no. 2122, 53:750a–52a. The rest of the part on "Offerings to the Buddha" (T. 53:752a–53b) contains citations from various sūtras extolling the virtues of giving gifts to the Buddha. While many Japanese studies of the ghost festival note the citations of *The Yü-lan-p'en Sūtra* and *The Pure Land Yü-lan-p'en Sūtra* in this section, none mentions the other portions of the document which concern the disposition of offerings.

In the great national temples like Hsi-ming and Tz'u-en ssu in Ch'ang-an, there are endowed fields and gardens in addition to land distributed on the basis of population, and everything that is given [during the ghost festival] is considered to be a national offering. Now every year when people send bowls of offerings and all sorts of items, with musicians and the like carrying the bowls and with more than one government official bringing bowls, what sort of items should be given to the guests? Furthermore, before the official bowls arrive, when offerings are made in front of the Buddha and various other offerings are made, what items should be used to make the offerings?

Tao-shih answers:

If there is common property, use that first. If there is no such property, then there is no alternative but to take items from the permanent property of the Sangha to treat the guests and to offer as food.

The third exchange concerns the justification for taking property belonging exclusively to the Sangha and sharing it with lay people in the form of a festival meal. Tao-shih answers:

According to the *Mahāsāṅghikavinaya*, the *Sarvāstivādavinaya*, and others, kings, great ministers, and workmen all hate stealing. In regard to the Sangha's profits and losses, if [34] you open things up to the laity and treat them with Sangha property, this does not count as an offense. If you do not share your expenditures with the laity, opening things up but not treating them, then they will deduce that there has been a loss in [the wealth of] the Buddha's Sangha. So it is no offense to open up [Sangha property] and let them see.

Now, since this is so, when the state sends bowls for offerings with officials and musicians, and the Emperor orders that Buddha bowls be sent, how can you not let them see [Sangha property]? If you do not let them see, it will lead to ridicule and reproach, calling forth sneers from outside the fold. [They will think], "Those who have left the householder's life seek only the possessions of others; they haven't even given up their own avarice." The common man sees what is near without understanding what is far. This is what is meant in saying, "Share your income and share

---

[34] Emending *fo* to *jo*.

your expenditures." The Buddha understood profit and loss, which is why he opened up the strictures in accord with circumstances.

The fourth question concerns the disposition of offerings made to the Buddha in the course of the ghost festival:

> *Question*: When permanent property of the Sangha is used to make the offerings of Buddha food in front of the Buddha, then after the service the offerings revert to the Sangha's permanent [property]—in this matter there is no doubt. What we do not know is what happens to the offerings when an outside donor offers bowls and other sundry items.
>
> *Answer*: This should be decided on the basis of the donor's circumstances and capability. If the donor makes the offering according to the sūtra, vowing[35] to bring salvation to his living and deceased relatives, then he makes offerings to the Sangha, those lowly and advanced [monks] of the ten directions who release themselves [in repentance] during the summer session. Only in this way can he save his deceased relatives, who will gain release from the three unpleasant paths of rebirth and ascend in purity to the paths of men and gods. Therefore, after making offerings to the Buddha, all of the food—the produce and raw items, rice and noodles that have been offered, etc.—becomes permanent [property] of the Sangha and is used in return to supply food for monks.

Tao-shih further allows that donors may alternatively choose to make offerings to the Buddha or to the Dharma. In these cases, a portion of the offering should revert to the Sangha.

The fifth and sixth questions raise doubts about the extravagance of ghost festival offerings. Responding to his questioner's concern that valuables and jewels exceed the simple offerings of food and incense allowed in *The Yü-lan-p'en Sūtra*, Tao-shih quotes from *The Pure Land Yü-lan-p'en Sūtra* to show that the lavish items given by King Bimbisāra to the Buddha and the Sangha were fully efficacious in bringing aid to his ancestors. While jewels and treasures are not necessary, they are perfectly acceptable as offerings.

The seventh and last question concerns the inclusion of flowers in offerings to the Buddha. Because Vinaya rules prohibited monks from adorning themselves with flowers, special precautions were needed to insure that flower offerings given to the Buddha (offerings which *were*

---

[35] Emending *yüan* to *yüan*[b].

allowed by the Vinaya) did not end up in the possession of the Sangha.[36] Flowers were permitted in the case of a lay donor supplying the offerings to the Buddha. Questions arose only when offerings at festivals had to be supplied by the Buddhist establishment itself.

In his response Tao-shih says that at small temples, flowers and fruits growing on the temple grounds—in Chinese eyes, temple land and its products belonged to the Buddhist Sangha—may be used for offerings to the Buddha. At larger temples, though, Tao-shih suggests that a distinction be maintained between the domain of the Buddha and the domain of the Sangha, with offerings of flowers to the Buddha being supplied out of the common property of the temple. Only when common resources are unavailable may Sangha-supplied flowers be given to the Buddha; while this kind of offering brings no relief to the ancestors (since no gifts are given to the Sangha), it effectively teaches charity and averts charges of Buddhist opulence. Tao-shih writes:

> If there is no common property, then there is no choice but to use permanent property of the Sangha, gathering various items of flowers, fruit, and all kinds of food to offer to the Buddha. This causes common people to give birth to good and to extinguish evil, and in this there is no loss. Although using permanent property of the Sangha cannot bring about the salvation of other people's living or deceased relatives, it does avoid the crime of being slandered and accused [of hoarding] by lay people.

Unlike most other entries in Tao-shih's encyclopedia, the document on offerings to the Buddha lacks a title and lists no author. A plausible argument may be made, however, for Tao-shih's authorship. Tao-shih was born around the year 600 and entered the monkhood at an early age.[37] Although it is unclear precisely which positions he held, Tao-shih was an important figure in the Buddhist etablishment in Ch'ang-an in the 650s and 660s: between 656 and 661 Tao-shih participated in the imperial reception of Hsüan-tsang's works, in 658 he was called by the emperor to live at Hsi-ming ssu, and in 664 he wrote a memorial to

[36] See, for example, Isaline B. Horner, trans., *The Book of the Discipline (Vinaya Pi-taka)*, 6 vols., Sacred Books of the Buddhists, Vols. 10, 11, 13, 14, 20, 25 (London: Luzac and Co., 1949–66), 5:170. This rule also figures prominently—as a potential source of clinging and duality—in the *Vimalakīrtinirdeśa*, in which unenlightened disciples of the Buddha try to shed flowers rained down upon them by a goddess; see *Wei-mo-chieh so-shuo ching*, trans. Kumārajīva (350–409), T. no. 475, 14:547c–48c.

[37] The *Ritsuon sōbō den* (completed 1689) by Eken reports that Tao-shih received full ordination in 615, which would place his birth sometime around the year 600, ZS. 64:177c.

the throne protesting a new edition of Taoist scriptures.[38] Tao-shih is reported to have written a short piece on the same subject discussed in the memorandum[39] and in at least one other case is known to have inserted his own writings, untitled and unattributed, into the body of his encyclopedia.[40] Tao-shih's position in the Sangha hierarchy, his interests in Vinaya and in the specific topic of the memorandum, and the precedent of smuggling his own pieces into the anthologies he compiled all lend weight to the likelihood that Tao-shih wrote the piece himself.

YANG CHIUNG'S "YÜ-LAN-P'EN RHAPSODY"
(692)

The large-scale celebration of the ghost festival in Lo-yang (the site of the capital between 690 and 701) in 692 provided the occasion for an important prose poem by the early T'ang writer, Yang Chiung (650– ca. 694). The *Chiu t'ang shu (Old T'ang History)* describes the event:

On the full moon of the seventh month in the first year of *Ju-i* [692], yü-lan bowls were sent out from the palace and distributed to Buddhist temples. [Empress Wu] Tse-t'ien went with the various officials to observe it at the Southern Gate. [Yang] Chiung presented his "Yü-lan-p'en Rhapsody." It was beautifully written and its words were striking.[41]

Lay people were not the only celebrants of the ghost festival in the T'ang. In most years, as in 692, the state supplied the offerings given at

[38] See *Sung kao-seng chuan*, T. no. 2061, 50:726c; Lung-hsi Li Yen's preface to *Fa-yüan chu-lin*, T. no. 2122, 53:269b; and *Sung kao-seng chuan*, T. 50:726c. A longer recension of Tao-shih's memorial is contained in *Fa-yüan chu-lin*, T. 53:703a–4c. A shorter recension is contained in *Ch'üan t'ang wen*, Hsü Sung (1781–1841) (Taipei: Ching-wei shu-chü, 1965), ch. 912, pp. 11993–94; and in *Fo-tsu li-tai t'ung-tsai*, Nien-ch'ang (d. 1341), T. no. 2036, 49:581b–c.

[39] Tao-shih's work, entitled *Li-fo i-shih (Ceremonial for Reverencing the Buddha)* is listed in the last chapter of *Fa-yüan chu-lin*, T. 53:1023c; and in *Sung kao-seng chuan*, T. 50:727a. The last chapter of *Fa-yüan chu-lin* did not assume its present form until ca. 800–1000, see Stephen F. Teiser, "T'ang Buddhist Encyclopedias: An Introduction to *Fa-yüan chu-lin* and *Chu-ching yao-chi*," *T'ang Studies* No. 3 (1985): 121. The fact that this text is cited for the first time at least 150 years after its alleged authorship may mean that the work was nothing but an extract from *Fa-yüan chu-lin* (completed in 668) that was later circulated independently.

[40] Tao-shih's memorial against the new edition of Taoist scriptures is inserted into *Fa-yüan chu-lin*, T. 53:703a–4c. See above for other recensions of his memorial.

[41] *Chiu t'ang shu*, Liu Hsü (887–946) (Peking: Chung-hua shu-chü, 1975), p. 5001.

the officially sponsored temples in the capital, and government officials were in attendance. Empress Wu's participation may also indicate that the imperial ancestors were singled out as beneficiaries of the offerings.

Yang Chiung's "Yü-lan-p'en Rhapsody" presents a vision of the festival illuminated by the stars and by the amber light of dawn. Yang, himself a stargazer of high repute,[42] evokes the cosmological and meteorological background of the early-autumn festival, a time when the western region of K'un-lun seems especially near. In Yang's rhapsody we feel the unearthly presence of spirits and magical birds, who are drawn noiselessly to the jewels and foods offered by Empress and commoner alike.

Outside of his surviving work, sources preserve few details of Yang Chiung's life. He was born in the year 650, and his family was from Hua-yin (present-day Shensi).[43] Yang held a succession of minor government posts, never rising to a position of power. He was called to the College for the Exaltation of Literature (Ch'ung-wen kuan) in the Palace of the Heir to the Throne in 681 and served as a local official in Ying-ch'uan and Tzu-chou (both in present-day Szechuan), among other posts.

It appears that Yang was best known for his acerbic personality and his elegant prose works. A Yüan-dynasty biography reports that Yang was in the habit of referring to some of his contemporaries as "unicorn lasts," a last or inverse mold around which was formed the shape of the mythical *ch'i-lin* ("unicorn"). The account reads:

> Whenever he heard of a pretentious courtier, he would call him a "unicorn last." When questioned about it, he responded, "One who plays at being a unicorn has to mark and draw all over himself to cover up his being an ass, to look like a different animal. But take away his skin and he's still an ass."[44]

[42] See Edward H. Schafer, *Pacing the Void: T'ang Approaches to the Stars* (Berkeley: University of California Press, 1977), pp. 36, 38, 86, 183.

[43] Yang's preface to his "Hun-t'ien fu" says that he was eleven years old in the fifth year of the Hsien-ch'ing era (660), which would probably place his birth in 650; *Ch'u-t'ang ssu-chieh wen-chi*, ed. Hsiang Chia-ta, Ssu-pu pei-yao ed. (Taipei: Chung-hua shu-chü, 1970), ch. 10, p. 1r. See also Yang Ch'eng-tsu, "Yang Chiung nien-p'u," *Tung-fang wen-hua (Journal of Oriental Studies*, Hong Kong) 13:1 (January 1975):57–72. Short biographies of Yang are contained in *Chiu t'ang shu*, p. 5001; and in *Hsin t'ang shu* (Peking: Chung-hua shu-chü, 1975), p. 5741. See also the material assembled in the appendix to his collected works, *Yang Ying-ch'uan chi*, Ssu-pu ts'ung-k'an, Series 1, Vol. 35 (Taipei: Commercial Press, 1967).

[44] *T'ang ts'ai-tzu chuan*, Hsin Wen-fang (ca. 1304) (Shanghai: Ku-tien wen-hsüeh ch'u-pan-she, 1957), p. 6.

Yang's collected works in thirty *chüan* survived into the tenth century, and a good many of them are still extant.[45]

Yang Chiung's "Yü-lan-p'en Rhapsody"[46] begins:

I.

Flowing essence proclaims the fall,
Hsi Ho reports the dawn:

The moon in full gaze, round face shining white;
The great gate opening, cool wind wisping along.
The four seas calm, the hundred streams clear,
Yin and *yang* well settled, heaven and earth deep-set.

Sweep out the hostel palace!
Clean up the storied pavilion!
Make up the august residence!
Set out the azure curtain!

The *luan* bird flies, the phoenix soars,
Sudden streaks of brilliance.
White clouds billow, rosy clouds unfurl,
Bright then gathering dark.

In the first stanza Yang begins to sketch the cosmological background to the seventh-month festival: the modulations of *yin* and *yang*, the first full moon of autumn, the arrival of Hsi Ho (the Chinese Phoebus

[45] See *Chiu t'ang shu*, p. 2075; and Wan Man, *T'ang-chi hsü-lu* (Peking: Chung-hua shu-chü, 1980), pp. 21–22. Yang's literary works are available in *Yang Ying-ch'uan chi; Ch'u-t'ang ssu-chieh wen-chi*, chs. 10–16; *Ch'üan t'ang wen*, chs. 190–97, pp. 2421–2516; *Ch'üan t'ang shih*, (Peking: Chung-hua shu-chü, 1960), ch. 50, pp. 610–17; and *T'ang-shih chi-shih* (Peking: Chung-hua shu-chü, 1965), pp. 98–99.

[46] The textual history of Yang Chiung's "Yü-lan-p'en Rhapsody" is a knotty issue. The ostensibly earliest version of the piece is contained in *I-wen lei-chü*, the compiler of which died over fifty years *before* Yang Chiung wrote the piece, *I-wen lei-chü*, Ou-yang Hsün (557–641), p. 80. This is the shortest recension of the piece. Encyclopedias from the eighth and tenth centuries closely follow this recension, with the addition of a forty-four-character section in the middle (marked as Section IV in my translation); see *Ch'u-hsüeh chi*, Hsü Chien (659–729), pp. 79–80; and *T'ai-p'ing yü-lan* (completed 983), Li Fang, p. 272b. In my translation I use the version in *I-wen lei-chü*, supplemented and collated with the version in *Ch'u-hsüeh chi*. Later recensions of Yang Chiung's rhapsody include an introductory section on the 692 celebration and a section at the end that more than doubles the length of the piece; see *Ku-chin t'u-shu chi-ch'eng* (completed 1725), Ch'en Meng-lei et al., 100 vols. (Taipei: Wen-hsing shu-tien, 1964), pp. 694–95; and *Ch'üan t'ang wen*, pp. 2426b–28a. My translation of the entire piece is extremely tentative.

Apollo),[47] and a cooling wind blown all the way from the great gate in the western K'un-lun Mountains. In this weather preparations are begun for the celebration of the ghost festival in the official precincts of Lo-yang, while the first of many magical birds soars through the clouds.

Yang continues:

II.

Set out the Dharma offering,
Adorn the yü-lan [bowls]:

How fertile the wondrous goods,
How prolific the art of creation;
The green lotus blossoms, yet not in summer,
The red fruit sways, yet not in winter.

Brass, iron, lead, tin,
Beautiful jade, red gems;
Bright as the Sweet Spring trees hung with jade,
Capped with golden bowls for catching dew.

The statutes document the three axes,
The forms pattern all varieties:
Above, incredible breadth modeled after heaven,
Below, rest and perseverance symbolizing earth.

In this stanza Yang Chiung assembles the jades and gems indigenous (again) to K'un-lun for the yü-lan-p'en offering.[48] Like the basins used to collect the life-prolonging dew of morning, these gifts reify and solidify the pure forces of the mysterious West. Yang also draws heavily on the symbolism of the *I-ching (The Book of Changes)* to intimate the potency of the gifts.[49] Like hexagrams and symbols (the "forms" being any pair of complementary opposites: heaven and earth, *yin* and *yang*, etc.), the items placed in the yü-lan bowl embody the universal process of change. Ghost festival offerings do not simply mirror the transfor-

---

[47] On the origins of Hsi Ho, see Mitarai Masaru, *Kodai chūgoku no kamigami: kodai densetsu no kenkyū*, Tōyōgaku sōsho, No. 26 (Tokyo: Sōbunsha, 1984), pp. 477–505.

[48] Jade-decked trees appear frequently in T'ang poetry. They grow in numerous places, including the K'un-lun Mountains and the Sweet Spring Palace, see PWYF, p. 2595c.

[49] Under the *k'un* hexagram, *The Book of Changes* notes, "The good fortune of rest and perseverance depends on our being in accord with the boundless nature of earth"; *Chou-i yin-te*, Harvard-Yenching Institute Sinological Index Series, Supplement No. 10 (reprint ed., Taipei: Ch'eng-wen Publishing Co., 1966), p. 3; translation from Richard Wilhelm, trans., *The I Ching or Book of Changes*, third ed., trans. Cary F. Baynes, Bollingen Series, No. 19 (Princeton: Princeton University Press, 1967), p. 388.

mations taking place in the three worlds ("axes") of heaven, earth, and man; they are the most luminous concrescences of that very process.
Yang continues:

III.

Exhaust strange powers,
Explore miracles:

Young sons and princes
Pull and heave as if bound;
Jade women, lustrous consorts—
They glide and stretch unending.

The singing western phoenix, the purple phoenix,
The dancing great phoenix, the kingfisher;
A deadly dragon, angered, fierce,
A mad elephant, raging, drunk.

Frightful spirits,
Hidden shades:

Even Li Lou's nimble eyes
Can't make out their profound subtlety,
And Artisan Shih's purity of heart
Isn't enough to root out their obscure secrets.

While other yü-lan-p'en literature attributes "mighty spiritual power" only to the assembly of monks, here all orders of being share in the numinosity of the festival. The more elusive members of the human world, the rarer and sacred members of the animal world,[50] and the mysterious spirits of the disembodied world all participate in the majesty of the day, while raging dragons and elephants evoke an atmosphere of force. The world abounds with these delights, yet they remain beyond the ken of even the most clearheaded.[51]

The marvels of the ghost festival are seen only indirectly, reflected in the clouds and star tracks of the firmament. Yang rhapsodizes:

[50] The four kinds of numinous birds are all types of phoenix. They appear in much Han and Six Dynasties literature and usually presage good events. The purple phoenix, for instance, appeared auspiciously as the Chou took power.

[51] Li Lou lived during the time of the Yellow Emperor. His eyesight was so good that he could discern a hair at one hundred paces. He is mentioned in *Mencius*, 4A:1; *Meng-tzu yin-te*, Harvard-Yenching Institute Sinological Index Series, Supplement No. 17 (reprint ed., Taipei: Ch'eng-wen Publishing Co., 1966), p. 26. Artisan Shih was a famous workman of ancient times; his full name was Shih Po. He is noted for his equanimity in Chapter Four of *Chuang-tzu*; see *Chuang-tzu yin-te*, Harvard-Yenching Institute Sinological Index Series, Supplement No. 20 (Cambridge: Harvard University Press, 1956), p. 11, ll. 64ff.

IV.

Teeming, thronging,
Misty, merging:
The five colors form beautiful patterns
Like fine, lustrous ether
Making streaks across a bank of clouds.

Growing, glistening,
Flourishing, flashing:
The three lights make a wondrous vision
Like paired jades and a string of pearls
Shining bright in the Milky Way.

(The "three lights" are the sun, moon, and stars; "paired jades" probably describes the sun and moon in the sky together, while "a string of
pearls" indicates the stars.)

Yang's rapture closes by descending from clouds and precipitous
crags to the service taking place in the foreground:

V.

How distant—
Mount T'ien-t'ai rising abruptly,
Surrounded by reddish clouds.
How near—
Steep, rough mountain standing alone,
Canopied with lotus blooms.

Shimmering, the imperial quarters in the jasper terrace,
Crimson, the immortals' home in the golden gate.

Towering—
Tall as Great Brahmā's among all the heavens.
Broad—
Spread far as the Ganges' sands among all the dharmas.

Above they sacrifice great storehouses to seven generations of
     ancestors,
Below they offer all kinds of animals to the Three Vehicles.

Mountain clouds and imperial offerings are brought together in the
end; the vault of heaven and earthbound temples alike serve as ritual
space for the confluence of forces that occurs in the ghost festival. The
"jasper terrace"—not only the beautiful terraces of Lo-yang, but also
the many mythical abodes of long-lived spirits, including the Queen

76

Mother of the West[52]—reaches the heavens and touches the clouds. In the end we are brought back to earth, much enriched for the flight, able to see the fuller significance of both the riches in the imperial offering and the meatier items offered by common folk.

Yang Chiung uses the occasion of the ghost festival to embark on a journey. The day is one of cosmic flux, of connection and communication, during which Mount K'un-lun, its treasures and immortals, are particularly close. The many references to mountains, clouds, and fabulous birds, as well as the mythical geography deriving from such sources as the *Huai-nan-tzu*, are part of the abundant store of symbol and myth from which T'ang authors drew their favorite flourishes. Phoenixes, dew drops, and different kinds of jade are all emblematic of the rarified state of purity so ill served by the epithet of "immortality." That such a "Taoist" theme is present in a prose poem on a "Buddhist" topic should surprise only those who assume such categories to be exclusive. To label these themes as "Taoist" (and not "Buddhist") is to obscure the specialness of the day, the closeness of distant mountains, the purity of mountain mists.

Yang Chiung's "Yü-lan-p'en Rhapsody" also shows—far more beautifully than a discussion of transactional analysis or ritual fields and dramas—that ghost festival offerings constituted not merely an economic system of exchange between parties living and dead, but more importantly an experience rich in luminosity and celestial significations. Making offerings was not a mechanical transaction, it was an act in which the actors quaked with awe and their prestations shone with brilliance. Festooning temples with banners and flowers was not an act of quiet decoration. Participants and the world in which they lived were transformed through the rituals of the ghost festival. How could it be otherwise with divine women, marvelous birds, and unseen specters converging under the first full moon of autumn?

Yang's rhapsody was well known in the T'ang, and it was preserved in a number of private and officially sponsored literary encyclopedias. Some of Yang's symbolism is also echoed in later poems on the ghost festival.

GOVERNMENT OFFERINGS ACCORDING TO THE *T'ang liu-tien* (CA. 739)

A work presented to Emperor Hsüan-tsung (r. 712–756) in 739, the *T'ang liu-tien (Administrative Rules of the Six Departments under the*

---

[52] See Wang Ch'i's comments on Li Po's series of poems, "Ch'ing-p'ing t'iao-tz'u," in *Li T'ai-po wen-chi*, ed. Wang Ch'i (ca. 1758) (n.p.: Pao-hu-lou, 1758), ch. 5, p. 22v.

T'ang), preserves a description of the bureau in charge of supplying the official offerings during the ghost festival. The responsibilities of the government office in question, the Central Office (Chung-shang shu) of the Imperial Workshop (Shao-fu chien), include the construction of the various tablets, clothes, musical instruments, and other objects used in state ritual.[53] In noting the duties of the Central Office throughout the year, the *T'ang liu-tien* states that, "during the seventh month . . . on the fifteenth day, the office furnishes yü-lan bowls."[54]

Some of the regulations in the *T'ang liu-tien* describe ideal measures that were not carried out during the T'ang, but in other respects it presents an accurate picture of administrative theory and practice under Hsüan-tsung.[55] While the rules in the *T'ang liu-tien* do not in every case represent actual government practice, there is no counterevidence to dispute the passage in question. Furthermore, the more specific the rule (like the one in question), the more likely that it represents actual practice. Hence, it may be concluded that the Central Office of the Imperial Workshop was probably responsible for supplying the objects used in imperial ghost festival offerings in the mid-T'ang dynasty.

THE CELEBRATION UNDER EMPEROR TAI-TSUNG IN 768

Emperor Tai-tsung's (r. 762–779) celebration of the ghost festival in 768 is the most thickly documented of all imperial celebrations during the T'ang dynasty. Tai-tsung's devotional style appears to be consistent with his unbounded patronage of the Buddhist establishment,

---

[53] On this office, see Robert des Rotours, trans., *Traité des fonctionnaires et Traité de l'armée, traduits de la Nouvelle histoire des T'ang (chap. XLVI–L)*, 2 vols., Bibliothèque de l'Institut des Hautes Etudes Chinoises, Vol. 6 (Leiden: E. J. Brill, 1948), pp. 462–67; and *Hsin t'ang shu*, pp. 1269–70.

[54] *T'ang liu-tien* (completed 639), ed. Chang Chiu-ling, Ssu-k'u ch'üan-shu chen-pen, Series 6, Vols. 117–19 (Taipei: Commercial Press, 1976), ch. 22, p. 10b. This passage is elided in the corresponding chapter of the *Hsin t'ang shu*, p. 1269. Rotours, *Traité des fonctionnaires*, p. 465, n. 2, writes, "in fact it is certain that the authors of the *Hsin t'ang shu* intentionally suppressed this passage, because they sought to do away with all evidence of Buddhism." The *T'ang liu-tien* and the *Hsin t'ang shu* also note the responsibilities of the Central Office for furnishing items on 2/2, the Cold Food Festival (105 days after the winter solstice), 5/5, 7/7, and the New Year Festival; see Rotours, *Traité des fonctionnaires*, pp. 463–66.

[55] The *T'ang liu-tien* incorporates segments of the revised laws promulgated in 719 and 737. See Denis C. Twitchett, "Hsüan-tsung," Chapter 7 of *The Cambridge History of China*, Vol. 3, Part 1: *Sui and T'ang China, 589–906*, ed. Denis C. Twitchett (Cambridge: Cambridge University Press, 1979), pp. 354, 414–15; and Robert des Rotours, "Le T'ang lieou-tien décrit-il exactement les institutions en usage sous la dynastie des T'ang?" JA 263:1–2 (1975):183–201.

which included temple construction, mass ordinations, large feasts, and special support of the Tantric monk Pu-k'ung chin-kang (Amoghavajra) (705–774).[56] Sources allow us to chart the route followed by the T'ang emperors' ancestral tablets as they were carried to and from the Palace Chapel in the imperial quarters of Ch'ang-an. The sources do not focus on the celebration of the festival at public, state-supported temples, but rather on the semiprivate rituals that Tai-tsung performed for his own ancestors, the preceding Sons of Heaven, in the context of the imperial ancestral cult. The rituals he performed were typical of other imperial celebrations during the T'ang. It also appears that Tai-tsung used the occasion to make special provisions for the salvation of his mother, who would not normally have been included in the formal imperial rites.

While many of the imperial festivities were shielded from public view, in most respects they resembled the popular celebration of the ghost festival. Music, dancing, and ornate banners filled the streets of the city, and large crowds must have joined the imperial procession—already swollen by ranks of officials and musicians—as it made its way to Chang-ching ssu just outside of Ch'ang-an.

The earliest (also the most complete) description of the celebration of 768 in Ch'ang-an is contained in the biography of Wang Chin (d. 781) in the *Old T'ang History*. Wang Chin, the younger brother of the famous poet Wang Wei (701–756), was the high official usually blamed for Tai-tsung's heavy patronage of Buddhism. According to Wang's biography:

> On the full moon of the seventh month Tai-tsung made yü-lan bowls in the Palace Chapel. They were decorated with golden kingfisher feathers and cost a million cash. He also set out ancestral tablets for seven generations from Kao-tsu on down. They were completely clothed in pennants and dragon parasols, with their venerable names written on the pennants so that people would know [which tablet represented which ancestor]. These tablets were carried out from the imperial precincts to be displayed in the Buddhist and Taoist temples. On this day all of the officials with their insignia were arrayed at the Gate of Bright Accord to await the procession. Banners and flowers, singing and dancing, and shouts of welcome filled the streets.

The celebration was an annual affair, but knowledgeable people

---

[56] For the institutional history of Buddhism during Tai-tsung's reign, see Stanley Weinstein, *Buddhism under the T'ang* (Cambridge: Cambridge University Press, 1987), pp. 77–89.

ridiculed its untraditional nature. The destruction of the teaching [of the Sage-Emperors] began with Wang.[57]

A thirteenth-century account by the Buddhist historian Chih-p'an (ca. 1260) adds a few details:

> In the seventh month an edict established the yü-lan-p'en assembly. Ancestral tablets for seven generations from Kao-tsu on down were taken from the Imperial Ancestral Temple and set out in the Palace Chapel. Banners and flowers, music and singing accompanied them all along the road, and all of the officials received them and paid obeisance. The celebration was an annual affair.
> The next day numinous fungus sprouted in two rooms of the Imperial Ancestral Temple.[58]

These two accounts provide a tantalizing picture of the nature of imperial celebrations during the T'ang. The spirit tablets of the imperial ancestors were taken from their usual niches in the Imperial Ancestral Temple (t'ai-miao) to the Palace Chapel (nei tao-ch'ang), where Tai-tsung made the yü-lan-p'en offering. In theory the Imperial Ancestral Temple was the locus of the emperor's ancestral cult, but during the T'ang few emperors actually performed ceremonies there.[59] Tai-tsung decided not to make ghost festival offerings in the Imperial Ancestral Temple, which was located in the Imperial City (huang-ch'eng), the cordon of government offices in the north-central part of Ch'ang-an.[60] Instead he chose to have his family's ancestral tablets brought to the Palace Chapel, which was located in the part of Ch'ang-an designated as the emperor's living quarters, the Palace of Great Illumination (Ta-ming kung).[61]

---

[57] Translation from Chiu t'ang shu, p. 3418. Cf. the translation by Kenneth K.S. Ch'en, "Filial Piety in Chinese Buddhism," HJAS 28 (1968):93, which deletes the historian's criticism in the last two sentences. The account (minus the last sentence) is also reproduced in T'ai-p'ing yü-lan, p. 272a–b.

[58] Fo-tsu t'ung-chi, T. no. 2035, 49:378; see also T. 49:451a.

[59] See Howard J. Wechsler, Offerings of Jade and Silk: Ritual and Symbol in the Legitimation of the T'ang Dynasty (New Haven: Yale University Press, 1985), esp. pp. 123–41.

[60] See T'ang liang-ching ch'eng-fang k'ao, Hsü Sung (1781–1848), in Tōdai no chōan to rakuyō: shiryō hen, ed. Hiraoka Takeo, T'ang Civilization Reference Series, No. 6 (Kyoto: Kyoto daigaku jinbun kagaku kenkyūjo, 1956), ch. 1, p. 11v.

[61] The Palace of Great Illumination was built under T'ai-tsung (r. 626–649), and Kao-tsung moved his residence there in 662. During the T'ang "Palace Chapel" appears to have been the generic term for the ritual space within the imperial living quarters in which any Buddhist or Taoist event was held. Seasonal observances like the ghost festival and the Buddha's birthday, irregular events like feasts, ordinations, and prayers for rain, as well as debates between Buddhists and Taoists were all held there. On the nei tao-ch'ang in T'ang times, see Ta-sung seng-shih lüeh, by Tsan-ning (919–1001), T. no. 2126,

The imperial ancestral cult was limited to the imperial family. Tai-tsung took part in the ghost festival for the sake of his own ancestors, with the proceedings largely closed to the public. Our sources indicate that when they were taken out of the emperor's family temple and placed in public view, the spirit tablets were so completely covered that their names, which were engraved on the tablets themselves, had to be written on the cloth-and-feather coverings so that people would know which tablet was which. Through these tablets, all of the T'ang emperors who preceded Tai-tsung (Kao-tsu [r. 618–626] and the six succeeding emperors) were present at the service held in the Palace Chapel.

The celebration of 768 was opened to the public only after the conclusion of the imperial service. After Tai-tsung had made his lavish offerings in the Palace Chapel, the tablets were paraded through the Palace of Great Illumination and eventually taken to public temples. While the procession still remained within the imperial precincts, a host of officials gathered at a small gate internal to the Palace of Great Illumination, the Gate of Bright Accord (Kuang-shun men), to join in the procession.[62] After bowing to the T'ang ancestors, the government officers took their place in the cortege as it made its way out of the imperial quarters.

The ceremony described above—Tai-tsung's offerings in the Palace Chapel and the procession of ancestral tablets through the Gate of Bright Accord—represents only one-half of the imperially sponsored celebration. Other sources show that the celebration continued outside the walls of Ch'ang-an at Chang-ching ssu. An eleventh-century collection of documents notes that in 768:

> In the seventh month [the emperor] sent special yü-lan bowls to Chang-ching ssu, which had recently been completed. To supplement [his repayment of] unbounded kindness [that his parents had bestowed], he decreed that all of the officials go to the temple and make a procession with incense.[63]

54:247b–c; Michihata Ryōshū, *Tōdai bukkyō shi no kenkyū* (Kyoto: Hōzōkan, 1957), pp. 24–28; and Naba Toshisada, "Tōdai ni okeru kokugi gyōkō ni tsuite" (1955), reprinted in *Tōdai shakai bunka shi kenkyū* (Tokyo: Sōbunsha, 1974), pp. 33–48. For the history of the *nei tao-ch'ang* in the Chin and Sui dynasties, see Yamazaki Hiroshi, *Zui tō bukkyō shi no kenkyū* (Kyoto: Hōzōkan, 1967), pp. 85–115.

[62] On the location of the Kuang-shun men, see *Ch'ang-an chih*, Sung Min-ch'iu (1019–1079), in *Tōdai no chōan to rakuyō*, ch. 6, p. 7v; and *T'ang liang-ching ch'eng-fang k'ao*, in *Tōdai no chōan to rakuyō*, ch. 1, p. 17r. Tai-tsung had had a Buddhist statue installed at the Kuang-shun men in 765, see *Fo-tsu t'ung-chi*, T. 49:377c.

[63] *Ts'e-fu yüan-kuei*, Wang Ch'in-jo (962–1025), 12 vols. (Peking: Chung-hua shu-chü,

Chang-ching ssu was located just outside of Ch'ang-an, near the north-ern end of the eastern city wall.[64] Chang-ching ssu had been established only the year before. It was named after Tai-tsung's mother, who was given the honorific name of "Chang-ching" (Dowager Who "Displays Respect"), and the temple was constructed to make merit on her be-half. The temple proved to be a thriving center of monastic and lay ac-tivity through the end of the T'ang dynasty.[65]

What is particularly noteworthy about the latter half of the 768 cer-emony is that it was probably not performed for the benefit of the em-peror's male ancestors, but for the sake of his mother, who had no of-ficial place in the imperial line residing at the Imperial Ancestral Temple. This second, maternal aspect of the celebration, performed after the rites affirming the patriliny, may well be the unmentioned in-sult that Liu Hsü equates with "the destruction of the teaching [of the Sage-Emperors]." While all versions of the yü-lan-p'en myth clearly show Mu-lien performing the service for his departed mother, most emperors apparently gave offerings only to their male ancestors.[66] In following Mu-lien's example, Tai-tsung was an exception: he used the ceremony of 768 to make extensive provisions for his mother's salva-tion.

Where Liu Hsü sees the destructive effects of the Buddhist and mat-rilineal slant given to the festival, Chih-p'an points to its miraculous results when he reports that, "The next day numinous fungus sprouted in two rooms of the Imperial Ancestral Temple." Sources prior to Chih-p'an's thirteenth-century account make no mention of this aus-picious sign, although the *Old T'ang History* reports that fungus did sprout in two rooms of the Imperial Ancestral Temple on the thirtieth day of the seventh month two years before, in 766.[67]

1960), 1:577a. See also *Tzu-chih t'ung-chien* (completed 1084), Ssu-ma Kuang, 10 vols., (Taipei: I-wen yin-shu-kuan, 1955), pp. 3496b–97a.

[64] See *Ch'ang-an chih*, Sung Min-ch'iu, in *Tōdai no chōan to rakuyō*, ch. 10, p. 12r.

[65] See *Tzu-chih t'ung-chien*, pp. 3493b–94b; and *T'ang hui-yao*, Wang P'u (922–982), Pai-pu ts'ung-shu chi-ch'eng, No. 27 (Taipei: I-wen yin-shu-kuan, 1969), ch. 48, p. 6r–v. For more background on the construction and later history of this temple, see Stanley Weinstein, *Buddhism under the T'ang* (Cambridge: Cambridge University Press, 1987), pp. 83–84.

[66] It is highly unlikely that Empress Wu was represented by a spirit tablet in the Im-perial Ancestral Temple after the reigns of her two sons, Chung-tsung (r. 705–710) and Jui-tsung (r. 710–712). If she was so represented, there would have been seven spirit tab-lets *in addition to* Kao-tsu's in the procession in the Palace Chapel in 768.

[67] In my opinion the most reasonable date for the fungus sprouting is 7/30/766. The *Old T'ang History* records the event for the seventh month of the year 766: "on the *kuei-wei* [thirtieth] day a fungus plant sprouted in two rooms of the Imperial Ancestral Tem-ple," *Chiu t'ang shu*, p. 283. It is my guess that this event was too well known and too

POEMS AND CELEBRATIONS UNDER EMPEROR TE-TSUNG
(r. 779–805)

The pattern of ghost festival celebrations under Emperor Te-tsung (r. 779–805) reflects the broader fluctuations in the official attitude toward the Buddhist establishment during the T'ang dynasty. It would appear that both state support for public celebrations as well as the emperor's own participation in the festival waned at the beginning and waxed at the end of Te-tsung's reign. While the sources allow only a spotty re-construction of celebrations during these years, they do preserve two noteworthy poems written on the occasion of the ghost festival in 791. One poem, by Te-tsung himself, draws on a largely Buddhist vocab-ulary to praise quiescence and the virtue of charity. The second poem, written by Ts'ui Yüan-yü, combines a mild rebuke of the emperor for his self-absorption with an appreciation of the cosmological signifi-cance of the early autumn ritual.

In his early years, Emperor Te-tsung sharply reduced the high level of spending on Buddhist and Taoist establishments characteristic of his father's rule.[68] In 780 he marked the second ghost festival of his reign by putting an end to celebrations in the palace. The *Old T'ang History* notes that, "On the fifteenth day of the seventh month in autumn, the practice of setting out yü-lan bowls in the palace was ended, and monks were not ordered to appear in the Palace Chapel."[69]

The banishment of Buddhist symbols and rituals from the imperial ancestral cult, which probably lasted for only eleven years, apparently had little or no effect on the popular celebrations of the ghost festival, for we find the Buddhist histories reporting that, sometime during his reign, the emperor himself went out to An-kuo ssu in northeast

---

useful—as an auspicious sign—for Buddhist historians to pass over in silence. Chih-p'an included the event in a Buddhist scheme by changing the date (from 7/30/766 to 7/16/768) so that it affirmed the efficacy of yü-lan-p'en offerings. Tsu-hsiu, a Buddhist his-torian who wrote the *Lung-hsing fo-chaio pien-nien t'ung-lun* in 1164, included the event in a Buddhist scheme by moving Tai-tsung's famous celebration of the festival to the day before the fungus sprouted. But Tsu-hsiu neglected to change the original sexagenary designation of the date, so that on his accounting the yü-lan-p'en offerings were made on the unlikely date of 7/29/766; see *Lung-hsing fo-chiao pien-nien t'ung-lun*, in Z. 2B, 3:3, p. 297rb. Weinstein, *Buddhism under the T'ang*, p. 83, accepts Tsu-hsiu's date of 766. (Tsu-hsiu incorrectly records the year as the first year of Ta-li. The year was in fact the second year of Yung-t'ai, since the reign name was not changed from Yung-t'ai to Ta-li until the eleventh month; see Tung Tso-pin, *Chung-kuo nien-li tsung-p'u*, 2 vols. [Hong Kong: Hong Kong University Press, 1960], 2:270.)

[68] For the institutional history of Buddhism during Te-tsung's reign, see Weinstein, *Buddhism under the T'ang*, pp. 88–89.

[69] *Chiu t'ang shu*, p. 780.

Ch'ang-an to observe yü-lan-p'en festivities.[70] A late source hints that imperial offerings in the Palace Chapel had been resumed in 786, but this possibility cannot be established with certainty.[71]

By the year 791 Te-tsung had in any event reverted to the practice, begun by his father in 768, of attending ghost festival services at Chang-ching ssu. Several sources preserve records of the event, which probably occurred on the night of the fourteenth:

On the seventh month of the seventh year [of Chen-yüan, i.e., 791], the Emperor visited Chang-ching ssu and composed a poem:

> People from all over crowd the imperial city,
> Lining the roads, forming many walls.
>
> For the Dharma-feast meeting in early fall,
> We drive out to visit the meditation bureau.
>
> I have heard tell that the immortal teaches
> Tranquility, honors no-birth.
>
> My offerings are baskets of the seven goods,
> To perfect charity before other actions.
>
> With name and form both silent
> How do pleasures maintain their glory?
>
> Autumn's golden wind fans a light breeze,
> Distant smoke thick and crystal blue.
>
> Pine garden peaceful, mossy;
> Bamboo hut, sonorous chimes.
>
> Pitch dark, utterly quiet thought—
> The Way triumphant, externals quelled.
>
> Consciousness at base is not for speaking—
> Whetting my brush, feeling again fills the void.

[70] *Fo-tsu t'ung-chi*, T. no. 2035, 49:451a. [Ta] An-kuo ssu was located in the eastern half of the Ch'ang-lo quarter of Ch'ang-an. It was established in 710 by Emperor Jui-tsung and contained murals painted by disciples of the famous painter, Wu Tao-hsüan (ca. eighth century). See *T'ang liang-ching ch'eng-fang k'ao*, in *Tōdai no chōan to rakuyō*, ch. 3, pp. 17v–18r.

[71] Chüeh-an (ca. 1354) in his *Shih-shih chi-ku lüeh*, T. no. 2037, writes that in 786, "The yü-lan-p'en assembly was reinstituted just like in Tai-tsung's time," T. 49:829c. Tai-tsung had celebrated the festival in both the Palace Chapel and at Chang-ching ssu, so if Chüeh-an's account is reliable, it would suggest that Te-tsung reinstituted celebrations in both places in 786. Other sources make no mention of the 786 celebration.

All of the officials were in agreement, and it was written on the temple walls. Later, Ching-chao Yin Hsüeh-ku asked permission to have the emperor's poem engraved in stone and filled in with gold.[72]

The festival in this year must have been a raucous event, as Te-tsung refers to crowds from the four corners[73] lining the streets leading to the temple. The emperor makes use of Buddhist terminology in portraying his offering as an act of charity[74] and in describing a path of meditation that ends in quiescence and a heightened state of awareness. For Te-tsung the Buddha's teaching of emptiness complements the mild autumn breeze and reverberating temple bells that penetrate the temple gardens. In the poem's precious ending, Te-tsung's moment of quiet, ineffable illumination gives way to expression as he picks up his brush to try his hand at verse.

Fortunately Te-tsung's poetic efforts gave rise to a fine piece by Ts'ui Yüan-yü, a poem entitled, "Accompanying the Sage's Poem Written on Chung-yüan at Chang-ching Ssu." Ts'ui was from Po-ling (present-day Shantung) and occupied various posts in the central government, including Auxiliary Secretary of the Board of Rites (Li-pu yüan-wai-lang) and Erudite in the Court of Imperial Sacrifices (T'ai-ch'ang po-shih). In both positions his responsibilities demanded a thorough knowledge of the protocol and practice of state-sponsored ritual.[75] I render his poem below:

> The mysterious Way cannot be expressed in basic speech,
> Taking different paths, assuming other names.
>
> But the Sage possesses its essentials,
> Fully transforming all creatures.

---

[72] Translation from *T'ang hui-yao*, Wang P'u, ch. 27, p. 14r; emended on the basis of the recension in *Ch'üan t'ang shih*, p. 7. The account in *T'ang hui-yao* is reproduced in ch. 29 of the *Yü hai*, Wang Ying-lin (1223–1296) (Taipei: Hua-wen shu-chü, 1964), pp. 607b–8a. The brief account in the *Old T'ang History* dates the event on the fourteenth, *Chiu t'ang shu*, p. 372.

[73] "People from all over" translates "*chao-t'i*," a transliteration of the Skt., "*catur deśa*," meaning "four quarters," often used in the expression "monks of the four quarters" (*chao-t'i seng* or *chao-t'i k'o*). See CWTTT, 12212.90.

[74] In *The Pure Land Yü-lan-p'en Sūtra*, King Bimbisāra offers "bowls of the seven jewels" (*ch'i-pao p'en-po*); *Ching-t'u yü-lan-p'en ching*, in Jan Jaworski, "L'Avalambana Sūtra de la terre pure," l. 52.

[75] For Ts'ui's biography, see *Chiu t'ang shu*, pp. 3766–67; *Hsin t'ang shu*, p. 5783; and *T'ang-shih chi-shih*, pp. 533–34. His surviving works are collected in *Ch'üan t'ang shih*, pp. 3521–22; and in *Ch'üan t'ang wen*, ch. 523.

A phoenix calls from the royal gardens,
Dragon palaces form outer walls;

Flower garlands arrayed in the rear halls,
Cloud chariots parked in the front chambers.

Pine, bamboo—full of the new season,
Porch windows cool and fresh.

Fond memories of K'ung-t'ung—
Flute music, play on.

Outside of form, complete silence;
Forgetting words, reason made pure.

If within the realm sincerity may be called great,
Then the empire will rest at ease.

Yielding comes from making things equal;
How can the brave heart of Yao maintain its glory?[76]

Ts'ui's poem gains its force by posing a Way of action as a conclusion to the Way of stillness touted in Te-tsung's poem. Ts'ui begins with an echo of the transcendent silence in Te-tsung's poem and then further explores how that silence may be used to order and harmonize the social world. While the Way itself remains transcendent to words, it finds instrumental expression in the actions and virtues of the Sage. Thus, the empire is ordered when the Sage—and certainly both Te-tsung and the Buddha fall under this hallowed rubric—cultivates responsiveness and yielding.[77] The virtues of quiescence and meditation are to be seen in their broader ramifications, in their effect upon the empire.

In his description of the Sage's experience, Ts'ui commands a much richer stock of allusions than does Te-tsung. The call of the phoenix is usually heard, for instance, when the Great Gate opens in K'un-lun,[78] and cloud chariots are a favorite mode of transport for sky-bound goddesses, holy men, and dragons. In Ts'ui's poem, as in Yang Chiung's

[76] *Ch'üan t'ang shih*, p. 3521.

[77] In his line, "If within the realm sincerity may be called great," Ts'ui alludes to the *Tao te ching*, ch. 25: ". . . the Way is great, heaven is great, earth is great, and the king is also great. Within the realm there are four things that are great, and the king counts as one"; *Lao-tzu tao te ching chu*, Hsin-pien chu-tzu chi-ch'eng, Vol. 3 (Taipei: Shih-chieh shu-chü, 1978), p. 14; translation following D. C. Lau, trans., *Lao Tzu, Tao Te Ching* (Harmondsworth: Penguin Books, 1963), p. 82. For Ts'ui, as for the Taoist and Buddhist sources to which he alludes, the perfection of virtue by the Sage is inevitably related to the social order.

[78] See PWYF, p. 643c.

"Yü-lan-p'en Rhapsody" written a century before, the ghost festival effects the rupture that brings the cool mountains of K'ung-t'ung (in Kansu and Honan) closer to hand.

The Transformation Text on Mu-lien Saving His Mother
from the Dark Regions
(CA. 800)

The "transformation text" (*pien-wen*) concerning Mu-lien narrates a story that had wide circulation in T'ang China. The value of this pro-simetric tale, which grew out of oral storytelling traditions, is that it demonstrates the particular kinds of appeal that the ghost festival and Mu-lien had for the popular imagination in medieval times. As a reflection of Chinese religion at the grass roots, *The Transformation Text on Mu-lien Saving His Mother* presents a view of the world in which gods, heroes, and concepts of foreign origin are fully synthesized with indigenous ones. The focus of the transformation text is different from that of the canonical sources. Its version of the Mu-lien myth is almost exclusively concerned with Mu-lien's tour of hell, sparing no detail in narrating the punishment of hell dwellers, the inexorable laws of karma, and the unbending magistrates who administer punishments. In the transformation text Mu-lien satisfies simultaneously the demands of filiality and world renunciation, wielding the powers of the shaman and those of the monk to deliver his mother from the tortures of hell.

A mature understanding of the significance of transformation texts in the social, literary, and religious history of China has emerged only in the past few decades. Building on the earlier work of those Chinese scholars who first edited the *pien-wen* manuscripts discovered at Tun-huang, current studies have begun to answer with more certainty questions concerning the literary form, the pictorial aspects, the audience, and the origins of transformation texts.[79]

[79] My summary in the next four paragraphs draws most heavily on the work of Victor H. Mair, including *Tun-huang Popular Narratives* (Cambridge: Cambridge University Press, 1983); and "Lay Students and the Making of Written Vernacular Narrative: An Inventory of Tun-huang Manuscripts," *Chinoperl Papers* No. 10 (1981):5–96. See also Mair's forthcoming study of the Indic origins and pan-Asian development of picture stories, *T'ang Transformation Texts*, Harvard-Yenching Monograph Series (Cambridge: Harvard University Press, forthcoming). See also Pai Hua-wen, "What is *Pien-wen*?" trans. Victor H. Mair, HJAS 44:2 (December 1984):493–514; and Kanaoka Shōkō, *Tonkō no bungaku* (Tokyo: Daizō shuppansha, 1971). For representative earlier studies, see Hsiang Ta, "T'ang-tai su-chiang k'ao," *Kuo-hsüeh chi-k'an* 6:4 (January 1950):1–42, reprinted in *T'ang-tai ch'ang-an yü hsi-yü wen-ming* (Peking: Sheng-huo tu-shu hsin-chih

Transformation texts represent a Chinese adaptation of the *chantefable* form characteristic of Buddhist sūtras and stories. Prose portions in *pien-wen* are often in the vernacular language, while their metrical sections are heptasyllabic, with varying rhyme schemes. The extant *pien-wen* manuscripts are neither scripts for the performance of stories nor independent literary pieces. Rather, they lie somewhere between the poles of a precise written record of an oral performance and an independently circulated written text. The Tun-huang manuscripts of this prosimetric form also reflect the less-than-advanced stage of literacy achieved by the lay students who copied them.

Both internal and external evidence confirms the pictorial aspect of *pien-wen* performance. Transformation texts almost always introduce long verse sections with the phrase (or one of its variants), "Please look at the place where [a particular event, e.g., Mu-lien's encounter with King Yama in hell] occurs, how does it go?" At these junctures in the performance, storytellers would direct their audience's attention to a new picture, which depicted the next scene described in the story. Contemporary accounts make it clear that some storytellers used painted scrolls that they turned to expose a succession of scenes, while some had recourse to the "transformation pictures" (*pien-hsiang*) adorning the walls of temples and monasteries.[80]

Other sources provide important clues concerning the performers and the audience of T'ang picture tales. They were recited, sung, and illustrated not by monks, but by professional entertainers, often female singers. The most frequent audience for these performances consisted neither of monks nor literate lay people, but the masses at large, those people who gathered in and around Buddhist temples during the numerous seasonal festivals (including the seventh moon) that punctuated the Chinese year. Common people flocked to these grand spectacles not simply to make offerings, but also to be part of a large, festive gathering, to purchase rare items and display their own family's wealth, and to hear the poems and watch the pictures depicting favorite stories from the popular tradition. Within the compass of popular Chinese lit-

---

san-lien shu-tien ch'u-pan, 1957), pp. 1–116; Cheng Chen-to, *Chung-kuo su-wen-hsüeh shih*, 2 vols. (1954; reprint ed., Taipei: Commercial Press, 1965), 1:180–270; Lo Tsung-t'ao, "Pien-ko, pien-hsiang, pien-wen," *Chung-hua hsüeh-yüan* No. 7 (March 1971):73–99; and Paul Demiéville, "Les Débuts de la littérature en chinois vulgaire," *Académie des Inscriptions et Belles-Lettres, Comptes rendus* (1952), reprinted in *Choix d'études sinologiques* (Leiden: E. J. Brill, 1973), pp. 121–29.

[80] For a picture scroll (narrating Śāriputra's battle with Raudrākṣa) with verses on the back, apparently for use by storytellers, see Akiyama Terukazu, "Tonkō-bon gōmahen emaki ni tsuite," *Bijutsu kenkyū* No. 187 (July 1956):1–35; and idem, "Tonkō ni okeru henbun to kaiga," *Bijutsu kenkyū* No. 211 (July 1960):1–28.

erature such *pien-wen* as *The Transformation Text on Mu-lien Saving His Mother* are unsurpassed in entertainment value.

Pien-wen not only entertained—*The Transformation Text on Mu-lien Saving His Mother* abounds with blood and entrails, metamorphosing animals, cosmic battles waged against the spooks and guardians of hell—they also educated. That is, the "transformations" or manifestations of Buddhas, gods, and heroes spoken of in these texts were also intended to enlighten their audience. Short of complete illumination, they edified and instructed common people in the ethics and cosmology of Chinese Buddhist folk religion. The *pien-wen* version of the Mu-lien tale demonstrated the efficacy of charity, the donation of gifts to monks by lay people. Through explicit lectures from the likes of King Yama and other functionaries of hell and through the example of particular kinds of hells corresponding to particular kinds of sinful acts, the transformation text drove home the inevitability of karmic retribution.

The Transformation Text on Mu-lien Saving His Mother relates the Mu-lien myth as it was told to the "masses," unfiltered by the monastic establishment and uncensored by Confucian tastes. It is an expression of the values and interests of the vast majority of Chinese people, who took part in the ghost festival as small donors and willing listeners, not as Buddhist converts or government officials. Its value is further enhanced by the large number of extant manuscripts, which, though not without lacunae and other problems, constitute a nearly complete text.[81] Lines from a "Mu-lien transformation" (*Mu-lien pien*) are quoted in a humorous dialogue between the poet, Po Chü-i (772–846),

---

[81] Victor H. Mair's translation in *Tun-huang Popular Narratives* further increases the value of this text. I have also consulted the translation by Iriya Yoshitaka, "Dai mokkenren meikan kyūbo henbun," in *Bukkyō bungaku shū*, ed. Iriya Yoshitaka, Chūgoku koten bungaku taikei (Tokyo: Heibonsha, 1975), pp. 54–81. Waley's incomplete but elegant translation may still be consulted with advantage; Arthur Waley, trans., *Ballads and Stories from Tun-huang: An Anthology* (London: George Allen and Unwin, 1960). My references are to the Chinese text in THPWC, pp. 714–55, usually following Mair's emendations. *The Transformation Text on Mu-lien Saving His Mother* is also collated in Chou Shao-liang, ed., *Tun-huang pien-wen hui-lu* (Shanghai: Shang-hai ch'u-pan kung-ssu, 1955), pp. 149–85. For other studies, see Aoki Masaru, "Tonkō isho *Mokuren engi, Dai mokkenren meikan kyūbo henbun*, oyobi *Gōma ōzabun* ni tsuite," *Shinagaku* 4:3 (October 1927):123–30, reprinted in *Shina bungaku geijutsu kō* (Tokyo: Kōbundō, 1942), pp. 172–82; Kuraishi Takeshirō, "*Mokuren henbun* shōkai no ato ni," *Shinagaku* 4:3 (October 1927):130–38; Kawaguchi Hisao, "Tonkō henbun no sozai to nihon bungaku: *Mokuren henbun, Gōma henbun*," *Nihon chūgoku gakkai hō* No. 8 (1957):116–33; Kanaoka Shōkō, *Tonkō no bungaku* (Tokyo: Daizō shuppansha, 1971), pp. 249–57; and idem, *Tonkō no minshū: sono seikatsu to shisō*, Tōyōjin no kōdō to shisō, Vol. 8 (Tokyo: Hyōronsha, 1972), pp. 189–232.

and a visitor that took place in 825 or 826 in Su-chou (present-day Kiangsu).[82] The current text of *The Transformation Text on Mu-lien Saving His Mother* may be dated roughly to the year 800, although the unwritten traditions on which it draws probably extend back several centuries before that.

The story of the founding of the ghost festival (the main focus of the canonical yü-lan-p'en sources) forms but a fraction of *The Transformation Text on Mu-lien Saving His Mother*. Instead, the audience's attention is given over almost entirely to Mu-lien's quest for his mother, Ch'ing-t'i. The transformation text begins with a brief account of Ch'ing-t'i's previous actions, her avaricious lies and refusal to donate food to monks, which land her in the deepest of all hells, Avīci Hell. Most of the story focuses on Mu-lien's efforts to find his dear, departed mother, whom he believes to be free of sin. He finds his father in Brahmā's Heaven, but not his mother. Descending beneath the surface of the continent of Jambudvīpa, Mu-lien questions a long succession of hell dwellers and bureaucrat-gods concerning her whereabouts. The narrative serves as a guidebook to the hells. It points out such important landmarks as the Watthellwedo River, which all sinners must cross, and it details the titles and functions of all of the members of the underworld bureaucracy from the lowliest gaolers and messengers to King Yama and the Magistrate of Mount T'ai. It spares few details in describing the tortures undergone by hell dwellers, while the heavens (Brahmā's Palace and the Heaven of Thirty-Three, where Ch'ing-t'i eventually achieves rebirth) are mentioned summarily in uninspired terms.

In *The Transformation Text on Mu-lien Saving His Mother*, Mu-lien emerges as a brave adventurer willing to risk anything for the salvation of his mother. While the Buddha does break down the gates of Avīci Hell to release Ch'ing-t'i, the hero of the story is clearly Mu-lien. It is Mu-lien, a merely human disciple, who braves the spears and flames of hell, and it is Mu-lien who undertakes the journey to the other world to communicate with ancestral spirits. The transformation text is not primarily concerned with abstract values like filiality or wisdom, with rebirth in the Pure Land or achieving the unproduced state of *nirvāṇa*,

---

[82] The dialogue between Po Chü-i and Chang Hu is first recorded by Meng Ch'i (ca. 886) in *Pen-shih shih*, contained in *Pen-shih shih, Pen-shih tz'u*, Chung-kuo wen-hsüeh ts'an-k'ao tzu-liao hsiao ts'ung-shu, Series 2, No. 2 (Shanghai: Ku-tien wen-hsüeh ch'u-pan-she, 1957), p. 23. See also Arthur Waley, *The Life and Times of Po Chü-i, 772–846 A.D.* (London: George Allen and Unwin, 1949), pp. 44, 219. The dialogue is also included in *T'ai-p'ing kuang-chi* (completed 978), Li Fang, 5 vols. (Peking: Jen-min wen-hsüeh ch'u-pan-she, 1959), p. 1948.

or with the exemplary enlightenment experience or soteriological role of the Buddha. Rather, the *pien-wen* story expresses the more concrete and visceral interests of the popular imagination: the experience of the spirit medium, the frightening realities of the underworld, and the rituals needed to help the ancestors escape suffering.

The transformation text reflects in its own way the fascinating synthesis of originally Chinese and Indian motifs characteristic of Chinese religion from medieval times onward. The hells that it describes are staffed by deities originating in Indian tradition as well as by indigenous bureaucrats, all of whom administer a single karmic law. Mu-lien holds the sword of the Chinese shaman at the same time as he tours the cosmos in the guise of a meditating monk. *The Transformation Text on Mu-lien Saving His Mother* also offers a dramatic and convincing account of the ultimate harmony of family life and monasticism. It is precisely his powers of meditation—the province of the monk—that enable Mu-lien to provide for the salvation of his ancestors. Mu-lien achieves the status of filial son because he is a monk and vice versa, thus demonstrating the potency of combining renunciation with worldly responsibility.

The myth related in *The Transformation Text on Mu-lien Saving His Mother* remained an enduring part of popular Chinese culture after the T'ang, its characters and plot forming the basis for plays and precious scrolls even in the twentieth century.

TSUNG-MI'S *Commentary on the Yü-lan-p'en Sūtra* (CA. 830)

The *Commentary on the Yü-lan-p'en Sūtra*, written by Tsung-mi (780–841), stands as eloquent testimony to the centrality of the ghost festival in early ninth-century Chinese society and to the genius of its author, a highly placed scholar-monk who gave systematic expression to the tradition of Sinicized Buddhism.[83] For Tsung-mi, the presuppositions

---

[83] Okabe Kazuo provides a good, brief introduction to the place of the yü-lan-p'en commentary in Tsung-mi's work in "Shūmitsu ni okeru kōron no tenkai to sono hōhō," IBK 15:2 (March 1967):574–78. On Tsung-mi see also Furuta Shōkin, "Keihō shūmitsu no kenkyū," *Shina bukkyō shigaku* 2:2 (1938):83–97; Kamata Shigeo, *Shūmitsu kyōgaku no shisōshiteki kenkyū: chūgoku kegon shisō shi no kenkyū* (Tokyo: Tokyo daigaku shuppansha, 1975); Takamine Ryōshū, *Kegon shisō shi*, second ed. (Tokyo: Hyakkaen, 1963), pp. 299–316; and Yamazaki, *Zui tō bukkyō shi no kenkyū*, pp. 223–37. For two recent studies in English, each of which significantly revises traditional views of Tsung-mi, see Yün-hua Jan, "Tsung-mi: His Analysis of Ch'an Buddhism," TP 58 (1972):1–54; and Peter N. Gregory, "The Teaching of Men and Gods: the Doctrinal and Social Basis of Lay Buddhist Practice in the Hua-yen Tradition," in *Studies in Ch'an and Hua-yen*, eds. Peter N.

and practice of the ghost festival represent a synthesis of core Chinese values with the tenets and rituals of Buddhism. In his lengthy commentary, over eleven times longer than the sūtra, the festival emerges not as an inchoate or sloppy mixture, but as the positive expression of a well-reasoned, all-encompassing hierarchy of values. The ghost festival is not viewed from the heights of an otherworldly philosophy or through the lens of meditative culture, approaches we might expect of such well-read monks as Tsung-mi. Instead, Tsung-mi demonstrates the relevance of the festival to the realities of social life of the vast majority of Chinese people. The regulating principle of the householder's life is never even questioned; Tsung-mi simply assumes the importance of the ancestors in Chinese family religion. For Tsung-mi filial devotion is the one consistent teaching of *The Yü-lan-p'en Sūtra*, and he articulates this concept through every source available to him, including Mahāyāna sūtras and the Chinese classics.

Tsung-mi's commentary also retains a singular place in the narrower world of Chinese Buddhist exegesis. By the Southern Sung dynasty, it had become the standard commentary on *The Yü-lan-p'en Sūtra*, spawning numerous subcommentaries and sub-subcommentaries.[84] For many of these later commentators it was Tsung-mi's language, not that of the original sūtra, which now deserved exegesis.

Tsung-mi, whose surname was Ho, was born in 780 in the prefecture of Kuo (present-day Szechuan).[85] As a youth he combined a traditional course of education as preparation for a career in government with a lay interest in Buddhist writings. At the age of twenty-seven he left the householder's life and began a period of travel and study with

Gregory and Robert M. Gimello, Studies in East Asian Buddhism, No. 1 (Honolulu: University of Hawaii Press, 1983), pp. 253–320.

[84] Tsung-mi's commentary was the basis for dozens of Chinese and Japanese subcommentaries. The extant Chinese subcommentaries include: *Lan-p'en ching shu-ch'ao yü-i (Further Meanings of the Commentary on the Lan-p'en Sūtra)*, Jih-hsin (ca. 1068, Z. 1, 94:4; *Yü-lan-p'en ching shu hsin-chi (A New Record of the Commentary on the Yü-lan-p'en Sūtra)*, Yüan-chao (1048–1116), Z. 1, 35:2; *Yü-lan-p'en ching shu hsiao-heng ch'ao (A Consideration of Filial Devotion in the Commentary on the Yü-lan-p'en Sūtra)*, Yü-jung (Sung), Z. 1, 94:4; *Yü-lan-p'en ching shu hui-ku t'ung-chin chi (A Record of the Commentary on the Yü-lan-p'en Sūtra Which Comprehends the Old and Understands the New)*, P'u-kuan (ca. 1178), Z. 1, 35:2; *Yü-lan-p'en ching hsin-shu (A New Commentary on the Yü-lan-p'en Sūtra)*, Chih-hsü (1599–1655), Z. 1, 35:2; *Yü-lan-p'en ching shu che-chung shu (Commentary Giving Equal Measure to [Tsung-mi's and Chih-hsü's] Commentaries on the Yü-lan-p'en Sūtra)*, Ling-yao (Ch'ing), Z. 1, 35:2; and *Yü-lan-p'en ching lüeh-shu (Condensed Commentary on the Yü-lan-p'en Sūtra)*, Yüan-ch'i (Ch'ing), Z. 1. 35:2.

[85] Biographical details in this paragraph and the next are drawn from *Sung kao-seng chuan*, T. no. 2061, 50:741c–43a; *Fo-tsu t'ung-chi*, T. no. 2035, 49:293c; and Takamine, *Kegon shisō shi*, pp. 299–316.

different teachers. He went to a monastery near Kuei-feng Mountain (near Ch'ang-an) for the first time in 821 and would return there frequently in later years. In 828 Tsung-mi lectured on Buddhism during the ritualized debates held on the emperor's birthday and was later bestowed a purple robe and the rank of Monk of Great Virtue. Tsung-mi died in 841 and was later granted the honorific title "Meditation Master of Concentration and Wisdom" (Ting-hui ch'an-shih).

Tsung-mi embraced many seemingly divergent trends in his life work, a distinction that is apparent in his posthumous elevation to the status of patriarch in two "schools" of Chinese Buddhism, Hua-yen and Ch'an. Tsung-mi read broadly in the Buddhist canon, and he wrote and lectured extensively on Hua-yen texts. He studied with meditation teachers and lived in seclusion during various periods of his life, writing important commentaries and compiling a lengthy collection of Ch'an texts. Tsung-mi also took an interest in the details of daily life and wrote several works on monastic ritual. Modern scholarship has recently portrayed Tsung-mi as a thinker of great catholicity, pluralistic in his acceptance of divergent forms of Buddhism, synthetic in his melding of thought and practice, and all-embracing in his affirmation of core Chinese values. As Peter Gregory writes, "By creating a framework in which Confucianism, Taoism, and Buddhism could be synthesized, Tsung-mi not only transcended the polemical intent of the earlier debates between the three teachings, but he also laid out a methodology by which Confucian terms—infused with Buddhist meaning—were later to be resurrected in the Confucian revival of the Sung dynasty."[86]

Tsung-mi's catholic interests are perhaps most apparent in his *Commentary on the Yü-lan-p'en Sūtra*, written between 822 and 841.[87] The first chapter of the commentary discusses the general significance of *The Yü-lan-p'en Sūtra*, while the second chapter contains a phrase-by-phrase exegesis.

Tsung-mi begins by singing the praises of filial devotion:

Beginning in formless chaos, filling all of heaven and earth, uniting men and spirits, connecting noble and poor; Confucians and Buddhists both revere it—it is the Way of filial devotion. Re-

[86] Gregory, "The Teaching of Men and Gods," p. 268.

[87] For the date, see Furuta, "Keihō shūmitsu no kenkyū," pp. 88–90. I have used the Taishō edition of Tsung-mi's commentary, *Yü-lan-p'en ching shu*, T. no. 1792, occasionally emended on the basis of Sung subcommentaries. The Taishō text is based on Ming and Tokugawa recensions, which were based on a copy belonging to Chu-hung (1535–1615).

sponding to filial sons' sincerity, saving parents from distress, re-paying broad heaven's kind virtue—it is the teaching of yü-lan-p'en.[88]

For Tsung-mi filial devotion is the Tao, the origin and goal of all teach-ings. It begins in the "formless chaos" (hun-tun), the primal condition devoid of names and dichotomies, expanding without discrimination to inform all processes and every form of life. It is a universal truth, the single Path followed by all religions, and it is precisely through yü-lan-p'en that this truth is made fully real.

After a section paying homage to the Buddha, Tsung-mi presents his own analysis of the sūtra. Śākyamuni established the ghost festival, says Tsung-mi, for several reasons: to repay the kindness his parents had shown in raising him, to repay Mu-lien's filial efforts, to teach fil-iality to others, and to establish an effective way of making merit. Here (and throughout his commentary) Tsung-mi quotes extensively from traditional Chinese as well as from Buddhist sources, exploring differ-ent dimensions of the concept of filial devotion. Tsung-mi proceeds to place The Yü-lan-p'en Sūtra within the systems of doctrinal classifica-tion current in the ninth century. Among the Three Baskets (Sūtra, Vi-naya, Abhidharma), it belongs in both the category of Sūtra, since it teaches a method of deliverance, as well as the category of Vinaya, since it teaches a means of control. Within the Five Vehicles (humans, gods, śrāvakas, pratyekabuddhas, and bodhisattvas), it constitutes a ve-hicle for humans and gods, a method of cultivating virtue through good deeds to achieve rebirth in the higher heavens.[89] Tsung-mi sum-marizes the basic teaching of The Yü-lan-p'en Sūtra in four concepts: "filial obedience, making offerings, rescuing those who suffer, and re-paying kindness."

In the second chapter of his commentary Tsung-mi notes the textual history of the sūtra and explains the meaning of the term "yü-lan-p'en":

"Yü-lan" is an expression of the western regions meaning "hang-ing upside-down."[90] This derives from the soul of the Honored

---

[88] Yü-lan-p'en ching shu, T. 39:505a. Cf. Jan, "Tsung-mi: His Analysis of Ch'an Bud-dhism," pp. 22–23.

[89] Okabe quite reasonably equates these two vehicles with the "Teaching of Men and Gods" (jen-t'ien chiao), which Tsung-mi formulates in his Yüan-jen lun (Inquiry into the Origin of Man), T. no. 1886; see Okabe, "Shūmitsu ni okeru kōron no tenkai to sono hōhō," p. 576. See also Gregory, "The Teaching of Men and Gods," passim.

[90] Tao-hsien occurs in Mencius, 2A: "At the present time, if a state of ten thousand char-iots were to practice benevolent government, the people would rejoice as if they had been

One's [Mu-lien's] mother being bogged down in the dark paths, suffering hunger and thirst and a fate akin to hanging upside-down. Even the mighty numinosity of her sagely son could not bring an end to her fiery fate. The Buddha ordered that a bowl filled with all kinds of food be offered to the Three Honored Ones [śrāvakas, pratyekabuddhas, bodhisattvas] out of respect for the luminous kindness of the great assembly and to deliver [those who suffer] from the affliction of hanging upside-down.[91]

Tsung-mi divides the sūtra into three sections: an introductory section on Mu-lien's unsuccessful effort to save his mother; a section on the principal teaching of the sūtra (the Buddha's establishment of the ghost festival as a method for aiding the ancestors); and a section on the propagation of the teaching, in which Mu-lien carries out the offering to the Sangha and his mother attains deliverance.[92]

In his exegesis Tsung-mi draws on the avadāna of Mu-lien's mother to explain how she arrived in hell, quoting, without attribution, from *The Pure Land Yü-lan-p'en Sūtra*. Hui-ching did not mention the previous lives of Mu-lien or his mother in his earlier *Commentary Praising the Yü-lan-p'en Sūtra*, and Tsung-mi's is the first commentary to take account of this version of the Mu-lien myth, a version made popular in the noncanonical *Pure Land Yü-lan-p'en Sūtra* and in *The Transformation Text on Mu-lien Saving His Mother*.

The length and the exegetical style of Tsung-mi's commentary make it difficult to summarize further, although in later chapters I shall draw frequently on its line-by-line comments.

THE SUPPRESSION OF YÜ-LAN-P'EN IN 844

A diary kept by the Japanese monk Ennin (793–863) preserves an important record of the celebration of the ghost festival in the temples of Ch'ang-an in the year 844. Ennin's record is noteworthy for several reasons. First, it confirms that the celebration of the ghost festival enjoyed great popularity among the T'ang people, who came in large

released from hanging upside-down"; *Meng-tzu yin-te*, Harvard-Yenching Institute Sinological Index Series, Supplement No. 17 (reprint ed., Taipei: Ch'eng-wen Publishing Co., 1966), p. 10; translation following D. C. Lau, trans., *Mencius* (Harmondsworth: Penguin Books, 1970), p. 76. For other Mencian terminology in *The Yü-lan-p'en Sūtra*, see Fujino Ryūnen, "Urabon kyō dokugo," *Ryūkoku daigaku ronshū* No. 353 (1956):340–45.

[91] *Yü-lan-p'en ching shu*, T. 39:506c–7a.

[92] Tsung-mi divides *The Yü-lan-p'en Sūtra* differently than does Hui-ching. *The Lecture Text on the Yü-lan-p'en Sūtra* also follows Tsung-mi's divisions.

95

CHAPTER 3

numbers to provide lavish offerings to Buddhist temples in the capital city. Second, it sheds significant light on the suppression of Buddhist institutions carried out during "Hui-ch'ang," the reign name given to the years of Emperor Wu-tsung's (r. 840–846) rule. The drastic measures of these years effectively crippled Buddhism as an institutional religion, destroying much of its economic base of support and emasculating the ranks of its monkhood. But Ennin's account also suggests that this T'ang-dynasty cultural revolution had only inconsequential effects on the practice of the ghost festival.

The effect of the Hui-ch'ang suppression on the practice of Chinese Buddhism is known to later history through the journal Ennin kept during his stay in China. This unparalleled literary artifact remains one of the best single sources on the practice of Buddhism in the T'ang dynasty and still serves as a lode tapped by social historians investigating political and institutional history, economics, and international relations in ninth-century China.

Born in 793 in eastern Japan, Ennin studied Tendai thought and practice under the eminent master Saichō (767–822) at Enryakuji on Mount Hiei.[93] After Saichō's death Ennin rose to some prominence as a teacher and lecturer, but went into seclusion at the age of forty. His hermitage ended early, however, when he was appointed to a Japanese delegation to China. The embassy arrived in China in 838, and for the next nine years Ennin trekked through much of eastern, central, and northern China, recording his peregrinations in his diary, *Nittō guhō junrei gyōki (The Record of a Pilgrimage to China in Search of the Law)*. In 847 Ennin returned to his homeland, where he was immediately accorded an honored place in the clergy. As the abbot of Enryakuji Ennin lectured to the clerical elite and taught Buddhist rituals to emperors. In his later years Ennin successfully introduced the use of *maṇḍalas* and the ceremony of consecration (Skt.: *abhiṣeka*) into mainstream Tendai practice. In recognition of his teaching and accomplishments, as well as his discipleship under Saichō, Ennin was posthumously bestowed the title of "Great Teacher of Compassion and Insight" (Jikaku daishi).

[93] Ennin's diary, *Nittō guhō junrei gyōki*, is still the best biographical source for his years in China. I have used the critical edition of the diary in Ono Katsutoshi, *Nittō guhō junrei gyōki no kenkyū*, 4 vols. (Tokyo: Suzuki gakujutsu zaidan, 1964–69). Ono's translation and notes are invaluable, as is Reischauer's translation, Edwin O. Reischauer, trans., *Ennin's Diary: The Record of a Pilgrimage to China in Search of the Law* (New York: Ronald Press Co., 1955). For Ennin's years in Japan, see *Zoku gunsho ruijū* (Tokyo: Zoku gunsho ruijū kanseikai, 1923–28), 8:684–700; Ono, *Nittō guhō junrei gyōki no kenkyū*, esp. 4:345–450; and Edwin O. Reischauer, *Ennin's Travels in T'ang China* (New York: Ronald Press Co., 1955), pp. 20–38.

96

The suppression of Buddhism witnessed by Ennin stretched over a number of years, culminating in a series of edicts promulgated in the year 845 which formalized and made even more severe many of the measures taken prior to that time.[94] The Buddhist clergy was repeatedly purged, limits were placed on ordinations into the Sangha, and private property belonging to monks was seized by state authorities. Pilgrimages to holy places were prohibited, as were donations to shrines, and local officials were directed to close most of the smaller temples within their jurisdiction. Finally, in the most damaging series of edicts, most of the property belonging to the larger Buddhist temples, including land, slaves, grain, cash, and cloth, was transferred to state coffers, bells and statues were melted down for copper coinage, and all monks under the age of forty were returned to lay life.

There can be no doubt that the Hui-ch'ang suppression dealt an unprecedented blow to Chinese Buddhist institutions, from which they never fully recovered. In the historical records the suppression rings out as the death knell to organized Buddhism. But the real effects of the suppression remain beyond the reach of analysis, largely because all of the surviving records of the suppression (Ennin's diary, Buddhist histories, and standard histories) are so heavily colored by the political interests of either the staunch defenders or the avowed enemies of the Buddhist establishment. Viewed in a broader context, the Hui-ch'ang suppression followed the pattern of the other well-known persecutions of Buddhism in 446 and 574, with a similar interplay between economic, political, and ideological factors. Furthermore, the years following the Hui-ch'ang suppression were marked by a strong infusion of money and land into the Buddhist church, which now received heavy official support under the revitalizing reign of Emperor Hsiuan-tsung (r. 846–859).[95]

If the effects of the suppression on Buddhism as an institution were less horrific than the Buddhist historians claim, its effects on noninstitutional forms of Buddhism were even less damaging. The practice of mortuary ritual, the annual round of festivals, feats of magic and curing

[94] On the Hui-ch'ang suppression, see Weinstein, *Buddhism under the T'ang*, pp. 114–36; Kamekawa Shōshin, "Kaishō no kaibutsu ni tsuite," *Shina bukkyō shigaku* 6:1 (July 1942):47–68; Kenneth K. S. Ch'en, "The Economic Background of the Hui-ch'ang Suppression of Buddhism," HJAS 19:1–2 (June 1956):67–105; Ono, *Nittō guhō junrei gyōki no kenkyū*, 4:544–63; and Reischauer, *Ennin's Travels*, pp. 217–71.

[95] Hsiuan-tsung's name is correctly transliterated as Hsüan-tsung. I follow standard practice in using the irregular form to avoid confusion with Emperor Hsüan-tsung (r. 712–756). For details on the rebuilding of Buddhist institutions under Hsiuan-tsung, see Weinstein, *Buddhism under the T'ang*, pp. 136–51.

by popular preachers—there exists little evidence showing that these forms of religious life were very much affected by the Hui-ch'ang suppression.

Ennin's description of the celebration of the ghost festival in 844 is a case in point. He writes:

> Offerings are made at the various temples in the city on the fifteenth day of the seventh month. At each temple [people] present flashy candles, colored cakes, artificial flowers, fruit trees, and the like, vying with one another in their rarities. Customarily the offerings are set out in front of the Buddha halls, and the whole city wanders among the temples at their pleasure. It is quite a flourishing festival.
>
> This year the offerings set out in the various temples surpassed those of normal years, but an edict ordered that all of the flowers, medicines, and the like offered at the Buddha halls of the various temples be taken to the Hsing-t'ang kuan to be sacrificed to the Celestial Venerables. On the fifteenth day the Son of Heaven visited the Taoist temple [i.e., the Hsing-t'ang kuan]. He summoned the people to come and see, but they scolded, "Seizing the Buddha's offerings to sacrifice to gods and spirits—who would dare come and watch?" The [Son of] Heaven was surprised that the people did not come. The various temples were extremely distressed that their offerings had been seized.[96]

According to Ennin the celebration of the ghost festival in Ch'ang-an in 844 drew a large number of people to Buddhist temples, where they made offerings typical of medieval times: fancy fruits, festive foods, specially decorated candles, and paper flowers. The ongoing suppression of Buddhism apparently had no effect on the major participants in the ghost festival. It is only at the instigation of the emperor that we see any change in public opinion. And, if Ennin's account may be trusted, Emperor Wu-tsung's order to seize the offerings given at Buddhist temples only served to strengthen the predilection of "the people" to give presents to the Sangha: attendance was minimal for the emperor's visit to the Hsing-t'ang kuan, a major Taoist temple located in the northeastern corner of Ch'ang-an.[97] Yü-lan-p'en was so well es-

---

[96] Ennin, *Nittō guhō junrei gyōki*, text in Ono, *Nittō guhō junrei gyōki no kenkyū*, 4:70; translation mostly following Ono, ibid., 4:72; cf. Reischauer, trans., *Ennin's Diary*, p. 344.

[97] The Hsing-t'ang kuan was built in 730 and restored in 806. It was located just opposite the [Ta] An-kuo ssu in the southwestern corner of the Ch'ang-lo quarter and just

tablished among the residents of the T'ang capital that most people boycotted the imperial celebration when it was moved to a Taoist setting.

Ennin's account also sheds important light on the logic of ritual transactions in Chinese religion. Neither the emperor nor the common people questioned the efficacy of making offerings to the Buddhist church or to the Taoist church. If the emperor had doubted the efficacy of such offerings, he would not have shifted the gifts from Buddhist to Taoist recipients. If the people had not believed that offerings to either church would bring results, they would not have made the offerings, nor would they have objected to the switch. The events of this year demonstrate that offerings in Buddhist temples to Buddhist deities and offerings in Taoist temples to Taoist deities were interchangeable. By taking advantage of this functional equivalence (as well as the popularity of making offerings on the fifteenth day of the seventh month), Emperor Wu-tsung insured that the celebration of the ghost festival in 844 would not be forgotten.

The Lecture Text on the Yü-lan-p'en Sūtra
(CA. 850)

The appeal of the ghost festival to a specifically Buddhist but nonmonastic audience may be judged from an untitled manuscript fragment kept in the Taiwan collection of Tun-huang manuscripts, the title of which may be reconstructed as *The Lecture Text on the Yü-lan-p'en Sūtra*.[98] The text is a record of a lecture on *The Yü-lan-p'en Sūtra* in which a monk presents an oral exegesis of the sūtra to a lay audience gathered for the specific purpose of receiving instruction on yü-lan-p'en. During the T'ang such lectures were an important means of propagating Buddhist teachings among lay people affiliated loosely with Buddhist temples. Surviving manuscripts of the "sūtra lecture text" genre serve as an index of which sūtras were most popular as lecture topics.[99] The thematic focus of *The Lecture Text on the Yü-lan-p'en Sūtra* is the concept of filial devotion, explained by reference to Mu-lien and by an ex-

south of the imperial living quarters in the northeastern corner of Ch'ang-an. See *T'ang liang-ching ch'eng-fang k'ao* in *Tōdai no chōan to rakuyō*, ch. 3, p. 18v.

[98] The text is Tun-huang MS. no. 32 in the Taiwan colletion, photographically reproduced in *Tun-huang chüan-tzu* (Taipei: Shih-men t'u-shu, 1976), Vol. 2. I reconstruct its title as *Yü-lan-p'en [ching] chiang-ching-wen*.

[99] Other popular sūtras for which there survive sūtra lecture texts include the *Vimalakīrtinirdeśa*, sūtra lecture texts included in THPWC, pp. 517–645; the *Diamond Sūtra*, sūtra lecture text in THPWC, pp. 426–50; *Fu-mu en-chung ching*, sūtra lecture texts in THPWC, pp. 672–94; and the *Lotus Sūtra*, sūtra lecture text in THPWC, pp. 488–516.

tended discussion of the hardships that parents undergo in the process of nurturing and raising children. Unfortunately the surviving text represents only a small fraction of an entire lecture on *The Yü-lan-p'en Sūtra*. The lecture text is not mentioned in earlier scholarship, so that until now its significance for the development of the ghost festival in medieval Chinese religion has not been explored.[100]

In style and content, *The Lecture Text on the Yü-lan-p'en Sūtra* reflects the interests of its audience, which was probably composed of lay people with a minimal level of literacy. As a genre, "sūtra lecture texts" (*chiang-ching-wen*) fall midway between the commentaries written for monks and well-educated lay people on the one hand and the transformation texts performed for the benefit of the unlettered masses on the other. Sūtra lecture texts grew out of the "popular lectures" (*su-chiang*) delivered by monks to lay people who periodically came to temples to receive instruction in Buddhist texts.[101] People who attended these lectures represent an audience more specialized than the commoners who merely made offerings at Buddhist temples and less specialized than monks, for whom Buddhism defined a distinctive form of social life. The actual surviving texts of the sūtra lecture text genre discovered at Tun-huang are either transcripts of these teaching sessions or notes compiled for use by the lecturer. Like transformation texts, they combine prose and verse portions, their language shows many traces of the vernacular, and they are oriented largely toward a nonmonastic audience. But in their exegesis they follow more closely the text of the sūtra, and they lack one essential characteristic of the transformation tale, the pictures around which the narrative was organized.

An investigation of the literary form of *The Lecture Text on the Yü-*

---

[100] Even the most recent book-length study of the myth of Mu-lien, Ch'en Fang-ying's *Mu-lien chiu-mu ku-shih chih yen-chin*, neglects *The Lecture Text on the Yü-lan-p'en Sūtra*. The lecture text is miscatalogued as a *pien-wen* in the catalogue of the Taiwan collection of Tun-huang manuscripts; Li Ch'ing-chih, *Kuo-li chung-yang t'u-shu-kuan so-tsang tun-huang chüan-tzu chiao-tu cha-chi* (N.p.: mimeograph, 1973), pp. 11r–v; see also P'an Ch'ung-kuei, "Kuo-li chung-yang t'u-shu-kuan so-tsang tun-huang chüan-tzu t'i-chi," *Hsin-ya hsüeh-pao* 8:2 (August 1968), pp. 368–69. See also Mair, "Lay Students and the Making of Written Vernacular Narrative," pp. 5–96, Item no. 598. Victor H. Mair first alerted me to the importance of this text, and Timothy Tsu generously helped in transcribing it and solving many problems of orthography.

[101] On sūtra lecture texts and popular lectures during the T'ang, see Kenneth K. S. Ch'en, *The Chinese Transformation of Buddhism* (Princeton: Princeton University Press, 1973), pp. 240–55; Reischauer, *Ennin's Travels*, pp. 183–87; Hsiang Ta, "T'ang-tai su-chiang k'ao"; and Mair, "Lay Students and the Making of Written Vernacular Narrative," pp. 5–6, 90–93.

lan-p'en Sūtra yields a general idea of how popular lectures were conducted. Near the beginning of the text the lecturer instructs his audience "to invoke Kuan-shih-yin Bodhisattva three [times],"[102] and the lecture was probably concluded with a similar ritual. The lecturer-exegete announces each section of the sūtra with the stock formula, "Please sing the next section of the sūtra. It reads. . . ."[103] At this point either a cantor or the audience recites a passage from the scripture, and then the lecturer explains the meaning of the passage. In his exegesis the lecturer usually uses poetry in seven-word lines. Whoever recorded *The Lecture Text on the Yü-lan-p'en Sūtra* (the lecturer himself or a note-taking listener) uses the words "The Buddha's Son [or Disciple]" (*fo-tzu*, Skt.: *Buddhaputra*) as a stage direction to indicate where the lecturer ("The Buddha's Disciple") begins his exegesis. The transition from the end of one exegetical section to the next is usually marked with a rhetorical question, "Now what about [e.g., Mu-lien attaining the Way]?"[104] Judging from the lecturer's promise to his "lay disciples" (*men-t'u*) that "I will explain [this topic] to my lay disciples on another day,"[105] it may be inferred that the sermon on the ghost festival formed part of a regular program of religious instruction.

The Lecture Text on the Yü-lan-p'en Sūtra opens with several verses setting forth the general idea of saving one's ancestors from the woeful states of existence. Following this preface, the preacher announces the title of the sūtra on which he will lecture, calling it "The Sūtra on the Purity of Yü-lan." The preacher also discusses the organization of the text, dividing it into three sections: "an introductory section," "[a section on] the principal teaching," and "a section on the propagation of the teaching."[106]

After these preliminaries, the lecture text presents a line-by-line exegesis of *The Yü-lan-p'en Sūtra*. Unfortunately the manuscript breaks off halfway through its explanation of the fourth sentence of the sūtra, although the few surviving sections provide helpful clues as to which subjects a lay audience found pertinent to the ghost festival.

The two major themes of the surviving portions of *The Lecture Text on the Yü-lan-p'en Sūtra* are charity and filial devotion. The virtue of charity is emphasized in the exegesis of the locale described in the sec-

[102] *The Lecture Text on the Yü-lan-p'en Sūtra*, in *Tun-huang chüan-tzu*, p. 1.

[103] *The Lecture Text on the Yü-lan-p'en Sūtra*, in *Tun-huang chüan-tzu*, pp. 2, 3, 4.

[104] *The Lecture Text on the Yü-lan-p'en Sūtra*, in *Tun-huang chüan-tzu*, p. 3.

[105] *The Lecture Text on the Yü-lan-p'en Sūtra*, in *Tun-huang chüan-tzu*, p. 2.

[106] Cf. *Tsung-mi Commentary*, T. no. 1792, 39:507a; and *Hui-ching Commentary*, T. no. 2781, 85:540a.

ond sentence of *The Yü-lan-p'en Sūtra,* the garden of Jetavana trees in the kingdom of Śrāvastī. The explanation notes that the garden was established through the pious contribution of the rich layman, Anātha-piṇḍika.

The bulk of the lecture text constitutes a sermon on the requirements and rewards of filial devotion. The text describes the generic filial son as one who waits diligently at his parents' side, always putting their comfort and needs ahead of his own. Mu-lien is identified as the paragon of devotion, since he used his powers of spiritual penetration to bring help to his poor suffering mother.

The Lecture Text on the Yü-lan-p'en Sūtra draws extensively on the concept of reciprocity to elucidate further the theme of serving one's parents and ancestors. Fully half of the surviving lecture text concerns the "ten kindnesses" (*shih-en*) bestowed by parents (especially mothers) upon their children. These "kindnesses" summarize the travails of childrearing. Children enter the world owing a debt to their parents. The debt must be repaid by providing them with material support in old age and with ritual aid (including yü-lan-p'en offerings) after their death. The "ten kindnesses," a frequent topic of late-T'ang apocrypha, are: (1) carrying the pregnancy safely to term, (2) enduring suffering as birth approaches, (3) forgetting sorrow in giving birth to a son, (4) taking the bitter and foregoing the sweet, (5) avoiding wetness and keeping the child dry, (6) nursing, feeding, and raising the child, (7) cleaning up the child's filth, (8) acquiring bad karma through actions for the child's benefit, (9) longing for the child when far away, and (10) being always compassionate and sympathetic.[107]

The one extant manuscript of *The Lecture Text on the Yü-lan-p'en Sūtra* lacks a colophon and any other data that would supply a certain date. It divides *The Yü-lan-p'en Sūtra* into the same three sections as does Tsung-mi, and, as noted above, it contains references to the "ten kindnesses," a concept that was quite popular in the late T'ang. On this admittedly slim basis, *The Lecture Text on the Yü-lan-p'en Sūtra* may be dated roughly to the year 850.

[107] The "ten kindnesses" form the main subject of several versions of *The Sūtra on the Importance of Kindness Bestowed by Parents (Fu-mu en-chung ching). The Lecture Text on the Yü-lan-p'en Sūtra* quotes from this source, many versions of which survive from the late T'ang. The list of ten kindnesses in the sūtra lecture text matches the list in *Fu-mu en-chung t'ai-ku ching,* printed from a Korean woodblock dating from the late fourteenth century and contained in Makita, *Gikyō kenkyū,* pp. 52–55. See Chapter Seven, below, for another discussion of this sūtra.

CHIH-YÜAN'S "HYMNS IN PRAISE OF LAN-P'EN"
(CA. 1020)

History does not preserve any record of the actual prayers used in the ghost festival during the medieval period, but later sources may be used to reconstruct loosely the mechanics of the ritual in the late T'ang. One such source, entitled *Lan-p'en li-tsan-wen* ("Hymns in Praise of Lan-p'en"), was written by the monk Chih-yüan (976–1028) and incorporated in a more complete liturgical text a century later. Although it was written and used after the medieval period covered in this chapter's survey, it is included here because it preserves the earliest surviving liturgy for ghost festival ceremonies. Chih-yüan's hymns, nominally addressed to the Three Treasures, were probably chanted by lay people as they made offerings in the temples of south China.

Chih-yüan, whose surname was Hsü, was born in 976 in Hang-chou (present-day Chekiang).[108] He entered the monkhood at an early age, studying T'ien-t'ai teachings and meditation under the monk Yüan-ch'ing (d. 996). He later took up residence at Mount Ku, which had a beautiful view of the surrounding lakes in Chekiang. Many students flocked there to hear his teachings. Chih-yüan was afflicted by growths on his neck, which also supplied the topic of many of his poems on suffering and retribution. His friends included the recluse-poet Lin Pu (965–1026) and the monk Tsun-shih (964–1032). He died in 1028 and was posthumously bestowed the title "Great Master of Dharma Wisdom" (Fa-hui ta-shih).

Chih-yüan's interests ranged far beyond the sectarian disputes within the T'ien-t'ai school for which he is best known in Buddhist historiography. He wrote several essays disputing the interpretations of

---

[108] Biographical details in this and the next paragraph are drawn primarily from Chih-yüan's biography in *Shih-men cheng-t'ung*, Tsung-chien (Sung), Z. 2B, 3:5, pp. 414rb–16rb. Shorter accounts and extracts from Chih-yüan's writings are included in *Fo-tsu t'ung-chi*, T. no. 2035, 49:418c–19a, 446c–47b; *Fo-tsu li-tai t'ung-tsai*, Nien-ch'ang (d. 1341), T. no. 2036, 49:661b–c; and *Wang-sheng chi*, Chu-hung (1535–1615), T. no. 2072, 51:136c–37a. Chih-yüan's autobiographical piece, "Chung-yung-tzu chuan" is contained in *Hsien-chü chi*, Z. 2A, 6:1, pp. 55va–57ra. Lists of Chih-yüan's works are contained in MBDJ, p. 3550b; and in the appendix to *Hsien-chü chi*, Z. 2A, 6:1, pp. 107va–8ra. For Chih-yüan's place in the schism pitting the "Non-mountain School" against the "Mountain School" (*shan-wai, shan-chia*) in T'ien-t'ai doctrine, see Michihata Ryōshū, *Chūgoku bukkyō shi*, second ed. (Kyoto: Hōzōkan, 1958), pp. 183–84, 205–6; Shimaji Taitō, *Tendai kyōgaku shi* (1933; reprint ed., Tokyo: Nakayama shobō, 1978), pp. 151–233; Chiang Wei-ch'iao, *Chung-kuo fo-chiao shih* (1933; reprint ed., Taipei: Ting-wen shu-chü, 1974), ch. 3, pp. 20–30; and Kuo P'eng, *Sung yüan fo-chiao* (Fukien: Fu-chien jen-min ch'u-pan-she, 1981), pp. 170–76.

T'ien-t'ai doctrine offered by Chih-li (960–1028), but he also wrote commentaries on Pure Land texts and on such core Mahāyāna sūtras as the *Heart, Nirvāṇa,* and *Diamond Sūtras.* Chih-yüan consistently taught the harmony of the Three Teachings, and the poems and letters collected in his *Hsien-chü pien* (roughly, *"Essays in Idleness"*) attest to his broad reading in all genres of Chinese literature. He also wrote a subcommentary on Tsung-mi's commentary on *The Yü-lan-p'en Sūtra, Lan-p'en ching shu chih-hua ch'ao (Collected Blossoms from the Commentary on the Lan-p'en Sūtra),* which is quoted extensively in a later subcommentary.[109]

Chih-yüan's "Hymns in Praise of Lan-p'en" forms the skeleton of a later work by Yüan-chao (1048–1116), who lived at Ling-chih ssu (present-day Chekiang) and also wrote his own subcommentary on Tsung-mi's commentary on *The Yü-lan-p'en Sūtra.*[110] Yüan-chao's *Lan-p'en hsien-kung i (Ceremonial for Lan-p'en Offerings)* combines Chih-yüan's "Hymns in Praise of Lan-p'en" with some brief invocations and explanatory passages. Chih-yüan's six hymns are addressed to the immediate recipients of ghost festival offerings: the Buddha, the Dharma (as embodied in sūtras), and the Sangha (represented by bodhisattvas, *pratyekabuddhas, śrāvakas,* and Mu-lien). I translate below the six hymns, each prefaced by an invocatory line:

I. With one mind we bow deeply to Śākyamuni Buddha, the Chief
   Teacher of Lan-p'en, who always repays familial kindness.

Over many kalpas of cultivation he perfected the Way of the sages,
At Mu-lien's sorrowful request he expounded the true vehicle.

His father the king[111] leapt into space to pay him respect;
Farmers and fishermen, hearing his words, set aside their plows and
   nets.

In cultivating the cause and collecting the fruit, he always takes refuge
   in filial devotion;
In transforming others and practicing it himself, he fully repays [his
   parents'] kindness.

We pray that he regard all sentient beings with his compassionate eye,
Causing them all, living and dead, to receive his gifts.

---

[109] Chih-yüan's commentary may be partially reconstructed from the citations in Jih-hsin's (ca. 1068) *Lan-p'en ching shu-ch'ao yü-i* (1068), Z. 1, 94:4.

[110] *Yü-lan-p'en ching shu hsin-chi,* Yüan-chao (1048–1116), Z. 1, 35:2.

[111] Or "Fathers and kings."

II. With one mind we bow deeply to the ultimate teaching of Lan-
p'en, the Sūtra Collection, which repays kindness and saves from
suffering.

The golden mouth speaks forth an unbounded teaching;
For repaying kindness there is only this fortuitous event [of yü-lan-
p'en].

To relieve suffering it specially calls upon monks who have freed
themselves;
It shows compassion in handing down the Lan-p'en Dharma.

Happily rejoicing and spreading the teaching, its words are complete;
With the translation of the Dharma, the Way becomes luminescent.

Kings and counselors, rich and poor, everyone carries it out,
The brilliance of its wondrous precepts surpasses sun and moon.

III. With one mind we bow deeply to the Bodhisattva Monks, those
sages and worthies who have freed themselves and gained the
Way.

Their compassion and wisdom practiced to the full, they are called
great men;

Seeking enlightenment above and transforming others below, they
move through the Sangha.

They aid beings, forever boarding the boat of the Six Perfections,
They benefit others, forever sending them to the shore of the Three
Emptinesses.[112]

Their internal realization would extend to all the Buddha realms;
In accord with conditions they sometimes manifest themselves in the
form of a *bhikṣu.*

And now as they descend to this sacred place,
We pray that they will release all of our living and dead relatives from
suffering.

IV. With one mind we bow deeply to the Monks who have
Awakened to Causality *[pratyekabuddhas]*, those sages and
worthies of the ten directions who have freed themselves and
gained the Way.

[112] The "Six Perfections" are giving, morality, patience, vigor, meditation, and wisdom. The "Three Emptinesses" are emptiness, marklessness, and desirelessness.

Their sharp wisdom is not passed down from masters or teachers;
By examining dependent origination they awaken to the unborn.

Preaching the Dharma and transmitting the lamp they call sectarian
   practice;
Cultivating the mind without companions, they evoke the parable of
   the *lin* [female "unicorn"].

With true emptiness completely realized, they regard splendor and
   decline;
With afflictions fully eliminated, they lend an ear to mild sounds.

And now as they descend to this sacred place,
We pray that they will release all of our living and dead relatives from
   suffering.

V. With one mind we bow deeply to the Monks who have Heard the
   Voice [of the Buddha, i.e., *śrāvakas*], those sages and worthies of
   the ten directions who have freed themselves and gained the
   Way.

In mountains and under trees, they complete the [summer] retreat;
Contemplating deeply the Four Noble Truths, they attain a surplus
   [of understanding].

Noisily they overturn fully the fruits of birth-and-death,
Silently they have already experienced the mind of *nirvāṇa*.

With the six penetrations and self-mastery, they pass over Māra's
   realm;
Roaming freely in the eight forms of liberation, they are called a field
   of merit.

And now as they descend to this sacred place,
We pray that they will release all of our living and dead relatives from
   suffering.

VI. With one mind we bow deeply to the Honorable Mu-lien, who
   entered the Way to repay his parents, giving rise to the teaching
   which profits life.

Most accomplished at spiritual penetrations, he abides among those
   who have nothing more to learn;
To repay his parents' kindness, he left the householder's life.

With just his own power it was hard to end his dear mother's
    misfortune;
He cried out in sorrow and sought instruction from the Thus-Come
    One.

He gave rise to the subtle words that bring aid to later generations,
And extolled the Way of filial devotion that profits all beings.

And now as he descends to this sacred place,
We pray that he will release all of our living and dead relatives from
    suffering.[113]

POSTSCRIPT: THE GHOST FESTIVAL AFTER T'ANG TIMES

A reasonable survey of the vagaries of the ghost festival in post-T'ang
China would fill several volumes. Sources for the study of Chinese social history began to proliferate after the T'ang, and the myth of Mu-
lien was repeated and reworked in a variety of new literary forms. In
light of its vitality after the medieval period, a highly selective survey
of the ghost festival in later times is offered here simply as a postscript.

Like many other forms of religion in late medieval China, the celebration of the ghost festival took on ritual forms deriving from the
Tantric tradition.[114] The influence of Tantra on the practice of the festival may be gauged primarily from the rapid production of liturgical
texts beginning in the late T'ang. Just how widespread these Tantric
practices were at that time is harder to judge, although certainly before
the Ming dynasty many rites performed during the ghost festival could
be traced back to liturgical texts attributed to the great Tantric masters,
Śikṣānanda (652–710) and Amoghavajra (705–774).[115] Such liturgical

---

[113] Translation from *Lan-p'en hsien-kung i*, Yüan-chao, Z. 2B, 3:2, p. 90ra–b.

[114] Yoshioka Yoshitoyo provides a comprehensive bibliographical survey of Tantric-
influenced texts on feeding hungry ghosts in *Dōkyō to bukkyō*, Vol. 1 (Tokyo: Nihon gakujutsu shinkōkai, 1959), pp. 369–432. Makita Tairyō traces the practice of feeding hungry ghosts from the Sung through the Ming in "Suirikue shōkō," *Tōhō shūkyō* No. 12
(July 1957):14–33.

[115] See, for example, *Chiu mien-jan o-kuei t'o-lo-ni shen-chou ching*, Śikṣānanda, T. no.
1314; and such texts attributed to Amoghavajra as *Chiu-pa yen-k'ou o-kuei t'o-lo-ni ching*,
T. no. 1313; *Shih chu o-kuei yin-shih chi shui-fa*, T. no. 1315; and *Yü-ch'ieh chi-yao chiu a-
nan t'o-lo-ni yen-k'ou kuei-i ching*, T. no. 1318. For a more complete listing, see Yoshioka,
Dōkyō to bukkyō, 1:412–30. See also Ferdinand Lessing, "Skizze des Ritus: Die Spiesung
der Hungergeister," in *Studia Sino-Altaica: Festschrift für Erich Haenisch zum 80. Geburtstag, in Auftrag der Deutschen Morgenländischen Gesellschaft* (Wiesbaden: Franz Steiner Verlag, 1961), pp. 114–19; and de Visser, *Ancient Buddhism in Japan*, 1:76–84.

texts as *Chiu-pa yen-k'ou o-kuei t'o-lo-ni ching (The Sūtra of Dhāraṇīs for Saving Hungry Ghosts with Burning Mouths)* record the *dhāraṇīs* to be spoken, describe the *mudrās* to be performed, and provide the names of the many Buddhas to be invoked in making offerings to hungry ghosts, mendicants, and the Three Jewels.[116] While these liturgies had no intrinsic connection to the fifteenth day of the seventh month, they were used at various rites throughout the year, including the ghost festival.

The Sung dynasties saw the growth of a liturgical tradition centering on the "Assembly of Water and Land" (*shui-lu hui*), a kind of mass dedicated to wandering spirits. Offerings to spirits haunting waterways were dumped into streams and rivers, while presents destined for souls suffering recompense in the hells were thrown onto the ground. This ritual too was practiced at irregular intervals throughout the year, including the fifteenth day of the seventh month. Tsun-shih (964–1032) was particularly active in propagating the Assembly of Water and Land.[117] Within a century after his death, the ritual had acquired an elaborate origin myth associating its rise with the patronage of the monk Pao-chih by Emperor Wu (r. 502–550) of the Liang dynasty.[118] In Ming times Chu-hung (1535–1615) was quite active in revitalizing and revising liturgies used in the assembly.[119]

The relative profusion of sources on daily life and customs beginning in the Northern Sung permits the reconstruction of many of the details of ghost festival celebrations in the newly arisen urban centers of China.[120] These sources show that from the eleventh through the thirteenth centuries, the seventh-moon festival brought together all classes of society in Buddhist temples and in markets where an astonishing va-

[116] T. no. 1313, 21:464b–65b.

[117] Texts on the Assembly of Water and Land written by Tsun-shih include *Chih-sheng-kuang tao-ch'ang nien-sung i*, T. no. 1951; and those collected in *Chin-yüan chi*, Z. 2A, 6:2. Tsung-hsiao (1151–1214) collects a number of important works in his *Shih-shih t'ung-lan*, Z. 2A, 6:3.

[118] See Makita Tairyō, "Hōshi oshō den kō," *Tōhō gakuhō* 26 (March 1956):64–89; and idem, "Suirikue shōkō," pp. 21–24.

[119] Some of Chu-hung's works on feeding hungry ghosts are included in chs. 18–21 of his *Yün-ch'i fa-hui* (Nanking: Ching-ling k'o-ching-ch'u, 1897). See also Chün-fang Yü, *The Renewal of Buddhism in China: Chu-hung and the Late Ming Synthesis* (New York: Columbia University Press, 1981), pp. 184–85.

[120] For a good overview, see Sawada Mizuho, *Jigoku hen: chūgoku no meikai setsu* (Kyoto: Hōzōkan, 1968), pp. 128–35. See also Jacques Gernet, *Daily Life in China on the Eve of the Mongol Invasion, 1250–1276*, trans. H. M. Wright (Stanford: Stanford University Press, 1970), p. 195.

riety of goods were sold. In most locales offerings were placed in bamboo bowls, some of which were decorated with drawings of Mu-lien saving his mother.[121] Sometimes the bottom half of a length of bamboo was splayed into several strips that served as legs; spirit money was then placed inside the top half, and the entire offering was transmitted to the other world by fire.[122] Sometimes the bamboo bowls were saved for use in divining the weather, in which case the bowl was flipped over onto the ground and the direction in which it ended up pointing was taken as a prediction of the coming winter: if pointing north, a cold one; if pointing south, a warm one; if pointing east or west, a temperate one.[123] Goods sold in markets included melons, lilac flowers, peaches, pears, poultry, rice, noodles, and paper goods (clothes and money) for use by the dead.[124]

Uncommon events were believed to occur on the full-moon festival of the seventh month. Legends report living persons ascending to mansions in the sky[125] and deceased relatives being allowed to leave the dark regions to visit their old homes on this day.[126] Even nonhumans went through unusual transformations during the ghost festival, as reported in a tenth-century collection of tales:

> Formerly in the T'ang, before he had assumed office, on chung-yüan Prefect Lu Yüan-yü set out banners and statues and placed a yü-lan [bowl] between them. All of a sudden he heard a chirping sound coming from the bowl. Yüan-yü looked and saw a tiny dragon barely an inch long, which was relaxed yet a little odd-looking, gentle and lovable. At this he took some water to moisten it. The dragon stretched out its legs and bristled its mane, growing several feet long. Yüan-yü took a great fright. A white

---

[121] *Shih-wu chi-yüan (chi-lei)*, Kao Ch'eng (ca. 1078–1085) (Taipei: Commercial Press, 1971), ch. 8, pp. 23r–v (pp. 585–86).

[122] *Sui-shih kuang-chi*, Ch'en Yüan-ching (S. Sung), *Sui-shih hsi-su tzu-liao hui-pien*, Vols. 4–7 (Taipei: I-wen yin-shu-kuan, 1970), ch. 30, pp. 1v–2r (pp. 970–71).

[123] *Lao-hsüeh-an pi-chi*, Lu Yu (1125–1210), in *Hsüeh-chin t'ao-yüan*, Pai-pu ts'ung-shu chi-ch'eng, No. 46 (Taipei: I-wen yin-shu-kuan), ch. 7, p. 1v.

[124] See *Shih-wu chi-yüan (chi-lei)*, ch. 8, pp. 23r–v (pp. 585–86); *Sui-shih kuang-chi*, ch. 30, pp. 1v–2r (pp. 970–71); *Tung-ching meng-hua lu*, Meng Yüan-lao (ca. 1235), in *Tung-ching meng-hua lu, wai ssu-chung* (Shanghai: Ku-tien wen-hsüeh ch'u-pan-she, 1957), pp. 49–50; *Lao-hsüeh-an pi-chi*, ch. 7, p. 1v; and *Wu-lin chiu-shih*, Chou Mi (ca. 1280), in *Tung-ching meng-hua lu, wai ssu-chung*, p. 381.

[125] See the story of Ts'ui Wei in *T'ai-p'ing kuang-chi*, pp. 216–20.

[126] See the story of Wang Tsu-te in *I-chien chih*, Hung Mai (1123–1202), 4 vols. (Taipei: Hsin-hsing shu-chü, 1960), p. 360.

cloud arose from the bowl, and the dragon left, following the cloud.[127]

In the Southern Sung capital of Hang-chou, those whose relatives had recently died went to sweep off their graves. Mountains of paper money were burned for use by ancestors in the underworld, and freshly printed sūtras on "Mu-lien, the Most Venerable" were sold in markets. And in K'ai-feng, according to Meng Yüan-lao (ca. 1235):

> In theaters,[128] having passed the seventh night [the festival marking the meeting of the Cowherd and Weaving Maiden], singing girls next staged the drama of Mu-lien saving his mother. It went straight through the fifteenth day with throngs of spectators.[129]

While no texts of the week-long drama (*tsa-chü*) on Mu-lien survive from Sung or Yüan times, it is clear that the Mu-lien myth took on new life in the genres of literature and drama that succeeded transformation texts after the T'ang. In fact the mythology of the ghost festival spread throughout so many genres that even a brief survey is beyond the scope of this study, and a few examples will have to suffice.[130]

It is generally thought that a play recorded by Cheng Chih-chen in the Ming dynasty preserves the general outline of the Northern Sung drama noted by Meng Yüan-lao. Cheng Chih-chen's work, entitled *Mu-lien chiu-mu hsing-hsiao hsi-wen* ("A Play on Mu-lien Practicing Filial Devotion by Saving His Mother"), adds significantly to the plot of the story contained in *The Transformation Text on Mu-lien Saving His Mother*.[131] In the play version Mu-lien's mother is not inherently

---

[127] Story of Lu Yüan-yü translated from *T'ai-p'ing kuang-chi*, p. 3438.

[128] I follow Sawada in emending *kou-ssu* to *kou-lan*; see Sawada, *Jigoku hen*, pp. 141–42.

[129] Translation from *Tung-ching meng-hua lu*, p. 49.

[130] For good overviews of the literary history of the Mu-lien myth in Sung and later times, see Chao Ching-shen, "Ch'üan-shan chin-k'o," in *Ming ch'ing ch'ü-t'an* (Shanghai: Ku-tien wen-hsüeh ch'u-pan-she, 1957), pp. 154–62; idem, "Mu-lien chiu-mu te yen-pien" (1946), reprinted in *Chung-kuo min-chien ch'uan-shuo yen-chiu*, ed. Wang Ch'iu-kuei (Taipei: Lien-ching ch'u-pan shih-yeh kung-ssu, 1980), pp. 219–36; Ch'en, *Mu-lien chiu-mu ku-shih chih yen-chin*; Ch'ien Nan-yang, "Tu jih-pen Kuraishi Takeshirō te Mokuren gyōkō gibun yen-chiu," *Min-su* No. 72 (August 1929):1–7; Kuraishi Takeshirō, "Moku-ren kyūbo gyōkō gibun ni tsuite," *Shinagaku* 3:10 (February 1925):5–24; Piet van der Loon, "Les Origines rituelles du théâtre chinois," *JA* 265:1–2 (1977):158–62; Sawada Mi-zuho, *Hōkan no kenkyū*, revised ed. (Kyoto: Kokusho kankōkai, 1975), pp. 123–26; and idem, *Jigoku hen*, pp. 141–48.

[131] I have consulted two editions of Cheng Chih-chen's play, one on microfilm from the National Library, Peking, in 8 ch., entitled *Hsin-k'an ch'u-hsiang yin-chu ch'üan-shan mu-lien chiu-mu hsing-hsiao hsi-wen*, Chin-ling shu-fang ed., ca. 1573–1620; and one in *Ku-pen hsi-ch'ü ts'ung-k'an ch'u-chi* (Shanghai: Commercial Press, 1954), Vols. 80–82.

greedy. Rather, after her husband dies, her evil brothers persuade her to give up a vegetarian diet and to withhold offerings from monks, actions for which she is reborn in hell. Mu-lien sets out to rescue his mother, but before the underworld search begins, the play includes a number of scenes portraying Mu-lien's journey to the west. Mu-lien, like the Tripiṭaka monk Hsüan-tsang in the novel *Hsi-yu chi (Journey to the West)*, enlists the aid of a monkey, he passes through the Black Pine Forest, and he depends at every turn upon the compassionate guidance of Kuan-yin. Cheng Chih-chen's play also marks the first appearance in ghost festival mythology of Mu-lien's fiancée, Ts'ao Sai-ying, who joins the Buddhist order of nuns after her betrothed becomes a monk.

Another important literary guise in which the myth appears is that of the "precious scroll" (*pao-chüan*), a genre that embellished popular stories in a form containing sections in vernacular prose and sections sung to the tune of folk songs and operas. In the early Ming *Mu-lien san-shih pao-chüan (The Precious Scroll on the Three Lives of Mu-lien)* was especially popular.[132] This tale adds two incarnations to the relatively simple life Mu-lien leads in the transformation text. First, Mu-lien was too successful in his battle with the armies of hell. When he broke open the gates of hell with his staff, eight million souls escaped from purgatory, but they must still be returned to purgatory to complete their karmic retribution. This provides the occasion for Mu-lien's second incarnation: he returns to the world above ground as the salt merchant-rebel leader Huang Ch'ao, whose peasant revolt between 874 and 884 effectively marked the end of the T'ang. As Huang Ch'ao, Mu-lien kills over eight million people, thus redressing the balance of karma he had disturbed by letting hell dwellers go free. The underworld administrator King Yama, however, judges that a large number of pig souls and sheep souls have still not been returned to their places in the underworld, and so Mu-lien is reborn on earth a third time—as a butcher, who quickly meets the quota set by King Yama. Eventually, both Mu-lien and his mother work out their karmic punishments and are reunited with Mu-lien's father in the heavens.

Mu-lien's transformations in Ch'ing and modern times make a fascinating story, but one which cannot be told here in this brief postscript. Sources for a survey of the mythology and practice of the ghost

---

[132] For bibliographical references on several *pao-chüan* on Mu-lien saving his mother, see Li Shih-yü, *Pao-chüan tsung-lu* (Peking: Chung-hua shu-chü, 1961), Item nos. 273–81, 332.

festival in the past three hundred years, however, are readily accessible. They include Chinese records of seasonal observances; detailed reports from Japanese ethnographers; appreciative accounts by visiting diplomats, missionaries, and wives; and the masterful study by the Dutch Sinologist and ethnographer, de Groot.[133]

[133] After local gazetteers, the imperial encyclopedia provides a convenient overview of local practices: *Ku-chin t'u-shu chi-ch'eng*, ch. 68, pp. 692–94. Suzuki's report on Taiwan and de Groot's on Amoy remain the best studies of modern practices: Suzuki Mitsuo, "Bon ni kuru rei," *Minzokugaku kenkyū* 37:3 (1972):167–85; and Jan J. M. de Groot, *Les Fêtes annuellement célébrées à Emoui*, 2 vols., trans. C. G. Chavannes, Annales du Musée Guimet, No. 12 (Paris: Ernest Leroux, 1886), pp. 404–35. Other accounts include: Juliet Bredon and Igor Mitrophanow, *The Moon Year: A Record of Chinese Customs and Festivals* (Shanghai: Kelly and Walsh, 1927), pp. 376–86; Valentine R. Burkhardt, *Chinese Creeds and Customs*, 2 vols. (Hong Kong: South China Morning Post, 1953–55), 2:53–64; F. J. Dymond, "The Feast of the Seventh Moon," *The East of Asia Magazine* 2:4 (December 1903):376–78; Wolfram Eberhard, *Chinese Festivals* (1952; reprint ed., Taipei: Wen-hsing shu-tien, 1963), pp. 129–33; Huang Yu-mei, "China's Ghost Festival," *Free China Review* 32:11 (November 1982):68–72; Claudine Lombard-Salmon, "Survivance d'un rite bouddhique à Java: la cérémonie du *pu-du (avalambana)*," BEFEO 62 (1975):457–86; Duane Pang, "The P'u-tu Ritual," in *Buddhist and Taoist Studies I*, eds. Michael Saso and David W. Chappell, Asian Studies at Hawaii, No. 18 (Honolulu: University Press of Hawaii, 1977), pp. 95–122; Reichelt, *Truth and Tradition in Chinese Buddhism*, pp. 92–114; Tanaka Issei, *Chūgoku saishi engeki kenkyū* (Tokyo: Tokyo daigaku shuppansha, 1981), pp. 230–41; Tun Li-ch'en, *Annual Customs and Festivals in Peking*, second ed., trans. Derk Bodde (Hong Kong: Hong Kong University Press, 1965), pp. 60–63; and de Visser, *Ancient Buddhism in Japan*, 1:84–88.

FOUR

The Mythological Background

IN MEDIEVAL TIMES the myth of Mu-lien saving his mother served to justify one of the most widespread of annual celebrations in China. The myth itself was elaborated in a variety of genres: entertaining picture stories recounted in the marketplace; short, dry sūtras accepted into the Buddhist canon; and a host of commentaries, hymns, lecture texts, and apocryphal sūtras. While they differ widely in form, all of these sources constitute a coherent group that can conveniently be called "yü-lan-p'en literature."

This chapter places yü-lan-p'en literature in the context of Chinese Buddhist mythology.[1] Most of the motifs of the mature yü-lan-p'en story were present in Chinese Buddhist mythology long before catalogues first noted the existence of *The Yü-lan-p'en Sūtra* and before historians first recorded the observance of the ghost festival. By surveying some of the antecedents of yü-lan-p'en literature, I hope to cast more light on the mythological context out of which the ghost festival emerged. In this and later chapters I also hope to show the dramatic and literary integrity of the various versions of the yü-lan-p'en story, suggesting that the constraints of genre and the demands of various audiences partly determined the shape of any one version. And rather than isolating specific motifs as essentially "Indian" or irreducibly "Chinese," I shall read the myths as they were enacted, read, and understood by Chinese of the first millennium: not as schizophrenic mixtures but as whole and healthy narratives.

[1] For the most recent and comprehensive study of the antecedents of the yü-lan-p'en myth, see Ch'en Fang-ying, *Mu-lien chiu-mu ku-shih chih yen-chin chi ch'i yu-kuan wen-hsüeh chih yen-chiu*, History and Literature Series, No. 65 (Taipei: Taiwan National University, 1983), pp. 7–22. See also the important studies by Ishigami Zennō, "Mokuren setsuwa no keifu," *Taishō daigaku kenkyū kiyō* No. 54 (November 1968):1–24; Iwamoto Yutaka, *Bukkyō setsuwa kenkyū*, Vol. 2, *Bukkyō setsuwa no genryū to tenkai* (Tokyo: Kaimei shoten, 1978), pp. 373–93, Vol. 4, *Jigoku meguri no bungaku* (which incorporates *Mokuren densetsu to urabon*) (Tokyo: Kaimei shoten, 1979), pp. 171–99; Lo Tsung-t'ao, *Tun-huang chiang-ching pien-wen yen-chiu* (Taipei: Wen shih che ch'u-pan-she, 1972), pp. 229–302 passim; Victor Mair, "Notes on the Maudgalyāyana Legend in East Asia," paper presented at the Mid-Atlantic Regional Meeting of the Association for Asian Studies, October 1984; and Ogawa Kan'ichi, *Bukkyō bunka shi kenkyū* (Kyoto: Nagata bunshōdō, 1973), pp. 165–71.

CHAPTER 4

An Example

In *The Yü-lan-p'en Sūtra* Mu-lien is a disciple of the Buddha, a meditator skilled in the powers of the seer, a traveler who reveals the structure
of the cosmos, and a figure instrumental in providing a means of salvation to his mother. None of these motifs was original to *The Yü-lan-
p'en Sūtra*; they all appear in a tale that had already been translated into
Chinese by the end of the fourth century. The tale is contained in the
Tseng-i a-han ching (The Additional Āgama, Ekottarāgama), a canonical
collection of short sūtras translated into Chinese by Gautama Saṃghadeva between 397 and 398. As one of the *Āgamas* (corresponding to the
Pāli *Nikāyas*), the *Tseng-i a-han ching* was part of the heritage common
to all schools of Buddhism in India and China, and it comes as close as
any Buddhist scripture to representing precanonical Buddhist beliefs of
the fourth century B.C.[2] For our purposes its value lies not in its "Indi-
anness," but in its antiquity and unassailable position in early Chinese
Buddhism.

The story related in the *Āgama*, which is summarized in the Appendix to this chapter, illustrates that many of the roles that Mu-lien plays
in later Chinese tradition had already been blocked out in early Chinese
mythology. In the *Āgama* tale, Mu-lien is portrayed as the quintessen-
tial shaman, one who uses his unusual martial and meditative powers
to travel through the universe. The story begins with Mu-lien responding to a cosmic disturbance: from their position under the Trikuta rocks that support Mount Sumeru, two nāga kings (Nanda and
Upananda) breathe fire throughout the continent of Jambudvīpa.[3] Mu-
lien is the only disciple of the Buddha powerful enough to engage the
nāga kings in battle, so he soars through the air to fight them on their
home ground of Mount Sumeru, the *axis mundi*. Mu-lien transforms
himself into a fourteen-headed nāga, he shrinks himself to an infinitesimal size, he changes a hailstorm of stones and knives into a canopy of
flowers and jewels, using his supernormal strength to persuade the der-
elict nāga kings to assume their proper place within the world order. In
the end, Mu-lien succeeds in convincing the nāga kings to relinquish
their position of power at the center of the world and to conform to the
harmonious Way of the Buddha.

[2] See Etienne Lamotte, *Histoire du bouddhisme indien, des origines à l'ère Śaka*, Publications de l'Institut Orientaliste de Louvain, No. 14 (1958; reprint ed., Louvain-la-Neuve:
Institut Orientaliste, 1976), pp. 167–71.

[3] De Visser cites Hardy's *Manual of Buddhism* (p. 44): "The Nāgas reside in the loka
(world) under the Trikuta rocks that support Meru, and in the waters of the world of
men"; Marinus Willem de Visser, *The Dragon in China and Japan* (1913; reprint ed., New
York: Philosophical Library, 1972), p. 2.

114

With the nāga kings vanquished, the *Āgama* narrative resumes its major theme: the ascension of the Buddha to the Heaven of Thirty-Three to preach to his mother.[4] Buddhist literature abounds with admonitions to "repay the kindness" (*pao-en*) that parents show to children through birth and nurturing, and in this story the Buddha himself carries out the teaching.[5] He goes to the Heaven of Thirty-Three and preaches the Dharma, bringing enlightenment to his mother and to all of the gods who reside there. Both the *Āgama* tale and the yü-lan-p'en myth give special attention to the mothers of monks. In the former, the mother of the Buddha is placed in one of the heavens, while in the latter, Mu-lien's mother awaits salvation from the torments of hell.

In both *Āgama* and yü-lan-p'en myths, Mu-lien performs a very particular function. He is a savior but not a Buddha; he plays the role of a bodhisattva in the Mahāyāna tradition without ever being called one. In the Āgama tale, Mu-lien converts errant nāga kings to the Buddhist Way. In the yü-lan-p'en myth, he defeats the armies of hell and brings aid to his mother. Yet unlike the fully Awakened One, Mu-lien's salvific power is not complete: the nāga kings are constantly in need of rehabilitation, and Mu-lien's powers alone are insufficient to free his mother from her sufferings in hell. The power of the Buddha or the Dharma or the Sangha is needed for true salvation. But while the Buddha's power is absolute in both myths, he also remains a more distant figure than does Mu-lien, who is fallible and hence more accessible.

Even in this abbreviated examination of the *Āgama* story of the Buddha preaching to his mother in the Heaven of Thirty-Three, the Mu-lien that emerges from the tale bears a strong resemblance to the Mu-lien presented in yü-lan-p'en mythology. In fact, early Chinese Buddhist mythology, comprising a rich corpus of materials translated into Chinese by the fourth or fifth century, provided many of the themes and symbols out of which the yü-lan-p'en myth was fashioned. Mu-lien's shamanic attributes will form the main topic of Chapter Five, and what Mu-lien sees on his spirit journey—the cosmos he maps out for his audience—will be explored in Chapter Six. The discussion in this chapter will be confined to only three topics as they are pre-

[4] The Heaven of Thirty-Three (Skt.: Trāyastriṃśa, Ch.: *san-shih-san t'ien* or *tao-li t'ien*) is located atop Mount Sumeru, still within the world of desire. Beings born there lead pleasurable lives but remain in need of salvation. Indra presides over this heaven from a central court. At each of the four corners are situated eight cities of gods, hence the name, "Heaven of Thirty-Three [palaces or gods]."

[5] Tsung-mi cites numerous canonical and apocryphal sources in which the Buddha preaches the necessity of "repaying the kindness," *Tsung-mi Commentary*, T. no. 1792, 39:508a–c.

sented in Chinese Buddhist mythology prior to the development of the ghost festival: Mu-lien's biography, hungry ghosts, and mothers.

MU-LIEN'S BIOGRAPHY

Mu-lien in Yü-lan-p'en Literature

Mu-lien is such an important figure in Buddhist mythology that a complete survey of the medieval Chinese understanding of his life as a disciple of the Buddha would require a book-length study.[6] By contrast, yü-lan-p'en literature tells us little about Mu-lien's career as a disciple of the Buddha. The main interest of yü-lan-p'en literature lies elsewhere: in Mu-lien's journey to the hells to save his mother and, to a lesser extent, in the events of his previous life.

The two earliest yü-lan-p'en sūtras, *The Sūtra on Offering Bowls to Repay Kindness* and *The Yü-lan-p'en Sūtra*, offer no information concerning Mu-lien aside from his vision of his mother as a hungry ghost, his discussions with the Buddha, and his performance of the first yü-lan-p'en ceremony.[7]

The Pure Land Yü-lan-p'en Sūtra contains a long section on Mu-lien's past life. The sūtra, in fact, is explicitly styled an "*avadāna*," the term used to designate a legend concerning the past lives of its subject.[8] The

---

[6] Akanuma, for instance, gives references to 92 episodes in the life of Mahāmoggallāna (Skt.: Mahā-Maudgalyāyana) in Pāli, Sanskrit, and Chinese sources; Akanuma Chizen, *Indo bukkyō koyū meishi jiten* (1931; reprint ed., Kyoto: Hōzōkan, 1967), pp. 375a–80b. Until a separate study on Mu-lien is undertaken, Migot's excellent study of Śāriputra remains quite helpful; see André Migot, "Un Grand Disciple du Buddha, Śāriputra: son rôle dans l'histoire du bouddhisme et dans le développement de *l'Abhidharma*," BEFEO 46:2 (1954):405–554, esp. 503–18.

[7] *The Sūtra on Offering Bowls to Repay Kindness*, T. no. 686, 16:780a; *The Yü-lan-p'en Sūtra*, T. no. 685, 16:779a–c.

[8] The text styles itself a *yin-yüan*, which, philologically speaking, should be translated *nidāna*. But Chinese usage in this case is rather loose, so I have followed Léon Feer and others in using "avadāna" to refer to a genre of Buddhist literature, whether the corresponding Chinese term is *yin-yüan, p'i-yü,* or *pen-sheng*. Feer defines avadāna as "a teaching intended to make clear the tie which links events of the present life to acts performed in previous existences, the present being considered as a product of the past. Thus all Avadānas are basically composed of two stories: the story of a real event—the story of a past event which determined it. This second story, the telling of which requires complete knowledge of other times, cannot be told by just anyone. It is only the omniscient Buddha who can call up such recollections; and as the Buddha is basically a healer, the explanation that he gives is necessarily followed by a warning, a precept, a practical teaching"; Léon Feer, trans., *L'Avadāna-Cataka: cent légendes bouddhiques*, Annales du Musée Guimet, No. 18 (Paris: Ernest Leroux, 1891), p. xi. On this genre see also Maurice Winternitz, *Geschichte der indischen Litteratur*, 2 vols. (Leipzig: C. F. Amelangs Verlag, 1912–20),

sūtra begins with a description of the audience and then says, "Having gathered the entire great assembly, [the Buddha] revealed to them the causes and conditions of Mu-lien's previous lives."[9] The sūtra then recounts the founding of the yü-lan-p'en ceremony, after which the Buddha's disciples request him to relate the story of Mu-lien's and his mother's past lives:

> At this time Ānanda and five hundred arhats rose from their seats and addressed the Buddha. They asked, "World-Honored One, what karmic acts did the mother of *bhikṣu* Mu-lien perform during her lifetime, what sin did she commit to be reborn as a hungry ghost and suffer punishment for three *kalpas?* On account of what causes and conditions was Mu-lien reborn in her house, and with this karmic result, how has he become a sage? We entreat the World-Honored One to explain the causes and conditions of Mu-lien's mother, so that the entire great assembly might hear it together."
>
> Then the World-Honored One told Ānanda and the five hundred householders: "The karmic retribution of the actions of all living beings is inconceivable. You should listen well!
>
> "Long ago, at a time five hundred *kalpas* ago, a Buddha named Lamplighter [Dīpaṃkara][10] appeared in the world, living in the country of Rādha.[11] At this time Mu-lien was born in the home of a brahmin, and his name was Lo-pu [Turnip].[12] His mother's name was Ch'ing-t'i.[13] When he was young, the son, Lo-pu, loved charity; the mother was very stingy and did not like charity. When the son, Lo-pu, was setting out on a long trip, he enjoined his mother, 'In the morning a number of guests will come looking for

2:215–29; J. S. Speyer, ed., *Avadānaçataka: A Century of Edifying Tales Belonging to the Hīnayāna*, (1909; reprint ed., The Hague: Mouton and Co., 1958), pp. i–xiv; and John Strong, *The Legend of King Aśoka: A Study and Translation of the "Aśokāvadāna"* (Princeton: Princeton University Press, 1983), pp. 22, 32–36.

[9] *The Pure Land Yü-lan-p'en Sūtra*, ll. 3–4.

[10] When Dīpaṃkara Buddha was in the world, a previous incarnation of Śākyamuni made offerings to him and received the prophecy that he would later attain Buddhahood.

[11] My reconstruction of Rādha is uncertain. The Chinese, Lo-t'o, may well be a mistaken rendering of Rājagṛha, which is usually transcribed phonetically as Lo-yüeh.

[12] Victor H. Mair suggests that the Chinese understanding of Mu-lien's name as "Turnip" is based on a mistranslation from the Sanskrit for "mung bean"; Victor H. Mair, trans. *Tun-huang Popular Narratives* (Cambridge: Cambridge University Press, 1983), pp. 224–25, second n. to l. 17.

[13] Mair reconstructs Nīladhi as the Sanskrit original of Ch'ing-t'i; *Tun-huang Popular Narratives*, p. 232, n. to l. 152.

me. Mother,[14] would you set out a meal for the guests, and, with respect and obedience,[15] see to it that each one is happy?' After her son left, many guests arrived, but the mother never had any intention to set out a meal. Instead she deceptively scattered rice, vegetables, and seasonings, strewing them all over the ground as if there had been a meal.

"When the son came back he asked his mother, 'This morning when the guests came, how did you treat them?'

"The mother answered, 'Don't you see how the [scraps from the] meal I served them are strewn all over the ground like this?' The mother spoke lies and falsehoods to deceive her son. She was stingy and lacked human feeling.

"The mother has been Mu-lien's mother for five hundred reincarnations, her avarice continuing to the present day. Mu-lien has been her son for five hundred reincarnations. . . . If I wanted to recount all of the examples of her avarice, a *kalpa* would not suffice for the telling of it. I have simply summarized one example of her stinginess to demonstrate to the great assembly the inconceivability of karmic retribution in the Three Times."[16]

Mu-lien's biography is given as an appendage to his mother's in *The Pure Land Yü-lan-p'en Sūtra*. The dramatic and didactic focus of the story is his mother's avarice and its ineluctable result: her continued rebirth as Mu-lien's mother who, in her last life, commits evil deeds that result in her rebirth as a hungry ghost. The only details about Mu-lien to be gained from the story are those concerning time, place, name, and piety: five hundred *kalpas* ago he was born into the household of a rich brahmin in Rādha, he was named "Turnip," and he was especially religious, practicing charity (*pu-shih*, Skt.: *dāna*) for the benefit of unspecified monks.

Hui-ching, who wrote his commentary on *The Yü-lan-p'en Sūtra* around the time of the composition of *The Pure Land Yü-lan-p'en Sūtra*, makes no mention of Mu-lien's previous life. He writes:

Mu-lien is his surname. His personal name is Kolita, which he was given because [before his birth, his parents] sacrificed to the spirit

[14] A-p'o, T'ang colloquial, might better be rendered informally as "Mom." This usage occurs frequently in *pien-wen*; see Iriya Yoshitaka, *"Tonkō henbun shū" kōgo goi sakuin* (Kyoto, 1961 [mimeographed]), p. 27b.

[15] Reading *kung-shun* rather than *kung-hsü*.

[16] The Three Times are past, present, and future. Translation from *The Pure Land Yü-lan-p'en Sūtra*, ll. 79–102; cf. *Tsung-mi Commentary*, T. 39:509c–10a.

of a Kolita tree.[17] Since people of that country honor the surname, he was called by his surname; hence "Mu-lien."[18]

Tsung-mi, writing in the early ninth century, includes in his commentary both types of biographical information discussed thus far: a linguistic and rather scholastic discussion of Mu-lien's Sanskrit and Chinese names, as well as the tale contained in *The Pure Land Yü-lan-p'en Sūtra* narrating the deeds of mother and son five hundred lifetimes ago. In his section on Mu-lien's name, Tsung-mi adds that an immortal who was an ancestor of Mu-lien often ate a kind of legume, and that the name of this legume, the *lu-tou*, is the meaning of Mu-lien's Sanskrit name, (Mahā-)Maudgalyāyana. He also provides Mu-lien with a paternity: he is the son of Fu Hsiang of the city of Rājagṛha.[19]

Tsumg-mi paraphrases the avadāna tale from *The Pure Land Yü-lan-p'en Sūtra*, prefacing the story with the words, "A sūtra says. . . ."[20] The fact that this is the only place in his commentary that Tsung-mi refers to *The Pure Land Yü-lan-p'en Sūtra*—and not even by name—suggests that this particular episode from Mu-lien's and his mother's lives was quite popular in Tsung-mi's time. In his retelling of the story, Tsung-mi makes no changes in plot or detail and occasionally interrupts the narrative to discuss the finer points of karma and rebirth. He asks, for instance:

> *Question*: From the time of Lamplighter Buddha until now [five hundred lifetimes], Mu-lien was not born from just one mother. Why was he partial in saving just Ch'ing-t'i [from the torments of hell]?
> *Answer*: There were deep karmic bonds between Ch'ing-t'i and Mu-lien. In this life she had been reborn again as his mother. He saved the mother who gave birth to him in this life; it is not the case that he saved that other Ch'ing-t'i from many lifetimes ago.[21]

The Transformation Text on Mu-lien Saving His Mother narrates a version of the story of Mu-lien's and his mother's previous lives more abbreviated than that of *The Pure Land Yü-lan-p'en Sūtra*. In this *pien-wen* version the story concerns Mu-lien's actions in *this* life, not in a previous one. As a young boy, Turnip believes in the Three Jewels. Before

[17] Following Tsung-mi, *Tsung-mi Commentary*, T. 39:507c.

[18] Translation from *Tsung-mi Commentary*, T. 85:541b.

[19] *Tsung-mi Commentary*, T. 39:507c. Mair reconstructs the Sanskrit for Fu Hsiang as Śūlakṣaṇa; *Tun-huang Popular Narratives*, p. 232, n. to l. 153.

[20] *Tsung-mi Commentary*, T. 39:509c; following the wording in the *Yüan-chao Commentary*, "*yu ching shuo*"; Z. 1, 35:2, p. 119vb.

[21] Translation from *Tsung-mi Commentary*, T. 39:509c–10a.

going abroad on business, he entrusts some money to his mother and asks her to use it to provide a vegetarian feast for the Buddha, Dharma, Sangha, and anyone who might come begging. Ch'ing-t'i hides the money and falsely claims to have held feasts while her son was away. As a result, when she dies she falls into Avīci Hell. After he completes the mourning obligations for her, Mu-lien enters the Sangha, quickly attains arhatship, and then embarks on a search for his deceased parents.[22]

In the *pien-wen* the episode of Mu-lien as a youth occurs at the beginning of the narrative, not in the middle as it does in the less theatrical Pure Land sūtra. The episode, ending with Ch'ing-t'i's falling into Avīci Hell (the hell of "No-Interval"), sets the stage for the action that follows. By placing her fall into Avīci Hell at the beginning of the story, *The Transformation Text on Mu-lien Saving His Mother* immediately arouses the interest of the audience. Mu-lien's goal—to save his mother from hell—is clearly established from the very start. The audience also knows just how evil his mother is and how terribly she suffers for her sins. With her hopes for salvation so bleak, an element of tension pervades the entire story as Mu-lien travels to the hells, battles armies of demons, and enlists the aid of the Buddha on the way to liberating his mother from torments. In this version of the yü-lan-p'en myth, the biographical details—Mu-lien's piety, his mother's avarice, and her rebirth in hell—are included for dramatic as well as thematic purposes.

Mu-lien in Other Genres of Literature

Chinese literature preserves many accounts of Mu-lien's previous lives that diverge from the accounts in yü-lan-p'en literature noted above. Collections of fables translated in the late third century by K'ang Seng-hui (d. 280) describe Mu-lien's previous incarnations as a king, a cygnet, an otter, a serpent, a minister of state, and an ascetic.[23]

A similar dichotomy characterizes biographies of Mu-lien in his rebirth as the boy Turnip: while yü-lan-p'en literature shows little interest in Mu-lien's previous career, Chinese Buddhist literature as a whole abounds with accounts of his monastic life. In particular, Mu-lien's

[22] THPWC, p. 714; Mair, trans., *Tun-huang Popular Narratives*, pp. 87–88.

[23] See the selections translated in Edouard Chavannes, trans., *Cinq Cents Contes et apologues: extraits du Tripitaka chinois*, 4 vols. (Paris: Libraire Ernest Leroux, 1910–11, 1934), 1:49, 72, 77, 93, 227, 304, 2:412. These selections are from two works translated by K'ang Seng-hui, *Liu-tu chi ching*, T. no. 152, and *Chiu tsa p'i-yü ching*, T. no. 206; cf. *Fa-yüan chu-lin*, T. 53:607a–b.

long-standing friendship with Śāriputra and the two friends' entry into the Buddhist order are discussed in numerous works.[24] In this section I shall survey some of these accounts. My survey is based primarily on the *Shih-chia p'u (The Genealogy of the Śākyas)* by Seng-yu (445–518), and Tao-shih's seventh-century *Fa-yüan chu-lin (Pearl Grove of the Dharma Garden)*. These two works occupy an important place in Chinese Buddhist historiography, their author-compilers having culled a large body of preexistent literature before writing works that conform to Chinese models.[25] Their versions of the story of Śāriputra and Mu-lien may thus be taken as accurate reflections of medieval Chinese perceptions of the two disciples.

Most accounts agree that Śāriputra and Mu-lien were close friends before they entered the Buddhist Sangha.[26] Upatisya (Śāriputra) was the youngest son of a rich brahmin of Nālandagrāmaka, and Kolita (Mu-lien) was the son of a rich brahmin of Kolitagrāmaka. They were inseparable friends and decided together to give up the householder's life and become disciples of a Vedic teacher. After spending some time under their teacher, Sañjaya,[27] they decide to pursue separately their search for the Way. Before splitting up they vow that, whichever one first hears the true Dharma, he will share his discovery with the other.

In all sources it is Śāriputra who first discovers the true Way to liberation.[28] By chance Śāriputra encounters a monk on his begging rounds. Śāriputra is so impressed by the monk's dignity and composure while begging that he pursues him to inquire about the Way he follows. The monk, named Aśvajit, is a disciple of the Buddha. He re-

---

[24] See Etienne Lamotte, trans., *Le Traité de la grand vertu de sagesse de Nāgārjuna (Mahā-prajñāpāramitāśāstra)*, 5 vols. (Louvain-la-Neuve: Institut Orientaliste, 1949–80), pp. 623–27, n. 2.

[25] On Seng-yu see Arthur E. Link, "Shih Seng-yu and His Writings," JAOS 80:1 (January–March 1960):17–43. On Tao-shih see Stephen F. Teiser, "T'ang Buddhist Encyclopedias: An Introduction to *Fa-yüan chu-lin* and *Chu-ching yao-chi*," *T'ang Studies* No. 3 (1975):109–28.

[26] Details in this paragraph are drawn from *Fa-yüan chu-lin*, T. 53:683a–b, which cites *Fo pen-hsing ching*, T. no. 193, 4:81a–c; and from *Ta chih-tu lun (Mahāprajñāpāramitāśāstra)*, T. no. 1509, 25:136b–c; cf. Lamotte, trans., *Traité*, pp. 623–33. Compare the account in *The Mahāvastu*, trans. J. J. Jones, 3 vols. (London: Luzac and Co., 1949–56), 3:56–61.

[27] Lamotte, trans., *Traité*, pp. 623–27, n. 2, notes that sources preserve two traditions on their teacher, Sañjaya. In one Sañjaya is inimical to the Buddha (as in *The Mahāvastu* account). In the other he is a precursor of the Buddha who, before dying, predicts the Buddha's birth (as in *Fa-yüan chu-lin*).

[28] In this paragraph I follow *Shih-chia p'u*, T. 50:47c–48a; see also *Ta chih-tu lun*, T. 25:136b–c (cf. Lamotte, trans., *Traité*, pp. 630–33); *Ssu-fen lü (Dharmaguptavinaya)*, T. no. 1428, 22:798b–99a; *Fo pen-hsing ching*, T. 4:81a; and *Fa-yüan chu-lin*, T. 53:683b.

sponds to Śāriputra with a very brief stanza encapsulating the Buddhist teaching on causality. Upon hearing these few words, Śāriputra has an enlightenment experience and attains insight into the nature of things. When Śāriputra returns, Mu-lien immediately notices a difference in his old friend. In *The Genealogy of the Śākyas*, Mu-lien questions Śāriputra closely:

"I've been observing you. Your sense and your countenance are different than usual. You must have already gained the sweet dew of a wondrous Dharma. Long ago we swore to each other that if one of us heard a wondrous Dharma, then he would enlighten the other—you have something you want to tell me?"

Śāriputra responded, "I have indeed gained a sweet-dew Dharma."

Mu-lien heard this and was happy beyond measure. "Wonderful," he cried. "Now you must tell me."

Śāriputra said, "When I was out just now I ran into a *bhikṣu*. He was wearing a robe and carrying a bowl and had entered town to beg for food. His senses were quiescent and his mighty deportment was perfectly restrained. Upon seeing him I respected him immensely, so I approached him and asked, 'I would have guessed that you only recently left the householder's life, yet you are able to restrain your senses so well. I would love to hear your response to some questions I want to ask. What is the name of your great master? What Dharma does he teach and propound?'

"Aśvajit composed himself and responded, 'My great master has gained every kind of knowledge. He is of the Sugar Cane clan,[29] a teacher of gods and men. He loves equally wisdom and the power of spiritual penetrations.[30] He has no equal.'

"Aśvajit continued, 'Since I am young and have practiced the Way for only a little while, how could I set forth the wondrous Dharma of the Thus-Come One? But I shall tell you what I know.' Then he spoke these lines:
'All dharmas basically
Are produced from causes and conditions and have no essence.
Whoever understands this
Will gain the true, full Way.' "

[29] "Sugar Cane clan" (*kan-che chung*) is another epithet for the clan of Gautama, the Sugar Cane Prince having been one of Śākyamuni's ancestors; see CWTTT, 22138.183 and MBDJ, pp. 691a, 2417b.
[30] After becoming disciples of the Buddha, Śāriputra will excel at wisdom and Mu-lien at spiritual penetrations.

Upon hearing Śāriputra speak these words, Mu-lien distanced himself from dust and left behind defilements, and in regard to all dharmas gained the purity of the Dharma eye.[31]

After this experience with one of the Buddha's disciples, Śāriputra and Mu-lien want to learn from the Buddha himself. Joined by their own group of two hundred disciples, they set out to join the Buddha's Sangha. Before they arrive, the Buddha sees them coming and prophesies their specialties:

At this time the World-Honored One saw Śāriputra and Mu-lien coming, leading all of their disciples one after the other. He said to the *bhikṣus* [in his audience], "You should all know that these two people leading their disciples have come to us seeking to leave the householder's life. The first is named Śāriputra, the second is named Mu-lien. In my Dharma they will be superlative disciples. Śāriputra will be first in wisdom, and Mu-lien will be unsurpassed in spiritual penetrations."[32]

Śāriputra and Mu-lien, together with their disciples, take the tonsure and don monk's robes. Upon hearing the Buddha preach the Four Noble Truths, Śāriputra and Mu-lien immediately attain arhatship.[33]

Different Mu-liens, Different Genres

The story of Śāriputra's and Mu-lien's entry into the Buddhist order was recorded in numerous versions in a wide range of sources in medieval China. It is, therefore, somewhat surprising that yü-lan-p'en literature contains only one reference to it, and a very tangential one at that. In his commentary on *The Yü-lan-p'en Sūtra*, Hui-ching glosses one particular passage by alluding not to Mu-lien, but simply to the episode of Śāriputra encountering Aśvajit.[34]

[31] Translation from T. 50:47c–48a.

[32] Translation from *Shih-chia p'u*, T. 50:48a–b. Cf. *Ta chih-tu lun*, T. 25:136c; Lamotte, trans., *Traité*, pp. 632–33.

[33] *Shih-chia p'u*, T. 50:48b.

[34] Hui-ching explains the phrase "his virtue is vast" (*ch'i te wang-yang*) with the gloss, "the wonderful appearance of a mighty deportment" (*sheng-mao chih wei-i*). He explains the gloss, in turn, by referring to the story of Śāriputra encountering Aśvajit: Aśvajit's deportment was so impressive that Śāriputra was led to attain arhatship. Hui-ching does not even mention Mu-lien here. He simply cites the episode of Śāriputra encountering Aśvajit to explain a passage in *The Yü-lan-p'en Sūtra* ("his virtue is vast") describing a hypothetical monk who receives yü-lan-p'en offerings. See *Hui-ching Commentary*, T. 85:542c–43b. In contrast to the language of *The Yü-lan-p'en Sūtra* and to Hui-ching's gloss, popular literature often uses the expression "*wei-i hsiang-hsü*" to describe a monk's

The disinterest—or blindness—shown by yü-lan-p'en literature toward this episode in Mu-lien's life may be explained in several ways. The various audiences of the yü-lan-p'en myth, especially the monkish ones, may well have known the story of Mu-lien's entry into the Sangha and may simply have deemed it unnecessary to repeat in their commentaries on *The Yü-lan-p'en Sūtra*. Mu-lien, in fact, does not come off well in the story: it is Śāriputra who has the encounter with Aśvajit, and Mu-lien's awakening occurs merely secondhand. Further, the teaching on causation that gives rise to the two friends' enlightenment, while not unimportant in Chinese Buddhist philosophy, was not as exciting or as hotly debated as such subjects as the immortality of the spirit, the practice of Buddhism, the nature of Buddha nature, or the division of the teachings.

Reasons for the absence of the story in the more popular versions of the yü-lan-p'en myth are probably of a different sort. The disciplined Mu-lien of the sources cited above looks nothing like the irrepressible Mu-lien of *The Pure Land Yü-lan-p'en Sūtra* or *The Transformation Text on Mu-lien Saving His Mother*. In his quest for the Way, the *disciple* Mu-lien finishes second, behind his friend, Śāriputra.[35] By contrast, the *shaman* Mu-lien knows no bounds; he travels to heaven and flings open the gates of hell. Mu-lien's lineage, the record of his study under different teachers and of his acceptance into the Buddhist order, was probably of little interest to people who came to watch storytellers illustrate Mu-lien's transformations. They were interested not in his legitimacy but in his powers. This may well explain why we do not find the story of Mu-lien's discipleship in the more dramatic forms of yü-lan-p'en literature and find only passing reference to it in the canonical yü-lan-p'en sources.

HUNGRY GHOSTS

Chinese Buddhist mythology abounds with stories of Mu-lien encountering those unfortunate beings reborn as hungry ghosts (*o-kuei*, Skt.:

---

stern composure; see Chiang Li-hung, *Tun-huang pien-wen tzu-i t'ung-shih*, revised ed. (Taipei: Ku-t'ing shu-ya, 1975), pp. 33–34.

[35] Migot suggests that in the Buddhist tradition, Śāriputra was associated with knowledge while Mu-lien was associated with power. Although both are deemed necessary for salvation, knowledge, especially in a monastic context, is rated first. Migot, "Un Grand Disciple du Buddha," p. 517, writes: "For certain people, *samādhi* [concentration], as a means of obtaining magical powers, is a goal which *in itself* is more important than the *Abhidharma* [scholarship] as a means of obtaining *prajñā* [wisdom]; some place knowledge in the foreground, others place powers in the foreground. Those who pursue powers address their devotions to Maudgalyāyana, those who pursue knowledge to Śāriputra."

preta). Sometimes residing in one or another chamber in hell, sometimes haunting mountains, valleys, or even cities, they wander about forever in search of food and drink. De Groot describes them well:

> Pretas are horrid monsters, disgusting objects, frightful wretches. They have long bristly hairs, arms and legs like skeletons. Their voluminous bellies can never be filled, because their mouths [or throats] are as narrow as a needle's eye. Hence they are always tormented by furious hunger. Their colour, blue, black, or yellow, is rendered more hideous still by filth and dirt. They are also eternally vexed by unquenchable thirst. No more but once in a hundred thousand years do they hear the word water, but when at last, they find it, it immediately becomes urine and mud. Some devour fire and tear the flesh from dead bodies or from their own limbs; but they are unable to swallow the slightest bit of it because of the narrowness of their mouths.[36]

His spiritual powers permit Mu-lien, more readily than other people, to see these creatures. A cycle of stories from the *Chuan-chi po-yüan ching (Sūtra of One Hundred Selected Legends, Avadānaśataka)*,[37] translated from Sanskrit into Chinese in the early third century by Chih Ch'ien (ca. 220–252), describes Mu-lien's experiences with *pretas*. In these encounters discussion invariably turns to the subject of the ghosts' evil actions in previous lives, as a result of which they now suffer the agonies of ghosthood.

In one of these avadāna tales, "The Legend of Pūrṇeccha Falling Down to Be Reborn As a Hungry Ghost," Mu-lien sees a hungry ghost with his body aflame, his stomach as large as a mountain, his throat as thin as a needle, and his hairs like sharp knives that prick his body. The ghost is running about seeking excrement for food, but is unable to obtain any. Mu-lien asks the reason why he suffers so, but the ghost is so hungry he cannot respond to Mu-lien's question. Mu-lien then relates what he has seen to the Buddha and asks, "What evil karma did he create that he now suffers such distress?" The Buddha explains that there was once a rich man of Rājagṛha who had made his fortune selling sugar-cane juice. A wandering monk came to his house, seeking some of the juice to cure an illness. The rich man had to depart because of a previous engagement, but before leaving he instructed his wife, Pūr-

[36] Jan J.M. de Groot, "Buddhist Masses for the Dead at Amoy," *Actes du sixième congrès international des orientalistes*, Part 4, Section 4 (Leiden: E. J. Brill, 1885), pp. 20–21.

[37] T. no. 200. For a comparison of the Chinese and Sanskrit versions, see Iwamoto Yutaka, *Bukkyō setsuwa kenkyū*, Vol. 1, *Bukkyō setsuwa kenkyū jōsetsu* (Tokyo: Hōzōkan, 1962), pp. 113–34. For a translation from the Sanskrit version, see Feer, trans., *Avadāna-Cataka*.

ṇeccha, to offer the monk the medicinal drink in his absence. After her husband left, however, Pūrṇeccha urinated secretly in the monk's bowl, added sugar-cane juice to it, and presented it to the monk. Knowing that she had defiled his bowl, he dumped out the drink and departed. After her death, Pūrṇeccha was reborn as the same hungry ghost whom Mu-lien had just encountered.[38]

A second legend, "The Legend of the Wife of the Elder, Worthy-and-Good, Falling Down to Be Reborn As a Hungry Ghost," sounds a similar theme. From his meditating position under a tree, Mu-lien sees a hungry ghost. The story describes the ghost in standard terms. When Mu-lien inquires why this fate has befallen him, the ghost directs the disciple to go ask the Buddha. The World-Honored One explains that long ago in a very prosperous country there lived a pious elder named "Worthy-and-Good" who loved practicing charity. The elder was on the point of leaving his house when a monk came begging, so he instructed his wife to give the monk some food. After Worthy-and-Good left, his wife was overcome by greed. Begrudging the monk his almsmanship, she decided to teach him a lesson. So she called him into her courtyard and, rather than giving him an offering, she had him locked up in an empty room without food for the whole day. As a result she was reborn as a hungry ghost for innumerable lifetimes, down to the time of her encounter with Mu-lien.[39]

Other legends from this avadāna collection follow the same pattern: Mu-lien, often in meditation, encounters a hungry ghost who, in a previous lifetime, was a greedy woman who refused to give donations to monks or who desecrated a food offering.[40]

Other sources, with titles like *Kuei wen mu-lien ching (The Sūtra on Ghosts Questioning Mu-lien)*, also picture Mu-lien in conversation with hungry ghosts.[41] In one legend Mu-lien meets five hundred hungry ghosts on the banks of the Ganges River. They all pay obeisance to him and ask him about the sins they had committed in previous lives. The ghosts step forward one-by-one to learn the karmic acts of past lives that have led to their current state of suffering. One was a diviner

[38] Story paraphrased from *Chuan-chi po-yüan ching*, T. 4:222b–23a. Cf. Feer, trans., *Avadāna-Cataka*, pp. 162–66, where the offender is not the rich man's wife but one of his male servants. The same theme is struck in the fourth legend in this decalogue, T. 4:223c–24a; cf. Feer, trans., *Avadāna-Cataka*, pp. 171–74.

[39] Paraphrased from T. 4:223a–b. Cf. Feer, trans., *Avadāna-Cataka*, pp. 166–68.

[40] E.g., the next two legends, T. 4:223b–c, 223c–24a.

[41] *Kuei wen mu-lien ching*, attributed to An Shih-kao (ca. 148–170), T. no. 734. See also the very similar *O-kuei pao-ying ching*, anonymous (ca. 317–420), T. no. 746; stories cited in *Ching-lü i-hsiang*, Pao-ch'ang (ca. 520), T. no. 2121, 53:73a–76a, 240b–44a; and Ch'en, *Mu-lien chiu-mu ku-shih chih yen-chin*, pp. 7–22.

(*hsiang-shih*) in a previous life who constantly misled people for his own gain so that now, whenever he takes a sip of water, his insides turn to fire; one was in charge of animal sacrifices in a previous life and is now attacked daily by dogs who eat all of the meat off his bones, only to have the flesh grow back when the wind blows; and so on.[42]

Early Chinese mythology not only recounts Mu-lien's special powers to see hungry ghosts and to know their past lives, but also includes a precedent for Mu-lien's major activity in the yü-lan-p'en myth: providing a communal feast to save departed souls from the torments of life as *pretas*. I translate below "The Legend of Mu-lien Entering the City and Seeing Five Hundred Hungry Ghosts" from the early third-century collection of one hundred avadāna tales:

> The Buddha was at Venuvana-kalandakanivāpa[43] in Rājagṛha. The time for begging having arrived, Mu-lien donned his robes, picked up his bowl, and entered the city to beg for food. At the city gates there happened to be five hundred hungry ghosts also entering. When they saw Mu-lien, their hearts were gladdened. They said to him, "We entreat you, Honored One, to be kind and to take pity on us. We will tell you our surnames and personal names, and you inform our relatives at our old homes. Tell them that we have received bodily form and fallen to the state of hungry ghost because we did not cultivate goodness and did not practice charity. We entreat you, Honored One, to collect riches and goods from our relatives and to set out a feast of delicacies for the Buddha and the Sangha. If the goods are insufficient, please instruct the *dānapati* [donors] communally to set out a feast on our behalf. This will bring us all deliverance from the state of hungry ghost."
>
> Mu-lien thought for a moment and then consented. He went on to ask them, "What karmic acts did you perform in a previous life to receive this unfortunate retribution?"
>
> All of the hungry ghosts answered Mu-lien with a single voice: "In a previous life we were all sons of elders in Rājagṛha. We were arrogant and indolent, hated charity, and craved worldly pleasures. We did not believe in the Three Jewels, the Teaching of the Highest Way. When we saw monks enter the city to beg for food, we ourselves gave nothing, and we restrained others from giving, [saying]: 'These holy men don't provide for themselves, they just sponge off of the people. If you give them something now, they'll

---

[42] The story occurs in Fa-hsien's (ca. 399–416) *Tsa-tsang ching*, T. no. 745, 17:557b–58c. It is also cited in *Ching-lü i-hsiang*, T. 53:243a–44a.

[43] This was the monastery complex donated by King Bimbisāra.

just come back again for more, and you'll end up wanting.' As a result of this karmic conditioning, after our death we fell into the state of hungry ghost, suffering this unfortunate retribution."

Mu-lien said to the hungry ghosts, "I will go now on your behalf and tell your relatives to make it a joint enterprise, to establish the observance of a communal feast. Then you can all come to the gathering."

The hungry ghosts said to the Honored One with a single voice, "Our current state is the fruition of past sins. Although we have received corporeal form, our bodies are like charred pillars, our stomachs like huge mountains, our throats like tiny needles. Our hairs are like sharp knives that slice into our bodies; the spaces between our joints are all aflame. Wherever we run in search of food or drink, we end up getting none; where sweet delicacies are set out [as offerings] and we dash off in that direction, the food turns to blood and pus. How could we possibly come to the gathering in our present bodily form?" Then Mu-lien, on behalf of the hungry ghosts, related all of the preceding events to their relatives. They were all deeply troubled when they heard it, and, joining forces, they all wished to set up a communal feast.

Then Mu-lien entered into concentration and looked for where the hungry ghosts were. He thoroughly searched the sixteen kingdoms,[44] but still did not see them. Next he searched through Jambudvīpa and the four empires[45] and then through a thousand world systems and three thousand great-thousand world systems,[46] but did not see them. He wondered why this was so and sought out the Buddha. "World-Honored One," Mu-lien said, "on behalf of all hungry ghosts, I just now exhorted people to make merit by coming together with their relatives and sponsoring a large communal feast. I have searched throughout the cosmos, but cannot find any [of the hungry ghosts]. With incomplete understanding I ask you, World-Honored One, where the hungry ghosts are."

The Buddha told Mu-lien, "Those hungry ghosts are all blown about by the wind of karma. This is not something that you, as a voice-hearer [śrāvaka], could understand. But now those hungry ghosts will partake of the communal feast you have established,

---

[44] The sixteen kingdoms of India.

[45] The "four empires" are the four continents surrounding Mount Sumeru.

[46] Three thousand great-thousand world systems comprise 1000 small world systems, 1000 middling world systems (each comprising 1000 small world systems), and 1000 great world systems (each comprising 1000 middling world systems), OBDJ, p. 643b.

and the burden of their past sins will be wiped out. I myself will dispatch them to the communal gathering."

On behalf of the hungry ghosts, Mu-lien set out all sorts of delicacies and invited the Buddha and the Sangha. The Buddha used his spiritual power to enable hungry ghosts to come to the communal feast. The *brahmins, kṣatriyas,* and lay people of Rājagṛha, having seen the foul and terribly fearful condition of the hungry ghosts, consequently gave up their greedy thoughts and developed an aversion to birth-and-death; their minds were opened and their thoughts liberated. Some attained the fruits of *srotāpanna* [stream-enterer], *sakṛdāgāmi* [once-comer], *anāgāmi* [non-returner], and *arhat.* Some produced the thought of *pratyekabuddhahood.* Some produced the thought of unsurpassed *bodhi.*

Then the World-Honored One, on behalf of the hungry ghosts, variously preached the Law and explained the sin of greed, giving rise to fervent belief and reverence. That night the lives [of the hungry ghosts] came to an end, and they were reborn in Trāyastrimśa Heaven [the Heaven of Thirty-Three].

Then they thought to themselves, "What meritorious karma did we make to attain rebirth in this Trāyastrimśa Heaven?" Upon consideration, they realized, "We have been reborn here because the Honored One, the Great Mu-lien, set up a communal gathering, inviting the Buddha and the Sangha on our behalf. We should go now and repay this kindness." After speaking these words they descended from heaven, adorning their bodies with heavenly caps and jeweled necklaces. They each brought incense and flowers to offer to the Buddha and to the Great Mu-lien. When they were done making offerings, they sat down facing the Buddha as he preached the Law. Their minds were opened and their thoughts liberated, and they each attained marks of the Way. They circumambulated the Buddha three times and returned to heaven.

The Buddha told Mu-lien, "Those five hundred hungry ghosts, if you would like to know, are the five hundred emperors."

Having heard what the Buddha said, the great assembly rejoiced and upheld it.[47]

This avadāna story supplies many of the motifs that appear later in yü-lan-p'en literature from the fifth through ninth centuries. The story begins with Mu-lien encountering hungry ghosts. Like the Mu-lien in the avadāna tales discussed above, this Mu-lien discusses with the

[47] Translation from *Chuan-chi po-yüan ching,* T. 4:224a–c. Cf. Feer, trans., *Avadāna-Cataka,* pp. 175–78.

ghosts their previous lives. Like Mu-lien's mother as she is presented in yü-lan-p'en literature, these ghosts were greedy in their previous lives, refusing to make donations to wandering monks. To alleviate their suffering Mu-lien establishes a communal feast. The feast is sponsored by the living relatives of the ghosts, who pool their resources and make donations to the Buddhas and the Sangha—just like the yü-lan-p'en feast.

Another motif found in both this story and in yü-lan-p'en literature is the intervention of the Buddha. Mu-lien first attempts to organize the feast all by himself: he directs the ghosts' descendants to set out offerings and to invite the Buddha and the Sangha, but the feast cannot be consummated because the hungry ghosts are unable to attend. Mu-lien, in fact, has lost track of them, and even after searching the cosmos he still cannot find them. Similarly, the yü-lan-p'en ritual at first remains unachieved: the food offering Mu-lien sends to his mother bursts into flame. In both cases Mu-lien's power alone is insufficient to alter the workings of karmic retribution. The five hundred ghosts as well as Mu-lien's mother must each suffer the consequences of their previous acts; they are prevented from enjoying the food sent by their relatives, and so they must wander about as hungry ghosts. The ritual succeeds only after the Buddha abrogates the laws of karma. In the avadāna story the Buddha uses special powers to bring the ghosts to the communal gathering, while in yü-lan-p'en myths he directs Mu-lien to rely upon the accumulated power of the Sangha. In both cases the rituals proceed without misfire only with the aid of the Buddha.

Finally, it should be noted that the five hundred ghosts in the story are reborn in the Heaven of Thirty-Three, which is where Mu-lien's mother is reborn in *The Transformation Text on Mu-lien Saving His Mother.*

MOTHERS AND MONKS

The foregoing survey of Chinese mythology has unearthed many of the motifs that recur later in yü-lan-p'en literature. Avadāna literature is a particularly rich storehouse of yü-lan-p'en themes: Mu-lien's frequent encounters with *pretas*, his knowledge of their sins in previous lives, his attempts to free them from suffering, and the role of the Buddha in completing this process. All that appears to be lacking is a precedent for Mu-lien saving not just any hungry ghost, but his *mother* as hungry ghost.

The kinship tie is, of course, a contingent matter. As some scholars are fond of reminding us, one man's ancestor is another man's ghost,[48] and, as the Buddhists would say, one man's hungry ghost may well have been his mother in a previous life. These relativities notwithstanding, prototypes of a son providing Mu-lien style for the salvation of his mother are indeed present in Chinese mythology. The *Āgama* story about Mu-lien and the nāga kings cited at the beginning of this chapter describes the paradigmatic filial son, the Buddha, ascending to the Heaven of Thirty-Three to liberate his mother from the cycle of birth-and-death by preaching the Dharma.

Another story comes from a much later source, the early eighth-century Chinese translation of the Vinaya rules of the Sarvāstivāda sect. The episode begins with Mu-lien reflecting on the kindness shown by parents to their children and on how difficult it is for children to make up for the hardships that parents endure in pregnancy, childbirth, and childrearing. One way to repay parents, Mu-lien knows, is to encourage them to follow Buddhist morality, thus ensuring a better rebirth or even a final release from the cycle of rebirth. With this in mind Mu-lien begins meditating to search for his deceased mother. Using his special powers of vision, Mu-lien sees his mother reborn in Marīci's heaven.[49] He wants to go there and preach the Dharma to her, but he knows that only the Buddha can do that. So he borrows the Buddha's cassock, and together the two of them use their supernatural powers to travel to Marīci's heaven. They arrive after seven days. The Buddha preaches to Mu-lien's mother and she attains the fruit of a stream-winner, thus beginning on the noble Way toward liberation from birth-and-death.[50]

A more striking precedent for Mu-lien saving his mother from ghosthood is to be found in an early avadāna tale. The similarity between the avadana tale and *The Transformation Text on Mu-lien Saving His Mother* extends to the last detail: in both, the final resting place of the mother (so far as the narrative goes) is the Heaven of Thirty-Three. One modern scholar, Lo Tsung-t'ao, even suggests that the Chinese

[48] See, for example, Arthur P. Wolf, "Gods, Ghosts, and Ancestors," in *Religion and Ritual in Chinese Society*, ed. Arthur P. Wolf (Stanford: Stanford University Press, 1974), pp. 131–82.

[49] Marīci (Ch.: Mo-li-chih) is the Indian god of fire, included by Buddhists in their pantheon of gods. According to tradition, Marīci travels in front of the sun, see MBDJ, pp. 4764c–65c. I am not sure where this heaven is located in the standard Buddhist cosmology. The authorship of three short sūtras on Marīci is attributed to Amoghavajra (705–774): T. nos. 1255a, 1255b, and 1258. For Marīci in later folk religion, see Henry Doré, S.J., *Researches into Chinese Superstitions*, 10 vols., trans. M. Kennelly, S.J. (1911–15; reprint ed., Shanghai: T'usewei Printing Press, 1914–33), 7:303–11.

[50] Summarized from *Ken-pen-shuo i-ch'ieh-yu-pu p'i-nai-yeh yao-shih*, trans. I-ching (635–713), T. no. 1448, 24:16a–b.

131

name of "Turnip," by which Mu-lien is popularly known, derives from an orthographic error in transcribing the meaning of the name of the protagonist-son, Uttara, in the avadāna tale.[51] The story, contained in Chih Ch'ien's third-century collection of tales, begins with an elder of Rājagṛha whose wealth was beyond measure. He took a wife and after ten (lunar) months of pregnancy she gave birth to a boy so fine and unequalled that his parents named him "Uttara" (Utterly-Good, or Superlative). After some time the boy's father died. Uttara was a pious Buddhist and had little interest in the acquisition of wealth or in the householder's life. One day the boy asked his mother's permission to become a monk. Since he was her only son she refused, insisting that only after her death could he follow his vow to become a monk. When Uttara threatened to swallow poison if he could not join the Sangha, his mother responded, "Don't say such things! Why do you want to leave the householder's life now? From now on, if you want to invite śramaṇas, brahmins, and others, I will follow your lead and give them offerings." Uttara was placated with this compromise, and for a while he frequently invited wandering ascetics, who came to the house in large numbers.

One day while Uttara was out, his mother became greedy. She scolded the monks who came to their house begging for food, and she scattered food and drink all over the ground. When Uttara returned, she showed him the scraps and claimed to have made offerings to many monks. When she died she was reborn as a hungry ghost.

The legend relates that after his mother's death, Uttara fulfills his wish to become a monk and soon attains the fruit of arhatship. One day, while sitting in meditation in a cave, a hungry ghost with a burning mouth appears before him. The ghost explains that in the last life she was his mother. She has been reborn in this terrible state, she explains, because of her greed and disrespect for monks in her previous incarnation. She describes her torments, which include always having luxuriant fruit trees wither as she runs toward them. Finally, she entreats Uttara to make offerings to the Buddha and the Sangha and to perform repentance rituals on her behalf.

Uttara prepares a feast as requested, inviting the Buddha and the Sangha. The hungry ghost appears at the gathering, and after hearing the Buddha preach the Dharma, she repents. That night she is reborn as a flying hungry ghost. Adorning herself, she returns to Uttara and asks for a more elaborate feast, one with finer offerings (such as mat-

[51] See Lo, *Tun-huang chiang-ching pien-wen yen-chiu*, p. 239.

tresses, not just food) and more recipients, which will free her from her ghostly body. The son complies, and that night she is reborn in the Heaven of Thirty-Three.[52]

This legend supplies many of the elements that were later made part of yü-lan-p'en literature. As in *The Pure Land Yü-lan-p'en Sūtra* and the transformation text, the greedy mother of a pious son feigns charity and is reborn as a hungry ghost as a result. Like all versions of the yü-lan-p'en myth, the avadāna tale shows the filial son sponsoring an ancestral feast in which offerings are made to monks, and the ritual succeeds in freeing the protagonist's mother from her torments. Furthermore, Uttara's mother is reborn in the Heaven of Thirty-Three, just like Mu-lien's mother in *The Transformation Text on Mu-lien Saving His Mother.*

Even the timing of the yü-lan-p'en festival—the fifteenth day of the seventh month, the day on which monks emerge from their summer retreat—has precedents in Chinese Buddhist mythology. Chapter Eleven of the *Kuan-ting ching* (*The Consecration Sūtra*), for instance, relates the story of a pious son named Na-she who conducts rituals for the salvation of his greedy parents, who have been reborn in hell. When the rituals fail to bring relief, the Buddha instructs Na-she to invite the Sangha to a feast at the end of their summer retreat and to present the monks with gifts of food, clothing, flowers, incense, gold, silver, and jewels. Na-she carries out the proto-yü-lan-p'en offering as directed, and his parents achieve rebirth in the heavens.[53]

Another story relating the origins of ancestral offerings on the seventh moon—although dedicated indiscriminately to both parents, not just the mother—brings the bodhisattva Kuan-yin into the picture. The story, contained in Wang Yen's (ca. 500) collection of ghost stories, *Ming-hsiang chi (Record of Good Fortune in the Dark Regions)*, describes the underworld experiences of the monk Hui-ta who, for several days after his death, journeyed through various hells before being resuscitated. In one chamber of hell he is taken before Kuan-yin, who preaches the benefits of making offerings on the full moon of the seventh month. Kuan-yin further specifies that offerings placed in bowls given to the Three Jewels should be inscribed with the name of the deceased person to whom the merit is dedicated:

[52] Summarized from *Chuan-chi po-yüan ching*, T. 4:224c–25b. Cf. Feer, trans., *Avadāna-Cataka*, pp. 178–82. In the Sanskrit and Tibetan versions Uttara's mother does not escape ghosthood.

[53] The story of Na-she is contained in the *Kuan-ting ching*, attributed to Śrīmitra (ca. 307–355), T. no. 1331, 21:530b–31b.

Whenever one makes merit on behalf of the deceased—for parents and siblings up to the seventh generation; wife's kin, extended family, friends and acquaintances; monk and lay alike—then the deceased undergoing suffering will achieve deliverance. On the full moon of the seventh month, when śramaṇa [ascetics] pass the new year, one should make offerings—the more, the better. If one provides vessels filled with offerings and labels each vessel with the recipient's name and a dedication to the Three Jewels, then the more merit one bestows, the quicker the blessings arrive.[54]

Conclusions

A concern with mothers, offerings to monks on the fifteenth day of the seventh month, Mu-lien's affinity for hungry ghosts—most of the elements of yü-lan-p'en literature had precedents in earlier Chinese mythology. Virtually all of the motifs that became part of the ghost festival in later times were already part of the corpus of stories, treatises, and histories of Chinese Buddhism prior to the fifth century. While most of the precedents are to be found in avadāna tales and other literature translated from Sanskrit and other Indic languages, indigenous sources (like Wang Yen's *Record of Good Fortune in the Dark Regions*) also preserve important antecedents. But perhaps the question of origins—Indian versus Chinese—is really beside the point in the case of fifth-century China. Avadāna tales translated from the Sanskrit took their place alongside Chinese miracle tales collected in encyclopedias, and together they constituted the copious fund from which yü-lan-p'en motifs were later drawn. The Mu-lien myth as it emerged in medieval times had many of its roots in this fully matured body of Chinese literature.

Moreover, the storehouse of mythology out of which the yü-lan-p'en myth developed appears to have spanned the poles of folk and elite. The variety of sources cited in this survey is unquestionably large; the antecedents of the yü-lan-p'en myth were probably distributed throughout Chinese society, just as the myth in its later medieval ver-

[54] Translation from *Ming-hsiang chi*, Wang Yen (ca. 500), contained in Lu Hsün, *Ku hsiao-shuo kou-ch'en* (Peking: Jen-min wen-hsüeh ch'u-pan-she, 1951), p. 407; based on the version in *Fa-yüan chu-lin*, Tao-shih (d. 683), T. no. 2122, 53:919b–20b. The story is also referred to in *Shih-shih yao-lan*, Tao-ch'eng (ca. 1019), T. no. 2127, 54:304b–c. Another biographical tradition on Hui-ta connects him with an Aśokan stūpa in K'uai-chi; see, for example, *Ming-seng chuan ch'ao*, copy made by Shūshō of Pao-ch'ang's (ca. 519) table of contents, Z. 2B, 7:1, p. 5rb; and *Kao-seng chuan*, Hui-chiao (497–554), T. no. 2059, 50:409b–10a.

sions was the common property of all social classes. Scholastic treatises like Kumārajīva's *Mahāprajñāpāramitāśāstra* related the entry of Mu-lien into the Buddhist order and spoke of his supernormal powers. The various rules for the conduct of monastic life contained stories of Mu-lien's discipleship and of his ascent to Marīci's heaven to deliver his mother. Chinese Buddhist historiography drew upon these sources and others to fill in the details of Mu-lien's life. And avadāna tales contain perhaps the greatest variety of motifs that later became popular in the celebration of the ghost festival. Such scholars as Chavannes and Iwamoto have long maintained that this last genre of tales and fables represents the most "popular" level of belief—popular in being most widespread and in coming closest to the unlettered masses.[55] It is thus likely that Mu-lien's frequent encounters with hungry ghosts, his role in establishing an ancestral festival for the benefit of the dead, and the story of a monk providing for the salvation of his mother were well known throughout Chinese society as early as the third century.

An awareness of the antecedents of yü-lan-p'en literature in Chinese mythology, however, is only the first step in assessing the significance of the ghost festival in medieval China. It remains to be seen just why the festival and its mythology took the shape that they did in later times. Some stories, like those concerning Mu-lien's career as a disciple of the Buddha, were ignored in later sources. Although it is recounted at length in many early accounts, Mu-lien's discipleship remains unmentioned in almost all yü-lan-p'en literature because it portrays in unflattering (or at least muted) light the hero of an epic adventure. Other episodes that are described only minimally in early sources come to dominate the narrative in later ones. By telling the story of Ch'ing-t'i's greed in *The Transformation Text on Mu-lien Saving His Mother*, for instance, storytellers were able to set up the ritual and cosmological rift which Mu-lien spends the rest of the story trying to mend. Thus, considerations of literary genre and the demands of dramatic form help to explain some of the permutations in yü-lan-p'en literature.

But other questions remain unsolved. Why, for instance, did Mu-lien, rather than Uttara, Na-she, or Śāriputra, become the central actor in the transformation texts and popular entertainments performed in T'ang and later dynasties? The data presented in this chapter help in formulating such questions, while discussions of shamanism, cosmol-

---

[55] See Chavannes, *Cinq Cents Contes et apologues*, 1:i-xx; and Iwamoto Yutaka, *Bukkyō setsuwa kenkyū*, Vol. 2, *Bukkyō setsuwa no genryū to tenkai* (Tokyo: Kaimei shoten, 1978), passim.

ogy, and other features of Chinese religion in later chapters are intended to help answer them.

APPENDIX: THE BUDDHA'S ASCENSION TO THE HEAVEN OF THIRTY-THREE TO PREACH TO HIS MOTHER

I summarize below the story of the Buddha's ascension to the Heaven of Thirty-Three contained in the *Tseng-i a-han ching (Ekottarāgama)*:[56]

Part One: Mu-lien Vanquishes and Converts Two Nāga Kings

Once, the Buddha resided with a large assembly in the kingdom of Śrāvastī in the Jetavana trees in the garden of Anāthapiṇḍika.[57] From his preeminent place in the Heaven of Thirty-Three, Indra descends to inform the Buddha that the Buddha's mother is in his heaven waiting to hear her son preach the Law. Having been reminded by Indra of his previous lectures on the value of enlightening and liberating one's parents, the Buddha silently consents to ascend to the Heaven of Thirty-Three and preach to his mother.

Before the Buddha is able to get off the ground, however, two nāga kings, Nanda and Upananda, cause a cosmic disturbance. Apparently because these nāgas reside at the base of Mount Sumeru, the *axis mundi*, and since monks usually ascend in meditation via this route, the nāgas had become angry. They thought to themselves, "All of these bald-headed monks are always flying about on top of us. We must come up with an expedient device to stop them from trespassing." So they breathed fire throughout Jambudvīpa, the world of men.[58] As the nāgas had hoped, their fiery wrath disturbs the peace of the Buddha's disciples. Monk after monk volunteers to fight the dragons, but the Buddha dissuades them from attempting it, warning them of the nāgas' ferocity.

Among the disciples of the Buddha only Mu-lien braves the chal-

---

[56] Summarized from *Tseng-i a-han ching*, trans. Gautama Saṃghadeva (ca. 383–397), T. no. 125, 2:703b–8c. For comparisons with the *Anguttaranikāya*, see Akanuma Chizen, *Kan-Pa shibu shiagon goshōroku* (Nagoya: Hajinkaku shobō, 1929). Parts Three, Four, and Five of the story are summarized in *Kao-seng fa-hsien chuan*, T. no. 2085, 51:859c–60a.

[57] The action of the three yü-lan-p'en sūtras also occurs here.

[58] Jambudvīpa is the continent located to the south of Mount Sumeru in our current world system. It is the continent on which humans live.

lenge. With a wave of his arm he flies off to Mount Sumeru. Once there he transforms himself into a large, fourteen-headed nāga king and, encircling the mountain fourteen times, tries to scare Nanda and Upananda with his mighty power. They respond by using their tails to splash water from the ocean, their fountains reaching up to the Heaven of Thirty-Three. Untouched, Mu-lien splashes them back. The nāgas next consider changing weapons from water to fire. Hoping to avoid any fire battle that would imperil people living on Jambudvīpa, Mu-lien again changes form, shrinking himself to an infinitesimal size. He succeeds in terrifying the poor nāga kings by running in and out of their mouths and noses. They are furious but unable to capture their tiny invader.

Resuming human form, Mu-lien sits atop their brows and lectures them, "You nāga kings should know that Mount Sumeru here is the pathway for all gods. It is not your own private dwelling place." Defeated by superior powers and now repentant, Nanda and Upananda wish to follow the Way of Mu-lien. He explains that his Way is that of the Buddha and that they must travel to Śrāvastī to take refuge in the Three Jewels in the presence of the Buddha himself. Together the three travel to Śrāvastī, and, after changing from nāga into human form,[59] Nanda and Upananda receive the lay precepts from the Buddha.

Part Two: Mu-lien Protects King Prasenajit,
Whom the Buddha Chastises

After the two nāga kings (temporarily in human form) and Mu-lien have rejoined the Buddha's following in Śrāvastī, King Prasenajit arrives for an audience with the Buddha. The king notices that among all of his subjects present there, only two do not bow down to him in the customary manner. The two nonconformists are the nāga kings in disguise. It seems that nāgas, because of their privileged position among sentient beings, bow down only to Buddhas, not kings. King Prasenajit takes umbrage at these two disrespectful seeming humans and wants to have them caught and killed. But before he is able to issue orders, the nāgas read his thoughts, beat a hasty retreat, and plot to ruin the king before he can ruin them.

Employing his own ability to read others' minds, the Buddha dis-

---

[59] Only humans may join the Buddhist order. As part of the initiation ceremony, novices are asked whether or not they are nāgas; see de Visser, *The Dragon in China and Japan*, p. 4; and Jean Phillipe Vogel, *Indian Serpent Lore, or the Nāgas in Hindu Legend and Art* (London: Arthur Probsthain, 1926), pp. 93–165.

patches Mu-lien to protect the king and defuse the conflict. Mu-lien sits in meditation atop King Prasenajit's palace, and from that position he transmutes the rain of stones and knives sent down by the nāga kings into flowers, food, fine clothing, and jewels.

The ignorant King Prasenajit, seeing beautiful offerings shower down from the heavens, assumes that they signify the coming of a sage (the Buddha) to the kingdom of a righteous, wheel-turning king (himself). Acting upon this conceit, the king takes the offerings to the Buddha so that he might fulfill his role as a universal monarch. The Buddha exposes the king's haughtiness and turns the offering to productive use as well: rejecting the king's claim to the status of a Cakravartin, he instructs him to hand over the gifts to his disciple, Mu-lien; and he lectures the king on his greed, informing him that in his next life he will be reborn again as a human being.

Part Three: The Buddha Preaches in
the Heaven of Thirty-Three

Having finished with King Prasenajit, the Buddha makes good on his original promise and ascends to the Heaven of Thirty-Three to preach the Dharma. His mother and Indra welcome the World-Honored One, and he preaches the Dharma. They all attain wisdom, and the Buddha gives them an added treat by allowing them to watch him enter *samādhi*.

Meanwhile the assembly at Śrāvastī, aware only of the Buddha's absence and not of his cosmic travels, has grown worried. Not even Ānanda, the Buddha's closest disciple, knows where he is. King Udyana suggests that a statue of the Buddha be made and that offerings be set before it, apparently in the hope that the Buddha will respond by reappearing. King Prasenajit, not to be outdone in displays of piety, also commissions a statue. Finally Ānanda asks another disciple, Aniruddha, to use his divine eye to search the cosmos for their master. Aniruddha looks over many heavens and all of the continents surrounding Mount Sumeru, but is unable to find the Buddha. At this point Ānanda begins to fear that perhaps the Buddha has entered nirvāṇa.

All of this time the Buddha has remained in the Heaven of Thirty-Three, bestowing boons upon the gods there and receiving their offerings. After three months he realizes that the residents of Jambudvīpa might have begun to miss him, so he dispatches a god to report on his whereabouts to Aniruddha. Aniruddha receives the message in a dream and uses his divine eye to confirm that the Buddha is in fact in the Heaven of Thirty-Three preaching to his mother.

Part Four: Mu-lien Retrieves the Buddha

At Ānanda's request, Mu-lien agrees to travel to the Heaven of Thirty-Three to pay respects to the Buddha on behalf of the assembly at Śrā-vastī. Mu-lien waves his arm and a moment later is welcomed by the gods of the heaven. The Buddha informs Mu-lien that he will return to the world of men, this time to the kingdom of Kāśi, after seven days. Mu-lien returns to Śrāvastī and reports to the Buddha's following. Overjoyed, they make preparations to greet the Buddha with lavish offerings and full-dress armies.

Seeing that the Buddha has given up the "spiritual feet" (*shen-tsu*) that allow him to fly, Indra asks the god Īśvara to construct three paths from the Heaven of Thirty-Three down to Kāśi. The Buddha, accompanied by all of the gods, follows the golden path in the center down to Kāśi. After a great welcome, the Buddha preaches to the assembled men and gods, who offer flowers, burn incense, and make music to delight the Buddha.

Part Five: A Disguised Nun Gains an Audience with the Buddha

In this last part, a pious nun named Uptalavarṇā impersonates a Cakravartin king so that she can have the honor of being the first person to greet the Buddha. The assembly of men and gods treats her like a Cakravartin rather than a nun, stepping aside to let her greet the Buddha first. As soon as she reaches him, she returns to her normal form. The Buddha praises her, but everyone else is upset at seeing a woman assume such an honored position. The kings finally gain their audience with the Buddha, and the story closes after they have been instructed to make statues and build temples for honoring the Buddha and making merit.

FIVE

Mu-lien as Shaman

IT IS a relatively simple task to document the many guises in which Mu-lien appeared in medieval China; it is quite a different matter to understand the strength of his appeal. The mythology of the ghost festival portrays Mu-lien as a paragon of filiality, as a devoted son willing to sacrifice his life for the sake of his ancestors. Given the importance of filial devotion throughout Chinese society, it is hardly surprising that a legend combining the theme of filiality with vivid descriptions of other worlds and cosmic battles should become a standard item in storytelling traditions. Chapter Four discussed some of the precedents of the yü-lan-p'en story in Chinese mythology, which provides most of the building blocks for the myth of Mu-lien saving his mother from hell.

But why should the hero of the ghost festival be Mu-lien rather than Śākyamuni Buddha, Uttara, or Na-she, all of whom were also identified in Chinese mythology as sons dedicated to their ancestors' salvation? The crucial difference, I would suggest, is that Mu-lien appeals to Chinese audiences because he plays the role of the shaman. Mu-lien's tour of hell, his visions of other worlds, his martial prowess—all present striking parallels to the actions of the shaman in Chinese religion and in Buddhism.

In the most common form of shamanic ritual in China, the spirit medium undertakes a tour of hell which he recounts to a small group using the vernacular language. The shaman communicates most often not just with any god or ghost, but with the ancestral spirits related to members of his audience. In the Buddhist tradition, the shaman's visionary experience and even his physical prowess are thought to be grounded in his meditative expertise; his ability to save people from suffering is based on his mastery of the techniques of consciousness training that are the special forte of the monk.

My argument in this chapter, simply put, is that Mu-lien is so popular in medieval China because he conforms to one of the most important forms of indigenous Chinese religion—shamanism—and because he conforms to the Buddhist ideal of the holy man. Historically speaking, the sources of Mu-lien's popularity are to be found in both pre-

Buddhist China and in the Buddhist tradition as a pan-Asian phenom-enon.

It would be misleading, however, to let history have the last word since the two traditions were effectively synthesized in China begin-ning in medieval times. Mu-lien's shamanic attributes, especially as they are portrayed in the more popular sources, attest to this union: Mu-lien rises from meditation, borrows the Buddha's staff, and then marshals the *yang* forces at his disposal to fight the armies of the under-world. Buddhist discipline and Chinese cosmology are thoroughly in-terfused. If there is a dichotomy—or rather, polarity—it has to do with the forms of shamanism acceptable to different classes of society. In monastic and poetic accounts, Mu-lien exercises the powers of the seer in his mystical roaming, while the oral traditions tend to concretize Mu-lien's martial abilities by focusing on his physical feats of strength.

"Shamanism" is, of course, a much-debated topic in comparative studies.[1] For the purposes of this discussion, the term may be used as an umbrella category for the set of symbols and rituals involving cosmic journeys and spirit-mediumship, which will be explored below not in general terms, but in their specifically Chinese and Buddhist contexts.

THE CHINESE BACKGROUND

The History of Shamanism in China

Spirit mediums, exorcisers, and diviners have been an essential part of Chinese religion at all levels of society for well over two millennia.[2]

---

[1] For two representative studies, see Mircea Eliade, *Shamanism: Archaic Techniques of Ecstasy*, revised ed., trans. Willard R. Trask, Bollingen Series, No. 74 (Princeton: Prince-ton University Press, 1964); and Ioan M. Lewis, *Ecstatic Religion: An Anthropological Study of Spirit Possession and Shamanism*, revised ed. (Harmondsworth: Penguin Books, 1978).

[2] Jan J.M. de Groot's study remains the best general treatment of Chinese shamanism. Entitled "The Priesthood of Animism," it constitutes Book II, Part V of *The Religious System of China*, 6 vols. (Leiden: E. J. Brill, 1892–1910), pp. 1187–1341. For historical studies of shamanism, see also: Kwang-chih Chang, *Art, Myth, and Ritual: The Path to Political Authority in Ancient China* (Cambridge: Harvard University Press, 1983), pp. 44–55; Henri Maspero, *China in Antiquity*, trans. Frank A. Kierman, Jr. (Amherst: Univer-sity of Massachusetts Press, 1978), pp. 111–19; Miyakawa Hisayuki, "Rikuchō jidai no fuzoku," *Shirin* 44:1 (January 1961):74–97; Edward H. Schafer, "Ritual Exposure in Ancient China," *HJAS* 14:1–2 (June 1951):130–84; P. Joseph Thiel, "Schamanismus im alten China," *Sinologica* 10:2–3 (1968):149–204; and Arthur Waley, *Chiu Ko—The Nine Songs: A Study of Shamanism in Ancient China* (London: Allen and Unwin, 1955). For sha-manism in modern Chinese culture, see Alan J.A. Elliott, *Chinese Spirit-Medium Cults in*

The significance of the term "*wu*" (usually translated "shaman") in the oracle bones of the Shang dynasty is still disputed,[3] but in the Eastern Chou period the term was clearly used to refer to the lowest class of the official priesthood of the ideal government supposed to have existed in earlier times. A text dating from the fourth century B.C. explains the shaman's role in ancient times:

> Anciently, men and spirits did not intermingle. At that time there were certain persons so perspicacious, single-minded, and reverential that their understanding enabled them to make meaningful collation of what lies above and below, and their insight to illumine what is distant and profound. Therefore the spirits would descend into them. The possessors of such powers were, if men, called *hsi* [shamans], and, if women, *wu* [shamannesses]. It is they who supervised the positions of the spirits at the ceremonies, sacrificed to them, and otherwise handled religious matters. As a consequence, the spheres of the divine and the profane were kept distinct. The spirits sent down blessings upon the people, and accepted from them their offerings. There were no natural calamities.[4]

By virtue of their inspired personalities and unusual abilities, shamans were chosen for the vocation of communicating with the gods, ancestors, and malevolent forces of the other world. Their religious and political calling was to insure the harmonious working of the cosmos by attending to "spiritual" matters. These *wu* were responsible for exorcising the forces that cause illness, for calling down spirits during state ceremony, for performing dances during droughts, and for invoking spirits during any great calamity.[5]

Singapore, Monographs on Social Anthropology, No. 14 (Norwich: London School of Economics and Political Science, 1955); Jack M. Potter, "Cantonese Shamanism," in *Religion and Ritual in Chinese Society*, ed. Arthur P. Wolf (Stanford: Stanford University Press, 1974); Ryū Shiman [Liu Chih-wan], *Chūgoku dōkyō no matsuri to shinkō*, Vol. 2 (Tokyo: Ōfūsha, 1984), pp. 20–234; Kristofer Schipper, *Le Corps taoïste: corps physique—corps social*, L'Espace interieur, 25 (Paris: Fayard, 1982), pp. 65–99, esp. pp. 70–79; and idem, "Vernacular and Classical Ritual in Taoism," JAS 45:1 (November 1985):121–57.

[3] See Akatsuka Kiyoshi, *Chūgoku kodai no shūkyō to bunka: In ōchō no saishi* (Tokyo: Kadokawa shoten, 1977), pp. 323ff.; Ch'en Meng-chia, "Han-tai tc shen-hua yü wu-shu," *Yen-ching hsüeh-pao* No. 20 (December 1936):485–576, esp. 536–38; and L. C. Hopkins, "The Shaman or Chinese Wu: His Inspired Dancing and Versatile Character," *Journal of the Royal Asiatic Society of Great Britain and Ireland* (1945, Parts 1 and 2):3–16.

[4] The *Kuo yü* (fourth century B.C.), cited in Derk Bodde, "Myths of Ancient China," in *Mythologies of the Ancient World*, ed. Samuel Noah Kramer (Garden City: Anchor Books, 1961), p. 390.

[5] See *Chou-li cheng-i*, (Taipei: Kuang-wen shu-chü, 1972), ch. 25, pp. 177c–78b;

With the unification of China and the development of a centralized state administration under the Ch'in and Han dynasties, the *wu* were made an uneasy but often-used part of the imperial state religion. Alternately patronized and persecuted by Chinese rulers, their honesty and excesses were debated by ministers, historians, and philosophers of Han times. While they were sometimes banished from the temples of the state religion and their activities among the people proscribed, the cosmological underpinnings of their activities were rarely called into question. Ngo Van Xuyet summarizes the common assumptions and divergent attitudes of the later Han literati with "Confucian" leanings (the *ju*) and of those technicians and diviners (*fang-shih*) who practiced spirit-mediumship. Both groups accepted the fact that shamans acted as intermediaries between this world and the other world. They disagreed, however, on the question of where and by whom such activities should be performed: by officials of the empire in state temples or by common thaumaturges in local and unofficial settings. Ngo writes that, "Undoubtedly, *ju* and *fang-shih* share the general belief in the existence of demons and spirits, but the first, prudent and reserved, do not seek to enter into private communication with this transcendent world and to act upon it with secret techniques that escape the edifice of official ceremony, as do a certain number of *fang-shih* whose rites, being of a private nature, are conducted outside of consecrated places."[6]

Shamans always maintained a following at the local level, even when their activities were proscribed by the state. Developing out of the state religion of Han times, shamanism became one of the major forms of "diffused religion" in medieval and modern China, a form of religious activity with its own specialists, yet one which was well integrated into ancestral religion and local cults. In these noninstitutionally religious settings—the family and the local temple—shamans cured illness, expelled pestilence, fought demons, became possessed by spirits, and performed divinations. Called by different names according to locality—*sai-kong* [Mandarin: *shih-kung*] in Fukien, *dang-ki* [Mandarin: *t'ung-chi*] and *fa-shih* in Taiwan—shamans entered into trances that car-

Edouard Biot, trans., *Le Tcheou-li ou Rites des Tcheou*, 2 vols. (Paris: Imprimerie Nationale, 1851), 2:102–4.

[6] Ngo Van Xuyet, *Divination, magie, et politique dans la Chine ancienne: essai suivi de la traduction des "Biographies des magiciens" tirées de "L'Histoire des Han postérieurs,"* Bibliothèque de l'Ecole des Hautes Etudes, Section des Sciences Religieuses, Vol. 78 (Paris: Presses Universitaires de France, 1976), p. 65. See also Kenneth J. Dewoskin, *Doctors, Diviners, and Magicians of Ancient China: Biographies of "Fang-shih"* (New York: Columbia University Press, 1983), pp. 1–39.

ried them through the heavens and hells of the other world. Such adventures were rarely private; assisted by an interpreter or master, shamans narrated their journeys to an assembled audience.

The Shaman's Spiritual Powers

Spirit-mediumship in China exhibits a seemingly dualistic tendency: the medium at times incarnates spirits in his or her own person and at other times sends his or her own spirit traveling to other realms. In the state cult, *wu* were responsible for invoking the spirits to whom rites were addressed, and in popular religion mediums called down spirits ranging from ancestral spirits and local gods of the temple to such luminaries as Kuan-ti and Kuan-yin.[7] In addition to possession proper, both Buddhist and Taoist accounts of mediums portray shamans calling down spirits to speak with them and to receive their inspiration.[8] Not only did shamans call down other spirits, but they also sent their own spirits traveling to other places. The ability to divide oneself into many forms, so as to be present in more than one place at once (*fen-hsing*), is attributed to advanced practitioners of Buddhism and Taoism, as is the ability to fly to other parts of the world or to have knowledge of distant events. Isabelle Robinet summarizes the shaman's ability to transform himself, or the science of "metamorphosis" (*pien-hua*) as conceived in Taoism:

> The Saint who knows how to transform himself is freed from corporal attachments and liberated from temporal-spatial bonds. He can travel a thousand miles in a moment, fly like a bird across the seas, etc. . . .
>
> Capricious, ethereal, and enigmatic, the Taoist vanishes or fades away only to reappear elsewhere or at another time. He does not die but retires to another region, hides himself, or flies away.[9]

The apparent tension between sending one's soul or spirit to another world and incarnating a spirit in this world in fact belies an underlying unity of structure, which can be seen in the language used to refer to

[7] See de Groot, *The Religious System of China*, pp. 1212–42 for medieval examples. For modern examples of local and ancestral spirits being called down by shamanesses, see Potter, "Cantonese Shamanism." For examples of mediums calling down gods who are higher in the pantheon, see Elliott, *Chinese Spirit-Medium Cults in Singapore*, pp. 73–79, 80–109.

[8] See Murakami Yoshimi, "*Kosō den* no shin'i ni tsuite," *Tōhō shūkyō* No. 17 (August 1961):11–12.

[9] Isabelle Robinet, "Metamorphosis and Deliverance from the Corpse in Taoism," HR 19:1 (August 1979): 48–49, 51.

the medium's activities. The medium not only "calls down spirits" (*chao-shen*) and allows people to "see spirits" (*chien-shen*), he also "sends his spirit roaming" (*yu-shen*).[10] Now the word *shen* has many meanings. In "calling down *shen*" and "seeing *shen*," it refers to the beings who reside in the heavens ("gods") or to a lower sort of spirit often associated with ghosts and specters. The medium possesses the special ability to communicate with, invoke, incarnate, and sometimes control these *shen* beings. Another sense of the word *shen* is operative in the expression "sends his *shen* roaming." Here the word refers to the more refined components of the person, those energies and elements which, at death and during times of illness or crisis, tend to separate from the body and ascend to the heavens.[11] Through special selection or initiation, the medium masters the art of liberating the *shen* parts of his or her person from the coarser parts so that they may move and fly about untrammeled.

Thus, the shaman is one who has special mastery over *shen*— spirits from afar, his own spirit, and spirituality in general. The shaman's special access to *shen*, then, implies that his mediumship works both ways: he can be possessed by spirits, and he is an adept at soul journeys.[12]

In their role as spirit mediums, shamans in China were associated with ancestral spirits perhaps more than with other kinds of spirits. When they incarnated the spirits of the dead, it was often the spirits of family members in their audience who possessed them. In their journeys to the dark regions, it was the kin of their listeners whom they most frequently encountered in the other world. Although they sometimes occupied a peripheral social position, shamans in China—like shamans among the Veddas of Sri Lanka, the Shona-speaking tribes of southern Zimbabwe, and the Kaffa people of southwestern Ethiopia— most often contacted ancestral spirits, and their pronouncements car-

[10] For examples of the first two usages, see de Groot, *The Religious System of China*, pp. 1214–15. For an example of the third usage, which might better be translated as "roams his spirit," see *Hui-ching Commentary*, T. no. 2781, 85:541b.

[11] See CWTTT, 25211, A: 1, 2, 4, 5.

[12] Some scholars have tried to make historical and typological distinctions between these two forms of mediumship, defining the first as mere "spirit possession" and the second as true "shamanism." See, for example, Eliade, *Shamanism*, pp. 5–8, 499–507. But this distinction does not appear valid even for Central Asian spirit-mediumship, to which the distinction was first applied. As Ioan M. Lewis, *Ecstatic Religion*, pp. 55–56, writes, "the Tungus evidence makes nonsense of the assumption that shamanism and spirit possession are totally separate phenomena, belonging necessarily to different cosmological systems and to separate historical stages of development." Demiéville also suggests the equivalence of the two forms of spirit travel; see Paul Demiéville, "Le Yogācārabhūmi de Sangharakṣa," BEFEO 44:2 (1954):381–82.

ried the authority of the central ancestral cult.[13] De Groot attributes the power and popularity of shamans in China to their special relation with ancestral spirits. He writes that, "the power of the Wu-ist priesthood to have intercourse with ancestors, even with the most exalted among them, and to reveal their will, was the great source of the influence of that priesthood among every class upon human conduct of every kind."[14] And Mu-lien's popularity in medieval Chinese religion, as I shall suggest below, was due in part to his performing the role of a spirit medium who made contact with his own ancestors in the other world.

The shaman's journey to other realms was made possible by the exercise of supernormal powers. The shaman's special powers include the abilities to penetrate physically the various planes of the cosmos in travel, to pierce through normal constraints and know events before they happen, to perceive sounds from all reaches of the universe, and to change oneself into an unbounded number of forms, be they animal, human, or god. While these powers are common to many forms of shamanism the world over, their elaboration in the Chinese context deserves further consideration.[15]

The powers of the shaman in medieval China came to be called "*shen-t'ung*," which may be translated provisionally as "spiritual penetrations." This term has many well-established nuances of meaning. Not only does the term have a very specific reference in Buddhist scholasticism (to be discussed below), it is also interpreted within the context of traditional Chinese cosmology. A twelfth-century lexicographer (and Buddhist monk), Fa-yün, explains the term by referring to the oldest and perennially popular Chinese manual of divination, *The Book of Changes*. He explains *shen*, "spiritual," by referring to the line from the *Changes* which says, "What *yin* and *yang* do not fathom is what is meant by *shen*." Fa-yün glosses *t'ung*, "penetration," with another quote from the *Changes*: "He [the sage-shaman] is still and unmoving. When he moves, he penetrates [all causes in the realm of all-under-heaven]."[16] The significance of this quotation from *The Book of*

---

[13] For a discussion of several cultures where shamans communicate mostly with ancestors, see Lewis, *Ecstatic Religion*, pp. 127–48.

[14] De Groot, *The Religious System of China*, pp. 1208–9.

[15] For a comparative study see Eliade, *Shamanism*, pp. 477–82.

[16] *Fan-i ming-i chi*, Fa-yün (1088–1158), T. no. 2131, 14:1177a; citing *Chou-i yin-te*, Harvard-Yenching Institute Sinological Index Series, Supplement No. 10 (reprint ed., Taipei: Ch'eng-wen Publishing Co., 1966), pp. 41a, 43a. Cf. Willard J. Peterson, "Making Connections: 'Commentary on the Attached Verbalizations' of the *Book of Change*," HJAS 42:1 (June 1982):104, 106. In the original context in the *Changes* the last quote probably refers to change or the *Changes* being still and unmoving.

Changes is manifold. The book itself, and especially the chapter from which the glosses are drawn, "Hsi-tz'u chuan" ("The Commentary on the Attached Verbalizations"), not only provides a technique for divination, it also claims to penetrate the processes of change and transformation in a uniquely illuminating way. As one scholar notes:

> In affirming the potency of *The Book of Changes*, the "Commentary" wants to persuade us not only that *The Book of Changes* is numinous, but also that it can be our medium, in a double sense. First, *The Book of Changes* in effect will be our *wu*, a shaman or diviner or "possessed person," who puts us in touch with *shen*, whether we interpret that word as spirits, divinities, demons, numinosity, or whatever. . . . *The Book of Changes* is the medium also in the sense of being the means of passing from the realm of what is intelligible to us to the realm of what is not directly or only imperfectly knowable.[17]

Situating the term "*shen-t'ung*" in the context of *The Book of Changes* helps to clarify the Chinese understanding of the shaman's powers. They are "*shen*" ("spiritual") in all senses of the term. The shaman's abilities are mysterious and occult, transcending the normal measures and modulations of change. The shaman's powers also pertain to the realm of the spirits, both the refined, in-dwelling parts of the person and the divinities of the other world. The notion of "*t'ung*" ("penetration") further specifies the shaman's forte: passing through one world to the next, he is able to travel beyond the seen world and to comprehend what lies hidden. The intentionally ambiguous rendering of "*shen-t'ung*" as "spiritual penetrations" helps preserve all of these nuances of the term.

THE BUDDHIST BACKGROUND

The portrayal of Mu-lien in ghost festival stories draws on two traditions of shamanism. On the one hand, Mu-lien's access to the dark regions and his concern with ancestral spirits mark him as a central figure in Chinese religion. His popularity in medieval times may be attributed, in part, to the indigenous tradition of shamanism. On the other hand, Mu-lien brings to the role of *wu* several features that derive from Buddhism. He is often pictured engaging in spirit travel in a distinctively Buddhist posture of meditation, and in many instances his pow-

---

[17] Peterson, "Making Connections," pp. 107, 108, modifying "*Change*" to "*The Book of Changes*."

ers are activated only after he borrows items belonging to the Buddha. In fact, Mu-lien's remarkable mastery of cosmic travel dates back to the earliest periods of Buddhism in India, when legends portrayed Mu-lien (Skt.: Mahā-Maudgalyāyana) as second only to the Buddha in the shamanic arts:

> In the early stages of Buddhist history cosmological motifs were established in the very center of the tradition through the visionary and meditative experiences of the Founder and his earliest disciples. The visionary experience that was a part of the Buddha's own Enlightenment process, and a special forte of the Buddha's great disciple Mahāmoggallāna [Skt.: Mahā-Maudgalyāyana], produced a series of vivid images of the heavenly realms in which men received retribution for their sins. The meditative experience . . . led to the development of conceptions of cosmic worlds corresponding to the various levels of meditative consciousness (*jhāna* [Skt.: *dhyāna*]) that especially holy men could achieve through mental discipline and concentration.[18]

In China the earliest yü-lan-p'en sūtras begin with Mu-lien's visionary experience:

> Thus have I heard. Once the Buddha resided in the kingdom of Śrāvastī, among the Jetavana trees in the garden of Anāthapiṇḍika. The Great Mu-lien began to obtain the six penetrations. Desiring to save his parents to repay the kindness they had shown in nursing and feeding him, he used his divine eye to observe the worlds.[19]

Mu-lien's world-piercing vision constitutes one of the "six penetrations," usually called the six "superknowledges" or "spiritual penetrations" (*shen-t'ung*, Skt.: *abhijñā*). Tsung-mi describes them:

> "The six penetrations." One: the penetration of spiritual realms, [so-called] because one knows and verifies the spiritual realms. It is also called the "as-you-wish" penetration, because your body goes wherever you want it to. Two: the penetration of the divine eye. Three: the penetration of the divine ear. These mean that one is able to see and to hear, close up and from afar, all sorts of sights

[18] Frank E. Reynolds and Mani B. Reynolds, *Three Worlds According to King Ruang: A Thai Buddhist Cosmology*, Berkeley Buddhist Studies Series 4 (Berkeley: Asian Humanities Press, 1982), p. 15.

[19] *The Yü-lan-p'en Sūtra*, T. no. 685, 16:779a–b. See also *The Sūtra on Offering Bowls to Repay Kindness*, T. no. 686, 16:780a.

and sounds within the walls [of a room] and from without. Four: the penetration of past lives, because one is able to know lives and events from previous existences. Five: the penetration of others' minds, because one knows [others' thoughts] whether their minds be settled or dispersed, with or without outflows. Six: the penetration of exhausted outflows, since one is able to know with one's bodily outflows exhausted. In all six there are no obstructions,[20] hence they are generally called "penetrations."[21]

As Tsung-mi points out, the first penetration goes by several names in Chinese Buddhist literature, all of them referring to the broadest of the shaman's powers, that is, his ability to fly to special realms by a number of means: self-transformation; meditative ecstasis; birdlike flight; or walking on his "spiritual feet" (*shen-tsu*), which allow him to traverse great distances.[22] His flight is special by virtue of his mode of transportation (*shen*-like feet) as well as his destination (*shen* realms). His abilities to penetrate the boundaries of the seen world also include the powers of invisibility and of manifesting his physical form at will. This faculty is also called "the penetration of the body," described as "flying about, hiding and manifesting [oneself]."[23]

The second and third penetrations involve a sharpening of the visual and auditory senses so that the eyes and ears perceive the most minute and distant of sense objects. The fourth power makes it possible to look back in time, usually by a retrogressive analysis from effect to cause, finally reaching the actions in previous lives that gave rise to rebirth in this life. The fifth penetration allows one to read the minds of other beings or, as one author writes, "to mirror like water [their] myriad

[20] Reading *yung*[a] for *yung*[b], following *Yüan-chao Commentary*, Z. 1, 35:2, 115ra.

[21] Translation from *Tsung-mi Commentary*, T. 39:507c–8a. Details of the six penetrations vary slightly in scholastic literature; see *A-p'i-ta-mo chü-she lun*, T. no. 1558, 29:142c–43a; Louis de La Vallée Poussin, trans., *L'Abhidharmakośa de Vasubandhu*, ed. Etienne Lamotte, 6 vols., *Mélanges chinois et bouddhiques*, Vol. 16 (Brussels: Institut Belge des Haute Etudes Chinoises, 1971), 5:98–103; and *Ta chih-tu lun*, T. no. 1509, 25:97c–98b; Etienne Lamotte, trans., *Le Traité de la grand vertu de sagesse de Nāgārjuna (Mahā-prajñāpāramitāśāstra)*, 5 vols. (Louvain-la-Neuve: Institut Orientaliste, 1949–80), pp. 328–33. For further references, see Lamotte, trans., *Traité*, pp. 1809–16. For the *abhijñā* in Pāli literature, see Paravahera Vajirañāna, *Buddhist Meditation in Theory and Practice: A General Exposition According to the Pāli Canon of the Theravāda School* (Colombo: M. D. Gunasena and Co., 1962), pp. 441–53.

[22] See MBDJ, pp. 1794b–95c.

[23] *Shih-shuo hsin-yü*, Liu I-ch'ing (403–444), Hsin-pien chu-tzu chi-ch'eng, Vol. 8 (Taipei: Shih-chieh shu-chü, 1978), p. 60; cf. Richard B. Mather, trans., *Shih-shuo hsin-yü: A New Account of Tales of the World* (Minneapolis: University of Minnesota Press, 1976), p. 119.

thoughts."[24] Only Buddhas attain the sixth penetration, which represents the culmination of wisdom and liberation over a long period of time.

The Meditative Context

The Buddhist conception of the shaman's arts is evident in the accounts of how Mu-lien first gained his powers. In *Fo wu-po ti-tzu tzu-shuo pen-ch'i ching (The Sūtra of the Five Hundred Disciples of the Buddha Explaining Their Previous Lives)*, an avadāna compilation from the early fourth century, Mu-lien tells of his previous lives. In one such life as a practicing ascetic he happened upon a monk who, starting from a position of meditation, could fly in the air. Upon seeing him, Mu-lien says:

> I then brought forth a vow
> That I too would gain spiritual feet,
> That I might gain them just as he had:
> Great power, great spiritual feet.

After many rebirths in Jambudvīpa and in various hells, Mu-lien's vow is fulfilled; when he becomes a disciple of the Buddha he becomes a champion at spiritual powers.[25] Unlike other mediums who attain their powers through special initiation, sickness, or inheritance, shamans who are disciples of the Buddha attain their powers because of bodhisattvalike vows made in previous existences. By the strength of these vows and through the workings of karma, Mu-lien is graced with spiritual feet.

The most common source of shamanic powers, however, was not a vow taken in a past life, but the practice of meditation. Scholastic treatises and popular tales alike view the medium's supernormal powers as grounded in meditative practice.

The *Āgama* story included in the Appendix to Chapter Four relates several instances of people exercising shamanic powers from a posture of meditation. In protecting King Prasenajit from the fury of the two nāga kings, for instance, Mu-lien changed a rain of stones and knives into flowers, food, clothing, and jewels. In performing these transformations, Mu-lien remained invisible, seated atop King Prasenajit's palace; he "sat atop the king's palace with his legs crossed, making his

[24] *Shih-shuo hsin-yü*, p. 60; cf. Mather, trans., *A New Account of Tales of the World*, p. 119.

[25] *Fo wu-po ti-tzu tzu-shuo pen-ch'i ching*, trans. Dharmarakṣa (ca. 265–313), T. no. 199, 4:190c–91a.

150

body invisible."[26] While engaged in meditation, Aniruddha, known for his supernormal eyesight, looked through the cosmos for the Buddha:

Seated with his legs crossed, [Aniruddha] composed his body and his thoughts, his mind unmoving. With his divine eye he observed the Heaven of Thirty-Three. . . . Then he arose from *samādhi*. . . .[27]

Yü-lan-p'en literature similarly leaves no doubt that Mu-lien's powers derive from his meditative experience. *The Transformation Text on Mu-lien Saving His Mother* describes how Mu-lien entered the Sangha after his mother's death:

Inheriting the good effects of his practices in former lives and listening to the Law [preached by the Buddha], he attained the fruit of *arhat*-ship. He then searched for his dear parent with his divine eye, but nowhere in the six paths of birth-and-death did he find her. Mu-lien arose from concentration full of sadness and inquired of the Buddha, "In which place is my dear mother enjoying happiness?"[28]

The first picture shown by storytellers in their recounting of *The Transformation Text on Mu-lien Saving His Mother*, in fact, depicted Mu-lien sitting in meditation in the mountains, and there are twenty-four lines of verse describing him sitting in meditation and calming his mind, his body erect and his respiration controlled.[29] Unfortunately none of the illustrations from this *pien-wen* survive.

Scholastic Buddhist literature affirms the origin of the spiritual powers in meditation and makes clear precisely when in the process of training the powers are believed to arise.[30] In the Buddhist scholastic

---

[26] *Tseng-i a-han ching (Ekottarāgama)*, trans. Gautama Saṃghadeva, T. no. 125, 2:704c.

[27] *Tseng-i a-han ching*, T. 2:706a.

[28] THPWC, p. 714; following Iriya Yoshitaka, trans., "Dai Mokkenren meikan kyūbo henbun," *Bukkyō bungaku shū*, Chūgoku koten bungaku taikei (Tokyo: Heibonsha, 1975), p. 54; cf. Victor Mair, trans., *Tun-huang Popular Narratives* (Cambridge: Cambridge University Press, 1983), p. 88.

[29] THPWC, p. 716; Mair, trans., *Tun-huang Popular Narratives*, p. 90.

[30] As many scholars have noted, the attribution of shamanic powers to accomplished ascetics was not unique to Buddhism. See Louis de La Vallée Poussin, "Le Bouddha et les abhijñās," *Le Muséon* 44 (1931):335–42; Carl Sigurd Lindquist, *Siddhi und Abhiññā: Eine Studie über die klassischen Wunder des Yoga* (Uppsala: A.-B. Lundequistska Bokhandeln, 1935) passim; Paul Demiéville, "Sur La Mémoire des existences antérieures," BE-FEO 27 (1927):283–98; and Mircea Eliade, *Yoga: Immortality and Freedom*, revised ed., trans. Willard R. Trask, Bollingen Series, No. 56 (Princeton: Princeton University

traditions transplanted in China, the spiritual penetrations are coordinated with a standardized system of meditation. Specifically, as the *Abhidharmakośa* says, "The first five penetrations depend upon the four *dhyānas*."[31] The picture of a monk exercising his shamanic powers from a meditating position is a common one at all levels of Chinese mythology, from *pien-wen* through scholastic literature. But the details of the meditative process—the specific stages of meditation and the attainment of specific powers—are spelled out systematically only in the more monkish literature. It is this attention to meditative detail that distinguishes Mu-lien as he is presented in monastic literature from Mu-lien as he is portrayed in more popular sources.

The system of meditation with which the supernormal powers are associated dates back to early Buddhism and is evident in works describing the Buddhist Path from the Pāli canon of the Theravāda school.[32] In medieval China the system was described in a variety of works used by monks and literati.

In this meditative system the practitioner ascends through four meditative states (*ch'an*, Skt.: *dhyānas*) by stripping away the emotional and intellectual activities that accompany normal, untrained consciousness. This process is begun after the meditator has calmed his mind, regulated his breath, and conquered such impediments to sustained medi-

---

Press, 1969), pp. 162–99, esp. pp. 173–85. La Vallée Poussin writes that, "India of the Buddha's time did not conceive of holiness, *arhattva*, unless it was accompanied by faculties of a magical order." Superknowledges were a common attribute of the holy man in sixth-century B.C. India, and in this context the Buddha was not exceptional in possessing them. In early Buddhism lower-level practitioners did not attain shamanic powers. Later, as Buddhism developed in India and Central Asia, it was believed that any practicing ascetic could attain them. At this stage, says La Vallée Poussin, there developed in scholastic Buddhism a need to distinguish the Buddha's superknowledges from those of other practitioners. See La Vallée Poussin, "Le Bouddha," pp. 335–42; quotation from p. 336. This historical process gave rise to the scheme of the six spiritual penetrations known in medieval China: anyone practicing ascetic arts could obtain the first five penetrations, but the powers of non-Buddhists did not last as long as those of Buddhists. See *Ta chih-tu lun*, T. 25:98a: "The [magical] creations of other schools never last more than seven days, while the mastery over creations by Buddhas and their disciples has an unlimited duration"; Lamotte, trans., *Traité*, p. 329. Furthermore, only Buddhas could obtain the sixth penetration, in which all defilements are exhausted. See *Ta chih-tu lun*, T. 25:264a–65b; Lamotte, trans., *Traité*, pp. 1817–27. Only Sages (*sheng*, Skt.: *āryas*) obtain the sixth penetration according to the *Abhidharmakośa*, T. 29:142c; La Vallée Poussin, trans., *L'Abhidharmakośa*, 5:100.

[31] T. 29:143a; La Vallée Poussin, trans., *L'Abhidharmakośa*, 5:101. For the reading of *ching-lü* as *ch'an-ting*, see OBDJ, pp. 722b–23a.

[32] See Vajirañāna, *Buddhist Meditation*, for canonical references. For later literature, cf. the *Visuddhimagga*, by Buddhaghosa (ca. 400); Bhikkhu Ñāṇamoli, trans., *The Path of Purification* (Colombo: A. Semage, 1956).

tative practice as desire, ill will, torpor, distraction, and perplexity. Having banished these hindrances, the practitioner is dissociated from sense desires and is able to enter the first *dhyāna*, which is marked by "inquiry, judgment, joy, happiness, and one-pointedness of mind."[33] Meditation progresses by letting go of inquiry and judgment, then joy, then happiness, so that in the fourth *dhyāna* only one-pointedness of mind remains. A scholastic compendium attributed by Kumārajīva to Nāgārjuna, the *Mahāprajñāpāramitāśāstra*, *(Ta chih-tu lun, Treatise on the Great Perfection of Wisdom)* describes the process:

> For the sake of all sentient beings the bodhisattva produces senti-ments of great compassion and cultivates *dhyāna* and concentra-tion. Attaching himself to the object of thought, he leaves the five desires, gets rid of the five hindrances, and enters the first *dhyāna*, that of great joy. Extinguishing inquiry and judgment, concen-trating his thoughts, he enters profoundly into internal peace, ob-tains subtle and marvelous joy, and enters the second *dhyāna*. Be-cause this profound joy distracts concentration, the bodhisattva leaves all joys, obtains complete happiness, and enters the third *dhyāna*. Leaving all suffering and happiness, getting rid of all wor-ries and joys, as well as the inhalation and exhalation of breath, he adorns himself with a pure and subtle indifference and enters the fourth *dhyāna*.[34]

The way in which the six spiritual penetrations are projected onto this map of the four *dhyānas* varies from one text to another. In the *Mahāprajñāpāramitāśāstra*, Kumārajīva notes the divergence of opin-ion: some people believe the penetrations arise in order from the divine eye (first) to the exhaustion of outflows (sixth), while others associate the first *dhyāna* with the divine ear, the second *dhyāna* with the divine eye, the third *dhyāna* with the penetration of "as-you-wish," and the fourth *dhyāna* with all of the penetrations.[35]

Such is the Buddhist view of the origin of the "spiritual penetra-tions" as elaborated in a stratum of Chinese Buddhist literature that ap-peals mostly to monks. While any ascetic can conceivably obtain the powers of the shaman, the most efficacious powers are obtained by fol-

[33] *Ta chih-tu lun*, T. 25:185c–86b; Lamotte, trans., *Traité*, pp. 1027–32. I have followed Lamotte's translation of technical terms from the *Ta chih-tu lun* here and in the following quotation.

[34] *Ta chih-tu lun*, T. 25:208b; Lamotte, trans., *Traité*, pp. 1237–38. The account in *Ssu-fen lü (Dharmaguptavinaya)*, trans. Buddhayaśas (ca. 408–412), is almost identical; T. no. 1428, 22:781a–b.

[35] *Ta chih-tu lun*, T. 25:265b; Lamotte, trans., *Traité*, p. 1827.

lowing the trail blazed by the Buddha.[36] This path, which consists of the progressive stripping away of the factors of consciousness, is described in terms of the four *dhyānas*. For monks and other preservers of the "Great Tradition" of Chinese Buddhism, then, the magical abilities of the shaman should be grounded in the Buddhist orthopraxis of meditation.

The Soteriological Context

If the shaman's powers originate in the act of meditation, they should also, according to the Buddhist view, be directed toward a specific end. Shamans should exercise their powers not for their own liberation, but for the salvation of others. This view of the soteriological grounding of the magician's powers is evident in yü-lan-p'en literature, in scholastic literature, in avadāna tales expressing an ambivalence toward supernormal powers, and in rules for the conduct of monks which restrict shamanic activities.

Hui-ching makes it quite clear that liberation from suffering is the unspoken goal of supernatural powers. Hui-ching even suggests that without the powers, saving others from suffering is a doomed enterprise. The soteriological purpose—that Mu-lien would use his powers for the salvation of others—is simply assumed. Hui-ching writes:

> *Question*: Why did Mu-lien not save his mother first, rather than saving her only after he gained the fruit of penetrations?
> *Answer*: At the time when he had not yet gained the fruit [i.e., the spiritual penetrations], defilements were not yet exhausted. As long as there are obstructions, one cannot save people from suffering.[37]

[36] The meditative origin of the penetrations is also evident in accounts of the experience of the paradigmatic meditator, the Buddha. The course of Śākyamuni's enlightenment experience under the Bodhi tree in Bodh-gayā is often described in terms of three watches of the night. In the first watch (again according to the *Ta chih-tu lun*) he obtained the penetration of "as-you-wish" and the knowledge of previous existences. With these powers he engaged in an activity central to the shamanic vocation, the subduing of demons: the Buddha conquered Māra and his army of gods and demons. As his meditation progressed, the Buddha gained the penetration of the divine eye and the knowledge of the divine ear in the second watch of the night. And in the third watch of the night he gained the penetration of knowing others' thoughts and the knowledge of the exhaustion of outflows. See *Ta chih-tu lun*, T. 25:265a; Lamotte, trans., *Traité*, p. 1824. Cf. the account in *Ssu-fen lü*, T. 22:781b–c, which only mentions the "three knowledges" (*san-ming*).

[37] *Hui-ching Commentary*, T. no. 1792, 85:541b. Tsung-mi attributes less power to Mu-lien than does Hui-ching. Tsung-mi writes, "Even the mighty numinosity of the sagely

For Hui-ching, as soon as one masters the requisite level of Buddhist discipline, the spiritual penetrations are automatically engaged in compassionate activities.

Sources also show special tolerance for anomalous, seemingly incomprehensible shows of magic, as long as they are performed in a soteriological context. The *Mahāprajñāpāramitāśāstra* states:

> Because he is detached from the five desires, has attained all of the *dhyānas*, and possesses benevolence and compassion, the bodhisattva takes hold of the spiritual penetrations on behalf of all beings and manifests extraordinary and marvelous things in order to purify the thoughts of sentient beings. Why is this so? Because if there were no extraordinary things, then he would not be able to cause many beings to attain salvation.[38]

Following the logic of Mahāyāna universalism, any expedient device, including a feat of magic, is justified when it is used in the appropriate setting.

By the same measure, adepts are criticized when they exercise their powers outside the context of salvation. In following the Buddhist Way, the cultivation of any religious practice always leaves open the possibility of clinging. Attaining higher states of absorption, scoring points in philosophical debate, gaining the spiritual penetrations—Buddhist literature abounds with stories of accomplished but ultimately ignorant practitioners whose pride in their achievements only hinders their march toward liberation. Mu-lien, best among the Buddha's disciples in the spiritual penetrations, not unexpectedly falls prey to conceit. One tale, from a late third-century avadāna collection, portrays a Mu-lien so haughty that he believes himself superior to the Buddha. The tale begins:

> Once, seated beneath a tree, Mu-lien tested his divine eye and saw eight thousand *Buddha-kṣetras* [Buddha lands]. He thought to himself, "The Thus-Come One can't even see what I can." So, taking lion strides, he went to where the Buddha was.
>
> The Buddha said to Mu-lien, "You are merely in the class of voice-hearers [*śrāvakas*]. Why do you now take lion strides?"
>
> Mu-lien told the Buddha, "I myself have seen eight thousand *Buddha-kṣetras* in the eight directions. I don't think that what the Buddha sees can compare with this. Hence the lion strides."

---

son [Mu-lien] could not bring to an end her fiery fate"; *Tsung-mi Commentary*, T. 39:506c–7a.

[38] *Ta chih-tu lun*, T. 25:264b; cf. Lamotte, trans., *Traité*, pp. 1819–20.

The Buddha proceeds to show Mu-lien his vanity. He does so not by scolding Mu-lien, questioning his logic, or impugning the efficacy of his powers, but by besting him at his own magic. The Thus-Come One emits rays of light from his body which illuminate unbounded Buddha lands as numerous as the grains of sand in many thousands of Ganges rivers.[39]

Shamanic powers per se are not questioned in this legend; the issue is not one of "no-magic" or "religion" versus "magic." The Buddha himself resorts to the same powers exercised by Mu-lien, and he does a better job at exercising them. What the Buddha objects to is Mu-lien's attitude toward the powers and the use to which he puts them. Mu-lien's haughty attitude shows in his deportment. He takes lion strides, which signify fearlessness and which indicate the way the Buddha walks as he leads an army of gods to wipe away hells and torments.[40] Rather than using his powers for the benefit of others, Mu-lien has let them go to his head. Furthermore, the Buddha makes his point in a particularly instructive way: he uses the same powers that Mu-lien did, only better; and he uses the powers for their proper purpose, as an expedient device for leading Mu-lien toward enlightenment.

The ambivalent attitude of the Buddhist establishment toward shamanic powers is evident in the rules for the conduct of monks. While accepting the reality and efficacy of shamanic powers, the Buddhist Sangha (throughout Asia) and state authorities (in China) sought to delimit the circumstances in which they could be used. Indian Vinaya texts preserve the frequent admonition:

> You are not, O *Bhikkus*, to display before the laity the superhuman power of *Iddhi*. Whoever does so, shall be guilty of a *dhukkhata* [wrongdoing].[41]

Such rules recognize the drawing power of shamans, but attempt to keep them contained within the ambit of the monkhood.

Buddhist monks are also prohibited by the codes and statutes of the T'ang government from practicing some skills of the shamanic trade among the populace. A statute from the *Tao-seng ko (Statutes for Taoist*

[39] *Chiu tsa p'i-yü ching*, trans. K'ang Seng-hui (d. 280), T. no. 206, 4:519b–c.

[40] For the Buddha walking with "lion strides" (*shih-tzu pu*), see *The Transformation Text on Mu-lien Saving His Mother*, THPWC, p. 738; Victor Mair, trans., *Tun-huang Popular Narratives*, p. 113.

[41] *Vinaya Texts*, Part III: *The Kullavagga, IV-XII*, trans., T. W. Rhys-Davids and Hermann Oldenberg, Sacred Books of the East, Vol. 20 (Oxford: Clarendon Press, 1885), p. 81. Cf. Isaline B. Horner, trans., *The Book of the Discipline (Vinaya-Pitaka)*, 6 vols. (London: Luzac and Co., 1949–66), 5:142.

and Buddhist Monks) of 650–655, for instance, makes it a minor crime for monks to claim falsely that they have achieved certain levels of sagehood, which would, in the popular view, qualify them as possessors of shamanic powers.[42] As noted in the previous section, the Chinese government often attempted to limit the influence of shamans. An imperial edict of 635, for example, prohibits those who "falsely claim to be doctors or shamans or who seek profit in the Ways of the left."[43] Chinese codes also prohibit monks from establishing their own sanctuaries outside of officially sponsored temples.[44]

Presumably, then, so long as it occurred within the system sanctioned by the state and administered by the Sangha, shamanic activity was tolerated, if not encouraged, by imperial and monastic authorities. In these cases the interests of the imperial government reinforced those of the Chinese Sangha. Both sought to restrict the exercise of shamanic powers to the right channels and the appropriate contexts.

MU-LIEN AS SHAMAN

The preceding sketch of the Chinese and the Buddhist figurations of the shaman should further our appreciation of Mu-lien's shamanic attributes in the mythology of the ghost festival, which may now be ex-

[42] The statute, quoted in the Japanese legal commentary *Ryō shūge*, refers to "those people who committed the crime of falsely claiming to have gained the Way of the Sage and whose trials have already been completed"; *Ryō no shūge*, 2 vols., ed. Koremune Naomoto (Tokyo: Kokusho kankōkai, 1912–13), 1:230. The Japanese code for monks and nuns, the *Sōni ryō*, probably dating from 717 to 724, specifically mentions shamans (*wu*, Ja.: *miko)*: "Monks and nuns who foretell good and bad fortune by divination and [geomantic or physiognomic] patterns and who practice the lesser paths, the shamanic arts, and the healing of sickness, shall all be returned to lay life. Those who follow the Buddhist Law in performing incantations to aid the sick are not included in this restriction." Translation from *Ritsuryō*, ed. Inoue Matsusada, Nihon shisō taikei, Vol. 3 (Tokyo: Iwanami shoten, 1976), p. 216. It remains unclear precisely what the corresponding passage said in the Chinese *Tao-seng ko*; see Futaba Kenkō, *Kodai bukkyō shisō shi kenkyū: nihon kodai ni okeru ritsuryō bukkyō oyobi han-ritsuryō bukkyō no kenkyū* (Kyoto: Nagata bunshōdō, 1962), pp. 196–98.

[43] The edict is cited in *Fo-tsu li-tai t'ung-tsai*, Nien-ch'ang (d. 1341), T. no. 2036, 49:569b–c.

[44] The term "sanctuary" (*tao-ch'ang*, Skt.: *bodhimaṇḍala*) has a wide range of meanings in China: the place where the Buddha achieved enlightenment (the Bodhi tree in Bodhgayā); the method of practice for achieving enlightenment; the place where one makes offerings to Buddhas; the place where one studies the Way; temples or monasteries; a Buddhist altar. See TFTT, p. 2368a–b. Akizuki claims that this prohibition was part of the 650–655 Chinese code; see Akizuki Kan'ei, "*Dōsō kō no fukkyū ni tsuite,*" *Tōhoku gakuin daigaku ronshū: rekishi-gaku, chiri-gaku* No. 4 (1952). Futaba, *Kodai bukkyō shisō shi kenkyū*, pp. 98–99, claims that it is present only in the Japanese code.

157

amined in greater detail. As an actor performing in front of a hetero-
geneous audience, much like the Buddha speaking with one voice to
many kinds of listeners, Mu-lien plays one character, the shaman. In
his mythic dimensions, Mu-lien combines in one convincing character
the two traditions of shamanism discussed above. The success of his
performance in medieval China, however, lies in his ability to suggest
some nuances of the role that appeal to a general Chinese audience—
spirit journeys, battles with ghosts and demons—and to express some
nuances of the role that appeal to those who follow a monastic way of
life, such as mastery of meditative techniques and the knowledge of
previous existences. In playing the *wu*, Mu-lien portrays a single (or
universal) type at the same time that he appeals to the particular concerns of different social classes.

Mu-lien's Journey

Mu-lien's journey to other worlds in search of his mother is described
variously in the different versions of the yü-lan-p'en story. In *The Yü-
lan-p'en Sūtra* and *The Sūtra on Offering Bowls to Repay Kindness*, simply
by exercising his divine eye Mu-lien is able to see his mother reborn as
a hungry ghost.[45] *The Pure Land Yü-lan-p'en Sūtra* further specifies the
meditative context of his ocular powers:

> Then Mu-lien used the divine power of his spiritual penetrations
> to enter the *samādhi*-concentration of the eighteen kings.[46] He vis-
> ualized where his mother might have been reborn; he expended
> his spiritual powers to their limit but still did not know where she
> was.[47]

These accounts portray Mu-lien's journey as primarily *visual* and as
a journey that occurs in the course of meditation. This style of shamanic experience appeals to an audience of meditators, to those who
shy away from the shaman's physical flight, rather than to a crowd

[45] *The Yü-lan-p'en Sūtra*, T. 16:779a–b; *The Sūtra on Offering Bowls to Repay Kindness*,
T. 16:780a.

[46] "*Samādhi*-concentration of the eighteen kings" (*shih-pa wang san-mei ting*) is problematic. As Jaworski points out, the eighteen kings are probably the kings of the eighteen
hells mentioned later in the text; Jan Jaworski, "L'Avalambana Sūtra de la terre pure,"
Monumenta Serica 1 (1935–36):101, n. 30. I have not found references to the eighteen kings
or to their *samādhi* in other texts; presumably it is a meditative state of concentration in
which one visualizes the eighteen courts of hell. I have reproduced the redundant "*samādhi*-concentration" in my translation.

[47] *The Pure Land Yü-lan-p'en Sūtra*, ll. 13–14; cf. Jaworski, "L'Avalambana Sūtra," p.
94.

gathered to hear spirits from another world speak through a medium. The more meditative and metaphoric versions, however, are not for that reason any less exciting than those describing physical transport. Even the commentaries—a genre which usually expresses difference only through paraphrase, rearrangement, and classical allusion—preserve an element of rapture. Hui-ching writes:

> Mu-lien transcended divisions and lodged in concentration. He sent his spirit roaming through the seven paths of enlightenment,[48] got rid of the three outflows,[49] and harvested as a fruit the six penetrations. He thoroughly manifested mature creations [by virtue of his power]. . . .
>
> With his divine eye Mu-lien then spied up and down the three worlds[50] and looked through the six paths [of rebirth]. He exhausted his spiritual power in search of his mother. . . .
>
> Next Mu-lien used his power of penetration to illuminate the three realms from top to bottom, to light up everything in all directions. So all-embracing was his search that he was able to see clearly [his mother's] *hun* [-spirit] suffering unspeakable distress in this path [of hungry ghosts].[51]

Mu-lien flies through space unhindered. Alluding to "concentration," Hui-ching is careful to hint that shamanic flight takes place in a meditative context. Having glossed Mu-lien as shaman and meditator, Hui-ching then describes the journey. In this case it is a journey as seen through the eyes of the traveler: we see the same sights as does Mu-lien with his divine eye, and we gain a sense of how far his vision reaches. Mu-lien's eyesight extends on a vertical scale from the highest heavens to the lowest hells, and his illumination fills the horizon in all directions. The nobility of sight is apparent in both the Chinese (*chao*) and English, "illumination," suggesting both a direct, unmediated vision and a brightness that dispels darkness and wipes out ignorance.[52]

[48] The seven "paths of enlightenment" (*chüeh-tao*) are probably the seven "constituents of enlightenment" (*chüeh-chih*, Skt.: *bodhyaṅga*). For an enumeration of them in scholastic sources, see MBDJ, pp. 1889a–90b.

[49] The three "outflows" or "remainders" (*lou*, Skt.: *āsrava*) are desire, existence, and ignorance. They signify attachment to the realm of form. See MBDJ, pp. 1700c–1701a.

[50] The three worlds are the worlds of desire, form, and no-form. In searching through these three worlds Mu-lien has searched the entire realm of birth-and-death.

[51] Translation from *Hui-ching Commentary*, T. 85:541b–c.

[52] Buddhas often emit rays of light before preaching, and bodhisattvas often use light to lead beings to salvation. See also Hans Jonas, "The Nobility of Sight: A Study in the Phenomenology of the Senses," *The Philosophy of the Body: Rejections of Cartesian Dualism*, ed. Stuart F. Spicker (Chicago: Quadrangle Books, 1970).

The Transformation Text on Mu-lien Saving His Mother employs a different style to convey the drama and cosmic significance of Mu-lien's journey. In this more popular rendition of the Mu-lien myth, Mu-lien travels not merely visually but physically to the world mountains, to the heavens and hells and nāga lairs of other worlds. It should be emphasized that there is not any contradiction between these two styles of cosmic travel, nor are the interests of different audiences necessarily exclusive. Furthermore, *The Transformation Text on Mu-lien Saving His Mother* includes *both* styles of travel, the visionary as well as the physical.[53]

The transformation text relates how Mu-lien uses his divine eye to look for where his parents may have been reborn. Unsuccessful, he embarks on a physical search of the cosmos, hoping to encounter bodily those who have thus far eluded his sight. He engages his shamanic powers of flight by hurling his begging bowl aloft and leaping after it:

> Mu-lien emerged from concentration
> And swiftly exercised his spiritual penetrations;
> His coming as quick as a thunderclap,
> His going like a gust of wind.
>
> . . . .
>
> Gaining freedom with his spiritual penetrations,
> He hurled his begging bowl and leapt into space;
> After just an instant
> He reached Brahmā's palace.[54]

This text portrays Mu-lien emerging from a state of meditation to begin a quest that will last for the duration of the performance. The quest carries Mu-lien to Brahmā's heaven, to the Buddha in Rājagṛha, through the various courts of hell, and eventually to the lowest of hells, where his mother suffers punishment for her sins. To travel to all of these levels of the cosmos, Mu-lien exercises the powers of the medium, which allow him to penetrate the karmic and physical barriers separating one plane from another. In this version of Mu-lien's quest, he activates the powers by tossing his bowl into the air and leaping into

---

[53] The Vinaya story (cited in Chapter Four) of Mu-lien's visit to his mother in Marīci's heaven also includes both meditative and physical journeys; *Ken-pen-shuo i-ch'ieh-yu-pu p'i-nai-yeh yao-shih (Mūlasarvāstivādavinayavastu)*, trans. I-ching (635–713), T. no. 1448, 24:16a–b.

[54] THPWC, p. 717; cf. Mair, trans., *Tun-huang Popular Narratives*, pp. 90–91. For similar accounts, see THPWC, pp. 729, 737, 739; Mair, trans., *Tun-huang Popular Narratives*, pp. 104, 112, 114.

space. This action begins the medium's journey. When he travels in this mode, he completes his trip—he successfully penetrates another level—almost instantaneously.

Such a homely item as an alms bowl is hardly incidental to the shaman's journey. The Buddha's twelve-ringed staff is particularly potent in helping its possessor break through obstructions and defeat hostile forces. In *The Transformation Text on Mu-lien Saving His Mother* Mu-lien borrows the Buddha's staff. In so doing he takes hold of the Buddha's awesome power, the power of the Buddhist holy man to venture into other realms and to bring deliverance to others:

> Having received the Buddha's mighty power, Mu-lien flung his body downwards, traveling swiftly as a winged arrow. In an instant, he arrived at the Avīci Hell.

Later, recounting his adventure to the Buddha, Mu-lien says:

> Receiving the Buddha's spiritual power, borrowing extra might, I was able to visit my dear mother in Avīci.[55]

Later in the tale, Mu-lien recites an incantation and rattles the Buddha's staff to decimate row after row of malevolent ogres.[56] In avadāna literature Mu-lien borrows both the Buddha's twelve-ringed staff and his seven-jeweled bowl as a way of gaining the spiritual powers necessary for visiting hell, while in other accounts of Mu-lien's travels it is the Buddha's cassock which gives him a boost in power.[57]

The Buddha's twelve-ringed staff might well have cosmological significance, since it represents a series of planes connected by a vertical

[55] THPWC, p. 730; cf. Mair, trans., *Tun-huang Popular Narratives*, p. 104; THPWC, p. 737; cf. Mair, trans., *Tun-huang Popular Narratives*, p. 112.

[56] THPWC, p. 730; Mair, trans., *Tun-huang Popular Narratives*, p. 105. This episode is discussed below.

[57] For the staff and bowl, see the avadāna fragment, *Mu-lien yüan-ch'i*, P. 2193, reproduced in THPWC, p. 704. In *Ken-pen-shuo i-ch'ieh-yu-pu p'i-nai-yeh yao-shih*, T. no. 1448, 24:16a–b, Mu-lien borrows the Buddha's cassock and the two of them together ascend to Marīci's heaven. In *The Transformation Text on the Subduing of Demons*, the Buddha's cassock gives Śāriputra the power needed to subdue demons; see *Chiang-mo pien-wen*, reproduced in THPWC, p. 381. In *The Journey to the West (Hsi-yu chi)* from Ming times, the Buddha gives the Tripiṭaka monk Hsüan-tsang his cassock, staff, and three tightening fillets. These items prevent the bearer from backsliding on the path to enlightenment, ward off poison and harm, and convert hostile demons to the Buddhist Path. The Buddha entrusts the items to Kuan-yin and asks her to bestow them on Tripiṭaka in Chapter Eight; the items are involved in numerous incidents after that. See Anthony C. Yü, trans., *The Journey to the West*, 4 vols. (Chicago: University of Chicago Press, 1977–83), 1:180–97 and passim.

axis. The staff might also be related to the swords and clubs often used in China during exorcisms performed by shamans.[58] The monk's robe signifies the authority of the Buddha and guarantees the continuity of his tradition, the robe transmitted to the sixth patriarch of Ch'an being the most notable example.[59] In contrast to the more abstract accounts of Mu-lien's journey, all of these symbols—bowl, staff, and robe—drive home the concrete side of the shaman's tour.

In addition to the meditative and visionary journeys portrayed in canonical and commentarial sources, in the popular tales discussed above Mu-lien embarks on a physical ecstasis. Freed from the usual constraints of space and time, Mu-lien reaches other worlds in a single stride or with the wave of an arm.[60] The corporeal details accentuate the physical side of shamanic travel. The shaman's powers are stressed in these accounts, his "might" and "supernatural power" being given concrete reference in such symbols as the robe, staff, and bowl. Together with the monkish portrayal of Mu-lien as meditator, these more popular representations of shamanic journeys cast additional, not necessarily fractious, light on the place of Mu-lien in medieval Chinese religion.

Mu-lien's Powers

In his travels Mu-lien exercises other powers usually associated with the shaman. Like the symbolism of his cosmic journeys, the language and style used to portray these powers appeal to several different audiences.

Mu-lien is equipped not only with a "divine eye" and a "divine ear," but also a "divine nose" by which he senses the odors and fragrances of other beings. An avadāna tale, for instance, relates how Mu-lien sat in meditation and, while in a contemplative state, saw a hungry ghost. Mu-lien simultaneously exercised his powers of vision (hungry ghosts are usually invisible or they reside in one of the hells) and also his supernormal powers of smell. The tale describes how Mu-lien

---

[58] For a description of the shaman's weapons see de Groot, *The Religious System of China*, 6:991–99.

[59] See Philip B. Yampolsky, *The Platform Sutra of the Sixth Patriarch* (New York: Columbia University Press, 1967), p. 133.

[60] Other stories show Mu-lien embarking on journeys by waving his arm; see the *Āgama* story cited in Chapter Four, T. 2:703c, 704b, 706c, 707a; and *The Mahāvastu*, trans. J. J. Jones, 3 vols., Sacred Books of the Buddhists, Vols. 17–19 (London: Luzac and Co., 1949–56), 1:46, 47.

sat with his legs crossed underneath a tree. Entering *samādhi*, he saw a hungry ghost. Its physical body was so smelly that it was impossible to get near it.[61]

Mu-lien's sharpened powers of perception, often exercised from a meditative state, allow him access to the sights, sounds, and smells of other worlds.

As noted in Chapter Four, numerous avadāna tales record Mu-lien's knowledge of the previous lives of hungry ghosts. This power, one of the "six spiritual penetrations" in the scheme of canonical Buddhism, is especially stressed in the avadāna literature, since stories in that genre draw a moral based on the unseen workings of karma. By contrast, knowledge of past incarnations is not stressed in any of the yü-lan-p'en myths; in these, it is the Buddha or Ch'ing-t'i herself who relates her uncharitable deeds in previous lives.

One last facet of shamanism mentioned in many accounts is Mu-lien's martial prowess, his ability to vanquish all comers by directly physical means or by intimidating them with his might. The word "*wei*" (which I have translated as "might" or "mighty"), is often used of Mu-lien (and sometimes of the Buddha and Sangha), indicating his ability "to inspire respectful fear."[62] This aspect of Mu-lien's power is especially stressed in the early Buddhist collections (e.g., the *Āgamas*), the apocryphal *Pure Land Yü-lan-p'en Sūtra*, and the Mu-lien transformation text.

Mu-lien's prowess as a warrior may well be a function of his mastery of the universal principles of change. In the Pure Land text, after his mother is reborn as a human being and reunited with her son, Mu-lien is so beside himself with joy that he issues fire and water from his body. He manifests in public the "eighteen transformations," which other *arhats* are technically capable of producing but rarely do.[63] Mu-lien is so thoroughly imbued with powers that are not by nature part of the system of Buddhist discipline that his energies seem to leak out almost against his will.

The *Āgama* story in which Mu-lien vanquishes Nanda and Upananda makes frequent reference to Mu-lien's "mighty power" (*wei-li*)

[61] *Chuan-chi po-yüan ching (Avadānaśataka)*, trans. Chih Ch'ien (ca. 220–252), T. no. 200, 4:223c.

[62] F. S. Couvreur, s.J., *Dictionnaire classique de la langue chinoise* (1890; reprint ed., T'ai-chung: Kuang-ch'i ch'u-pan-she, 1966), p. 206a.

[63] See *The Pure Land Yü-lan-p'en Sūtra*, ll. 32–33. On the "eighteen transformations" (*shih-pa pien*), see TFTT, p. 199c.

and "mighty spirituality" (*wei-shen*).[64] After changing into a fourteen-headed nāga and then into a tiny marauder, Mu-lien returns to his normal human form. The two nāga kings, themselves well accomplished in the arts of transformation, are especially amazed that a mere human being could so soundly defeat them. The nāgas exclaim:

> This is Mu-lien the *śramaṇa*, not a nāga king. How odd! How strange! He possesses great mighty power which enables him to do battle with the likes of us.[65]

Nor is Mu-lien simply a filial son in *The Transformation Text on Mu-lien Saving His Mother*. Here too he fights battles with opposing armies and manifests the awe-inspiring power of the shaman in very tangible ways. Taking hold of the Buddha's staff, Mu-lien wields the power of the Buddha:

> Mu-lien recited the Buddha's name like sands of the Ganges,
> [And said] "The hells are my original home";
> He wiped his tears in mid-air and shook the metal-ringed staff,
> And ghosts and spirits were mowed down on the spot like stalks
>   of hemp.[66]

CONCLUSIONS

Mu-lien's example illustrates a trend in Chinese religion that has until recently received little scholarly attention. As Buddhism and Taoism developed as institutional religions in the first several centuries A.D., they were perforce compelled to build upon a preexisting base. The "shamanistic substrate," as one scholar has called it, was an essential component of that indigenous background.[67] What better way to popularize enlightenment or immortality than by showing that the spirit medium resident in every village was, underneath it all, working for Buddhist or Taoist ends? Similarly, propagators of institutionalized religions in China were eager to show that the saints hallowed by their own traditions used the same methods as the local shaman.

The influence of shamanism on Taoism has not escaped the notice of some scholars. Discussing "the religion of the people," Kristofer Schipper writes:

[64] *Tseng-i a-han ching*, T. no. 125, 2:703c, 704a, 706c.

[65] Ibid., 2:704a.

[66] THPWC, p. 730; mostly following Mair, trans., *Tun-huang Popular Narratives*, p. 105.

[67] Piet van der Loon, "Les Origines rituelles du théâtre chinois," JA 265:1–2 (1977): 168.

It is indeed reluctantly, for lack of anything better, that I use the term "shamanism" improperly to take account of a socio-cultural fact broad-ranging, rich, poetical, and refined. If we were to limit ourselves to the references furnished by classical literature, we would ignore practically all popular cults. But Chinese shamanism has survived into our time, no doubt, as the poor relation of religion, but with enough vitality that we can recognize it once more. It is the *substrate* of the entire system of practices and beliefs of Taoism; it is its rival and, in modern China, its inseparable complement. In all epochs, Taoism defined itself first of all in relation to it.[68]

Taoist adepts have always demonstrated a strong interest in the magical powers of the shaman, modeling their actions on those of Lao-tzu, who, beginning in the Han dynasty, was believed to have changed bodily form numerous times.[69]

Regrettably, the history of Buddhism has rarely been read as a process of accommodation to the indigenous tradition of shamanism. Nevertheless, the influence of shamanism on Buddhism—from the bottom up, as it were—is undeniable. The same kind of shamanic influence evident in ghost festival mythology may also be seen in the selection of Buddhist texts for translation into Chinese: meditation texts dealing with supernormal powers were a first priority in the translation of Sanskrit works.[70] In the view of T'ang Yung-t'ung, Chinese interest in Buddhist meditation practices in the early period centered on supernatural powers:

[68] Schipper, *Le Corps taoïste*, p. 18.

[69] Ko Hung, writer on alchemy, practitioner of the arts of long life, and biographer of the mid-fourth century, notes several techniques for "penetrating the spiritual [realm]" (or "getting in touch with spirits," *t'ung-shen*) in his *Pao-p'u tzu*. These techniques include one-pointedness of mind and the ingestion of elixirs containing gold; *Pao-p'u tzu* (*nei-p'ien*, ch. 18), Ko Hung (ca. 277–357), Hsin-pien chu-tzu chi-ch'eng, Vol. 4 (Taipei: Shih-chieh shu-chü, 1978), pp. 93, 94. Through his comprehension of the Way of change, Lao-tzu travels throughout the cosmos in accord with its greater patterns. According to the *Lao-tzu pien-hua ching* (*Classic of the Metamorphoses of Lao-tzu*), Lao-tzu can "make himself brilliant or somber, sometimes present, sometimes gone, he can become large or small, coil up or stretch himself out, raise or lower himself, extend vertically or horizontally, go forwards or backwards"; translated in Anna K. Seidel, *Le Divinisation de Lao tseu dans le Taoïsme des Han*, Publications de l'Ecole Française d'Extrême-Orient, Vol. 68 (Paris: Ecole Française d'Extrême-Orient, 1969), p. 63. See also Robinet, "Metamorphosis," pp. 39–48.

[70] See T'ang Yung-t'ung, *Han wei liang-chin nan-pei-ch'ao fo-chiao shih* (reprint ed.; Taipei: Ting-wen shu-chü, 1976), pp. 95–98; and Murakami, "*Kosō den* no shin'i ni tsuite," pp. 4, 16 n. 3.

CHAPTER 5

According to the Buddhist Dharma, there are two results of meditation and concentration. The first consists of attaining release
and entering *nirvāṇa*. The second is obtaining spiritual penetrations. Most of the meditators of the Han and Wei emphasized the
spiritual penetrations.[71]

Further, many Buddhist figures popular in medieval times were well
known for their practice of shamanic arts, including prophesy, healing,
and spirit journeys.[72]

Influence in the other direction—the Buddhist contribution to the
development of ecstatic religion in China—is no less important. While
shamans may well be "holders of specific gifts of the body and spirit,"[73]
in the Buddhist tradition their charisma is not essentially antithetical to
institutional control. Specifically, one acquires the "spiritual penetrations" by following a formalized technique of meditation. The shaman's career is carefully regulated: he undergoes a special course of
training symbolized by levels of *dhyāna*. Progress along the path is
judged by norms recorded in the narrative, scholastic, and technical literature of Buddhism. This formalized technology of meditation is recognized not only by a religious elite, but also by the unlettered, who
see Mu-lien exercising his powers from a meditating position and who
hear of his dependence on the superior might of the Buddha.

We need not assume a dichotomy between the two different kinds of
representation given Mu-lien in the mythology of the ghost festival.
Some nuances of Mu-lien's role appeal to members of the Buddhist establishment, government officials, and other literati, while some of his
attributes appeal to nonspecialists—those who belong neither to a privileged social class nor to a distinctive religious group. It may well be his
versatility, his ability to combine different interests in a single reper-
toire, that accounts for Mu-lien's appeal at all levels of Chinese society.

At one end of the continuum Mu-lien plays to an audience of commoners. His miracle-working powers attest to his divinity, while his
physical labors mark him as human. His frolics provoke the Buddha to
chastise his mischievous pursuit of the magical arts. As a shaman who
makes contact with the spirit of his deceased mother, he fulfills an am-
bition common to all classes in traditional China, where the relation

[71] T'ang, *Fo-chiao shih*, p. 144.

[72] Fo-t'u-teng (ca. 310) and Wan Hui (ca. 705) are notable Buddhist exemplars of this
skill. See Arthur F. Wright, "Fo-t'u-teng: A Biography," HJAS 11:3–4 (December
1948):340, 350, 354. Wan Hui is reported to have traveled over ten thousand *li* in one day;
see *Sung kao-seng chuan*, Tsan-ning (919–1001), T. no. 2061, 50:823c–24c.

[73] Max Weber, *From Max Weber: Essays in Sociology*, trans. and eds. H. H. Gerth and
C. Wright Mills (New York: Oxford University Press, 1946), p. 245.

between the living and the "dead" is of paramount concern. The mythology of the ghost festival serves to express these popular interests and to reiterate the unruly aspects of shamanism in Chinese religion.

At the other end of the continuum, Mu-lien's performance is oriented toward the upholders of state and Sangha authority. The Chinese government always attempted to control, only rarely to prohibit, the exercise of shamanism. Mediums and their masters performed in state-sponsored temples under imperial patronage. And for those who viewed their Buddhism as a distinguishing mark in Chinese society, Mu-lien's power was rooted in his experience of meditation and was exercised for the benefit of all sentient beings. The monastic establishment considered Mu-lien and his type to be exemplars of Buddhist practice. In expressing the values embraced by both the Sangha and the state, the myth of Mu-lien gave voice to the ideals of institutionalized religion in China.

Mu-lien secured a central place in Chinese religion because he combined in one person forms of shamanism acceptable to different classes of society. His journeys were simultaneously physical and ethereal, his powers both martial and figurative. Mu-lien linked two poles of Chinese society, just as he served as the medium between two different worlds.

SIX

The Cosmology of
the Ghost Festival

MU-LIEN was not simply a world traveler and invoker of spirits. He was also a teacher, and the subject he taught was the layout of the worlds he visited. Fa-hsien (ca. 399–416) explains:

> Each of the *arhats* among the disciples of the Buddha was best at one activity. Śāriputra, for instance, was best at wisdom, taking delight in preaching the subtle, wondrous Dharma. Mu-lien was best at shamanic travel [literally, "spiritual feet"]. He often rode the spiritual penetrations along the six paths of rebirth, viewing the good and evil retribution suffered by sentient beings and returning to explain it to humans.[1]

While Mu-lien may have been unique in possessing the power to travel to other realms of the cosmos, he never tried to keep his adventures secret. As Fa-hsien suggests, Mu-lien publicized his forays widely, using his own experience of rebirth and karmic retribution as the basis for his teachings.

This chapter explores the "worldview" or "cosmology" that Mu-lien taught. Such terms are used advisedly, since the worldview that Mu-lien teaches is not spelled out in a separate philosophical treatise, nor is it formulated in a clean doctrinal package. Rather, it is expressed in the different genres of yü-lan-p'en literature, and it is assumed in the performance of ghost festival rituals. Although it never takes the form of explicit tenets of belief, the cosmological system presents a sophisticated explanation of evil and a consistent framework of ethics.

This chapter takes most of its details from *The Transformation Text on Mu-lien Saving His Mother*, since that text describes Mu-lien's travels in the greatest detail. After recounting the cosmology of the transformation text I shall then trace its history, looking both backward and forward in time. Viewed strictly in historical terms, the cosmology reflected in the transformation text combines elements drawn from both

[1] *Tsa-tsang ching*, Fa-hsien (ca. 399–416), T. no. 745, 17:557b.

168

indigenous Chinese traditions and Indian Buddhist sources. But in China these two traditions remained separate only briefly; they appear fully synthesized in the worldview of *The Transformation Text on Mu-lien Saving His Mother*, a synthesis that had probably been achieved a few centuries before the first celebration of the ghost festival. In chronological terms a schizophrenic reading of medieval Chinese cosmology, seeing it as the grafting of Buddhist branches onto an inhospitable Chinese trunk, is simply wrong, at least after the fourth century. I hope to avoid any artificial bifurcation of the worldview of Chinese folk religion, a sphere in which the distinction between canonical Buddhism and indigenous traditions—or between Great Tradition and Little Tradition—had little relevance.[2]

Since this chapter is concerned primarily with the underworld, a brief discussion of Chinese terms for the underworld may be in order. Early texts refer to the "yellow springs" (*huang-ch'üan*) as a source of life located underground. By the third century B.C. the term denoted the underground residence of the deceased: "those who are killed go to the yellow springs; they die but do not perish."[3] By the beginning of the common era, many texts refer to Mount T'ai (T'ai-shan, in present-day Shantung) as the abode of the dead. Known also as the "Eastern Peak" (*tung-yüeh*), Mount T'ai was viewed as the source of light and life. It was the place where the spirits of the dead gathered and the

[2] My attempt to give an historical account of the cosmology of the ghost festival must be regarded as merely tentative. The primary sources for such a study are quite scattered: transformation texts, funerary inscriptions and prayers, biographies, and collections of folklore. While Buddhologists have done much work on the cosmological systems in canonical and scholastic sources, their accounts apply more to the theoretical monk of the Great Tradition than to the vast majority of Chinese people. See Iwamoto Yutaka, *Bukkyō setsuwa kenkyū*, Vol. 4, *Jigoku meguri no bungaku* (Tokyo: Kaimei shoten, 1979), pp. 200–224; Willibald Kirfel, *Die Kosmographie der Inder nach den Quellen dargestellt* (Bonn: Kurt Schroeder, 1920), pp. 178–207; Randy Kloetzli, *Buddhist Cosmology: From Single World System to Pure Land: Science and Theology in the Images of Motion and Light* (Delhi: Motilal Banarsidas, 1983); Louis de La Vallée Poussin, "Cosmogony and Cosmology (Buddhist)," *Encyclopaedia of Religion and Ethics*, 13 vols., ed. James Hastings (Edinburgh: T. and T. Clark, 1912), 4:129–38; Alicia Matsunaga, *The Buddhist Philosophy of Assimilation: The Historical Development of the Honji-Suijaku Theory* (Rutland: Tuttle and Co., 1969), pp. 40–59; Daigan and Alicia Matsunaga, *The Buddhist Concept of Hell* (New York: Philosophical Library, 1972); and Sadakata Akira, *Shumisen to gokuraku: bukkyō no uchūkan* (Tokyo: Kōdansha, 1973). The only book-length study of popular Chinese cosmology is Sawada Mizuho's *Jigoku hen*, which outlines afterlife concepts in medieval and modern times. I shall draw frequently on this pioneering work; *Jigoku hen: chūgoku no meikai setsu* (Kyoto: Hōzōkan, 1968); see also Michihata Ryōshū, *Chūgoku bukkyō shisō shi no kenkyū* (Kyoto: Heiryakuji shoten, 1979), pp. 78–188.

[3] MDKJ 47926.572, quoting the *Kuan-tzu*.

site where the emperor performed the *feng* and *shan* sacrifices of Chinese state religion. Chang Hua (232–300) writes:

> Mount T'ai is also called Heaven's grandson, meaning that he is the grandson of [August] Heaven, Emperor [on High]. He is in charge of summoning people's *hun* and *p'o*. He is in the East, the originator and completer of all things; hence he knows the length of people's lives.[4]

By the third or fourth century A.D. the Magistrate of Mount T'ai occupied an important position in the bureaucracy that administered the laws of karma: he assigned deceased spirits to their next realm of rebirth.[5]

In yü-lan-p'en literature the most common term referring to the underworld is "*ti-yü*," which may be translated more literally as "earthly (or subterranean) prison." Tao-shih (d. 683) explains the two components of the term, noting that "subterranean" refers to what lies under the continent of Jambudvīpa, connoting the lowest of all realms of rebirth, while "prison" implies restraint or lack of freedom, suggesting that existence there is devoid of joy and happiness.[6] "Ti-yü" is often used as a translation of the Sanskrit term for hell, *naraka*, meaning "devoid of happiness." In this study I translate "ti-yü" as "hell" or "hells."[7]

THE COSMOLOGY OF *The Transformation Text on Mu-lien Saving His Mother*

In theory Mu-lien's powers enable him to teach the layout of the entire realm of the six paths of rebirth as they are defined in Buddhist sources: rebirth as a god in the heavens, as a human on earth, as an *asura*, as an animal, as a hungry ghost, or as a hell dweller. (Sometimes the *asuras* are not included and only five paths are specified.) Kumārajīva writes:

[4] *Po-wu chih*, Chang Hua (232–300), in *Chih-hai*, Pai-pu ts'ung-shu chi-ch'eng, No. 54 (Taipei: I-wen yin-shu-kuan, 1967), ch. 6, p. 4r. Cf. Edouard Chavannes, *Le T'ai Chan: essaie de monographie d'un culte chinois*, Annales du Musée Guimet, Vol. 21 (Paris: Ernest Leroux, 1910), p. 406.

[5] For studies of Mount T'ai, see Chavannes, ibid.; Ono Shihei, "Taisan kara hōto e," *Bunka* 27:2 (1963):80–111; and Sakai Tadao, "Taisan shinkō no kenkyū," *Shichō* 7:2 (1937):70–118.

[6] *Fa-yüan chu-lin*, T. no. 2122, 53:322b.

[7] For the most part I shall follow Chinese usage in not distinguishing between the purgatorial realms (e.g., the ten courts of the underworld) through which all spirits must pass on their way to rebirth and the hells proper, the tortuous prisons further underground in which only those who have committed evil acts are reborn.

What the divine eye sees: sentient beings and all things in the six terrestial and subterrestial paths. Whether near or far, gross or subtle, there is no form that the divine eye cannot illuminate.[8]

Yü-lan-p'en literature, however, focuses only on the lower reaches of the cosmos, especially on the paths of hungry ghost and hell dweller into which Mu-lien's mother has been reborn. The canonical sūtras summarily describe Ch'ing-t'i's condition as a hungry ghost: she is hungry, she is so thin that her skin hangs off her bones, and the food offering sent by Mu-lien bursts into flames as soon as it touches her lips.[9] The Pure Land Yü-lan-p'en Sūtra varies the story only slightly: when other hungry ghosts see the bowl of food Mu-lien has sent to his mother, they beg Ch'ing-t'i to share it with them, but her greed remains so strong that she sits on top of the bowl to prevent them from getting even one grain of rice.[10]

In yü-lan-p'en literature—in fact in medieval Chinese literature broadly speaking—it is The Transformation Text on Mu-lien Saving His Mother from the Dark Regions that provides the most detailed and edifying descriptions of the underworld. The transformation text (pien-wen) spares no detail in relating Mu-lien's descent through the horrible chambers of hell, and it follows Mu-lien and his mother as they move upward in the scheme of rebirth, finally reaching the heavens. I summarize Mu-lien's and Ch'ing-t'i's travels below.[11]

The story in the transformation text begins with a quick account of how Ch'ing-t'i's selfish actions in a previous life led to her rebirth in Avīci Hell. By this narrative device Mu-lien's mother is placed in the most horrid and the most distant hell, the one in which any filial son

---

[8] Ta chih-tu lun, Kumārajīva (350–409), T. no. 1509, 25:98a; Etienne Lamotte, trans., Le Traité de la grand vertu de sagesse de Nāgārjuna (Mahāprajñāpāramitāśāstra), 5 vols. (Louvain-la-Neuve: Institut Orientaliste, 1949–80), p. 330. See also Yüan-chao Commentary, Z. 1, 35:2, p.115ra. On the "six paths of rebirth" (liu-ch'ü or liu-tao), see OBDJ, pp. 1837c–38a. For important studies of their place in art and literature, see Paul Mus, La Lumière sur les six voies: tableau de la transmigration bouddhique (Paris: Travaux et Mémoires de l'Institut d'Ethnologie, 1939); and William R. LaFleur, The Karma of Words: Buddhism and the Literary Arts in Medieval Japan (Berkeley: University of California Press, 1983), pp. 26–59. Like early Indian Buddhist texts, Chinese sources from monastic and folk milieux refer sometimes to five paths and sometimes to six.

[9] The Sūtra on Offering Bowls to Repay Kindness, T. no. 686, 16:780a; The Yü-lan-p'en Sūtra, T. no. 685, 16:779b.

[10] The Pure Land Yü-lan-p'en Sūtra, in Jan Jaworski, "L'Avalambana Sūtra de la terre pure," Monumenta Serica 1 (1935–36): ll. 97–100.

[11] Ta Mu-chien-lien ming-chien chiu-mu pien-wen, THPWC, pp. 714–55; Victor Mair, trans., Tun-huang Popular Narratives (Cambridge: Cambridge University Press, 1983), pp. 87–121.

would least expect his parents to be reborn. The audience is kept in suspense for over one-half of the tale as Mu-lien searches first the heavens and then the hells for his dear mother.

Mu-lien first ascends to Brahmā's palace, a heaven located above the Heaven of Thirty-Three and above Maitreya's Tuṣita Heaven, though still within the world of form. Here Mu-lien finds his father. Beings in this heaven are still subject to the laws of birth and death, but they enjoy many pleasures and few pains. Satisfied that his deceased father now leads a happy life, Mu-lien pushes on in search of his mother.

The transformation text next shows Mu-lien passing through the gates of the yellow springs and descending to the underworld, to "the dark roads" (ming-lu) of Jambudvīpa. With neither a sibyl nor Beatrice as guide, Mu-lien first encounters a group of hungry ghosts who are unable to return to the human world because of a bureaucratic error. They know nothing about his mother, so Mu-lien leaves them and goes to the great King Yama (Yen-lo wang), from whom he hopes to gain news of his mother's whereabouts.

Mu-lien expects Yama to have passed sentence on his mother, since all people who perform some good and some bad actions during their lifetime are taken to King Yama for judgment after death. The king of the underworld is honored to have such a holy man as Mu-lien in his court, and he soon has all of his officers and assistants working on the case of Mu-lien's mother. The first figure in Yama's court to provide some information is Ti-tsang (Skt.: Kṣitigarbha) Bodhisattva. He apprises Mu-lien of the likelihood that his mother is in hell due to the number of sins that she committed in her lifetime.[12]

King Yama next summons three other officers, the Karma Official, the Examiner of Fate, and the Officer of Records, who are all administrative assistants in charge of the records of sinners sent to the hells for punishments. The Karma Official reports:

> Three years have already passed since Lady Ch'ing-t'i died. The casebooks on the adjudication of her sins are all contained in a volume of the Magistrate of Mount T'ai, the Recording Office of Affairs of Heaven's offices.[13]

King Yama then hands Mu-lien over to yet another group of functionaries, the Two Pages of Good and Evil [Rebirth]. These boys usually act as messengers between the office of the Magistrate of Mount T'ai

---

[12] Ti-tsang's role in the plot structure appears redundant, since the Buddha had already told Mu-lien that his mother had been reborn in Avīci Hell.

[13] THPWC, p. 721; Mair, trans., Tun-huang Popular Narratives, p. 95.

and the underworld ruled by King Yama. King Yama instructs them to escort Mu-lien to another court of hell, the one ruled by the General of the Five Paths (Wu-tao chiang-chün).

En route to the General's court, Mu-lien crosses the great river which runs through the underworld, the Nai-ho (which, as Victor Mair suggests, might best be translated as "The Wathellwedo River" to convey the Chinese pun).[14] On the banks of the river stand groups of people who have recently died. Repenting the evil they committed while alive, they lament their fate and bemoan the uselessness of their descendants' mortuary offerings. Some ghosts have removed their clothes and are beginning to cross the river, and picture texts dating from the early tenth century portray recently deceased people being forced by ox-headed gaolers to cross the river during the second week after death.[15]

Having crossed the Wathellwedo River, Mu-lien arrives at the last barrier before entering the hells, the gate ruled by the General (also called the Spirit or Ghost) of the Five Paths. All beings sentenced to the hells must pass through this gate, and the general, as Officer of Names, asks his assistants about Ch'ing-t'i. They report that Ch'ing-t'i passed through their court three years before, having been summoned by a warrant from Avīci Hell.

At this point in the narrative Mu-lien has not yet entered the realm of hell proper. The subterranean prisons for the punishment of evil deeds still lie ahead. The infernal regions discussed thus far—the court of King Yama and his aides, the Wathellwedo River, the court of the General of the Five Paths—constitute a transitional space. All of the souls whom Mu-lien encounters in these regions are going somewhere, they are en route from death to their next assigned rebirth in one of the hells. Homesick, dragged away from their loved ones by the minions of death, they are yet unsure of their final destination. The administration of the underworld has not finished adjudicating their cases so they simply wait, as fearful of punishment as they are sure of its inevitability.

[14] Mair, trans., *Tun-huang Popular Narratives*, p. 235, n. to l. 309; cf. Iriya Yoshitaka, "Dai Mokkenren meikan kyūbo henbun," *Bukkyō bungaku shū*, ed. Iriya Yoshitaka (Tokyo: Heibonsha, 1975), pp. 7–8, n. 28.

[15] See Tokushi Yūshō and Ogawa Kan'ichi, "*Jūō shōshichi kyō* santoken no kōzō," *Seiiki bunka kenkyū*, 6 vols., ed. Seiiki bunka kenkyūkai (Tokyo: Hōzōkan, 1958–63), 5:264–91; also reproduced in Ogawa, *Bukkyō bunka shi kenkyū* (Kyoto: Nagata bunshōdō, 1973), pp. 80–154. These picture texts describe the torments undergone by the deceased in the ten courts of hell and prescribe Buddhistic sacrifices during the seven-day periods following death. I discuss these texts and their significance in greater detail below.

The bureaucratic machinery supposed to move people through the courts of hell is far from swift. The paper work involved in processing the dead is, as it were, mountainous. Mu-lien's inquiry concerning his mother's whereabouts gives rise to a search of the records kept at Mount T'ai, in King Yama's court, in the court of the General of the Five Paths, and in the hells. The narrative portrays a bureaucratic system made even more unwieldy by its extensiveness. The transformation text describes a hierarchy reaching from the heavens down into the hells, including even gods who have no direct bearing on the plot. Ti-tsang Bodhisattva, for instance, tells Mu-lien something that he had already heard from the Buddha, that his mother has been reborn in one of the hells. It appears that the narrators of the Mu-lien transformation text are as concerned with mapping out a convincing and familiar map of the underworld as they are with following the course of a unilinear *Heilsgeschichte*.

The Transformation Text on Mu-lien Saving His Mother continues with Mu-lien's passage into the hells. The tale describes Mu-lien's general impression of the hells:

Mu-lien's tears fell, his thoughts wandered aimlessly,
The karmic retribution of sentient beings is like being tossed in the
    wind;
His dear mother had sunk into a realm of suffering,
Her *hun* and *p'o* had by that time long since dissipated.

Iron disks continuously plunged into her body from out of the air;
Fierce fires, at all times, were burning beneath her feet;
Every place on her chest and belly had been stripped to shreds,
Every inch of her bones and flesh had charred to a pulp.

Bronze-colored crows pecked at her heart ten thousand times over,
Molten iron poured on top of her head for a thousand turns;
You might well ask whether the forest of swords up ahead were the
    most painful,
But how could it compare with the cleaving mill which chops men's
    waists in two?[16]

With some trepidation, Mu-lien advances to the first hell to inquire about Ch'ing-t'i. The warden of the first hell replies that his chamber contains only male inmates, and that Mu-lien should continue his search in the hells further down the line.

[16] THPWC, p. 725; mostly following Mair, trans., *Tun-huang Popular Narratives*, p. 99.

Next Mu-lien enters the Knife Hill and Sword Forest Hell. People who destroy or steal property belonging to the Sangha are reborn in this hell, where they are forced to climb up a hill covered with knives and to walk through a forest densely packed with swords, getting horribly sliced up in the process. Ch'ing-t'i is not in this hell or in the next one that Mu-lien visits, the Copper Pillar and Iron Bed Hell. In the first of many tortures, residents of this hell are laid on iron beds and have nails driven through their bodies, while others have their hands bound together so that they embrace hot copper pillars that burn away their chests.

The warden of the next hell informs Mu-lien that his mother resides in Avīci Hell, and a demonlike *yakṣa* prince advises Mu-lien to quit his search, citing the inexorable torments of Avīci. Daunted by the *yakṣa's* description of Avīci's tortures, yet unwilling to give up his quest to save his mother, Mu-lien returns to the Buddha for help. The Buddha provides moral support and material aid in the form of his metal-ringed staff.

Armed with the Buddha's staff, Mu-lien darts back down to the entrance to Avīci, the deepest of the hells. When the ogre guards of Avīci stand in his way, the Buddha's disciple topples them all with a shake of his staff. The text relates Mu-lien's entry into Avīci:

Mu-lien walked forward and came to a hell. When he was something over a hundred paces away from it, he was sucked in by the fiery gases and nearly tumbled over. It was Avīci Hell with lofty walls of iron which were so immense that they reached to the clouds. Swords and lances bristled in ranks, knives and spears clustered in rows. Sword trees reached upward for a thousand fathoms with a clattering flourish as their needle-sharp points brushed together. Knife mountains soared ten thousand rods in a chaotic jumble of interconnecting cliffs and crags. Fierce fires throbbed, seeming to leap about the entire sky with a thunderous roar. Sword wheels whirled, seeming to brush the earth with the dust of starry brightness. Iron snakes belched fire, their scales bristling on all sides. Copper dogs breathed smoke, barking impetuously in every direction. Metal thorns descended chaotically from midair, piercing the chests of the men. Awls and augers flew by every which way, gouging the backs of the women. Iron rakes flailed at their eyes, causing red blood to flow to the west. Copper pitchforks jabbed at their loins until white fat oozed to the east. Thereupon, they were made to crawl up the knife mountains and enter the furnace of coals. Their skulls were smashed to bits, their

175

bones and flesh decomposed; tendons and skin snapped, liver and gall broke. Ground flesh spurted and splattered beyond the four gates; congealed blood drenched and drooked the pathways which run through the black clods of hell. With wailing voices, they called out to heaven—moan, groan. The roar of thunder shakes the earth—rumble, bumble. Up above are clouds and smoke which tumble, jumble; down below are iron spears which jangle-tangle. Goblins with arrows for feathers chattered-scattered; birds with copper beaks wildly-widely called. There were more than several ten thousands of gaolers and all were ox-headed and horse-faced.[17]

Mu-lien advances into this pit of interminable torment by breaking down the gates. Impressed by his power, jailers politely escort him to the warden of Avīci. Mu-lien informs the warden that he has come in search of his mother, and the warden himself expedites Mu-lien's request by going personally to each of the seven compartments of Avīci to ask if Ch'ing-t'i is there. Finally, in the seventh and last compartment, where she is nailed to a steel bed with forty-nine long spikes, Ch'ing-t'i meekly answers the warden's call.

Mother and son are finally reunited in a bittersweet embrace. Ch'ing-t'i tearfully confesses her evil actions in her previous life and laments the inevitable recompense of all acts, good or bad. Blinded by devotion and pity, Mu-lien offers to suffer the punishments of Avīci in his mother's place so that she might be released. The warden of Avīci rejects the offer, explaining that compassion and familial sentiment cannot displace the law of karma; all decisions come from the Impartial King, and each person must suffer retribution for his or her own acts.

Mu-lien is so distraught at the sight of his mother being led back to her compartment in Avīci that he sobs and pummels himself into unconsciousness. When he awakes he flies off to the Buddha to explain his mother's terrible plight: since he alone is powerless, perhaps the World-Honored One might intercede to liberate her. Beseeching the Buddha to provide illumination, Mu-lien champions the importance of familial affection, likening the Buddha to the "compassionate father and mother of all sentient beings."[18] The Buddha responds by offering a short homily on the inescapable effects of karma; then he himself embarks for Avīci to save Mu-lien's mother. Accompanied by gods, spirits, kings, and guardians, the Buddha utterly transforms the hells,

---

[17] THPWC, p. 731; following Mair's reconstruction and translation of this difficult and often corrupt passage; *Tun-huang Popular Narratives*, pp. 105–6.

[18] THPWC, p. 737.

changing knife hills into lapis lazuli and liberating all of the sinners being tortured there.

While everyone else in the hells gains rebirth in the heavens, Mu-lien's mother is reborn as a hungry ghost. Her sins were so nefarious, it seems, that she can move upward in the paths of rebirth only one step at a time. The transformation text next shows Mu-lien's frustrated attempts to bring relief to his mother: the food he sends her turns to fire, as does the Ganges River when he leads her there for a drink.

Ch'ing-t'i becomes a black dog in Rājagṛha in her next rebirth, which Mu-lien secures by providing yü-lan-p'en offerings in the ceremony specially instituted by the Buddha. In contrast to the canonical sources, in which the establishment of the ghost festival constitutes the climax of the story, the transformation text includes the festival almost as an afterthought, as one more device included hurriedly in the denouement after the Buddha has already rescued Ch'ing-t'i from Avīci Hell.

In fact two more ritual acts are needed in the *pien-wen* before Mu-lien's mother takes her place in the heavens. Ch'ing-t'i, in the body of a black dog, chants and makes repentance in front of a *stūpa* in Rājagṛha. The merit from this act allows her to slough the dogskin and emerge as a human being again. Thus, Mu-lien's mother is finally released from the torments of rebirth in the three lower paths of hell dweller, hungry ghost, and animal.

Ch'ing-t'i and Mu-lien then perform a second act of devotion by circumambulating the Buddha three times. The Buddha examines Ch'ing-t'i's karmic situation and determines her recompense to be complete. At this, gods, goddesses, and nāgas welcome her to a happy rebirth in the Heaven of Thirty-Three.

My retelling of the story in this chapter has dwelled at length on Mu-lien's odyssey from one magistrate to the next in the various courts of hell; slightly less space was devoted to Mu-lien's travel in the various hells and very little space at all to his mother's rebirth in the Heaven of Thirty-Three. The varying degrees of elaboration in my recounting are modeled after the *pien-wen* narrative, which focuses almost exclusively on the infernal bureaucracy and the lowest paths of rebirth.

The transformation text devotes most of its narrative to the purgatorial courts of the underworld and to the sufferings of those beings reborn in the hells, which suggests that the map of the territory that Mu-lien covers in his quest—the picture of the underworld around which the narrative is constructed—is at least as important as the motivation and goals of that quest. The cosmographic aspect of Mu-lien's journey in the *pien-wen* cannot be overstressed, especially in light of the recog-

177

nition, made only in the past few years, of the visual or scenic half of this genre of storytelling. The center of activity of the cosmic map drawn in the story is the underworld: the subterranean court of King Yama, the sinners being forced to cross the Wathellwedo River, the critical passage guarded by the General of the Five Paths, the instruments of torture used in all the hells, and the especially gruesome tortures of Avīci. Far from teaching the evanescence of life and the inevitability of rebirth in one of the six paths, the popular entertainment impresses upon its audience the torments and tortures of an underworld that seems horrifyingly permanent.

All paths of rebirth shown in the transformation text are governed by the laws of karmic retribution and administered by a bureaucracy staffed by bodhisattvas, gods, kings, generals, magistrates, scribes, messengers, wardens, demons, and ghosts. While some components of the system are drawn from indigenous Chinese traditions and others from the myths and rituals of Indian and Central Asian Buddhism, what must be stressed above all is that the law and its adminstrators are part of one indissoluble framework. In popular religion the "yellow springs," a term for the underworld used in China since at least the third century B.C., denotes the same realm as the "dark paths of Jambudvīpa," a term of Buddhist provenance. Similarly, Ti-tsang Bodhisattva, a relative newcomer to the Middle Kingdom, administers precisely the same laws as does his superior, the autochthonous god of Mount T'ai. Both are part of the same bureaucracy.

Even the Buddha's compassion and unequalled power do not negate the rule of karmic law. The yü-lan-p'en myth certainly presents an ambiguous message concerning karmic retribution, but the ambiguity in no way pits an essentially *Buddhist* law of karma against an unchanging *Chinese* preference for the special treatment of family members. In the *pien-wen*, Śākyamuni himself descends to Avīci Hell to liberate its prisoners from the karmic fate to which they have consigned themselves. The officers of hell also make special exceptions for the preeminent disciple of the Buddha, Mu-lien, who shares some of the Buddha's power and compassion; the bureaucrats investigate Ch'ing-t'i's case with unusual dispatch, treating her son as an honored guest.

But these examples of the bending of the causal law are never clearcut. In fact, as exceptions they tend to confirm the overarching law according to which each individual suffers recompense for his or her own deeds. Like all sentient beings, Ch'ing-t'i must pass through the gate guarded by the General of the Five Paths and she must suffer in Avīci according to her actions in her previous life. Since her sins were more serious than most people's, she can move upward in the system of rebirth only one stage at a time, while the other inmates of Avīci Hell are reborn directly in the heavens. Even the Buddha's power and compassion are not strong enough to cancel Ch'ing-t'i's karmic burden. In the last episode of the transformation text, the World-Honored One can only survey her karmic record to certify that she herself has paid off all her karmic debts. Thus, even the Buddha plays a functional and subordinate role in the administration of the laws of karma.

GHOST FESTIVAL COSMOLOGY IN CONTEXT

In some respects the cosmology of *The Transformation Text on Mu-lien Saving His Mother* diverges little from the worldview of medieval Chinese religion. Its hells are run according to the same bureaucratic logic evident in China for over two thousand years, and its portrayal of King Yama merely adds a new name to the popular vision of the underworld. But in other respects the cosmology of the transformation text articulates concepts and images unprecedented in Chinese religion. Its hells prefigure the system that later became the basic worldview of Chinese popular religion, and its references to Ti-tsang Bodhisattva reflect new developments in folk belief.

Turning from a synchronic to a diachronic analysis, this section places the cosmology of the ghost festival in the context of Chinese religion. While my account does not a priori exclude a consideration of the worldview of "elite" Chinese religion—such a concept being at best propaedeutic—it does take most of its data from sources on which Buddhist monks and other literati have usually cast a doubtful eye.

The Enumeration of Hells

The Transformation Text on Mu-lien Saving His Mother mentions several distinct courts and passages in the underworld, including King Yama's court, the Magistrate of Mount T'ai, the Wathellwedo River, and the gate of the General of the Five Paths. It also pictures four separate hells through which Mu-lien travels: a hell in which only men reside, the Knife Hill and Sword Forest Hell, the Copper Pillar and Iron Bed Hell, and Avīci Hell with at least seven compartments. Considered separately these elements of the eighth-century transformation text offer few innovations in Chinese religion. Considered together as a system, however, they represent an important stage in the development of Chinese cosmology.

The enumeration of hells in the transformation text differs from both earlier and later cosmology. Specifically, it does not contain any

179

of the standard numbers of hells common in sixth-century China: systems of five, eight, eighteen, thirty, or sixty-four hells. Its purgatorial courts remain unnumbered and sometimes indistinct, and it contains four compartments of hell proper, also unnumbered. But it also differs from the system that started to become popular in the tenth century. This later system contains ten separate purgatorial courts and remains a distinctive feature of Chinese culture even in modern times.

The encyclopedia compiled by Pao-ch'ang in the early sixth century, *Ching-lü i-hsiang (Different Aspects of the Sūtras and the Vinaya)*, provides a convenient summary of the hell systems current in China prior to the date of *The Transformation Text on Mu-lien Saving His Mother*. Pao-ch'ang's encyclopedia quotes from the *Wen ti-yü ching (Sūtra of Questions on Hell)*, which probably dates from the late second century. *The Sūtra of Questions on Hell* contains a list of sixty-four hells,[19] while another source quoted by Pao-ch'ang, the *Ching tu san-mei ching (Sūtra on the Samādhi of Purity and Deliverance)*, contains a list of thirty hells.[20] Pao-ch'ang also cites fifth-century sources with lists of eighteen hells and of eight hells.[21] And sources from the Taoist canon contain systems of nine and of twenty-four hells.[22]

[19] *Ching-lü i-hsiang*, T. no. 2121, 53:267a–68b. The *Wen ti-yü ching*, in one *chüan*, is also called the *Wen ti-yü shih ching*. It does not survive as a separate work. Extracts from it are cited in *Ching-lü i-hsiang* and in other T'ang Buddhist encyclopedias. All catalogues attribute its authorship to K'ang Chü in the year 187; see *Ta-t'ang nei-tien lu*, Tao-hsüan (596–667), T. no. 2149, 55:224c; *Ta-chou k'an-ting chung-ching mu-lu*, Ming-ch'üan (ca. 695), T. no. 2153, 55:415a; *K'ai-yüan shih-chiao mu-lu*, Chih-sheng (ca. 669–740), T. no. 2154, 55:483a and 641c. See also Tokiwa Daijō, *Go-kan yori sō-sei ni itaru yakkyō sōroku* (1938; reprint ed., Tokyo: Kokusho kankōkai, 1973), p. 531.

[20] *Ching-lü i-hsiang*, T. 53:259a–b. Catalogues list four different translations of the *Ching tu san-mei ching*, ranging from one *chüan* to four *chüan*: 1) Translation by Chih-yen (ca. 394–427), and Pao-yün (376–449), *Ta-t'ang nei-tien lu*, T. 55:258a; 2) Translation by Guṇabhadra (394–468), ibid., 55:258c; 3) Translation by T'an-yao (ca. 462), ibid., T. 55:268c; 4) Translation by the second son of Emperor Wu of the Ch'i Dynasty, the Prince of Ching-ling, Hsiao Tzu-liang (ca. 490), *Chung-ching mu-lu*, Fa-ching (594), T. no. 2146, 55:127a. The first *chüan* of a text by this title is contained in Z. 1, 87:4; it corresponds to S. no. 4546, and Makita Tairyō has collated both of them in his *Gikyō kenkyū* (Kyoto: Kyoto daigaku jinbun kagaku kenkyūjo, 1976), pp. 254–61. Other manuscripts of this text include S. no. 5960, S. no. 2301, and several manuscripts in the Peking collection; see Makita, *Gikyō kenkyū*, pp. 247–54; and Tokiwa Daijō, *Yakkyō sōroku*, pp. 268, 317–18.

[21] The *Kuan-fo san-mei hai ching*, by Buddhabadra (359–429), T. no. 643, lists eighteen hells, each containing eighteen minor hells; *Ching-lü i-hsiang*, T. 53:263b–67c. The *Ch'ang a-han ching (Dīrghāgama)*, translated by Buddhayaśas (ca. 408–12) and Chu Fo-nien (ca. 365), lists eight hells, each containing sixteen minor hells; *Ching-lü i-hsiang*, T. 53:260b–62a.

[22] See Sawada, *Jigoku hen*, pp. 18–20.

As is well known, the system of eight hells was the "orthodox" Buddhist cosmology contained in the scholastic treatises of the Sarvāstivāda school and in all of the Mahāyāna philosophical traditions that developed out of this tradition of dharma-analysis.[23] In China this standard cosmology is contained in such sources as the *Mahāprajñāpāramitāśāstra (Treatise on the Great Perfection of Wisdom)*, translated by Kumārajīva in the early fifth century; the *Dīrghāgama*, translated by Buddhayaśas in the early fifth century; the *Cheng-fa nien-ch'u ching (Sūtra on the Fixation of Thought of the True Law)*, attributed to Gautama Prajñāruci in the mid-sixth century; and Abhidharma treatises like the *Mahāvibhāṣā* and the *Abhidharmakośa*. All of these sources enumerate the hells, beginning with the one closest to the surface of the continent of Jambudvīpa, on which humans live, and ending with Avīci Hell, which is furthest from the surface of the earth. The eight hells are: (1) The Hell of Resuscitation, where people constantly die and are resuscitated for more torture, (2) The Black Rope Hell, (3) The Crowded Hell, (4) The Screaming Hell, (5) The Great Screaming Hell, (6) The Hell of Fiery Heat, (7) The Hell of Great Heat, and (8) Avīci Hell, or the Hell of No-Interval.[24] Yü-lan-p'en literature (and later Chinese religion generally) reflects very little of this canonical system of hells. Avīci Hell is kept as the lowest and most gruesome of hells (this is where Ch'ing-t'i is reborn because of her sins), and the sense of progressing deeper under the earth is also maintained in *The Transformation Text on Mu-lien Saving His Mother*. But aside from these characteristics and the intensification of some of the tortures described in the canonical sources, yü-lan-p'en literature preserves little of the canonical system.

Looking forward in time, it is noteworthy that the hells described in the transformation text share many features with the underworld of later popular Chinese religion. The dark regions through which Mulien travels, like those of later folk religion, are administered not just by King Yama, but also by bureaucrats who have resided in China for

---

[23] For brief surveys of the standard Buddhist cosmology, see Kloetzli, *Buddhist Cosmology*; Michihata, *Chūgoku bukkyō shisō shi no kenkyū*, pp. 200–224; Sawada, *Jigoku hen*, pp. 9–14; Matsunaga, *The Buddhist Concept of Hell*, pp. 21–73; and Louis de La Vallée Poussin, "Cosmogony and Cosmology (Buddhist)," 4:129–38.

[24] *Ta chih-tu lun*, T. 25:175b; *Ch'ang a-han ching*, T. 1:121b–27a; *Cheng-fa nien-ch'u ching (Saddharmasmṛtyupasthānasūtra)*, trans. Gautama Prajñāruci, T. no. 721, 17:27a ff.; *A-p'ita-mo chü-she lun (Abhidharmakośa)*, Vasubandhu, trans. Hsüan-tsang (602–664), T. no. 1558, 29:58b; and *A-p'i-ta-mo ta-p'i-p'o-sha lun (Mahāvibhāṣā)*, trans. Hsüan-tsang, T. no. 1545, 27:865a–66c. See also *The Mahāvastu*, trans. J. J. Jones, 3 vols., Sacred Books of the Buddhists, Vols. 17–19 (London: Luzac and Co., 1949–56), 1:6–21, where Mu-lien visits the eight hells.

many centuries, like the Magistrate of Mount T'ai. The bureaucratic apparatus—casebooks, karma mirrors, logbooks, and other steno-graphic paraphernalia—is also more developed in the underworlds of the *pien-wen* and of later religion than in the hells of canonical Buddhism discussed above. And, while the yü-lan-p'en system of hells is not divided systematically into ten courts as in the later scheme, some of the officials of hell whom Mu-lien encounters in the *pien-wen* play important administrative roles in the later system.

The ten courts of hell are the subject of *Yen-lo-wang shou-chi ssu-chung yü-hsiu sheng-ch'i[-chai] wang-sheng ching-t'u ching (The Sūtra on the Prophecy of King Yama to the Four Orders concerning the Seven [Rituals] to Be Practiced Preparatory to Rebirth in the Pure Land).*[25] This sūtra was excluded from the official canon of Chinese Buddhism, but is known to us through some two dozen Tun-huang manuscripts, most of which date from the early tenth century. The action of the sūtra is set in the Indian city of Kuśinagara, where both Indian and Chinese gods have gathered to hear the Buddha deliver one of his last sermons. After delivering a prophecy to King Yama, the Buddha prescribes offerings to the ten kings of hell. The Buddha preaches that after one's death, if one's descendants make offerings to the ten kings, then the deceased will escape punishment for previous sins and be reborn in the heavens. Seven of these sacrifices are to be conducted during the first forty-nine days after death, the offerings destined for the first seven kings of purgatory; offerings should also be sent to the eighth king one hundred days after death, to the ninth king one year after death, and to the tenth king three years after death. King Yama promises the Buddha that he will dispatch envoys riding black horses from the dark regions to go to the homes of the deceased to see whether or not their descendants make offerings.

The Sūtra on the Prophecy of King Yama continues with a brief descrip-

[25] The Four Orders are monks, nuns, male, and female lay devotees. The text is P. no. 2003, reproduced in Tokushi and Ogawa, "*Jūō shōshichi kyō* santoken no kōzō," 5:255–96. I have consulted five other manuscripts of this text: one from the Nakamura Shodō Hakubutsukan, also reproduced in Tokushi and Ogawa, ibid., copy dated 936; S. no. 3961, in THPT 32:569–76; T. no. 3143 (from the Kōyasan collection), T. 92:645–62 (Zuzō, Vol. 7); S. no. 4530, in THPT 36:474–75, copy dated 909; and S. no. 5544, in THPT 43:361–63, copy dated 911 (?). The earliest of these texts are not illustrated and are in prose; they are probably earlier in date than the majority of manuscripts, which have both (spoken) prose and (sung) poetry portions and contain illustrations. For important studies, see also Niida Noboru, "Tonkō hakken *jūō kyō* token ni mietaru keihō shiryō," *Tōyō gakuhō* 25:3 (May 1938):63–78; and Matsumoto Eiichi, *Tonkō-ga no kenkyū*, 2 vols. (Tokyo: Tōhō bunka gakuin, 1937), 1:402–16, 2: Plates 115–18.

tion in prose and verse and a picture of each of the ten courts of hell. The ten kings and the corresponding periods of sacrifice are:

1. The Far-Reaching King of Ch'in: first 7 days after death
2. The King of the First River: 8–14 days after death
3. The Imperial King of Sung: 15–21 days after death
4. The King of the Five Offices: 22–28 days after death
5. King Yama: 29–35 days after death
6. The King of Transformations: 36–42 days after death
7. The King of Mount T'ai: 43–49 days after death
8. The Impartial King:[26] 100 days after death
9. The King of the Capital: one year after death
10. The King of the Cycle of the Five Paths: three years after death

The ten courts of hell have been a universal feature of Chinese folk religion since the Sung dynasty, with *The Sūtra on the Prophecy of King Yama* representing the earliest elaboration of the system.[27]

The Sūtra on the Prophecy of King Yama presents a fascinating synthesis—one very similar to that of the Mu-lien transformation text—of Indian and Chinese deities. Among those who have come to India in the last days of the Buddha to hear him preach are the Magistrate of Mount T'ai and such members of the medieval Chinese underworld as the Officer of Fate, the Officer of Records, and the Great Spirit of the Five Ways. They have come to hear the Buddha's prophecy concerning their superior, King Yama, and to receive orders on how to carry out their duties. In the context of Chinese religion, their inclusion in the audience at Kuśinagara is perfectly natural; having awakened to the laws that govern birth-and-death, the Buddha is their chief, the one to whom they come to receive orders. The Chinese-style bureaucrats are

---

[26] Reading *p'ing-teng* for *p'ing-cheng*, in keeping with the later title of this king; see *Yü-li ch'ao-chuan ching-shih*, attributed to Tan Ch'ih-tsun (Peking: Wen-yüan-chai, 1872).

[27] The ten courts were made the subject of a particular genre of morality book in later imperial China, the "Jade Register" (*yü-li*), signifying the account books kept by the bureaucrat-gods of heaven and hell in which each person's good and bad actions are recorded. Scholars date the first examples of this genre of hell literature to the mid-twelfth and the late thirteenth centuries. See Sawada, *Jigoku hen*, pp. 32–34; and Yoshioka Yoshitoyo, "Chūgoku minkan no jigoku jūō shinkō ni tsuite," in *Bukkyō bunka ronshū*, Vol. 1, ed. Kawasaki daishi kyōgaku kenkyūjo (Tokyo: Kawasaki daishi heikanji, 1975), p. 269. For an English translation of one of these books, see G. W. Clarke, "The Yü-li, or Precious Records," *Journal of the Royal Asiatic Society of Great Britain and Ireland* 28:2 (1893):233–400. See also Yoshioka Yoshitoyo, *Dōkyō to bukkyō*, Vol. 2 (Tokyo: Toshima shobō, 1970), pp. 167–227; Sakai Tadao, *Chūgoku zensho no kenkyū* (Tokyo: Kōbundō, 1960), pp. 359–69; and Wolfram Eberhard, *Guilt and Sin in Traditional China* (Berkeley: University of California Press, 1967), pp. 24–59.

functionaries in the universal system governing the rebirth of all beings in the five (or six) paths of existence. *The Sūtra on the Prophecy of King Yama* harks back to the beginnings of the system, with the gods of the underworld traveling to the Buddha to receive instructions. *The Transformation Text on Mu-lien Saving His Mother* portrays the gods carrying out their duties, with Mu-lien and the Buddha descending temporarily to modify their operations. "Chinese" figures have a natural place in India, just as "Indian" figures have a comfortable position in China. In both of these popular texts, the figures of the underworld have lost their nationalistic character. Gods of both Indian and Chinese origin participate in a unitary system in which exclusivizing questions of cultural origins have no meaningful place.

It should be noted, however, that the hells in the yü-lan-p'en text are not as systematized as are the hells of the Yama text and of later Chinese religion. The transformation text suggests but does not explicitly state that the courts of King Yama and the General of the Five Paths are merely transitional areas, places through which the deceased must pass before being assigned a course of rebirth. The intermediary nature of the ten courts is made explicit in *The Sūtra on the Prophecy of King Yama*, which deals *only* with the purgatorial aspect of the underworld and not with its lower paths of rebirth, the hells. Relationships between the infernal courts are also more clearly specified in the Yama sūtra, where the spirit of the deceased passes through all ten courts in succession, beginning the day after death and ending when rebirth is achieved (forty-nine days or three years later). In these respects the representation of the underworld in the transformation text marks the beginning of a process of systematization that achieved fruition in later Chinese religion.

The transformation text further prefigures the development of the system of ten courts of hell in that five of the courts through which Mu-lien passes are similar or identical to the purgatorial courts of later tradition. Early in his journey Mu-lien encounters people being forced to cross the Wathellwedo River. The later Yama text places this river in the second court of hell, presided over by the King of the First River.[28] In both systems the spirit of the deceased is portrayed as crossing a dangerous river early in the journey through purgatory. Like most medieval Chinese literature on hell the yü-lan-p'en text also refers to two officials who each have their own court in the later system, King Yama (in the fifth court) and the Magistrate of Mount T'ai (in the seventh).

---

[28] In later tradition the name of the river is changed from *ch'u* ("first") to Ch'u^b (place name), hence "The King of the Ch'u River"; see the texts cited in Yoshioka, "Chūgoku minkan no jigoku jūō shinkō ni tsuite," supra.

The transformation text mentions, though obliquely, one of the kings who appears in the later system, the Impartial King. The warden of Avīci Hell simply refers to him in passing, while in later tradition he is shown presiding over the eighth court of the underworld. Finally, *The Transformation Text on Mu-lien Saving His Mother* anticipates the later system in its portrayal of the last purgatorial court, located at the entrance to hell proper. In the transformation text the court consists of a gate ruled by the General of the Five Paths through which all those ready for rebirth (in the five paths) must pass. In later texts the gate becomes the tenth court of purgatory, ruled by "The King of the Cycle of the Five Paths" (or "The King Who Turns the Wheel [of Rebirth] in the Five Paths," Wu-tao chuan-lun wang), marking the threshold between purgatorial existence and rebirth.

Other Features of the Underworld

The figure of King Yama looms large in *The Transformation Text on Mu-lien Saving His Mother*, and in this respect the text reflects a well-established Chinese tradition. In China King Yama plays at least one of the major roles that he had earlier played in India: as ruler of the underworld, he keeps records of people's actions in their previous lives.[29] Yama probably came to play this role in China as early as the second century A.D. *The Sūtra of Questions on Hell* contains a passage describing Yama's domain. In this text Yama rules over an intermediary zone, the area where people reside en route from death to rebirth. While there, people have a uniquely intermediary psychophysical constitution. They are composed of the "aggregates" or "heaps" (Skt.: *skhandas*, Ch.: *yün* or *yin*), as are living people, but in the liminal state the residents of the underworld are composed of correspondingly liminal aggregates. As the sūtra describes it:

> To the north, south, east, and west of King Yama's city are arrayed all of the hells. Although there is light from the sun and moon, it is not bright; the prisons are so black that light does not illuminate them. After human life has ended the spirit is reborn with intermediary aggregates.[30] One with intermediary aggre-

[29] For an overview of Yama's roles in India, China, and Japan, see Alicia Matsunaga, *The Buddhist Philosophy of Assimilation*, pp. 34–48.

[30] In other contexts "intermediary aggregates" (*chung-yin*) might better be rendered as "purgatory" or "purgatorial," equivalent to *ch'iu-yu, i-ch'eng*, and *chung-yu* (Skt.: *antarā-bhava*); see *Chu-ching yao-chi*, T. no. 2123, 54:114c–15a, quoting the *Hsin p'o-sha lun*; MDKJ, 73.36, 73.44; and MBDJ, pp. 3648a–50a. Since the next sentence places *chung-yin* between *ssu-yin* and *sheng-yin*, I have rendered the term as "aggregates" or *skandhas*,

gates has already given up the aggregates of death but has not yet attained the aggregates of rebirth. Sinners take on a body composed of intermediary aggregates and enter the city of Naraka, which is where all those who have not yet received punishment gather together. Blown about by the winds of fortune according to the severity of their karma, they receive bodies either large or small. Blown by ill-odored winds, people who have committed evil receive coarse, ugly forms. Blown by fragrant winds, people who have performed good receive fine, ethereal bodies.[31]

From his central court in the city of Naraka, Yama rules over his prisoners, the recently deceased who await judgment. In *The Sūtra of Questions concerning Hell* this process of judgment is carried out impersonally and pneumatically, while in other texts the adjudication of past actions appears to be Yama's personal administrative responsibility. An early sixth-century text, for example, notes that King Yama "determines one's basic life span in the august records and inspects the city registers in Heaven's offices."[32]

The transformation text also makes occasional reference to Ti-tsang Bodhisattva,[33] who resides in or near Yama's court, and who tells Mu-lien that his mother has probably been reborn in the deepest of the hells. In fact Ti-tsang probably came to assume his place in the dark regions just prior to the date of *The Transformation Text on Mu-lien Saving His Mother* (ca. eighth century). Ti-tsang was well known among some segments of Chinese society as early as the sixth century, in part through the efforts of Hsin-hsing (540–594) and his Teaching of Three Stages (*san-chieh chiao*).[34] Rituals involving divination and repentance were connected with Ti-tsang, as were such scriptures as the *Ta fang-kuang shih-lun ching (The Great Extended Sūtra on the Ten Wheels)*, dating

---

which are the psychophysical components of the person that perdure from one moment and one lifetime to the next.

[31] *Wen ti-yü ching*, K'ang Chü (ca. 187), cited in *Ching-lü i-hsiang*, T. no. 2121, 53:259b; and in *Fa-yüan chu-lin*, T. no. 2122, 53:377b.

[32] "Hsi t'ai-shan wen" ("A Warning to Mount T'ai") is contained in the *Hung-ming chi*, Seng-yu (445–518), T. no. 2102, 52:92a, where it is attributed to Chu Tao-shuang. Modern scholars have suggested, however, that Chu Tao-shuang is a pseudonym and that Seng-yu himself authored the piece; see *Gumyō shū kenkyū*, 2 vols., ed. Kyoto daigaku jinbun kagaku kenkyūjo chūsei shisō shi kenkyūhan (Kyoto: Kyoto daigaku jinbun kagaku kenkyūjo, 1973–75), 2:748, n. 1.

[33] For recent studies on Ti-tsang, see Sakurai Tokutarō, ed., *Jizō shinkō*, Minshū shūkyō shi sōsho, Vol. 10 (Tokyo: Yūzankaku shuppan, 1983); Hayami Tasuku, *Jizō shinkō* (Tokyo: Hanawa shobō, 1975); and Manabe Kōsai, *Jizō bosatsu no kenkyū* (Kyoto: Sanmitsudō, 1960).

[34] See Yabuki Keiki, *Sangaikyō no kenkyū* (Tokyo: Iwanami shoten, 1927), pp. 638–58.

from the fifth century, and the *Chan-ch'a shan-o yeh-pao ching (Sūtra on Divining Good and Evil Karmic Retribution)* from the late sixth century.[35]

While these sources attest to Ti-tsang's popularity, it is only beginning in the seventh century that Ti-tsang's position in hell is sketched out in any detail. The *Ta-sheng ta-chi ti-tsang shih-lun ching (Sūtra of the Great Collection of the Greater Vehicle on Ti-tsang's Ten Wheels)*, translated by Hsüan-tsang (602–664), and especially the *Ti-tsang p'u-sa pen-yüan ching (Sūtra on the Former Vows of Ti-tsang Bodhisattva)*, by Śikṣā-nanda (652–710), tell the story of Ti-tsang's compassionate actions in previous lives.[36] In several of his previous lives Ti-tsang vowed to end the suffering of any sentient being in need, and in one incarnation as a woman she descended to hell, Mu-lien style, to save her mother. These and other sources from T'ang times portray Ti-tsang residing in the underworld; they stress his compassionate efforts to free people from the torments of hell, often in contrast to King Yama's stern and impartial administration.[37]

Another source, the *Huan-hun chi (Record of a Returned Spirit)*, relates the adventures of a monk from K'ai-yüan ssu named Tao-ming who, in the year 778, was mistakenly summoned to hell by King Yama's assistants. Another person named Tao-ming was the intended subject of the infernal warrant, and Tao-ming from K'ai-yüan ssu is eventually able to rectify the mistake and return to life. While still in hell, though, he encounters Ti-tsang Bodhisattva, who complains that people have been drawing inaccurate pictures of him. Ti-tsang asks the monk to make known his true appearance on earth and promises that anyone who chants his name will have their sins wiped away and that anyone who gazes upon his picture will gain merit. Upon his return to life, Tao-ming relies on his encounter with Ti-tsang to publicize the correct representation of the hell-dwelling bodhisattva.[38]

Ti-tsang has little or no bearing on the ghost festival in medieval times. His function in the transformation text appears redundant, since Mu-lien already suspects that his mother has been consigned to hell. Ti-tsang's inclusion in *The Transformation Text on Mu-lien Saving His Mother* may well be an epiphenomenon of folk interest in Ti-tsang as a compassionate savior dwelling in the underworld. Further details con-

---

[35] *Ta fang-kuang shih-lun ching*, T. no. 410; *Chan-ch'a shan-o yeh-pao ching*, attributed to P'u-t'i-teng (ca. 590–618), T. no. 839. See also Makita Tairyō, *Gikyō kenkyū* (Kyoto: Kyoto daigaku jinbun kagaku kenkyūjo, 1976), pp. 108–17.

[36] T. nos. 411 and 412, respectively.

[37] See Sawada, *Jigoku hen*, pp. 113–15.

[38] *Huan-hun chi*, S. no. 3092, in THPT 25:667–68; printed text reproduced in *Tun-huang i-shu tsung-mu so-yin* (Peking: Commercial Press, 1962), p. 172.

cerning Ti-tsang are not mentioned in the transformation text perhaps because they were already known to its audience and could simply be assumed by storytellers.[39]

The transformation text depicts an underworld that is hopelessly bureaucratic. The strength of the bureaucratic model in China's politico-religious system, evident from the earliest periods of Chinese history, hardly bears repeating here.[40] The present discussion attempts merely to highlight a few instances of the bureaucratic logic underlying medieval Chinese cosmology and to suggest that the transformation text shares the same logic. This continuity serves as both an index and an explanation of the strong appeal that *The Transformation Text on Mulien Saving His Mother* had in medieval China.

The narrators of the transformation text drew a hierarchical picture of the other world. In describing the geography of the underworld they made clear the relative ranks of King Yama and the Two Pages of Good and Evil, and they showed lackeys and pen pushers following the dictates of the wardens of the various hells. Some medieval accounts address the issue explicitly, explaining the hierarchy of the other world by comparing it to the hierarchy of this world. Thus T'ang Lin (ca. 600–659) relates the tale of Mu Jen-ch'ien, who was educated about the infernal bureaucracy by one of its members, a functionary named Ch'eng Ching, who had been sent to the world of the living on official business.[41] The ghostly administrator explains to his friend, Mu Jen-ch'ien:

> The Emperor of Heaven has complete control over the six paths; this is what is meant by [calling his administration] "Heaven's offices." King Yama is like you humans' Son of Heaven. The Magistrate of Mount T'ai is like the President of the Department of State Affairs. The spirits who record [destinies] in the five paths are like the various functionaries in the Department of State Affairs.[42]

[39] Sawada also notes that after Sung times the celebration of Ti-tsang's birthday (on 7/30) in north China was part of the ghost festival, while in south China the two were kept separate; *Jigoku hen*, p. 123.

[40] See, for example, David N. Keightley, "The Religious Commitment: Shang Theology and the Genesis of Chinese Political Culture," HR 17:3–4 (February–May 1978):211–25.

[41] Ch'eng Ching may be an orthographic pun for *ch'eng-ying*, "making (or casting) a shadow," an appropriate name for a specter who has returned to the world of the living.

[42] *Ming-pao chi*, T. no. 2082, 51:793b. See also the biography of Mu attributed to Ch'en Hung in *T'ang-tai ts'ung-shu* (Taipei: Hsin-hsing shu-chü, 1968), pp. 537a–39a.

The bureaucracy of the other world operates on a contractual basis. Ti-tsang Bodhisattva, for instance, made vows in the past to save from the torments of hell any sentient being who would invoke his name. Likewise, the ten kings of hell contracted to obviate the purgatorial period for anyone who provides them with offerings. Dealings with the underworld are "rational"—in the Weberian sense of a clear and direct relation between means and ends—in that the purpose of such offerings is clearly specified: ancestors will be saved from the torments of hell if their descendants make offerings. Correct performance of the specified rituals (giving gifts to gods and monks) brings the promised result of deliverance from hell, just as incorrect performance results in punishment. The gods carry out their duties in accord with the rules and exemplary cases described in myth.

The duties of Chinese bureaucrat-gods are routinized often by reference to the calendar; they descend (or ascend) to the world of the living on specified days to perform their appointed duties. Beginning in the fifth century, for instance, each of the "Three Primordials" (san-yüan) descended on a particular day (the fifth or fifteenth day of the first, seventh, and tenth months) to judge people's actions. On these days people performed repentance rituals and gave offerings to the gods, who returned to their offices at the end of the day.[43] The descent of the "Middle Primordial" (chung-yüan) fell on the fifteenth day of the seventh month, so that early in its history the festival held on this day was associated with the routine visit of the gods. The founding of the ghost festival on the fifteenth day of the seventh month and the set of seven week-long offerings to the ten kings of hell as described in *The Sūtra on the Prophecy of King Yama* provide other examples of the bureaucrat's schedule.

The task of recordkeeping is made easier by a system of quantification. In the background of the hierarchy described in *The Transformation Text on Mu-lien Saving His Mother* lies the concept that each person is born with an alotted life span (*pen-ming*), which is largely determined by actions in one's previous life, and which will be lengthened or shortened according to one's actions in this life.[44] The duties of those who administer justice in the other world consist of recording debits and credits against each person's karmic account. *The Sūtra on the Samādhi of Purity and Deliverance* describes the system:

[43] See Yoshioka Yoshitoyo, *Dōkyō to bukkyō*, Vol. 2 (Tokyo: Toshima shobō, 1970), pp. 274–77; and Chapter Two, above.

[44] See Ching-lang Hou, *Monnaies d'offrande et la notion de trésorie dans la religion chinoise* (Paris: College de France, Institut des Hautes Etudes Chinoises, 1975), pp. 97–126.

In hearing investigations and reporting sinful and meritorious acts, the spirits take no notice of status. Every month they make six reports, every year they make four investigations. On the days when the four investigations are made, they use the eight kings.[45] On these days the heavenly kings investigate their cases by comparing all of the people under the jurisdiction of their heaven. Those with meritorious actions have their life span increased, those with sinful actions have it reduced. In regulating the length of life they do not miss even by a hair's breadth.

People are blind and deluded, and in the end they do not know [their fate]. If you do not perform good actions now, you will be remanded to hell.[46]

The gods whom Mu-lien encounters in the dark realms are part of the same system. They maintain the logbooks and court records in which each person's actions are tallied, adjusting their life spans and using the calculus of karma to decide their mode of rebirth.

CONCLUSIONS

Other chapters of this study examine the mythological, shamanic, and ritual aspects of the ghost festival. In this chapter I have focused on its cosmology, its conception of how the world is put together and how the various levels of being are ordered. I have tried to indicate the complexity as well as the the comprehensibility of the worldview espoused and assumed in yü-lan-p'en literature, especially in its most developed and most popular medieval version, *The Transformation Text on Mu-lien Saving His Mother*. I have also tried to convey the philosophical sophistication of this worldview which, by virtue of its karmic laws and bureaucratic form of organization, was capable of absorbing and ordering—without contradiction—a number of different gods. In this analysis the cosmology of medieval Chinese religion emerges not as a tenuous combination of Chinese bureaucrats and Indian gods, but as a consistent and integrated system.

I have also placed the cosmology of the ghost festival in its historical context. The hells through which Mu-lien travels are not the hells of scholastic Buddhism, which were known in China before the emer-

---

[45] The "eight kings" are probably the gods who receive offerings at the eight seasonal junctures of the year, see TFTT, p. 126b.

[46] *Ching tu san-mei ching*, cited in *Ching-lü i-hsiang*, T. 53:259b. See Makita, *Gikyō kenkyū*, p. 260, for the corresponding passage in other versions of the *Ching tu san-mei ching*.

gence of the ghost festival. Rather, the underworld through which Mu-lien travels is closer to the hell system of later (post-T'ang) Chinese religion. Mu-lien's tour foreshadows the later portrayal of separate courts of hell, each administered by a king, and it includes five of the ten courts contained in the later system. Yü-lan-p'en mythology draws on a long tradition in portraying King Yama as the ruler of the under-world, responsible for processing those who have recently died, while Mu-lien's encounter with Ti-tsang Bodhisattva probably reflects a more recent (sixth-eighth century) motif in Chinese religion.

At various points I have alluded to the presumed audience of *The Transformation Text on Mu-lien Saving His Mother*, attempting to show how the cosmology expressed in the text appeals not to an audience composed of the elite or the professionally religious, but to those whose religious actions were an undifferentiated part of family and communal life. One way to give this discussion a sharper focus is to address the question of audience: to whom did the cosmology of *The Transformation Text on Mu-lien Saving His Mother* appeal?

Yü-lan-p'en literature does not focus on the upper reaches of the cos-mos. While some texts do mention Amitābha's Pure Land and the Heaven of Thirty-Three or refer more generally to rebirth in heaven as a happy experience, they all dwell almost exclusively on the hells. This underworldly orientation appealed neither to monks nor to those com-moners who defined their salvation in distinctively Buddhist terms.

Chinese monks were especially interested in a cosmology in which meditation brought access to the higher planes of existence, the various heavens denoting the realms seen or experienced in concentration. Cosmology was grounded in meditative culture; as one ascended through the four levels of *dhyāna*, one ascended through the various levels of heaven.[47] The hells were likewise demythologized, their ter-rors viewed as products of false discrimination or as useful and instruc-tive products of the imagination.[48] Among all the cave paintings in the meditation chambers at Tun-huang—rooms intended for use by med-itating monks—there is not a single picture of hell.[49] Ultimately both heaven and hell were to be seen as impermanent, devoid of own-being, and marked by suffering. At best the hells were a peripheral feature in the monastic life, be it scholastic or meditative.

[47] See Chapter Five for examples and Sadakata, *Shumisen to gokuraku*, pp. 66–67, for a convenient diagram.

[48] Daigan and Alicia Matsunaga, *The Buddhist Concept of Hell*, esp. pp. 47–73, adopt this perspective in explaining the hells.

[49] See Kanaoka Shōkō, "Tonkōbon jigoku bunken kanki awasete bakkōkutsu no sei-kaku o ronzu," *Komazawa daigaku bukkyōgakubu ronshū* No. 13 (October 1982):51–52.

Nor did the cosmology of the transformation text have much to offer those lay Buddhists who sought salvation in primarily Maitreyan or Amidist terms. Medieval yü-lan-p'en sources, in fact, do not mention Maitreya's Tuṣita Heaven, either as a place of rebirth or as a domain visited by Mu-lien. Yü-lan-p'en literature thus shares few interests with the Maitreyan cults popular in China through the sixth century.[50] The worldview reflected in the transformation text similarly had few points of contact with the development of Pure Land Buddhism.[51] Amitābha's Pure Land is located outside of the system of heavens and hells through which Mu-lien travels. And although *The Pure Land Yü-lan-p'en Sūtra* does speak of "Pure Land conduct" (*ching-t'u chih hsing*), it places Ch'ing-t'i's rebirth in the human realm, not in the Pure Land.[52] Yü-lan-p'en literature focuses neither on Maitreya's nor Amitābha's realms; it tends not to focus on the heavens at all. Furthermore, in the rituals of the ghost festival, offerings and invocations were made to a number of different Buddhas, bodhisattvas, and gods, while Maitreyan and Amidist rituals tended to concentrate on their respective deities.

With its stress on the torments of hell, the cosmology of the transformation text appealed to the majority of unlettered Chinese in medieval times, to those people whose primary religious concern was their ancestors' current status and their own future prospects in the other world. This conclusion is corroborated by other evidence concerning the audience for artistic representations of hell in medieval times.

A brief examination of sources describing paintings and painters from the middle T'ang suggests that pictorial representations of hell had their greatest effect upon the common person in the marketplace. Chang Yen-yüan's (ca. 847–874) *Li-tai ming-hua chi (Record of Famous Painters through the Ages)* describes the paintings remaining in the Buddhist temples of Ch'ang-an and Lo-yang that were not destroyed in the Hui-ch'ang (841–846) suppression of Buddhism. The account lists seven "transformation pictures" (*pien-hsiang*) of hell:

[50] For a review of medieval Chinese sources on Maitreya, see Kanaoka Shōkō, "Tonkō bunken yori mitaru Miroku shinkō no ichi sokumen," *Tōhō shūkyō* No. 53 (May 1979):22–48; and Matsumoto Bunzaburō, *Miroku jōdo ron* (Tokyo: Heigo shuppansha, 1911).

[51] Of the multitude of sources on Pure Land Buddhism in China, see especially Ogasawara Senshū, *Chūgoku jōdo kyōka no kenkyū* (Kyoto: Heiryakuji shoten, 1951); Tsukamoto Zenryū, *Tō chūki no jōdokyō* (1933; reprint ed., Kyoto: Hōzōkan, 1955); and Julian F. Pas, "Shan-tao's Commentary on the *Amitāyur-Buddhānusmṛti-Sūtra*" (Ph.D. dissertation, McMaster University, 1973).

[52] *The Pure Land Yü-lan-p'en Sūtra*, ll. 5–6, 27, 72.

At Tz'u-en ssu . . . to the southeast of the pagoda on the outside of the center gate, a transformation [picture] of hell painted by Chang Hsiao-shih; already peeled off.

At Pao-sha ssu . . . in the western corridor, a transformation of hell painted by Ch'en Ching-yen.

At the Monastery of the Three Stages [at Ching-yü ssu] . . . on the eastern wall, a transformation of hell painted by Chang Hsiao-shih.

At Ching-kung ssu . . . to the east of the center gate, a [picture] of hell including captions painted by Wu [Tao-hsüan].

At Hua-tu ssu . . . a transformation of hell painted by Lu Leng-ch'ieh; only a little bit of two figures remains.

At Ching-fa ssu . . . behind the hall, a transformation of hell painted by Chang Hsiao-shih.

(The above temples in Ch'ang-an.)

At the Monastery of the Three Stages at Fu-hsien ssu . . . a transformation of hell by Wu; it contains a sickly nāga that is most sublime.

(The above temples in Lo-yang.)[53]

Tales concerning two of the painters of hell pictures, Chang Hsiao-shih and Wu Tao-hsüan (both active in the eighth century), provide some insights into the popular lore surrounding visions and pictures of hell. An early twelfth-century source describes Chang Hsiao-shih:

He was an excellent painter. Having once died and returned to life, he was especially skilled in painting pictures of hell. These were all [scenes of] what he had seen on his journey in the dark world and could not be compared to pictures drawn from imagination. Wu Tao-hsüan saw his paintings and emulated them in his transformation pictures of hell.[54]

Like many of the literary accounts of tours of hell, artistic renderings of the other world were frequently believed to be the result of personal experience.[55]

---

[53] *Li-tai ming-hua chi*, Chang Yen-yüan, Hua-shih ts'ung-shu, Vol. 1 (Taipei: Wen-shih-che ch'u-pan-she, 1974), pp. 43–54. See also Kanaoka Shōkō, "Tonkōbon jigoku bunken kanki," pp. 50–51.

[54] *Hsüan-ho hua-p'u*, anonymous (preface dated 1120) Hua-shih ts'ung-shu, Vol. 1 (Taipei: Wen-shih-che ch'u-pan-she, 1974), p. 384.

[55] Chinese ghost stories often use such devices as a death and subsequent resuscitation, a shaman's journey, or a dream to introduce their subject matter. The same conventions apply to artistic representations of the underworld. See Maeno Naoaki, "Meikai yūkō," *Chūgoku bungaku hō* 14 (April 1961):38–57; 15 (October 1961):33–48; and Donald E.

Chang Hsiao-shih based his pictures of hell on his own travels there, and the pictures were so convincing that others imitated his style. These imitations were, in turn, quite convincing. Later sources indicate that Wu Tao-hsüan's renderings of hell had a noticeable effect on the residents of Ch'ang-an. Folklore collected in the tenth century reports the general reaction to Wu's picture of hell painted at Ching-kung ssu in 736, noting that, "Everyone in the capital saw it and they all feared punishment and cultivated goodness; butchers and wine sellers in the two markets did not do any business."[56] Whatever the actual effect upon trade in meat and liquor in Ch'ang-an for the year 736, this tale does suggest that those who viewed pictures of hell drawn on temple walls in Ch'ang-an were neither court officials, nor highly placed literati, nor monks, but rather the common folk, people who normally purchased meat and liquor in the city's markets. It is also clear that representations of hell, like the terrifying descriptions of the underworld in oral tales, were designed not so much to command philosophical assent as to change the way people acted.

With its emphasis on the trials and tortures of hell and the cumbersome bureaucracy responsible for carrying them out, the cosmology of *The Transformation Text on Mu-lien Saving His Mother* was directed primarily toward neither the higher classes of Chinese society nor those who practiced the more sectarian forms of Buddhism. In the practice of meditation monks pursued heavenly realms different from those in which commoners sought rebirth, and in defining the canon of Chinese Buddhism monks and literati excluded the more popular descriptions of hell, dubbing them "counterfeit" or "apocryphal" (*wei*[b]) and "deluded" (*i-huo*).[57] Those who sought rebirth in Maitreya's Tuṣita Heaven or in Amitābha's Pure Land turned to pictures and texts with a focus more narrow than that of yü-lan-p'en literature.

The cosmology of the ghost festival as it is reflected in *The Transfor-*

Gjertson, "The Early Chinese Buddhist Miracle Tale: A Preliminary Survey," JAOS 101:3 (July–September 1981):287–301.

[56] *T'ai-p'ing kuang-chi*, Li Fang (925–996) (Peking: Jen-min wen-hsüeh ch'u-pan-she, 1959), ch. 212, p. 829. The same account is contained in *Fo-tsu t'ung-chi*, Chih-p'an (ca. 1260), T. no. 2035, 49:375a. For a brief biography and a list of ninety-three paintings by Wu Tao-hsüan that were extant in the Sung imperial repository, see *Hsüan-ho hua-p'u*, pp. 387–90.

[57] See the entries for the *Yen-lo wang tung-t'ai-shan ching* (*Sūtra on King Yama and the Eastern Mount T'ai*) in *Chung-ching mu-lu*, T. no. 2146, 55:138c; *Ta-t'ang nei-tien lu*, T. no. 2149, 55:335c; *Ta-chou k'an-ting chung-ching mu-lu*, T. no. 2153, 55:473b; *K'ai-yüan shih-chiao lu*, T. no. 2154, 55:676b; and the entries for the *Yen-lo wang shuo i ti-yü ching* (*Sūtra Spoken by King Yama on Avoiding Hell*) in *Ta-chou k'an-ting chung-ching mu-lu*, T. 55:473b; and *K'ai-yüan shih-chiao lu*, T. 55:676b.

mation Text on Mu-lien Saving His Mother grew out of a social milieu different from the circles composed exclusively of monks, literati, or lay people of a sectarian bent. Without alienating any of these specialized audiences, the cosmology of the ghost festival appealed most strongly to the vast majority of unlettered Chinese, those who made offerings to Buddhas, bodhisattvas, and the functionaries of hell as an integral part of family life and as a regular part of mortuary ritual.

195

SEVEN

Buddhism and the Family

FROM THE VERY BEGINNING the myth of Mu-lien saving his mother from hell betrays an ambivalent attitude toward traditional Chinese family life. *The Yü-lan-p'en Sūtra* opens with a ritual act gone awry:

> [Mu-lien] saw his departed mother reborn among the hungry ghosts: she never saw food or drink, and her skin hung off her bones. Mu-lien took pity, filled his bowl with rice, and sent it to his mother as an offering. When his mother received the bowl of rice, she used her left hand to guard the bowl and her right hand to gather up the rice, but before the food entered her mouth it changed into flaming coals, so that in the end she could not eat. Mu-lien cried out in grief and wept tears. He rushed back to tell the Buddha and laid out everything as it had happened.[1]

Normally Mu-lien's offering would have been one of the most unexceptional of ritual acts that any Chinese person could have performed for the sake of his or her ancestors. The presentation of food (and paper money, paper clothes, and other necessities of daily life) constituted the backbone of Chinese family religion, which was premised upon the mutual dependence of descendants and ancestors. In the context of Chinese religion, such offerings to senior generations were so much a part of everyday life that they were rarely questioned or made an explicit topic of debate.

But this is precisely what the myth in the sūtra does: it disputes the efficacy of traditional Chinese mortuary ritual, it questions the very basis of Chinese family religion and funerary ritual by beginning with an episode showing the failure of ancestral food offerings. For all its questioning of the traditional methods, however, the myth does not reject them entirely. Rather the myth remains ambiguous (as does the ritual): it couples an acceptance of the earlier forms of mortuary ritual with the admonition that more—something new—is needed.

The Yü-lan-p'en Sūtra insists that the Sangha be added to the circle of reciprocity between descendants and ancestors. The Buddha instructs Mu-lien and all other devoted sons to make offerings to the assembly

[1] *The Yü-lan-p'en Sūtra*, T. no. 685, 16:779b.

of monks as they emerge from their summer retreat. Rather than sending gifts directly to their ancestors, people should henceforth use the Sangha as a medium: benefits will pass through monks to the inhabitants of the other world. In fact monks possess the distinctive ability to multiply the blessings that reach the ancestors in hell. Having renounced the bonds of kinship, Buddhist ascetics generate a store of power made even greater over the course of the summer meditation retreat. For the price of a small offering during the ghost festival families may tap that power, directing its benefits to their less fortunate members.

The spread of the ghost festival in medieval China signals the movement of the Buddhist monkhood into the very heart of family religion. Monks were not simply accessories to the continued health of the kinship group; their role was nothing less than essential for the well-being of the family. One way in which Buddhism was domesticated in China—particularly clear in the ghost festival—was through the inclusion of monks as an essential party in the cycle of exchange linking ancestors and descendants.

This chapter explores the conditions and implications of this epochal realignment of Chinese society. The recognition of this historical fact runs counter to the traditional wisdom, according to which monks were always strangers to the Chinese family. But to view monks as outsiders is to be blinded by the prejudice of most historiography, which was written by a class of people who viewed the Buddhist institution as a leech upon the body politic. Questioning the traditional view, however, does not necessitate accepting its opposite. We need not simply accept the bias of the Sangha, which viewed monastic life as superior to other forms of existence. Rather, we must construe Chinese society as a changing and complex whole which, in the T'ang dynasty, brought together lay people and monks as participants in the central ancestral cult.

THE BONDS OF KINSHIP

The ghost festival highlights the way in which Buddhism during the medieval period came successfully to make an issue of the traditional forms of Chinese religion. Prior to the influx of Buddhist practices and concepts, the Chinese family as a socioreligious institution could be defined as a self-contained continuum of descent. Hugh Baker writes:

> Descent is a unity, a rope which began somewhere back in the remote past, and which stretches on to the infinite future. The rope

197

at any one time may be thicker or thinner according to the number of strands (families) or fibres (male individuals) which exist, but so long as one fibre remains the rope is there. The fibres at any one point are not just fibres, they are representatives of the rope as a whole. That is, the individual alive is the personification of all his forebears and of all his descendants yet unborn. He exists by virtue of his ancestors, and his descendants exist only through him. . . . [2]

In the first few centuries A.D., Buddhism was consigned to a position in Chinese society outside the continuum of descent that constituted the family. By the fourth or fifth century, however, Buddhism as a social institution had been woven—albeit ambiguously, as a differently colored strand—into the rope of descent. World renouncers were made a critical part of family religion, and the offerings made during the ghost festival affirmed the existence of the Buddhist Sangha as an economic institution. But I would argue that none of these affirmations of new social forms entailed a negation of the old ones: the ancestors were still cared for, the family was still enriched, the goals of filial devotion were still secured. A variety of sources attest to the fact that Buddhism as an organized religion could not survive in medieval China without adjusting itself to the structures of diffused religion.

Both the mythology and the rituals of the ghost festival affirm the mutual dependence of ancestors and descendants. In *The Transformation Text on Mu-lien Saving His Mother*, Mu-lien joins the priesthood and begins the perilous quest for his mother only after he has completed the three-year mourning period for his deceased parents prescribed by ancient Chinese tradition. Before he sets out on the monastic path, Mu-lien fulfills the traditional obligations:

> From the time his parents passed away, Turnip
> Completed the three-year mourning period of ritual sorrow:
> Listening to music did not make him happy—his appearance
>   became emaciated;
> Eating fine foods gave him no pleasure—he wasted away to skin
>   and bones.[3]

---

[2] Hugh D.R. Baker, *Chinese Family and Kinship* (New York: Columbia University Press, 1979), pp. 26–27.

[3] Translation from *The Transformation Text on Mu-lien Saving His Mother*, in THPWC, p. 714; mostly following the translation by Victor Mair, trans., *Tun-huang Popular Narratives* (Cambridge: Cambridge University Press, 1983), p. 88. The passage here alludes to Confucius's description of proper mourning behavior: "The gentleman in mourning finds no pleasure in fine food, no happiness in music, and no comforts in his own home";

Death does not sever the link between family members, it simply changes the way in which older and younger generations fulfill their obligations to one another.

Living descendants are also able to carry out their duties by making annual offerings to their ancestors. In *The Yü-lan-p'en Sūtra*, the Buddha assures Mu-lien that as a result of making offerings during the ghost festival one's current parents, one's forebears stretching back seven generations, and one's six kinds of relatives will all "obtain release from the evil paths of rebirth; at that moment they will be liberated and clothed and fed naturally."[4] Clothing and food may strike the reader as tangential to salvation, but in fact such concerns are an important part of Chinese family religion. Those who pass through purgatory on their way to rebirth and those reborn in hell are without exception hungry and very often naked, and offerings to the ancestors in traditional China always included food and some form of money. The specific mention of ancestors' clothing in *The Yü-lan-p'en Sūtra* may indicate that the practice of sending them paper clothes, quite common in the Sung dynasty, had already begun in the fourth or fifth century.[5] In any event the descendant's ritual act was clearly thought to have a

Lun-yü yin-te, Harvard-Yenching Institute Sinological Index Series, Supplement No. 16 (reprint ed., Taipei: Chinese Materials and Research Aids Service Center, 1966), p. 36; cf. D. C. Lau, trans., *The Analects (Lun yü)* (Harmondsworth: Penguin Books, 1979), p. 147.

[4] *The Yü-lan-p'en Sūtra*, T. 16:779b. The wording in *The Sūtra on Offering Bowls to Repay Kindness*, T. no. 686, 16:780a, is the same except it speaks of the five kinds of relatives. Elsewhere *The Yü-lan-p'en Sūtra* notes that one's elders, both those living and those reborn in the woeful states, will experience one hundred years of happiness, long life, and one hundred years without sickness, all as a result of their descendants properly carrying out yü-lan-p'en offerings; *The Yü-lan-p'en Sūtra*, T. 16:779b, c. Ancestors stretching back seven generations "will be reborn in the heavens; born freely through transformation, they will enter into the light of heavenly flowers and receive unlimited joy"; *The Yü-lan-p'en Sūtra*, T. 16:779b. In *The Pure Land Yü-lan-p'en Sūtra*, ancestors are believed to transcend entirely the process of rebirth: "seven generations of parents will pass beyond the sufferings of seventy-two *kalpas* of birth-and-death"; *The Pure Land Yü-lan-p'en Sūtra*, in Jan Jaworski, "L'Avalambana Sūtra de la terre pure," *Monumenta Serica* 1 (1935–36), ll. 38–39, 53–54, 60–61, 69–70. And according to Tsung-mi (780–841), "The living will enjoy long life in the human realm, never experiencing sickness or pain. The spirits of the dead will be dispatched to the heavens, forever cut off from the dark paths"; *Tsung-mi Commentary*, T. no. 1792, 39:512a.

[5] By the seventh century paper money was a regular component of ancestral sacrifices. See Ching-lang Hou, *Monnaies d'offrande et la notion de trésorie dans la religion chinoise* (Paris: College de France, Institut des Hautes Etudes Chinoises, 1975), pp. 5–6. Tao-shih (d. 683) includes a section on the clothing worn in heaven in *Fa-yüan chu-lin*, T. no. 2122, 53:286a–b. It is hard to tell whether or not Tao-shih's interest in otherworldly fashion and the reference in *The Yü-lan-p'en Sūtra* are truly representative of medieval times.

salutary effect on the day-to-day lives of the ancestors in the other world.

Instructions in the canonical sources list the items given for use by monks: "Gather food of the one hundred flavors and five kinds of fruit, basins for washing and rinsing, perfume, oil lamps, and mattresses and bedding; take the sweetest, prettiest things in the world and place them in the bowl and offer it to the Sangha, those of great virtue of the ten directions."[6] Other sources imply that in actual practice people sometimes dispensed with monks as intermediaries and gave items directly to their ancestors. In his sixth-century record of seasonal observances, Tsung Lin observes that many people gave gifts that far exceeded the offerings stipulated in *The Yü-lan-p'en Sūtra*, "pushing their skillful artistry to the point of [offering] cut wood, carved bamboo, fine candles, and pretty cuttings [of paper] patterned after flowers and leaves."[7] Numerous accounts from the Sung dynasty describe "meat delicacies," offerings clearly not intended for monks, and a number of paper items that were transmitted to the ancestors by fire: paper money, paper clothes, and drawings of Mu-lien.[8]

Descendants were enjoined to make offerings to aid their ancestors as a way of "repaying the kindness" (*pao-en*) that parents show to children by bringing them into the world and nurturing and supporting them through childhood. The influence of reciprocity and filiality on all forms of Chinese culture is, of course, a vast and important topic. The discussion here focuses on how this idea was elaborated in literature related to the ghost festival.[9]

---

[6] *The Yü-lan-p'en Sūtra*, T. 16:779b; following Tsung-mi's reading of the items, *Tsung-mi Commentary*, T. 39:510c–11a.

[7] *Ching-ch'u sui-shih chi*, Tsung Lin (ca. 498–561), in Moriya Mitsuo, *Chūgoku ko saijiki no kenkyū* (Tokyo: Teikoku shoin, 1963), p. 361.

[8] "Meat delicacies" are noted in *I-chien chih*, Hung Mai (1123–1202), 4 vols. (Peking: Chung-hua shu-chü, 1981), 1:360. See Chapter Three for references to other Sung accounts. Sawada Mizuho argues that the nature of the offerings and the fact that they were placed in a combustible bowl made of bamboo (not a ceramic bowl as may have been the case in earlier times) show that in the Sung dynasty, ghost festival offerings were intended for the ancestors; Sawada Mizuho, *Jigoku hen: chūgoku no meikai setsu* (Kyoto: Hō-zōkan, 1968), p. 133.

[9] Scholars such as Lien-sheng Yang have stressed the importance in Chinese society of the notion of reciprocity involved in aiding one's ancestors; see Lien-sheng Yang, "The Concept of 'Pao' as a Basis for Social Relations in China," *Chinese Thought and Institutions*, ed. John K. Fairbank (Chicago: University of Chicago Press, 1957), pp. 291–301. For the classic study of filiality in Chinese Buddhism, see Michihata Ryōshū, *Bukkyō to jukyō rinri* (Kyoto: Heiryakuji shoten, 1968). See also Kenneth K.S. Ch'en, "Filial Piety in Chinese Buddhism," HJAS 28 (1968): 81–97; and idem, *The Chinese Transformation of Buddhism* (Princeton: Princeton University Press, 1973), pp. 14–64.

The earliest canonical sources, *The Yü-lan-p'en Sūtra* and *The Sūtra on Offering Bowls to Repay Kindness*, both begin with a description of Mu-lien entering into meditation to save his parents and "to repay the kindness [they had shown] in nursing and feeding him."[10] In both sū-tras, as the title of the second one makes clear, the act of providing bowls filled with offerings during the ghost festival is viewed as a means of repaying one's parents by insuring their well-being. In his commentary to *The Yü-lan-p'en Sūtra*, Tsung-mi comments exten-sively on the short phrase, "repaying kindness." He contrasts the method of repayment in the "outer [non-Buddhist] teachings," which stress the passing down of physical form through the patriliny, with Buddhist modes of reciprocation, which are more concerned with the transmigrating counsciousness and with repaying the mother, since the mother bears the larger share of duties in birth and nurturing. Tsung-mi also mentions three well-known paragons of filiality, Meng Tsung, Tung An, and Tung Yung, just as Hui-ching in his earlier commentary had compared Mu-lien to the disciple of Confucius best known for fil-iality, Tseng-tzu.[11] Tsung-mi quotes extensively from non-Buddhist sources (such as the *Shih-ching [The Book of Songs]*) as well as Buddhist ones to explain the notion of repaying kindness. Foremost among the Buddhist sources he mentions is the *Fu-mu en-chung ching (Sūtra on the Importance of Kindness Bestowed by Parents)*. In this text the Buddha ex-pounds the hardships endured by parents, describing in detail the ten lunar months of pregnancy. The only way to repay one's parents, says the Buddha, is by making yü-lan-p'en offerings, giving to the Three Jewels, and copying the sūtra.[12] In this view, younger generations can

[10] *The Yü-lan-p'en Sūtra*, T. 16:779a; *The Sūtra on Offering Bowls to Repay Kindness*, T. 16:780a.

[11] For the comparison of Mu-lien with Tseng-tzu, see *Hui-ching Commentary*, T. no. 2781, 85:541b. Meng Tsung (third century) and Tung Yung (second century) were two of the twenty-four paragons of filiality. On Tung Yung, see *Hsiao-tzu chuan*, Liu Hsiang (80–9 B.C.), in *Huang-shih i-shu k'ao*, Ts'ung-shu ching-hua, Vol. 35 (Taipei: I-wen yin-shu-kuan, 1971), pp. 1v–2v; "Hsiao-tzu Tung Yung," S. no. 2204, in THPT 17:246b–47b; Arthur Waley, trans., "The Ballad of Tung Yung," in *Ballads and Stories from Tun-huang: An Anthology* (London: Allen and Unwin, 1960); the materials collected in *Tung Yung, Ch'en Hsiang ho-chi*, ed. Tu Ying-t'ao, Min-chien wen-hsüeh tzu-liao ts'ung-shu, No. 5 (Shanghai: Shang-hai ch'u-pan kung-ssu, 1955), pp. 5–161; and Kanaoka Shōkō, *Tonkō no bungaku* (Tokyo: Daizō shuppansha, 1971), pp. 237–48. Elsewhere (T. 39:506b–c) Tsung-mi mentions another of the twenty-four paragons, Wang Hsiang (second cen-tury).

[12] This sūtra was quite popular in the late T'ang, when a number of different texts with similar titles circulated. These texts include: *Fu-mu en nan-pao ching*, An Shih-kao (ca. 148–170), T. no. 684; *Fu-mu en-chung ching*, S. nos. 2084, 1907, printed in T. no. 2887. See also *Fu-mu en-chung ching chiang-ching wen*, P. no. 2418, printed in THPWC, pp. 672–

repay their elders by sending them aid during the ghost festival. The celebration of the seventh moon affirms the mutual obligations that link the generations.

From other quarters, however, Buddhism cast doubt upon—but did not fully undermine—the familial structure of Chinese society. A strict reading of the doctrine of karma throws into question the efficacy of traditional ancestral offerings. In his *Commentary on the Yü-lan-p'en Sū-tra* Tsung-mi describes the way in which inhabitants of hell are responsible for their own pitiable state, with little hope for deliverance through the aid of their descendants. He writes:

> The recompense of the fruit follows of necessity; it is comparable to shadows and echoes following from objects and sounds. Even with parents and close relatives one cannot stand in for the other [and suffer the other's karmic retribution]. Therefore all wise people must themselves be diligent. Even if they have good karmic affinities [from previous lives], they should not make idle mistakes.
>
> One morning, when you leave this world, who will pay you reverence? If you depend upon your sons and grandsons, then of seven parts you will receive only one. It is worse still if you have no filial sons—you will be contrite, but without any posthumous [support].[13]

Tsung-mi uses the strict interpretation of karma for rhetorical and persuasive ends. He mentions the possibility of merit transfer (offerings from one's descendants), but disparages the results, which, in popular belief, were thought to be only one-seventh of the full offering.[14] Tsung-mi hints that the harsh rule of karma overrides the paltry com-

---

94; and Makita Tairyō, *Gikyō kenkyū* (Kyoto: Kyoto daigaku jinbun kagaku kenkyūjo, 1976), pp. 50–55. Only T. no. 2887 mentions yü-lan-p'en offerings, T. 85:1403c. For studies of this genre, see Arai Keiyo, "On shisō kara mita *Urabon kyō* to *Fubo onchō kyō* no kankei," in *On*, ed. Nakamura Hajime, Bukkyō shisō, Vol. 4 (Kyoto: Heiryakuji shoten, 1979), pp. 149–72; Akizuki Kan'ei, "Dōkyō to bukkyō no *Fubo onchō kyō*," *Shūkyō kenkyū* 39:4 (March 1966):23–44; Tokushi Yūshō, "*Fubo onchō kyō* no ibun ni tsuite," *Shūkyō kenkyū* N.S. 5:4 (July 1932):116–23; and P'an Ch'ung-kuei, "Ts'ung tun-huang i-shu k'an fo-chiao t'i-ch'ang hsiao-tao," *Hua-kang wen-k'o hsüeh-pao* 12 (March 1980):197–267.

[13] *Tsung-mi Commentary*, T. 39:509a–b.

[14] Yü-jung quotes from the *Sui-yüan wang-sheng ching*; *Yü-jung Commentary*, Z. 1, 94:4, p. 403va. In the *Sui-yüan wang-sheng shih-fang ching-t'u ching*, which constitutes Chapter 11 of the *Kuan-ting ching (Consecration Sūtra)* attributed to Śrīmitra (ca. 307–355), T. no. 1331, the Buddha speaks of a man who neither believes in the Three Jewels nor upholds the precepts. After he dies, when his relatives undertake to cultivate merit on his behalf, "then out of seven parts he will receive only one"; *Kuan-ting ching*, T. 21:530a, also 531b.

fort obtainable, even in the best of circumstances, through the ancestral cult.

In *The Transformation Text on Mu-lien Saving His Mother* the gloomy interpretation of karma is propounded by the functionaries of hell. These arbiters of karmic justice speak a universal language, insisting that laws were not made to be broken and that no one can bend the rules to evade the results of his or her actions. In this context, the whole administration of heaven and hell represents an elaboration in bureaucratic metaphor of the laws of karma. The gods and their underlings merely carry out the "decisions" that all people unwittingly make for themselves through their own deeds. When Mu-lien first descends to hell, King Yama lectures him:

> Mount T'ai's verdicts are, in the end, difficult to alter,
> For all were sanctioned by heaven's bureaucrats and earth's pen pushers.
> The karmic retribution for sinners follows from causes and conditions;
> Who is there who could rush in to save them?

And later, after Mu-lien offers to take his mother's place in Avīci Hell, the warden replies:

> If your mother has sinned, she will receive punishment,
> And if you, oh teacher, have sinned, you will bear punishment.
> [The records of sins written on] gold tablets and jade tokens cannot be wiped off or washed away,
> In the end, there is no one who can readily alter them.[15]

THE POWER OF MONKS

The mythology of the ghost festival not only casts doubt upon the utility of traditional ancestral offerings, it also indicates a more effective mechanism for securing the welfare of the family. The development of the ghost festival signals the addition of the Sangha as an intermediary party to the system of obligation linking descendants and ancestors. The canonical sources give very explicit instructions concerning the circuit of exchange. The Buddha instructs Mu-lien "to make offerings to the assembly of monks, those of great virtue of the ten directions," and "to place food and drink of the one hundred flavors in the yü-lan

[15] Translations from THPWC, p. 720; mostly following Mair, trans., *Tun-huang Popular Narratives*, p. 94; and from THPWC, p. 735; mostly following Mair, trans., *Tun-huang Popular Narratives*, p. 110.

bowl and give it to monks of the ten directions who have released themselves."[16] The Buddha's instructions to the Sangha are also quite detailed:

> Then the Buddha decreed that the assembled monks of the ten directions should first chant a prayer on behalf of the family of the sponsor for seven generations of ancestors, that they should practice meditation and concentrate their thoughts, and that they should then receive the food. In receiving the bowls, they should first place them in front of the Buddha's *stūpa*; when the assembled monks have finished chanting prayers, they may then individually partake of the food.[17]

Monks also play a mediating role in the ritual described in a later source, the *Lan-p'en hsien-kung i (Liturgy for the Offering of Lan Bowls)*. In this liturgy, containing prayers used in the eleventh century, lay people pay respects to the Three Jewels: the Buddha, the Dharma, and the Sangha. Included under the category of "Sangha" are three types of monks (bodhisattvas, *pratyekabuddhas*, and *śrāvakas*) and Mu-lien. Prayers made to each of these four subgroups of the Sangha end with the phrase:

> And now as they [e.g., bodhisattvas] descend to this sacred
>   place,
> We pray that they will release all of our living and dead [relatives]
>   from suffering.[18]

Monks augment the flow of benefits to the ancestors by virtue of their special powers. It is well known that monks in China have always been associated with meritorious karma. But it is not enough simply to point out that monks and nuns were habitually thought to have a beneficial influence on the workings of karma. Our explanation should also seek the causes and conditions of that special power. My contention is that the Sangha's unique contribution depends upon the curious dialectic of asceticism: precisely because they have renounced the family, monks are able to enrich the family. Having dedicated themselves to an ascetic way of life that claims to deny the principle of procreation, monks simultaneously contribute a regenerative force to that very

[16] *The Yü-lan-p'en Sūtra*, T. 16:779b, c.

[17] *The Yü-lan-p'en Sūtra*, T. 16:779c. *The Sūtra on Offering Bowls to Repay Kindness*, T. 16:780a, omits the chanting of prayers and the preliminary offering to the Buddha. The Buddha also instructs donors to make prayers for their parents' happiness and their ancestors' rebirth in heaven; *The Yü-lan-p'en Sūtra*, T. 16:779c.

[18] *Lan-p'en hsien-kung i*, Z. 2B, 3:2, p. 90ra.

world they appear to transcend. I would argue that in the medieval Chinese ghost festival there is a clear echo of the relationship between asceticism and eroticism as it is articulated in Indian mythology:

> *Tapas* (asceticism) and *kāma* (desire) are not diametrically opposed like black and white, or heat and cold, where the complete presence of one automatically implies the absence of the other. They are in fact two forms of heat, *tapas* being the potentially destructive or creative fire that the ascetic generates within himself, *kāma* the heat of desire.[19]

In medieval China this opposition is spelled out most often in social terms as the difference between a monastic way of life and a life lived within the family. Renunciation and procreation are not diametrically opposed, but are joined together as part of the same cycle. The power of monks—their ability to enrich substantially the welfare of the family—depends upon their social placement outside of the family. It is this power that is referred to, in a variety of sources, with the standard locution, "the mighty spiritual power of the assembly of monks" (*chung-seng wei-shen chih li*).

The power of Buddhist monks reaches its annual peak precisely on the fifteenth day of the seventh lunar month, which is the last day of the ninety-day summer retreat. This critical juncture marks the end of the retreat (*an-chü*, Skt.: *varṣā*), during which monks undertake more strenuous religious practice and reduce their contacts with lay society. As noted in Chapter Two, the Chinese Sangha followed Indian precedents in setting aside three months out of the year for the intensive practice of meditation and for study. Monks in China also adopted the Indian ceremony performed at the end of the retreat, in which monks "released themslves" (*tzu-tzu*, Skt.: *pravāraṇa*) by inviting other monks to give voice to any complaints or infractions of discipline that may have occurred during the long hot period of isolation. Themes of renewal and regeneration are evident in this culminating ritual, which was not open to lay people. Monks "released themselves" in several senses: they loosened the rules of discipline, they unleashed the ascetic energies built up during retreat, they submitted to criticism from other monks, and through their repentance they let loose the positive forces of purification and renewal.

In China the regenerative aspects of the monastic retreat are especially clear. Throughout Asia, the ending of the summer retreat

[19] Wendy Doniger O'Flaherty, *Asceticism and Eroticism in the Mythology of Śiva* (London: Oxford University Press, 1973), p. 35.

marked the beginning of the monastic year. In China, the "Buddhist New Year" (*fa-la*) falls precisely six months after the secular New Year, celebrated on the fifteenth day of the first lunar month. As Tsan-ning (919–1001) says of the Buddhist New Year:

> Having left the secular world, *bhikṣus* do not use the secular year in making calculations. Thus, [the fifteenth day of the seventh month] is counted as the summer New Year.[20]

While the secular and Buddhist New Year celebrations are perfectly opposed in timing, they are identical in structure: monks close themselves off from the rest of the world during the period leading up to the summer New Year, just as families close their doors to all visitors in the days before the winter New Year. When the new year arrives, they both open their doors in celebrations of renewal. For monks, 7/15 is "the day on which the Buddhist year is full and complete."[21] Following the example of the early disciple, Upāli (who, according to some legends, recited the entire Vinayapiṭaka at the Council of Rājagṛha), Chinese monks lit incense and made offerings to the rules for monastic discipline. Then they literally punctuated the passing of the monastic year by placing a "dot" (*tien*) in the scrolls containing the Vinaya.[22]

The ascetic power given vent in the ghost festival derives not only from the social position of monks and from the course of the monastic schedule, but also from the modulations of the natural world. The renewal and release of energy by monks is also synchronized with the rhythms of nature. Chinese sources preserve an interesting explanation for the monks' retreat. Tsung Lin writes:

> On the fifteenth day of the fourth month, monks and nuns hang up [their clothes] and suspend [their bowls] and go to the meditation area. This is called "beginning the summer" and "beginning the strictures."
> Since summer is the season of growth and nurturing, they fear

---

[20] *Ta-sung seng-shih lüeh*, Tsan-ning (919–1001), T. no. 2126, 54:251a. See also *Shih-shih yao-lan*, Tao-ch'ang (ca. 1019), T. no. 2127, 54:298c–99a.

[21] See *Meng-liang lu*, Wu Tzu-mu (ca. 1275), in *Tung-ching meng-hua lu, wai ssu-chung* (Shanghai: Ku-tien wen-hsüeh ch'u-pan-she, 1957), p. 160.

[22] On Upāli as compiler of the Vinaya, see *Kao-seng chuan*, Hui-chiao (497–554), T. no. 2059, 50:403a; and Etienne Lamotte, *Histoire du bouddhisme indien, des origines à l'ère Śaka*, Publications de l'Institut Orientaliste de Louvain, No. 14 (1958; reprint ed., Louvain-la-Neuve: Institut Orientaliste, 1976), pp. 188–93. On the practice of marking the Vinaya with a dot each year, see Wayne Pachow, "A Study of the Dotted Record," JAOS 85:3 (September 1965), reprinted in *Chinese Buddhism: Aspects of Interaction and Reinterpretation* (Lanham: University Press of America, 1980), pp. 69–86; and *Lung-hsing fo-chiao pien-nien t'ung-lun*, Tsu-hsiu (ca. 1164), Z. 2B, 3:3, pp. 242va–43ra.

that walking about outside [the monastery] will harm plant and animal life, so they hold a retreat for ninety days.[23]

According to Tsung Lin, monks undertake a period of special austerity and increased isolation to avoid interfering with the growth of plant and animal life. This theory explicitly connects the monastic and agricultural cycles. Summer is the time when both plants and monks develop their potency and store up their energy. The beginning of autumn—also the Buddhist New Year—is the time when these energies are released and harvested by society at large.

Given the convergence of agricultural fertility and monastic regeneration, it should not be surprising to find human fecundity also associated with the ghost festival. The association, contained in a late T'ang work, concerns not just any human birth, but rather the birth of the Buddha. According to Han O (T'ang dynasty), Śākyamuni was incarnated in his mother's womb on the fifteenth day of the seventh month in the year 686 B.C., to be born nine months later.[24] While the synchronicity of the Buddha's conception with the appearance of the seventh moon was probably not common knowledge in medieval China, the date undoubtedly marked a number of culturally significant conjunctions. The coming of harvest, sending provisions to the ancestors, and giving offerings to monks at the end of the summer retreat formed part of the yearly cycle of events on which most people's lives were based.

Paralleling the ripening of plant life, monks build up their virtue in isolation from lay society. They conclude the period of intensified effort by bestowing their power upon lay society. In exchange for material gifts from descendants, they channel their "mighty spiritual power" to benefit the ancestors. Hui-ching writes:

> The principle of the performance of releasing oneself[25] penetrates in all ten directions. In harmony and unity the Sangha is completed[26] without mixing the secular and the sacred. Its spirituality [shen] is like the bounding ocean, unfathomable as caves and marshes. Its might [wei] is like the flaming earth, producing un-

[23] *Ching-ch'u sui-shih chi*, in Moriya, *Chūgoku ko saijiki no kenkyū*, pp. 349–50; see also Moriya, trans., *Keiso saijiki*, Tōyō bunko, Vol. 324 (Tokyo: Heibonsha, 1978), p. 139. The same theme is noted in Vinaya sources in Chinese; see *Ssu-fen lü*, trans. Buddhayaśas (ca. 408–412), T. no. 1428, 22:830b–c.

[24] See *Sui-hua chi-li*, Han O (T'ang), in *Sui-shih hsi-su tzu-liao hui-pien* (Taipei: I-wen yin-shu-kuan, 1970), 3:88.

[25] *Tzu-tzu chieh-mo*, Skt.: *pravāraṇa-karma*.

[26] Tsung-mi and others understood "Sangha" (literally "assembly") to mean "harmony and unity," *Tsung-mi Commentary*, T. 39:510a.

CHAPTER 7

limited merit. This is how it is able to get rid of greed, thievery, and the experience of suffering and [to cause ancestors] to be re- born in the heavens in freedom according to their wishes, imme- diately attaining liberation.[27]

Monks multiply the blessings given to ancestors by virtue of their iso- lation from the secular world. They enter the cycle of family religion not simply as a third party on equal footing with ancestors and de- scendants, but as world renouncers; and they enter the circuit of ex- change just at the time of year when their virtue, born of homelessness, is at a peak. The power that they bring to the world of the family is so great precisely because they normally stand outside of it.

CONCLUSIONS

The earliest critics of Buddhism in China focused their attack on the Sangha.[28] By renouncing the claims of kinship and reproduction, monks appeared to deny the most important socioreligious institution in Chinese society, the family. Since they were exempt from the taxes and labor services exacted from other adults and since the Sangha pos- sessed large quantities of land and precious metals, monks were also viewed with suspicion by state authorities. Nevertheless, despite these antagonisms, the Buddhist monkhood did not exist merely as an un- easy appendage to indigenous social, economic, political, and religious institutions. The Sangha interacted with indigenous social institutions during the medieval period, and both were transformed in the process. The ghost festival offers a particularly clear illustration of how Bud- dhist monks, having entered China as complete outsiders, soon took their place at the center of Chinese religious life.

To understand the position of the Sangha vis-à-vis the family, it has been necessary to take a view of Chinese society more inclusive than the picture drawn in traditional sources. What is required is a view of Chinese society as a complex whole, in which different groups are linked by a system of exchange, broadly conceived. In the classic dis- cussion of such a system, Marcel Mauss writes:

[27] *Hui-ching Commentary*, T. 85:542a–b.

[28] For early criticisms of Buddhist monasticism, see the *Li-huo lun*, attributed to Mou Yung (ca. third century), in *Hung-ming chi*, Seng-yu (445–518), T. no. 2102. See also Paul Pelliot, "Meou-tseu, ou les doutes levées," TP 19 (1920), pp. 255–433; the essays col- lected in *Ssu-shih-erh chang ching yü mou-tzu li-huo lun*, ed. Chang Man-t'ao, Hsien-tai fo- chiao hsüeh-shu ts'ung-k'an, Vol. 11 (Taipei: Ta-sheng wen-hua ch'u-pan-she, 1978), pp. 97–395; and Erik Zurcher, *The Buddhist Conquest of China: The Spread and Adaptation of Buddhism in Early Medieval China*, revised ed. (Leiden: E. J. Brill, 1972), 1:254–85.

It is groups, and not individuals, which carry on exchange, make contracts, and are bound by obligations. Further, what they exchange is not exclusively goods and wealth, real and personal property, and things of economic value. They exchange rather courtesies, entertainments, rituals, military assistance, women, children, dances, and feasts; and fairs in which the market is but one element and the circulation of wealth but one part of a wide and enduring contract.[29]

I have tried to show how the ghost festival performs just such a function in Chinese society: as a system of exchange, it links those who stand within the family to those who stand outside it. *Neither group stands outside of society.* As James A. Boon remarks:

> monasticism achieves what Durkheim called "organic solidarity" with an incremental level of differentiation: reciprocity between two specialist sectors or categories, one producing merit and release, the other producing successors and subsistence. Neither lay nor monk alone can reproduce the socioreligious totality.[30]

Rituals of the ghost festival articulate a "total" socioreligious system, "total" in the sense that it serves ends commonly called "religious" as well as ends commonly called "social." By virtue of their detached charity filial sons earn merit, and the act of offering goods to monks brings the ancestors a better rebirth or release from the round of birth-and-death altogether. In addition to these "sacred" ends, the cycle of exchange also serves goals commonly called "secular." Monks receive food, clothing, and money, which allow them to survive in economic terms, while fertility and glory—more descendants and greater ancestors—accrue to the kinship group.

The ghost festival not only links the family and the Sangha considered as social groups, it also mediates the principles upon which these forms of life are based. As seen in the cycle of exchange, kinship and monasticism are complementary, not opposed, principles. Those who have renounced the family are not antagonistic toward householders; they have left one social group and joined another. The festival requires that both groups cooperate in reestablishing harmony and creating a greater good.

[29] Marcel Mauss, *The Gift: Forms and Functions of Exchange in Archaic Societies*, trans. Ian Cunnison (New York: W. W. Norton and Co., 1967), p. 3.

[30] James A. Boon, "Incest Recaptured: Some Contraries of Karma in Balinese Symbology," in *Karma: An Anthropological Inquiry*, eds. Charles F. Keyes and E. Valentine Daniel (Berkeley: University of California Press, 1983), p. 218.

The case of the ghost festival tends to confirm the analysis of Jacques Gernet, who has shown that in medieval China, "economy" and "religion" do not form two separate spheres. Good acts pay off debts, offerings of money get rid of sin.[31] Material offerings given during the festival have religious value because they are part of a cycle of exchange at once economic and religious.

All gifts are convertible into one form of merit or another, be it material or soteriological. Merit is the unitary concept underlying the different forms of value, and merit making is the mechanism through which gifts are transformed. In Chinese usage, "merit" (*fu* or, more technically, *kung-te*) implies both spiritual and material blessings. "Merit" describes the future happiness or liberation to be attained as a result of a meritorious action, and it also refers to the concrete blessings—long life and wealth—that flow from good acts.[32]

The notion of a cycle of exchange is not simply a product of our own conceptual system. It is also articulated at length in indigenous terms. Early Indian texts describe a "field of merit" (Skt.: *puṇyakṣetra*) corresponding to the circuit of gifts: one makes offerings and obtains merit just as one plants seeds and gathers the harvest. While the concept is mentioned in texts originating in India, it is developed at greater length in Chinese Buddhism.[33]

Tsung-mi explains the idea in his commentary on *The Yü-lan-p'en Sūtra*. He writes:

> [*The Yü-lan-p'en Sūtra*] reveals superior fields [of merit]. It is like worldly people who want to obtain a granary so abundantly stocked with the five grains[34] that they are never in want. They

[31] Jacques Gernet, *Les Aspects économiques du bouddhisme dans la société chinoise du Ve au Xe siècle* (Saigon: Ecole Française d'Extrême-Orient, 1956), esp. pp. 287–90, 297–98.

[32] According to Jean Filliozat, the Sanskrit term for merit, *puṇya*, also has a broad semantic domain which includes both the tangible benefits of a good act as well as the "happiness" that accompanies the performance of the act; "Sur Le Domaine sémantique de *puṇya*," *Indianisme et Bouddhisme: mélanges offerts à Mgr. Etienne Lamotte*, Publications de l'Institut Orientaliste de Louvain, No. 23 (Louvain: Insitut Orientaliste, 1980), pp. 101–16.

[33] For an overview, see Tokiwa Daijō, *Shina bukkyō no kenkyū*, Vol. 2 (Tokyo: Shunjūsha, 1941), pp. 471–98. In its doctrinal form the concept of a "field of merit" (*Ch.: fu-t'ien*) served as an explanation of and justification for acts of charity, while in practice it came to be identified with such institutions of social welfare as hospitals, famine-relief efforts, hostels, and the building of roads and bridges. See Michihata Ryōshū, *Tōdai bukkyō shi no kenkyū* (Kyoto: Hōzōkan, 1957), pp. 381–440; and idem, *Chūgoku bukkyō to shakai fukushi jigyō* (Kyoto: Hōzōkan, 1967).

[34] According to Yüan-chao the five grains are: hemp, two kinds of millet, wheat or

must gather the seeds from grain, use an ox and plow to till the fields, and plant the seeds. If they do not plant them, they will run out. It is the same with the Dharma. The heart of compassion, the heart of respect, and the heart of filiality[35] are the seeds. Food, clothing, and valuables are the ox and plow. The destitute and the sick, the Three Jewels, and parents are the field.

There are disciples of the Buddha who want to obtain a store-consciousness[36] with all kinds of merit so splendid that it is never exhausted. They must pull together the hearts of compassion, respect, and filiality; take food, clothing, valuables, and their own lives; and donate them respectfully for the support and aid of the destitute and the sick, the Three Jewels, and parents. This is called "planting merit." If they do not plant merit, they will be poor; lacking merit and wisdom, they will enter the dangerous path of birth-and-death.[37]

Now seeds are fresh or dried, and fields are fertile or barren, just as hearts of compassion, respect, and filiality are earnest or slack; destitution is mild or severe; sickness is minor or serious; Buddhas are true or transformational; transformation [-Buddhas] dwell in the world or enter *nirvāṇa*; the Dharma is smaller or greater; the teaching is provisional or ultimate; monks uphold [the precepts] or break them; parents are those who gave birth or those stretching back seven generations. As can readily be seen, each of these corresponds to fertile or barren fields.

---

barley, and beans, *Yüan-chao Commentary*, Z. 1, 35:2, p. 108va. According to Yü-jung they are: millet, rice, beans, hemp, and barley, *Yü-jung Commentary*, Z. 1, 94:4, p. 191rb.

[35] I have interpreted Tsung-mi's usage along Mencian lines, translating *pei-hsin, ching-hsin*, etc., as "heart of compassion," "heart of respect," etc. The terms might just as easily be interpreted along Buddhist lines as "thought [Skt.: *citta*] of compassion," "thought of respect," etc.

[36] Here Tsung-mi draws on the broader implications of the concept of *ālaya-vijñāna* (Ch.: *tsang-shih*). In Yogācāra thought the *ālaya-vijñāna*, in which the seeds of all thought and action are stored, "constitutes the cohesion of each autonomous series of instants conditioned by the development of one and the same causality, thus providing us with the illusion of the individual, the person"; Paul Demiéville, "Araya," in *Hōbōgirin: dictionnaire encyclopédique du bouddhisme d'après les sources chinoises et japonaises*, ed. Paul Demiéville and Jacques May (Tokyo: Maison Franco-Japonaise, 1927–), 1:35. By storing seeds in a granary future survival is assured; by storing seeds in the store-consciousness continued existence in the realm of birth-and-death is assured; and by storing seeds of merit liberation is assured.

[37] In the text there follows a sentence which I believe to be an early interpolation by a copyist since it begins with "*wei*" and because the commentary by Yüan-chao has some variations. The sentence reads: "The field in which merit is planted is called a 'field of merit' just as the field in which grains are planted is called a 'field of grain.' "

211

The yü-lan assembly combines all three kinds of fertile fields, which is why we call it "superior." Making offerings to those pure ones of great virtue who release themselves [in repentance] on the day on which Buddhas rejoice shows the superiority of the field of respect. Repaying the kindness of parents shows the superiority of the field of kindness.[38] One's parents being in difficult straits [i.e., the hells] shows the superiority of the field of compassion. [The Buddha] preached this sūtra in order to reveal these superior fields.[39]

The metaphor of "planting merit" organically links all of the participants in the cycle of exchange. In referring to compassion, respect, and filiality, Tsung-mi alludes to the gift giver's intention: charity should be directed toward others and not motivated by thought of reward. The production of merit, like any small-scale agricultural enterprise, is a cooperative venture requiring the participation of all members. For the harvest to be successful, donors must be well intentioned, monks and parents must be receptive, and the goods must be efficacious. If any of these elements is deficient, the crop will not grow.

Tsung-mi also refers to a variety of recipients or "fields" in which to plant merit: monks, living parents, and ancestors. While ghost festival offerings are given to all three parties, each party stands in a different relation to the donor. Donors show respect to those nonkin who rank above them in status, monks. Donors act out of filiality to repay the kindness shown by their parents. And donors display compassion toward those in less fortunate circumstances than themselves, the deceased who live in hell as hungry ghosts.

In the metaphor of the field of merit, merit grows naturally from the seeds planted in the field. Clothing and cash produce merit, not through a transformation of their unchanging nature, but through the maturation of qualities inherent in them from the very start. Merit is actualized money (without merit in the storehouse of consciousness, one is poor), just as money is potential merit waiting to be invested in a salvific venture.

In China Buddhist monks rarely stood completely outside of society, but only outside of one particular social group, the family. In the ghost festival we see the monk standing fully within society, his renunciation serving key social and religious ends. Buddhist monasticism has often been viewed as an asocial institution. Traditional Chinese critics of Buddhism have viewed it as standing outside the square of the so-

---

[38] The field of kindness is equivalent to the field of filiality.

[39] Translation from *Tsung-mi Commentary*, T. 39:506a.

cially constructed worlds of family and state, while many modern scholars have adopted the methods and attitudes of Weber in dubbing it "otherworldly." In their view, the monk is seen in the abstract, "an idealized and isolated figure." Considered in context, however, renunciation does not mean a lapse into a social vacuum. Instead, it marks "a change-over from one condition of life to another."[40] The monk does not leave society, but only one segment of it, and even then he remains linked to the family through the cycle of exchange. In the ritual circuit of the festival, the monk plays an indispensable role in furthering subsistence and salvation; he actively assumes a place at the very center of Chinese family religion.

[40] Sukumar Dutt, *Buddhist Monks and Monasteries of India: Their History and Their Contribution to Indian Culture* (London: George Allen and Unwin, 1962), p. 45.

213

EIGHT

Concluding Perspectives

A Sociological Perspective

WHILE THERE can be little doubt that the ghost festival pervaded the entire social landscape of medieval China, the question of how to portray that landscape—as Buddhist, Taoist, or just plain "folk"—remains to be answered. Common people were indeed drawn to the entertainments and offerings held at the temples of organized religion in China, and there existed both Buddhist and Taoist legends concerning the origin of the festival. The Taoist name for the celebration, "chung-yüan" (Middle Primordial), drew upon a traditional notion of trinitarian rule and mass repentance, linking the seventh-month festival to a universe conceived in distinctively Taoist terms. Similarly, the Buddhist name of "yü-lan-p'en" never escaped suspicion of its Indian origins, and the myth of Mu-lien rescuing his mother from the torments of hell made it clear that salvation for the ancestors was effected only through the intervention of the Buddha and the Sangha.

But the ghost festival could hardly have become so widely practiced if it were associated primarily with either of China's two institutional religions. After the T'ang dynasty both the Buddhist and the Taoist names for the festival lagged in popularity. In Sung literature and Ming gazetteers names for the festival tend to emphasize its soteriological intention ("The Ghost Festival," "Releasing Hungry Ghosts with Burning Mouths," "The Universal Passage of Hungry Ghosts Out of Hell," "Gathering Orphaned Souls") or to specify the kind of food given as offerings ("Sending Grains," "The Melon Festival").[1] The name used most commonly in official sources, "The Fifteenth Day of the Seventh Month" (ch'i-yüeh shih-wu-jih), also stripped the event of its Buddhist and Taoist associations, indicating merely the calendrical significance of the day. The ghost festival precisely bisected the secular year, which was inaugurated by the New Year celebration on the fifteenth day of the first lunar month. Rituals of renewal had been held at the half-year mark in China for several centuries before the development of either Buddhism or Taoism. The melding of social divisions in a festive gath-

---

[1] See the discussion in Chapter One, above.

214

ering, the regeneration of plant and animal life, and the key fructifying role of ancestors were all hallmarks of earlier celebrations. If the institutional versions of the ghost festival are so clear to us in T'ang sources, that is largely because the Buddhist and Taoist forms gained their strength from the celebrations that were carried on underneath and outside of organized religion.

Such considerations imply that while it flourished in a multitude of social settings in the medieval era, the ghost festival was primarily an expression not of Buddhism or of Taoism but of that other category—religion in its diffused form as it was practiced by the largest class of people, the "folk." Tying the ghost festival to the anchor of "popular religion," however, is not a straightforward exercise in sociological analysis. For "popular religion" and "folk religion" are most often used as leftover categories: whatever is not part of Buddhism or Taoism or state religion must fall into this convenient bin. As one scholar has noted, "Whether it is presented, bluntly, as 'popular superstition' or categorized as 'lower forms of belief,' it is assumed that 'popular religion' exhibits modes of thinking and worshiping that are best intelligible in terms of a failure to be something else."[2]

The view that "popular religion" represents something marginal is not unique to modern scholars; it is a bias shared by most written sources on Chinese religion, which were compiled by the self-conscious bearers of institutional religion in its Buddhist, Taoist, and imperial forms. But as long as Chinese religion is viewed from the top downward, the most persistent forms of ritual activity will be relegated to the unchanging and lackluster heap of "popular religion."[3]

[2] Peter Brown, *The Cult of the Saints: Its Rise and Function in Latin Christianity*, The Haskell Lectures on History of Religions, New Series, No. 2 (Chicago: University of Chicago Press, 1981), p. 19.

[3] The suggestion that we dispense with the dichotomy between folk and elite no longer represents an innovation. Similar calls have been made from a number of quarters, from scholars arguing for a pyramidical conception of institutional religion in China, for the breakdown of any simple division between "elite" and "popular," and for the analysis of "heterodoxy" and "orthodoxy" or "local religion" and "national religion." See Erik Zürcher, "Buddhist Influence on Early Taoism: A Survey of Scriptural Evidence," TP 66:1–3 (1980):84–147; David Johnson, "Communication, Class, and Consciousness in Late Imperial China," in *Popular Culture in Late Imperial China*, eds. David Johnson, Andrew Nathan, and Evelyn Rawski (Berkeley: University of California Press, 1985), esp. pp. 67–68; and Raoul Birnbaum, "Thoughts on T'ang Buddhist Mountain Traditions and Their Context," *T'ang Studies* 2 (Winter 1984):5–23. It appears that we have now come full circle, for the distinction between the "Great Tradition" of the literate few and the "Little Tradition" of the illiterate many was originally made with the intention of showing how they were interrelated rather than dichotomous; see McKim Marriott, "Little Communities in an Indigenous Civilization," in *Village India:*

This study has instead attempted to explore the many meanings that the ghost festival assumed for different groups—on their own ground, rather than as poor reflections of the Great Traditions—within Chinese society.

There remain significant limits to the conclusions to be drawn from a close-grained analysis of the place of the ghost festival in medieval Chinese society. In the third through ninth centuries Chinese society, as best as can be determined, was stratified not simply along class lines, but also by variations in literacy and in affiliation with institutional religion. A mere determination of class still leaves important questions unsettled. Granted that peasants constituted the majority of those providing offerings to monks in temples, the question remains whether ritual served to alienate or rather to fulfill the needs of that class. Did the ghost festival tend to conceal the true nature of class society, masking the economic control that large landholders (the great families and the Buddhist church) exercised over all segments of society? Or did Mu-lien's tour of hell and the payment of spirit money to the bureaucrats of the dark regions teach people instead to understand and even to manipulate the political apparatus that governed their lives? One suspects that both alternatives may have been true, but given the state of the field, the issue is less likely to be decided on the basis of evidence (since relatively little is available) than by political orientation.[4]

Social divisions in China were further complicated by differences in language: class culture could not be determined straightforwardly on the basis of which languages one spoke and which literatures one read. Patrick Hanan writes:

> The Classical, vernacular, and oral languages are media and cannot be directly equated with class-differentiated cultures in society. One can conceive of a "high" oral literature performed at court which could not be associated with a "low," or popular, culture. But in general, the Classical and oral literatures do reflect somewhat different emphases within Chinese culture. If the potential publics for the three literatures are thought of as concentric circles, the circle of the Classical literature will be surrounded by

---

Studies in the Little Community, ed. McKim Marriott, Comparative Studies of Cultures and Civilizations, No. 6, *The American Anthropological Association Memoir* 57:3 (June 1955): Part 2, No. 83.

[4] For an Althusserian analysis and a response, see Stephan D.R. Feuchtwang, "Investigating Religion," in *Marxist Analyses and Social Anthropology*, ed. Maurice Bloch (London: Malaby Press, 1975), pp. 61–82; and Emily Martin Ahern, *Chinese Ritual and Politics*, Cambridge Studies in Social Anthropology, No. 34 (Cambridge: Cambridge University Press, 1981), esp. pp. 92–108.

the somewhat larger circle of the vernacular, while both will be engulfed by the vastly larger circle of the oral, the only true mass literature of premodern times. . . . The differences lie not in distinct systems of philosophical and religious belief but in different emphases among attitudes and values.[5]

Attitudes and values were further diffracted according to one's relationship to organized religion. Members of the same class with the same rudimentary level of literacy, for example, would have quite different interpretations of the protagonist of *The Transformation Text on Mu-lien Saving His Mother from the Dark Regions*, depending on whether they were monks or members of a lay Buddhist society on the one hand or unaffiliated lay people on the other.

Rather than consign the ghost festival to the amorphous lump of "popular religion," I have documented and assessed the festival as it appears at all levels of Chinese society. Yet Chinese society itself appears so ridden with variation in class, literacy, and religiosity, that my analysis may well appear lost in details, its clarity threatened by the complexity (or chaos) of the social landscape.

But we are left with something more (or, as Chuang-tzu would say, something less) than chaos. I would suggest that in paying attention to the social context of Chinese religion, we must take pains to employ concepts more detailed than just "popular religion," with its inherently dichotomous and top-heavy assumptions. Specifically, as I have attempted to do in the later chapters of this study, we must address the enduring components of Chinese socioreligious life: mythology, ritual, cosmological conceptions, religious virtuosi, the ancestral cult. A better understanding of Chinese culture will be achieved only when these forms of Chinese religion are explored against the background of Chinese society.

A RITUAL PERSPECTIVE

While one style of analysis pursued in this study breaks down the ghost festival, emphasizing its different meanings in different social contexts, another style of analysis, equally important, necessitates a more synthetic view.[6] It is true that the crowd drawn to temples for the celebra-

[5] Patrick Hanan, *The Chinese Vernacular Story* (Cambridge: Harvard University Press, 1981), pp. 12–13. See also Johnson, "Communication, Class, and Consciousness in Late Imperial China," pp. 34–72.

[6] This section extends the arguments made in an earlier essay; see Stephen F. Teiser, "Ghosts and Ancestors in Medieval Chinese Religion: The Yü-lan-p'en Festival as Mortuary Ritual," HR 26:1 (August 1986):47–67.

tion of the full moon of the seventh month was far from homogeneous. Participants came from all classes, all levels of literacy, and from homes as well as monasteries. But if the festival attracted a crowd distinguished by its plurality, the festival was also a complex whole. The ghost festival was a multivalent symbolic event that drew together different classes, united a variety of social forces, and expressed a curious blend of values. Viewing the festival as ritual—specifically, the kind of rite that marks a socially valued passage—allows a deeper appreciation of the integrity of the event.

To most interpreters, the ghost festival betrays ambiguity: it joins together two sides that in a strictly rational world would otherwise be kept separate. Tsung-mi devotes a portion of his *Commentary on the Yü-lan-p'en Sūtra* to a discussion of mortuary ritual, in which he attempts to distinguish Buddhist from Confucian rituals:

> Confucians place the coffin in the grave, preserving the material form. Buddhists chant, recite, and hold posthumous feasts, serving the departed consciousness. . . . Confucians practice internal purity and external calm, thinking of [their ancestors'] utterances and actions. Buddhists set out offerings and expound sūtras, aiding [their ancestors'] karmic retribution.[7]

The beauty of Tsung-mi's analysis is that it makes a Buddho-Confucian out of everyone. The separation between the "Confucians" and the "Buddhists" is illusory from the very start. "Buddhism" and "Confucianism" arise only by abstracting from the actual ritual, which involves *both* burial and commemoration, meditative repose and communal recitation. Other Buddhist apologists and historians augment the polarization inherent in Tsung-mi's account, viewing the ghost festival as a contradictory mix of interests, the stress on family being opposed to the higher Buddhist goal of deliverance from the cycle of rebirth.[8] Confucian defenders of indigenous customs have postulated the same dichotomy, but with the opposite valuation. Yen Chih-t'ui (531–591), for instance, applauded the way in which the ghost festival strengthened the solidarity of the kinship group, but he remained critical of the offerings—part of the same ritual—intended to appease hungry ghosts.[9]

For other interpreters the emotional ambivalence of the festival es-

---

[7] *Tsung-mi Commentary*, T. no. 1792, 39:505b.

[8] See, for example, Tsuda Sōkichi, *Shina bukkyō no kenkyū* (Tokyo: Iwanami shoten, 1957); and Michihata Ryōshū, *Bukkyō to jukyō* (Tokyo: Daisan bunmeisha, 1976).

[9] See Ssu-yü Teng, trans., *Family Instructions for the Yen Clan: "Yen-shih chia-hsün" by Yen Chih-t'ui*, T'oung Pao Monograph No. 4 (Leiden: E. J. Brill, 1968), p. 211.

calates to a scandal of rationality. In this view participants in the ghost festival use faulty logic, since they simultaneously hold incommensurate notions of the afterlife:

> In many ways Buddhism and ancestor worship were contradictory. . . . The idea of re-birth is clearly contrary to the concept of a continuing ancestral spirit. Could one logically go on worshipping an ancestor who had been reborn as an animal or as another person?[10]

But the two voices of the ghost festival—one expressing fear of ghosts, the other proclaiming admiration for ancestors—need not be diagnosed as indications of schizophrenia. The two sides of ghost festival symbolism, summed up in the friction between ghost and ancestor, may well suggest something far more healthy, interesting, and intelligent. Accepting, rather than explaining away, the ambivalences of the ghost festival requires a closer look at the relationship between ghosts and ancestors.

It would appear that the rituals of the ghost festival embrace not an illicit pairing of opposites, but a continuum defined by ghosts at one end and by ancestors at the other. In his seminal study of symbolic classification in a community near Taipei, Arthur Wolf writes:

> The important point is that however they arrange their [spirit] tablets, people in San-hsia recognize a continuum of obligation that runs from those dead to whom the living are obligated by descent to those to whom they are hardly obligated at all. The dead at one end of the continuum are true ancestors; the dead at the other end are almost ghosts.[11]

This line of analysis may be pursued still further in the case of the ghost festival. As a performance, the festival does more than just mirror the concerns of society with the class of strangers (ghosts) and the class of loved ones (ancestors). My suggestion is that, like other rites of passage, the ghost festival effects a transition from one status to the next.

It may well be argued that the ghost festival marks not one passage, but four. Through the offerings given to please and appease them, the

---

[10] Hugh D.R. Baker, *Chinese Family and Kinship* (New York: Columbia University Press, 1979), p. 98.

[11] Arthur P. Wolf, "Gods, Ghosts, and Ancestors," in *Religion and Ritual in Chinese Society*, ed. Arthur P. Wolf (Stanford: Stanford University Press, 1974), p. 159. The quotation cited here tends to contradict Wolf's later portrayal (p. 169) of "the extreme contrast . . . between the gods and ancestors on the one hand, and ghosts on the other."

"dead"—that class of beings whose vitality is disturbing but never in doubt—are moved from the threatening category of ghost to the honored position of ancestor. For the living the festival marks a second passage, the successful completion of the first half of the year. For monks whose lives are regulated by a calendar inverse to the secular one, the ghost festival marks not only the end of the old year and the inauguration of the new one, but also the release of ascetic vigor built up in retreat. A fourth passage is marked in the agricultural cycle, in which the harvest is synchronized with the last bloom of *yang* forces in the face of autumn's chilling winds.

The ghost festival shares many of the features regularly identified with rites of passage. Since they surround the transition from one social world to the next, rites of passage comprise an unavoidable sequence of phases. In the first phase the individual is separated from his or her previous status. Plucked out of the flow of normal time but not yet having arrived at a secure station, the individual is in transit, and symbols of liminality are especially pronounced in this phase. The second phase occurs when the individual crosses beyond the threshold and is incorporated into a new group. Themes of integration and rebirth are typical of this second phase of aggregation.[12]

The phasic nature of rites of passage goes far toward explaining the ambiguous symbolism of the ghost festival; it allows us to make sense out of the presence of both ghosts and ancestors in the festival. The celebration of the seventh moon marks the passage of the dead from the liminal stage, where they are troublesome, threatening, and feared as ghosts, to the stage of incorporation, in which they assume a place of honor within the family. In the liminal phase the dead lack clothes, they have subhuman bodies, they have difficulty eating, they are constantly in motion. Ghosts are a species in transition. The dead person's *hun* and *p'o* spirits are unstable, waiting to be assigned their next rebirth. Ghost festival offerings are frequently dedicated to this dangerously shifting group of "all sinners in the six paths of rebirth" (*i-ch'ieh liu-tao tsui-jen*). But offerings are also made to the dead in the phase of incorporation, after they have joined the group of ancestors stretching back seven generations. As ancestors they have successfully completed the journey

[12] My summary of rites of passage here draws especially on Arnold van Gennep, *The Rites of Passage*, trans. Monika B. Vizedom and Gabrielle L. Caffee (Chicago: University of Chicago Press, 1960); Robert Hertz, *Death and the Right Hand*, trans. Rodney Needham and Claudia Needham (Glencoe: Free Press, 1960); and Edmund Leach, "Two Essays concerning the Symbolic Representation of Time," in *Rethinking Anthropology*, London School of Economics Monographs on Social Anthropology, No. 22 (London: Athlone Press, 1961).

from life, through death, to rebirth. They are welcomed back into the family as its immortal progenitors, creators and maintainers of the values necessary to sustain the life of the kinship group.

Far from indicating a confusion of categories or an accident of history, the coupling of apprehension about ghosts with the propitiation of kin represents a necessary ambivalence about the dead. The ghost festival articulates the fear that the dead have not been resettled and might continue to haunt the community as strangers, at the same time that it expresses the hope that the dead be reincorporated at the head of the family line. By analyzing the processual structure of the ghost festival ritual, we are better able to understand how it holds together as a coherent system.

AN HISTORICAL PERSPECTIVE

To the relativities of class and the aggregating function of ritual must be added the vagaries of history. The ghost festival developed on the basis of earlier celebrations, but its most familiar features appeared only in the fourth or fifth century, largely through the influence of the mythology, rituals, and social forms of Buddhism. During the T'ang dynasty the myth of Mu-lien rescuing his mother from the fires of hell gripped the Chinese imagination, which came easily to accept the fact that its filial hero, Mu-lien, was not simply a follower of the Buddha but a monk, one who had formally renounced the comforts and duties of kinship. Toward the end of the medieval period, however, Buddhism started to assume a different profile in Chinese society. Although the power of the Buddhist church began to wane, nevertheless Buddhist ideas and practices were woven more effectively into the fabric of social life. Thus the decline of Buddhism as an institutional religion coincided with the greatest diffusion of Buddhist influence throughout Chinese society. The historical course of the ghost festival offers several insights into this broader pattern of change.

The reigning paradigm teaches that Chinese Buddhism reached its peak in the late medieval period under the T'ang dynasty. Buddhism entered China in the first century of the common era as a religion of foreign merchants and missionaries, and several centuries passed before the Chinese were able to translate properly the ideas of the Indian religion. But once Buddhism was understood, it was quickly modified to suit Chinese tastes. This process of "sinicization" is thought to be represented most clearly in several phenomena of the T'ang dynasty: the brilliant career of the pilgrim and translator, Hsüan-tsang (602–664); the ascendancy of the Ch'an school, marking the union of Taoist

221

spontaneity with a mature understanding of Mādhyamika emptiness; the poetry and outlook on life of Po Chü-i (772–846); and the ingenuity of numerous doctrinal formulations (*p'an-chiao*, "division of the teachings") used to comprehend and systematize the entire history of Buddhism. Paul Demiéville summarizes the standard view:

> Under the T'ang (from 618 to 909), who assumed the heritage of the Sui and made China for three centuries the most brilliant empire of the world, Chinese Buddhism reached its apogee. To speak nowadays of a fervent Buddhist, one still says in vernacular Chinese, "a Buddhist of the T'ang." At this time there is no art nor literature that could not in some measure be called Buddhist; economic life is renewed under the influence of the Buddhist church, in which the embryo of capitalism is born; and as for philosophical thought in this age, one is at pains to find any outside of Buddhism.[13]

With social conditions always exerting a strong pressure on the trajectory of Buddhism, periods of severe decline often followed the high points. The rebellion of An Lu-shan between 755 and 763 effectively marked the end of centralized power, and the Huang Ch'ao rebellion between 874 and 884 brought destruction and social chaos unprecedented in the T'ang. Between these two cataclysms came the suppression of Buddhist institutions that peaked in the year 845, from which only the Ch'an and Pure Land schools emerged intact. If the T'ang dynasty represents the high point, it also contains some of the most violent convolutions in the institutional history of Buddhism in China.

A consideration of the diachronic dimension of the ghost festival, however, casts some doubt on the historical veracity of the standard model, which tends to undervalue the significance of important developments both before and after the T'ang. In assessing the cosmology presented in the legends of the ghost festival, this study has drawn attention to the synthesis of Indian and Chinese conceptions of the afterlife, a synthesis that was achieved in the first few centuries A.D., before the ghost festival first appears in the written records. The standard

---

[13] Paul Demiéville, "Le Bouddhisme chinois," *Encyclopédie de la Pléiade, histoire des religions* (Paris: Gallimard, 1970), 1:1275, reprinted in Demiéville, *Choix d'études bouddhiques* (Leiden: E. J. Brill, 1974), p. 391. For other discussions of the special characteristics of Chinese Buddhism during the T'ang dynasty, see Robert M. Gimello, "Chih-yen (602–668) and the Foundations of Hua-yen Buddhism" (Ph.D. dissertation, Columbia University, 1976), esp. pp. 93–130; and Peter N. Gregory, "Chinese Buddhist Hermeneutics: The Case of Hua-yen," *Journal of the American Academy of Religion* 51:2 (June 1983):231–49.

model places this synthesis much later, in the Sung dynasty, after the institutional strength of Buddhism had declined.[14] Later periods of Buddhist history are made even more problematic, since they tend to be judged by the monochromatic ideal of doctrinal innovation against which they invariably fall short. Yet surely the rich story of post-T'ang Buddhism contains as many examples of innovation and renewal as of decline.[15]

The accepted paradigm is not so much wrong as it is one-sided. Most studies of Buddhism during its golden age concentrate on doctrine.[16] But if Buddhism did indeed reach its peak during the T'ang, its manifestations must be sought in less rarified realms of Chinese culture; the graph we draw of Buddhism's path must include more dimensions than just time and thought. In fact, the more pervasive influence of Buddhism on Chinese society is to be seen in domains that are not distinctively Buddhist.

The account of the ghost festival sketched in these pages offers several important lessons concerning the historical process through which "religious phenomena translate themselves into a reorganization of the social."[17] Not only was the festival instrumental in bringing about far-reaching changes in Chinese society, it also serves—now as part of a narrative written in the historical style—as a convenient lens for viewing several of these transformations.

The emergence of the ghost festival in medieval times signifies an important alteration in the traditional calendar. While the festival was undoubtedly established on the basis of earlier celebrations held in the middle of the seventh month, beginning in medieval times the festival held on that day would henceforth never escape association with insti-

[14] According to Arthur F. Wright, "Before Buddhism divine retribution was believed to fall upon families; Buddhism then introduced the idea of karmic causation, but this was on an individual basis. Finally the two were interwoven into the view that has prevailed since the Sung period; that divine retribution works on a family basis *and* through a chain of lives"; Arthur F. Wright, *Buddhism in Chinese History* (Stanford: Stanford University Press, 1959), p. 105.

[15] See, for example, Judith A. Berling, *The Syncretic Religion of Lin Chao-en* (New York: Columbia University Press, 1980); and Chün-fang Yü, *The Renewal of Buddhism in China: Chu-hung and the Late Ming Synthesis* (New York: Columbia University Press, 1981).

[16] Important exceptions to this generalization include: Kenneth K.S. Ch'en, *The Chinese Transformation of Buddhism* (Princeton: Princeton University Press, 1973); Jacques Gernet, *Les Aspects économiques du bouddhisme dans la société chinoise du Ve au Xe siècle* (Saigon: Ecole Française d'Extrême-Orient, 1956); Michihata Ryōshū, *Tōdai bukkyō shi no kenkyū* (Kyoto: Hōzōkan, 1957); and Stanley Weinstein, *Buddhism under the T'ang* (Cambridge: Cambridge University Press, 1987).

[17] Gernet, *Les Aspects économiques du bouddhisme*, p. xiii.

CHAPTER 8

tutional religion. The affiliation of the festival with organized religion is unmistakable in the medieval period, when offerings were made regularly to Buddhist (and Taoist) monks at their temples. After the medieval period the linkage was maintained more indirectly: if celebrations were carried out less often within the walls of the temple, the timing of the festival was still synchronized with the end of the summer retreat for monks.

The medieval ghost festival also sheds important light on the history of Chinese mortuary practices. The condition of the dead, formerly pictured only in hazy generalities, was now defined in horrifying detail. The stories that were told about the founding of the festival relate the journey of deceased spirits through the courts of hell, where they undergo questioning, judgment, and torture before being assigned to their next rebirth. The mythology of the ghost festival provides numerous examples of how Buddhist landmarks in the other world (King Yama's court, Avīci Hell, the karma mirror that reflects past deeds) became permanent additions to Chinese topography. The worldview reflected in the medieval ghost festival constituted a mature synthesis of Indian deities and concepts with Chinese ones, lacking only the numerical systematization of hells characteristic of postmedieval religion. The portrait of the hells drawn in yü-lan-p'en literature was also important for didactic purposes: in showing the torments suffered by the dead it supplied unequivocal justification for performing the key ritual of the ghost festival, which was designed to secure a pleasurable rebirth for one's kin.

The influence of the ghost festival on Chinese society is enshrined most clearly in the domain of family religion. In early medieval China, monks were viewed as ungrateful profligates whose egotism drove them to reject the family while reaping the material benefits accorded them by Chinese law. But beginning in the T'ang, as seen most clearly in the transactions of the ghost festival, monasticism was accepted, though never without complaint, as a necessary complement to family life. In the rituals of the ghost festival, householder and ascetic are both needed to maintain the harmonious workings of nature and to further the welfare of the living and the dead. By virtue of the soteriological efficacy that monks alone command, the Sangha was made an essential part of Chinese family religion. Precisely because they had shed the bonds of kinship, monks gained the power to produce even greater blessings for the family. The history of the ghost festival documents the addition of the role of world renouncer to the social world of traditional China, illustrating the way in which Buddhism prepared its own transformation, synthesis—and, after the medieval period, its diffusion—throughout the entire fabric of Chinese society.

Character Glossary of
Chinese, Korean, and Japanese Words

a-p'o 阿婆

an-chü 安居

[Ta] An-kuo ssu 大安國寺

An Lu-shan 安祿山

bon 盆

bon odori 盆踊り

ch'an 禪

ch'an-ting 禪定

Chang-ching ssu 章敬寺

Chang Hsiao-shih 張孝師

Chang Hu 張祜

ch'ang 嚐

Ch'ang-an 長安

ch'ang-chu seng-wu 常住僧物

Ch'ang-lo 長樂

Ch'ang-shan 常山

chao 照

chao-shen 召神

chao-t'i 招提

chao-t'i k'o/seng 招提客 / 僧

chen 眞

Chen-yüan 眞元

Ch'en Ching-yen 陳淨眼

Ch'en Hung 陳鴻

Cheng Ssu-hsiao 鄭思肖

Ch'eng Ching 成景

ch'eng-ying 成影

Chi-kuo ssu 紀國寺

chi-ssu 祭祠

Chi-tsang 吉藏

Ch'i 齊

ch'i-lin 麒麟

ch'i-pao p'en-po 七寶盆鉢

ch'i te wang-yang 其德汪洋

ch'i-yüeh shih-wu-jih 七月十五日

chia-ch'ih-na 迦絺那

chiang-ching-wen 講經文

ch'iang-ku 搶孤

chien-shen 見神

Ch'ien-niu 牽牛

Chih-lang 智郎

Chih-li 智禮

Chih-nü 織女

Chih-yen 智嚴

Chih-yüan 智圓

Ching-fa ssu 淨法寺

ching-hsin 敬心

Ching-kung ssu 景公寺

Ching-ling 竟陵

ching-lü 靜慮

ching-t'u chih hsing 淨土之行

Ching-yü ssu 淨域寺

"Ch'ing-p'ing t'iao-tz'u" 清平調詞

Ch'ing-t'i 清提

ch'iu-yu 求有

Chou 周

Chu-hung 袾宏

Chu Tao-shuang 竺道爽

ch'u 初

Ch'u 楚

ch'u-liu 貙劉

chüeh-chih 覺枝

Chüeh-chiu 覺救

chüeh-tao 覺道

Chung-shang shu 中尙署

chung-yin 中陰

chung-yu 中有

chung-yüan 中元

chung-yüan jih 中元日

"Chung-yung-tzu chuan" 中庸子傳

Ch'ung-fu ssu 崇福寺

Ch'ung-wen kuan 崇文舘

225

Daianji 大安寺

"Daianji shizai chō" 大安寺資財帳

Ennin 圓仁

Enryakuji 延曆寺

Fa-chü 法炬

Fa-hui ta-shih 法慧大師

fa-la 法臘

fa-shih 法師

Fang 房

Fang Hsüan-ling 房玄齡

fang-shih 方士

fang yen-k'ou 放焰口

fen-hsing 分形

feng 封

fo 佛

Fo-t'u-teng 佛圖澄

fo-tzu 佛子

fu 福

fu-ch'u 祓除

Fu Hsiang 輔相

Fu-hsien ssu 福先寺

fu-t'ien 福田

Gentō 玄棟

Hang-chou 杭州

Hiei 比叡

Ho 何

Hong Sŏng-mo 洪錫謨

hsi 覡

hsi[b] 禊

Hsi Ho 義和

Hsi-ming ssu 西明寺

"Hsi t'ai-shan wen" 檄太山文

"Hsi-tz'u chuan" 繫辭傳

Hsi-yu chi 西遊記

hsiang-shih 相士

Hsiao-p'en pao-en ching 小盆報恩經

Hsiao Tzu-liang 蕭子良

Hsien-ch'ing 顯慶

hsien-fo 獻佛

hsin 心

Hsin-hsing 信行

Hsing-t'ang kuan 興唐觀

Hsiuan- [Hsüan-] tsung 宣宗

Hsü 徐

Hsüan-tsang 玄奘

Hsüan-tsung 玄宗

Hua 華

Hua-tu ssu 化度寺

Hua-yen 華嚴

Hua-yin 華陰

Huang Ch'ao 黃巢

huang-ch'eng 皇城

huang-ch'üan 黃泉

Hui-ch'ang 會昌

Hui-chao 慧沼

Hui-ching 慧淨

Hui-ta 慧達

hun 魂

"Hun-t'ien fu" 渾天賦

hun-tun 混沌

i-ch'eng 意成

i-ch'ieh liu-tao tsui-jen 一切六道罪人

i-huo 疑惑

jen-t'ien chiao 人天教

Jikaku daishi 慈覺大師

jo 若

ju 儒

Ju-i 如意

ju-tsang 入藏

K'ai-yüan ssu 開元寺

kan-che chung 甘蔗種

Kao 高

K'ao-tsu 高祖

kou-lan 勾欄

kou-ssu 構肆

Ku 孤

kua-chieh 瓜節

K'uai-chi 會稽

Kuan-la ching 灌臘經

Kuan- [shih-] yin 觀世音

Kuan-ti 關帝

kuan-ting 灌頂

Kuan-tzu 管子

Kuang-shun men 光順門

226

kuei-chieh 鬼節

Kuei-feng 圭峯

kuei-wei 癸未

k'un 坤

K'un-lun 崑崙

kung-hsü 恭須

kung-shun 恭順

kung-te 功德

K'ung Ying-ta 孔穎達

Kuo 果

kuo-chia kung-yang 國家供養

lan-p'en 蘭盆

Lao-tzu pien-hua ching 老子變化經

Li-fo i-shih 禮佛儀式

Li Lou 離婁

Li-pu yüan-wai-lang 禮部員外郎

Liang 梁

lien 鍊

Lien-yün ch'an-yüan 連雲禪院

lin 麟

Lin Pu 林逋

Ling-chih ssu 靈芝寺

Ling-hu Ch'u 令狐楚

liu-ch'ü 六趣

liu-tao 六道

Lo-pu 羅卜

Lo-t'o 羅陀

Lo-yang 落陽

Lo-yüeh 羅閱

lou 漏

Lu Kung 盧拱

Lu Leng-ch'ieh 盧稜伽

lu-tou 菉豆

Lu Yüan-yü 盧元裕

luan 鸞

Lung-hsi Li Yen 隴西李儼

mang-hon il 亡魂日

men-t'u 門徒

Meng Tsung 孟宗

ming-lu 冥路

Mo-li-chih 摩利支

Mu-chien-lien 目揵蓮

Mu Jen-ch'ien 睦仁蒨

Mu-lien 目蓮

Mu-lien pien 目蓮變

Na-she 那舍

Nai-ho 奈河

Nara 奈良

nei tao-ch'ang 內道場

o-kuei 餓鬼

obon お盆

paek-chong il 百種日

p'an-chiao 判教

Pao-chih 寶誌

pao-chüan 寶卷

pao-en 報恩

Pao-sha ssu 寶利寺

Pao-yün 寶雲

pei-hsin 悲心

pen-ming 本命

pen-sheng 本生

p'en 盆

p'en-tso-na 盆佐那

p'i-yü 譬喻

pien-hsiang 變相

pien-hua 變化

pien-wen 變文

p'ing-cheng 平正

p'ing-teng 平等

Po Chü-i 白居易

Po-ling 博陵

p'o 魄

Pu-k'ung chin-kang 不空金剛

pu-shih 布施

P'u-kuang ssu 普光寺

p'u-tu 普渡

Saichō 最澄

san-chieh chiao 三階教

san-kuan 三官

san-ming 三明

san-shih-san-t'ien 三十三天

san-yüan 三元

shan 禪

shan-wai, shan-chia 山外山家

Shao-fu chien 少府監

shen 神

shen-tsu 神足

shen-t'ung 神通

sheng 聖

sheng-mao chih wei-i 盛貌之威儀

sheng-yin 生陰

shih-en 十恩

Shih-i lun 釋疑論

shih-kung 師公

shih-pa pien 十八變

shih-pa wang san-mei ting 十八王三
    昧定

Shih Po 石伯

shih-tzu pu 獅子步

Shōsōin 正倉院

shui-lu hui 水陸會

Sōni ryō 僧尼令

Ssu-chung ssu 四衆寺

ssu-yin 死陰

su-chiang 俗講

Su-chou 蘇州

sung ma-ku 送麻穀

Ta-li 大歷

Ta-ming kung 大明宮

Ta-p'en ching-t'u ching 大盆淨土經

Ta-t'ung 大同

Tai-tsung 代宗

T'ai-ch'ang po-shih 太常博士

t'ai-miao 太廟

T'ai-shan 泰／太山

T'ai-shang tao-chün 太上道君

T'ai-yüan 太圓

T'an-yao 曇曜

T'ang Lin 唐臨

tao-ch'ang 道場

tao-hsien 倒懸

tao-li t'ien 忉利天

Tao-ming 道明

Tao-seng ko 道僧格

Te-tsung 德宗

Tempyō 天寶

Tempyō shōhō 天平勝寶

Ti-tsang 地藏

ti-yü 地獄

tien 點

Ting-hui ch'an-shih 定慧禪師

Tongguk sesigi 東國歲時記

tsa-chü 雜劇

Ts'ai Tzu-huang 蔡子晃

tsang-shih 藏識

Ts'ao Sai-ying 曹塞英

Tseng-tzu 曾子

Ts'ui Wei 崔煒

Ts'ui Yüan-yü 崔元翮

Tsun-shih 遵式

Tsung Lin 宗懍

Tsung-mi 宗密

Tu-t'o ssu 度脫寺

Tung An 董黯

tung-fang p'u-sa 東方菩薩

tung-yüeh 東嶽

Tung Yung 董永

t'ung 通

t'ung-chi 童㐱

t'ung-shen 通神

T'ung-t'ai ssu 同泰寺

t'ung-yung chih wu 通用之物

Tzu-chou 梓州

tzu-tzu 自恣

tzu-tzu chieh-mo 自恣羯磨

Tz'u-en ssu 慈恩寺

urabon 盂蘭盆

Wan Hui 萬迴

Wang Chin 王縉

Wang Hsiang 王祥

Wang Tsu-te 王祖德

Wang Wei 王維

wei 威

wei[b] 僞

wei[c] 謂

wei-i hsiang-hsü 威儀序序

wei-li 威力

wei-shen 威神

Wŏrin sŏkpo 月氏釋譜

wu 巫

Wu 武

wu-hsing 五行

Wu-t'ai 五台

Wu-tao chiang-chün 五道將軍

Wu-tao chuan-lun wang 五道轉輪王

Wu Tao-hsüan 吳道玄

Wu-tsung 武宗

yang 陽

Yang Chiung 楊炯 / 炯

Yen Chih-t'ui 顏之推

Yen-lo wang 閻羅王

Yen-lo wang shuo i ti-yü ching 閻羅王
　說逸地獄經

Yen-lo wang tung-t'ai-shan ching 閻羅王
　東太山經

yin 陰

Yin Yao-fan 殷堯藩

yin-yüan 因緣

Ying-ch'uan 盈川

yu ching shuo 有經說

yu-shen 遊神

yü-lan 盂蘭

yü-lan[b] 魚籃

yü-lan[c] 盂籃

Yü-lan ch'ing-ching ching 盂蘭清淨經

yü-lan fo-p'en 盂蘭佛盆

yü-lan hui 盂蘭會

yü-lan-p'en 盂蘭盆

yü-lan-p'en[b] 筷籃盆

yü-li 玉歷

yüan 元

yüan[b] 願

Yüan-ch'ing 源清

Yüan-shih t'ien-tsun 元始天尊

Yüeh-ling 月令

yün 蘊

yung 雍

yung[b] 擁

Yung-t'ai 永泰

Bibliography

I. PRIMARY SOURCES

A. Works in Buddhist and Taoist Collections

A-p'i-ta-mo chü-she lun 阿毘達磨俱舍論 *(Abhidharmakośa).* Vasubandhu, translated by Hsüan-tsang 玄奘 (602–664). T. no. 1558. Translation by La Vallée Poussin, *L'Abhidharmakośa.*

A-p'i-ta-mo ta p'i-p'o-sha lun 阿毘達磨大毘婆沙論 *(Mahāvibhāṣā).* Translated by Hsüan-tsang 玄奘 (602–664). T. no. 1545.

Chai-chieh lu 齋戒錄. Ca. late seventh century. TT. no. 464.

Chan-ch'a shan-o yeh-pao ching 占察善惡業報經. P'u-t'i-teng 菩提燈 (ca. 590–618). T. no. 839.

Ch'ang a-han ching 長阿含經 *(Dīrghāgama).* Translated by Buddhayaśas (ca. 408–412) and Chu Fo-nien 竺佛念 (ca. 365). T. no. 1.

Cheng-fa nien-ch'u ching 正法念處經 *(Saddharmasmṛtyupasthānasūtra).* Translated by Gautama Prajñāruci (ca. 538–543). T. no. 721.

Chien-cheng lun 甄正論. Hsüan-i 玄嶷 (ca. 690–705). T. no. 2112.

Chih-sheng-kuang tao-ch'ang nien-sung i 熾盛光道場念誦儀. Tsun-shih 遵式 (964–1032). T. no. 1951.

Chin-ch'üeh ti-chün san-yüan chen-i ching 金闕帝君三元眞一經. Late fourth century. TT. no. 253.

Chin-yüan chi 金園集. Tsun-shih 遵式 (964–1032). Z. 2A, 6:2.

Ching-lü i-hsiang 經律異相. Pao-ch'ang 寶唱 (ca. 516). T. no. 2121.

Chiu mien-jan o-kuei t'o-lo-ni shen-chou ching 救面然餓鬼陀羅尼神祝經. Śikṣānanda (652–710). T. no. 1314.

Chiu-pa yen-k'ou o-kuei t'o-lo-ni ching 救拔焰口餓鬼陀羅尼經. Amoghavajra (705–774). T. no. 1313.

Chiu tsa p'i-yü ching 舊雜譬喻經. Translated by K'ang Seng-hui 康僧會 (d. 280). T. no. 206.

Chu-ching yao-chi 諸經要集. Tao-shih 道世 (d. 683). T. no. 2123.

Ch'u san-tsang chi-chi 出三藏記集. Seng-yu 僧祐 (445–518). T. no. 2145.

Chuan-chi po-yüan ching 撰集百緣經 *(Avadānaśataka).* Translated by Chih Ch'ien 支謙 (ca. 220–252). T. no. 200. Cf. translation from Sanskrit by Feer, *L'Avadāna-Cataka.*

Chung a-han ching 中阿含經 *(Madhyamāgama).* Translated by Gautama Saṃghadeva (ca. 383–398). T. no. 26.

Chung-ching mu-lu 眾經目錄. Fa-ching 法經 (ca. 594). T. no. 2146.

Chung-ching mu-lu 眾經目錄. Yen-tsung 彥琮 (ca. 602). T. no. 2147.

231

Chung-ching mu-lu 衆經目錄. Ching-t'ai 靜泰 (ca. 665). T. no. 2148.

Dai nihon bukkyō zensho 大日本佛教全書. 100 vols. Tokyo: Suzuki gakujutsu zaidan, 1970–73. Abbreviated as ZS.

Dai nihon zoku zōkyō 大日本續藏經. 150 cases. 1905–12; reprint ed., Shanghai: Commercial Press, 1923. Abbreviated as Z.

Fa-yüan chu-lin 法苑珠林. Tao-shih 道世 (d. 683). T. no. 2122.

Fan-i ming-i chi 翻譯名意集. Fa-yün 法雲 (1088–1158). T. no. 2131.

Fan-wang ching 梵網經. Attributed to Kumārajīva (350–409), probably written ca. 431–481. T. no. 1484. Translations by Ishida, *Bommō kyō*; and de Groot, *Le Code du Mahāyāna en Chine*.

Fo pen-hsing ching 佛本行經. Pao-yün 寶雲 (376–449). T. no. 193.

Fo-tsu li-tai t'ung-tsai 佛祖歷代通載. Nien-ch'ang 念常 (d. 1341). T. no. 2036.

Fo-tsu t'ung-chi 佛祖統記. Chih-p'an 志磐 (ca. 1260). T. no. 2035.

Fo wu-po ti-tzu tzu-shuo pen-ch'i ching 佛五百弟子自說本起經. Dharmarakṣa (ca. 265–313). T. no. 199.

Fu-mu en-chung ching 父母恩重經. T. no. 2887.

Fu-mu en nan-pao ching 父母恩難報經. An Shih-kao 安世高 (ca. 148–170). T. no. 684.

Hsien-chü pien 閑居編. Chih-yüan 智圓 (976–1028). Z. 2A, 6:1.

Hsin-sui ching 新歲經 (*Pravāraṇasūtra*). Chu T'an-wu-lan 竺曇無蘭 (ca. 381–395). T. no. 62.

Hsü kao-seng chuan 續高僧傳. Tao-hsüan 道宣 (596–667). T. no. 2060.

Hung-ming chi 弘明集. Seng-yu 僧祐 (445–518). T. no. 2102.

I-ch'ieh-ching yin-i 一切經音義. Hsüan-ying 玄應 (737–820). T. no. 2128.

K'ai-yüan shih-chiao lu 開元釋教錄. Chih-sheng 智昇 (ca. 669–740). T. no. 2154.

Kao-seng chuan 高僧傳. Hui-chiao 慧皎 (497–554). T. no. 2059.

Kao-seng fa-hsien chuan 高僧法顯傳. Fa-hsien 法顯 (ca. 416). T. no. 2085.

Ken-pen-shuo i-ch'ieh-yu-pu p'i-nai-yeh an-chü shih 根本說一切有部毘奈耶安居事 (*Mūlasarvāstivādavinayavarṣāvastu*). Translated by I-ching 義淨 (635–713). T. no. 1445.

Ken-pen-shuo i-ch'ieh-yu-pu p'i-nai-yeh sui-i shih 根本說一切有部毘奈耶隨意事 (*Mūlasarvāstivādavinayapravāraṇavastu*). Translated by I-ching 義淨 (635–713). T. no. 1446.

Ken-pen-shuo i-ch'ieh-yu-pu p'i-nai-yeh yao-shih 根本說一切有部毘奈耶要事 (*Mūlasarvāstivādavinayavastu*). Translated by I-ching 義淨 (635–713). T. no. 1448.

Kokuyaku issaikyō, wakan senjutsubu 國譯一切經和漢撰述部. 101 vols. Tokyo: Daitō shuppansha, 1958–63.

Ku-chin i-ching t'u-chi 古今譯經圖記. Ch'ing-mai 靖邁 (ca. 645–665). T. no. 2151.

Kuan-fo san-mei hai ching 觀佛三昧海經. Buddhabhadra (359–429). T. no. 643.

Kuan-ting ching 灌頂經. Śrīmitra (ca. 307–355). T. no. 1331.

Kuei wen mu-lien ching 鬼問目連經. An Shih-kao 安世高 (ca. 148–170). T. no. 734.

Lan-p'en ching shu-ch'ao yü-i 蘭盆經疏鈔餘義. Jih-hsin 日新 (ca. 1068). Z. 1, 94:4.

Lan-p'en ching shu chih-hua ch'ao 蘭盆經疏撻華鈔. Chih-yüan 智圓 (976–1028). Not extant; largely reproduced in *Lan-p'en ching shu-ch'ao yü-i*.

Lan-p'en hsien-kung i 蘭盆獻供儀. Yüan-chao 元照 (1048–1116). Z. 2B, 3:2.

Li-huo lun 理惑論. Mou Yung 牟融 (ca. third century). In *Hung-ming chi* 弘明集. Seng-yu 僧祐 (445–518). T. no. 2102. Translation by Pelliot, "Meou-tseu."

Li-tai san-pao chi 歷代三寶記. Fei Ch'ang-fang 費長房 (ca. 561–597). T. no. 2034.

Ling-pao ta-lien nei-chih hsing-ch'ih chi-yao 靈寶大鍊內旨行持機要. Thirteenth century. TT. no. 407.

Liu-tu chi ching 六度集經. K'ang Seng-hui 康僧會 (d. 280). T. no. 152.

Lung-hsing fo-chiao pien-nien t'ung-lun 隆興佛教編年通論. Tsu-hsiu 祖琇 (ca. 1164). Z. 2B, 3: 3–4.

Mi-sha-sai-pu ho-hsi wu-fen lü 彌沙塞部和醯五分律 *(Mahīśāsakavinaya)*. Translated by Buddhajīva (ca. 423–424). T. no. 1421.

Miao-fa lien-hua ching 妙法蓮華經 *(Saddharmapuṇḍarīkasūtra)*. Translated by Kumārajīva (350–409). T. no. 262. Translation by Hurvitz, *Scripture of the Lotus Blossom of the Fine Dharma*.

Ming-pao chi 冥報集. T'ang Lin 唐臨 (ca. 600–659). T. no. 2082.

Ming-seng chuan ch'ao 明僧傳抄. Shūshō 宗性; copy of table of contents of work by Pao-ch'ang 寶唱 (ca. 519). Z. 2B, 7:1.

Mo-li-chih p'u-sa lüeh nien-sung fa 摩利支菩薩略念誦法. Amoghavajra (705–774). T. no. 1258.

Mo-li-chih-t'ien ching 摩利支天經. Amoghavajra (705–774). T. no. 1255b.

Mo-li-chih-t'ien p'u-sa t'o-lo-ni ching 摩利支天菩薩陀羅尼經. Amoghavajra (705–774). T. no. 1255a.

Mo-lo wang ching 末羅王經. Chü-ch'ü Ching-sheng 沮渠京聲 (ca. 455–464). T. no. 517.

Nan-hai chi-kuei nei-fa chuan 南海寄歸內法傳. I-ching 義淨 (635–713). T. no. 2125.

O-kuei pao-ying ching 餓鬼報應經. Anonymous (ca. 317–420). T. no. 746.

Pan-ni-yüan hou kuan-la ching 般泥洹後灌臘經. Attributed to Dharmarakṣa (ca. 265–313). T. no. 391.

Pao-en feng-p'en ching 報恩奉盆經 *(The Sūtra on Offering Bowls to Repay Kindness)*. Anonymous (317–420). T. no. 686.

Pieh-i tsa a-han ching 別譯雜阿含經 *(Saṃyuktāgama)*. Anonymous (ca. 350–431). T. no. 100.

Pien-cheng lun 辯正論. Fa-lin 法琳 (572–640). T. no. 2110.

Ritsuon sōbō den 律苑僧寶傳. Eken 慧堅 (ca. 1689). ZS. Vol. 64.

Sangoku denki 三國傳記. Gentō 玄棟 (ca. 1407). ZS. Vol. 832. Also in Ikegami Jun'ichi 池上洵一, *Sangoku denki* 三国伝記. 2 vols. Tokyo: Miyai shoten, 1976–82.

233

Shih-chia p'u 釋家譜. Seng-yu 僧祐 (445–518). T. no. 2040.

Shih chu o-kuei yin-shih chi shui-fa 施諸餓鬼飲食及水法. Amoghavajra (705–774). T. no. 1315.

Shih-men cheng-t'ung 釋門正統. Tsung-chien 宗鑑 (Sung). Z. 2B, 3:5.

Shih-shih chi-ku lüeh 釋氏稽古略. Chüeh-an 學岸 (ca. 1354). T. no. 2037.

Shih-shih t'ung-lan 施食通覽. Tsung-hsiao 宗曉 (ca. 1204). Z. 2A, 6:3.

Shih-shih yao-lan 釋氏要覽. Tao-ch'eng 道誠 (ca. 1019). T. no. 2127.

Shih-sung lü 十誦律 *(Sarvāstivādavinaya)*. Translated by Kumārajīva (350–409). T. no. 1435.

Shou hsin-sui ching 受新歲經 *(Pravāraṇasūtra)*. Dharmarakṣa (ca. 265–313). T. no. 61.

Ssu-fen lü 四分律 *(Dharmaguptavinaya)*. Translated by Buddhayaśas (ca. 408–412). T. no. 1428.

Sui-tzu-i san-mei 隨自意三昧. Hui-ssu 慧思 (515–577). Z. 2A, 3:4.

Sui-yüan wang-sheng shih-fang ching-t'u ching 隨願往生十方淨土經. Chapter Eleven of *Kuan-ting ching* 灌頂經. Attributed to Śrīmitra (ca. 307–355). T. no. 1331.

Sung kao-seng chuan 宋高僧傳. Tsan-ning 贊寧 (919–1001). T. no. 2061.

Ta chih-tu lun 大智度論 *(Mahāprajñāpāramitāśāstra)*. Kumārajīva (350–409). T. no. 1509. Translation by Lamotte, *Le Traité de la grand vertu de sagesse*.

Ta-chou k'an-ting chung-ching mu-lu 大周刊定眾經目錄. Ming-ch'üan 明佺 (ca. 695). T. no. 2153.

Ta fang-kuang shih-lun ching 大方廣十輪經. Anonymous (ca. 412–439). T. no. 410.

Ta-sheng chuang-yen ching lun 大乘莊嚴經論 *(Mahāyānasūtrālaṃkāra)*. Translated by Prabhāmitra (565–633). T. no. 1604.

Ta-sheng ta-chi ti-tsang shih-lun ching 大乘大集地藏十輪經. Translated by Hsüan-tsang 玄奘 (602–664). T. no. 411.

Ta-sung seng-shih lüeh 大宋僧史略. Tsan-ning 贊寧 (919–1001). T. no. 2126.

Ta-t'ang hsi-yü chi 大唐西域記. Hsüan-tsang 玄奘 (602–664). T. no. 2087. Translation by Beal, *Si-yu-ki*.

Ta-t'ang nei-tien lu 大唐內典錄. Tao-hsüan 道宣 (596–667). T. no. 2149.

T'ai-chi chi-lien nei-fa i-lüeh 太極祭鍊內法儀略. Cheng Ssu-hsiao 鄭思肖 (1239–1316). TT. no. 548.

T'ai-shang huang-lu-chai i 太上黃錄齋儀. Tu Kuang-t'ing 杜光庭 (850–933). TT. no. 507.

T'ai-shang tung-hsüan ling-pao chih-hui tsui-ken shang-p'in ta-chieh ching 太上洞玄靈寶智慧罪根上品大戒經. TT. no. 457.

T'ai-shang tung-hsüan ling-pao san-yüan p'in-chieh kung-te ch'ing-chung ching 太上洞玄靈寶三元品戒功德輕重經. Ca. fifth century. TT. no. 456.

T'ai-shang tung-hsüan ling-pao san-yüan yü-ching hsüan-tu ta-hsien ching 太上洞玄靈寶三元玉京玄都大獻經. Ca. sixth century. TT. no. 370.

T'ai-shang tung-hsüan ling-pao yeh-pao yin-yüan ching 太上洞玄靈寶業報因緣經. TT. no. 336.

T'ai-shang tzu-pei tao-ch'ang hsiao-tsai chiu-yu ch'an 太上慈悲道場消災九幽懺. TT. no. 543.

Taishō shinshū daizōkyō 大正新修大藏經. 100 vols. 1924–34; reprint ed., Taipei: Hsin-wen-feng ch'u-pan kung-ssu, 1974. Abbreviated as T.

Tao-tsang 道藏. 1120 vols. Shanghai: Commercial Press, 1924–26. Abbreviated as TT. References use the numbering system in the Harvard-Yenching index, *Tao-tsang tzu-mu yin-te.*

Ti-tsang p'u-sa pen-yüan ching 地藏菩薩本願經. Translated by Śikṣānanda (652–710). T. no. 412.

Tsa a-han ching 雜阿含經 *(Saṃyuktāgama)*. Translated by Guṇabhadra (394–468). T. no. 99.

Tsa tsang ching 雜藏經. Fa-hsien 法顯 (ca. 399–416). T. no. 745.

Tseng-i a-han ching 增一阿含經 *(Ekottarāgama)*. Translated by Gautama Saṃghadeva (ca. 383–397). T. no. 125.

Wang-sheng chi 往生集. Chu-hung 袾宏 (1535–1615). T. no. 2072.

Wei-mo-chieh so-shuo ching 維摩詰所說經 *(Vimalakīrtinirdeśa)*. Translated by Kumārajīva (350–409). T. no. 475.

Wen-shih ching shu 溫室經疏. Hui-ching 慧淨 (578–ca. 645). S. no. 2497, printed as T. no. 2780.

Wen-shih hsi-yü chung-seng ching 溫室洗浴衆僧經. An Shih-kao 安世高 (ca. 148–170). T. no. 701.

Wen ti-yü ching 問地獄經. K'ang Chü 康巨 (ca. 187). Not extant; fragments quoted in *Ching-lü i-hsiang*, T. no. 2121 and in *Fa-yüan chu-lin*, T. no. 2122.

Wu-shang pi-yao 無上秘要. Completed 583. TT. no. 1130.

Yao-hsiu k'o-i chieh-lü ch'ao 要修科儀戒律鈔. Chu Fa-man 朱法滿 (ca. early seventh century). TT. no. 463.

Yü-ch'ieh chi-yao chiu a-nan t'o-lo-ni yen-k'ou kuei-i ching 瑜伽集要救阿難陀羅尼焰口軌儀經. Amoghavajra (705–774). T. no. 1318.

Yü-ch'ieh shih ti lun 瑜伽師地論 *(Yogacārabhumiśāstra)*. Translated by Hsüan-tsang 玄奘 (602–664). T. no. 1579.

Yü-lan-p'en ching 盂蘭盆經 *(The Yü-lan-p'en Sūtra)*. Attributed to Dharmarakṣa (ca. 265–313). T. no. 685. Translation by Chavannes, *Dix Inscriptions.*

Yü-lan-p'en ching hsin-shu 盂蘭盆經新疏. Chih-hsü 智旭 (1599–1655). Z. 1, 35:2.

Yü-lan-p'en ching lüeh-shu 盂蘭盆經略疏. Yüan-ch'i 元奇 (Ch'ing). Z. 1, 35:2.

Yü-lan-p'en ching shu 盂蘭盆經疏 *(Tsung-mi Commentary)*. Tsung-mi 宗密 (780–841). T. no. 1792.

Yü-lan-p'en ching [shu] che-chung shu 盂蘭盆經疏折中疏. Ling-yao 靈耀 (Ch'ing). Z. 1, 35:2.

Yü-lan-p'en ching shu hsiao-heng ch'ao 盂蘭盆經疏孝衡鈔 *(Yü-jung Commentary)*. Yü-jung 遇榮 (Sung). Z. 1, 94:4.

Yü-lan-p'en ching shu hsin-chi 盂蘭盆經疏新記 *(Yüan-chao Commentary)*. Yüan-chao 元照 (1048–1116). Z. 1, 35:2.

Yü-lan-p'en ching shu hui-ku t'ung-chin chi 盂蘭盆經疏會古通今記. P'u-kuan 普觀 (ca. 1178). Z. 1, 35:2.

Yü-lan-p'en ching tsan-shu 盂蘭盆經讚述 *(Hui-ching Commentary).* Hui-ching 慧淨 (578–ca. 645). P. no. 2269, printed as T. no. 2781.

Yüan-jen lun 源人論. Tsung-mi 宗密 (780–841). T. no. 1886.

B. Other Primary Sources

Ch'ang-an chih 長安志. Sung Min-ch'iu 宋敏求 (1019–1079). Text in *Tōdai no chōan to rakuyō: shiryō hen* 唐代の長安と落陽資料篇. Edited by Hiraoka Takeo 平岡武夫. T'ang Civilization Reference Series, No. 6. Kyoto: Kyoto daigaku jinbun kagaku kenkyūjo, 1956.

Chiang-mo pien-wen 降魔變文. Numerous Tun-huang MSS; reproduced in THPWC.

Chin-ku-yüan chi 金谷園記. Li Yung 李邕 (d. 746). Text in Moriya, *Chūgoku ko saijiki no kenkyū.*

Ching-ch'u sui-shih chi 荊楚歲時記. Tsung Lin 宗懍 (ca. 498–561). Edited by Tu Kung-chan 杜公瞻 (ca. 581–624). Text in Moriya Mitsuo 守屋美都雄, *Chūgoku ko saijiki no kenkyū* 中國古歲時記の研究. Tokyo: Teikoku shoin, 1963. Translation by Moriya, *Keiso saijiki.*

Ching-tu san-mei ching 淨度三昧經. Manuscript fragments include: S. nos. 4546 (printed in Z. 1, 87:4), 2301, 5960; Peking nos. 902, 3563, 3565, 3751.

Ching-t'u yü-lan-p'en ching 淨土盂蘭盆經 *(The Pure Land Yü-lan-p'en Sūtra).* Ca. 600–650. P. no. 2185, printed and translated in Jaworski, "L'Avalambana sūtra" and in Iwamoto, *Jigoku meguri no bungaku.*

Chiu t'ang shu 舊唐書. Liu Hsü 劉昫 (887–946). Peking: Chung-hua shu-chü, 1975.

Chou-i yin-te 周易引得. Harvard-Yenching Institute Sinological Index Series, Supplement No. 10. Reprint ed., Taipei: Ch'eng-wen Publishing Co., 1966.

Chou-li cheng-i 周禮正義. Taipei: Kuang-wen shu-chü, 1972. Translation by Biot, *Le Tcheou-li ou Rites des Tcheou.*

Ch'u-hsüeh chi 初學記. Hsü Chien 徐堅 (659–729). Peking: Chung-hua shu-chü, 1962.

Ch'u-t'ang ssu-chieh wen-chi 初唐四傑文集. Edited by Hsiang Chia-ta 項家達 (Ch'ing). Ssu-pu pei-yao ed. Taipei: Chung-hua shu-chü, 1970.

Chuang-tzu yin-te 莊子引得. Harvard-Yenching Institute Sinological Index Series, Supplement No. 20. Reprint ed., Cambridge: Harvard University Press, 1956.

Ch'üan t'ang shih 全唐詩. Edited by P'eng Ting-ch'iu 彭定求 (1645–1719). 12 vols. Peking: Chung-hua shu-chü, 1960.

(Ch'in-ting) Ch'üan t'ang wen 欽定全唐文. Hsü Sung 徐松 (1781–1848). Taipei: Ching-wei shu-chü, 1965.

Dai nihon komonjo, hennen monjo 大日本古文書編年文書. Edited by Tokyo teikoku daigaku shiryō hensanjo. Tokyo: Tokyo teikoku daigaku, 1901–40.

Fu-mu en-chung ching chiang-ching-wen 父母恩重經講經文. P. no. 2418, printed in THPWC, pp. 672–94.

Fu-mu en-chung t'ai-ku ching 父母恩重胎骨經. Korean xylograph from blocks engraved between 1375 and 1388. Reproduced in Makita, *Gikyō kenkyū*.

Hsiao-tzu chuan 孝子傳. Attributed to Liu Hsiang 劉向 (80–9 B.C.). In *Huang-shih i-shu k'ao* 黃氏遺書考, by Huang Shih 黃氏. *Ts'ung-shu ching-hua* 叢書菁華, Vol. 35. Taipei: I-wen yin-shu-kuan, 1971.

Hsiao-tzu Tung Yung 孝子董永. S. no. 2204, reproduced in THPT 17: 246b–47b.

Hsin t'ang shu 新唐書. Ou-yang Hsiu 歐陽修 (1007–1072). Peking: Chung-hua shu-chü, 1975.

Hsüan-ho hua-p'u 宣和畫譜. Anonymous (preface dated 1120). *Hua-shih ts'ung-shu* 畫史叢書, Vol. 1. Taipei: Wen-shih-che ch'u-pan-she, 1974.

Huan-hun chi 還魂記. Anonymous. S. no. 3092, reproduced in THPT 25: 667–68; printed version in *Tun-huang i-shu tsung-mu so-yin*, p. 172.

I-chien chih 夷堅志. Hung Mai 洪邁 (1123–1202). 4 vols. Peking: Chung-hua shu-chü, 1981.

I-wen lei-chü 藝文類聚. Ou-yang Hsün 歐陽詢 (557–641). Taipei: Hsin-hsing shu-chü, 1960.

(Ch'in-ting) Ku-chin t'u-shu chi-ch'eng 欽定古今圖書集成. Compiled in 1725 by Ch'en Meng-lei 陳夢雷 et al. 100 vols. Taipei: Wen-hsing shu-tien, 1964.

Lao-hsüeh-an pi-chi 老學庵筆記. Lu Yu 陸游 (1125–1210). In *Hsüeh-chin t'ao-yüan* 學津討源. Pai-pu ts'ung-shu chi-ch'eng, No. 46. Taipei: I-wen yin-shu-kuan, 1965.

Lao-tzu tao-te ching chu 老子道德經注. Hsin-pien chu-tzu chi-ch'eng, Vol. 3. Taipei: Shih-chieh shu-chü, 1978.

Li-chi cheng-i 禮記正義. Taipei: Kuang-wen shu-chü, 1971.

Li-tai ming-hua chi 歷代名畫記. Chang Yen-yüan 張彥遠 (ca. 847–874). In *Hua-shih ts'ung-shu* 畫史叢書, Vol. 1. Taipei: Wen-shih-che ch'u-pan-she, 1974.

Li T'ai-po wen-chi 李太白文集. Edited by Wang Ch'i 王琦 (ca. 1758). N.p.: Pao-hu lou, 1758.

Liang shu 梁書. Yao Ssu-lien 姚思廉 (557–637). 2 vols. Peking: Chung-hua shu-chü, 1973.

Lun-yü yin-te 論語引得. Harvard-Yenching Institute Sinological Index Series, Supplement No. 16. Reprint ed., Taipei: Chinese Materials and Research Aids Service Center, 1966. Translation by Lau, *The Analects (Lun yü)*.

Meng-liang lu 夢梁錄. Wu Tzu-mu 吳自牧 (ca. 1275). In *Tung-ching meng-hua lu, wai ssu-chung* 東京夢華錄外四種. Shanghai: Ku-tien wen-hsüeh ch'u-pan-she, 1957.

Meng-tzu yin-te 孟子引得. Harvard-Yenching Institute Sinological Index Series, Supplement No. 17. Reprint ed., Taipei: Ch'eng-wen Publishing Co., 1966.

Ming-hsiang chi 冥祥記. Wang Yen 王琰 (ca. 500). Portions cited in *Fa-yüan chu-lin* and in Lu, *Ku hsiao-shuo kou-ch'en*.

Mu-lien chiu-mu hsing-hsiao hsi-wen 目連救母行孝戲文. Cheng Chih-chen 鄭之珍 (Ming). Microfilm of Ching-ling shu-fang text kept in National Library, Peking: *Hsin-k'o ch'u-hsiang yin-chu ch'üan-shan mu-lien chiu-mu hsing-hsiao hsi-wen* 新刻出相音注勸善目連救母行孝戲文. Also in Vols. 80–82 of *Ku-pen hsi-ch'ü ts'ung-k'an ch'u-k'an* 古本戲曲叢刊初刊. Shanghai: Commercial Press, 1954.

Mu-lien yüan-ch'i 目連緣起. P. no. 2193, reproduced in THPWC.

Nihon shoki 日本書記. Nihon koten bungaku taikei, Vols. 67–68. Tokyo: Iwanami shoten, 1967, 1965. Translation by Aston, *Nihongi.*

Nittō guhō junrei gyōki 入唐求法巡禮行記. Ennin 圓仁 (793–864). Text in Ono, *Nittō guhō junrei gyōki no kenkyū.* Translation by Ono and by Reischauer, *Ennin's Diary.*

Pao-p'u-tzu 抱樸子. Ko Hung 葛洪 (ca. 277–357). Hsin-pien chu-tzu chi-ch'eng, Vol. 4. Taipei: Shih-chieh shu-chü, 1978.

Pei shih 北史. Li Yen-shou 李延壽 (ca. 629). 10 vols. Peking: Chung-hua shu-chü, 1974.

Pen-shih shih 本事詩. Meng Ch'i 孟棨 (ca. 886). In *Pen-shih shih, Pen-shih tz'u* 本事詩本事詞. Chung-kuo wen-hsüeh ts'an-k'ao tzu-liao hsiao ts'ung-shu, Series 2, No. 2. Shanghai: Ku-tien wen-hsüeh ch'u-pan-she, 1957.

Po-shih liu-t'ieh shih-lei chi 白氏六帖事類集. Po Chü-i 白居易 (772–846). 2 vols. Taipei: Hsin-hsing shu-chü, 1969.

Po-wu chih 博物志. Chang Hua 張華 (232–300). In *Chih-hai* 指海. Pai-pu ts'ung-shu chi-ch'eng, No. 54. Taipei: I-wen yin-shu-kuan, 1967.

Ritsuryō 律令. Edited by Inoue Matsusada 井上光真. Nihon shisō taikei, Vol. 3. Tokyo: Iwanami shoten, 1976.

Ryō no shūge 令集解. Edited by Koremune Naomoto 惟宗直本. 2 vols. Tokyo: Kokusho kankōkai, 1912–13.

Shih-shuo hsin-yü 世說新語. Liu I-ch'ing 劉義慶 (403–444). Hsin-pien chu-tzu chi-ch'eng, Vol. 8. Taipei: Shih-chien shu-chü, 1978. Translation by Mather, *Shih-shuo hsin-yü: A New Account of Tales of the World.*

Shih-wu chi-yüan (chi-lei) 事物紀源集類. Kao Ch'eng 高承 (ca. 1078–1085). Taipei: Commercial Press, 1971.

Sui-hua chi-li 歲華紀麗. Han O 韓鄂 (T'ang). In *Sui-shih hsi-su tzu-liao hui-pien* 歲時習俗資料彙編, Vol. 3. Taipei: I-wen yin-shu-kuan, 1970.

Sui-shih kuang-chi 歲時廣記. Ch'en Yüan-ching 陳元靚 (S. Sung). In *Sui-shih hsi-su tzu-liao hui-pien* 歲時習俗資料彙編, Vols. 4–7. Taipei: I-wen yin-shu-kuan, 1970.

Ta mu-ch'ien-lien ming-chien chiu-mu pien-wen 大目乾連冥間救母變文. Numerous Tun-huang MS sources; collated in THPWC, pp. 714–55. Translations by Mair, *Tun-huang Popular Narratives*; Iriya, *Bukkyō bungaku shi*; and Waley, *Ballads and Stories.*

T'ai-p'ing kuang-chi 太平廣記. Li Fang 李昉 (925–996). 5 vols. Peking: Jen-min wen-hsüeh ch'u-pan-she, 1959.

T'ai-p'ing yü-lan 太平御覽 (completed 983). Li Fang 李昉 (925–996). 12 vols. Taipei: Hsin-hsing shu-chü, 1959.

T'ang hui yao 唐會要. Wang P'u 王溥 (922–982). Pai-pu ts'ung-shu chi-ch'eng, No. 27. Taipei: I-wen yin-shu-kuan, 1969.

T'ang liang-ching ch'eng-fang k'ao 唐兩京城坊考. Hsü Sung 徐松 (1781–1848). Reproduced in *Tōdai no chōan to rakuyō: shiryō hen* 唐代の長安と洛陽資料篇. Edited by Hiraoka Takeo 平岡武夫. T'ang Civilization Reference Series, No. 6. Kyoto: Kyoto daigaku jinbun kagaku kenkyūjo, 1956.

T'ang liu-tien 唐六典. Chang Chiu-ling 張九齡 (673–740). Ssu-k'u ch'üan-shu chen-pen, Series 6. Taipei: Commercial Press, 1976.

(Ku) T'ang lü shu-i 故唐律疏義. Kuo-hsüeh chi-pen ts'ung-shu ed. Taipei: Commercial Press, 1968. Partial translation by Johnson, *The T'ang Code.*

T'ang-shih chi-shih 唐詩紀事. Chi Yu-kung 計有功 (ca. 1121–1161). 2 vols. Peking: Chung-hua shu-chü, 1965.

T'ang-tai ts'ung-shu 唐代叢書. Taipei: Hsin-hsing shu-chü, 1968.

T'ang ts'ai-tzu chuan 唐才子傳. Hsin Wen-fang 辛文房 (ca. 1304). Shanghai: Ku-tien wen-hsüeh ch'u-pan-she, 1957.

Tsa-ch'ao 雜抄. Ca. 800. P. 2721, reproduced in Naba, "Tō shōbon zashō kō."

Ts'e-fu yüan-kuei 册府元龜. Wang Ch'in-jo 王欽若 (962–1025). 12 vols. Peking: Chung-hua shu-chü, 1960.

Tun-huang chüan-tzu 敦煌卷子. 6 vols. Taipei: Shih-men t'u-shu, 1976.

Tun-huang pao-tsang 敦煌寶藏. Edited by Huang Yung-wu 黃永武. Taipei: Hsin-wen-feng ch'u-pan-she, 1981–. Abbreviated as THPT.

Tun-huang pien-wen chi 敦煌變文集. Edited by Wang Ch'ung-min 王重民. 2 vols. Peking: Jen-min wen-hsüeh ch'u-pan-she, 1957. Abbreviated as THPWC.

Tun-huang shih-shih hsieh-ching t'i-chi yü Tun-huang tsa-lu 敦煌石室寫經提記與敦煌雜錄. Edited by Hsü Kuo-lin 許國霖. Shanghai: Commercial Press, 1937.

Tung-ching meng-hua lu 東京夢華錄. Meng Yüan-lao 孟元老 (ca. 1235). In *Tung-ching meng-hua lu, wai ssu-chung* 東京夢華錄外四種. Shanghai: Ku-tien wen-hsüeh ch'u-pan-she, 1957.

Tung Yung, Ch'en Hsiang ho-chi 董永沈香合集. Edited by Tu Ying-t'ao 杜穎陶. Min-chien wen-hsüeh tzu-liao ts'ung-shu, No. 5. Shanghai: Shang-hai ch'u-pan kung-ssu, 1955.

Tzu-chih t'ung-chien 資治通鑑. Ssu-ma Kuang 司馬光 (ca. 1084). 10 vols. Taipei: I-wen yin-shu-kuan, 1955.

Wei shu 魏書. Wei Shou 魏收 (506–572). 5 vols. Peking: Chung-hua shu-chü, 1974.

Wu-lin chiu-shih 武林舊事. Chou Mi 周密 (ca. 1280). In *Tung-ching meng-hua lu, wai ssu-chung* 東京夢華錄外四種. Shanghai: Ku-tien wen-hsüeh ch'u-pan-she, 1957.

Yang Ying-ch'uan chi 楊盈川集. Ssu-pu ts'ung-k'an, Series 1, Vol. 35. Taipei: Commercial Press, 1967.

Yen-lo-wang shou-chi ssu-chung yü-hsiu sheng-ch'i [-chai] wang-sheng ching-t'u ching 閻羅王授記四衆預修生七齋往生淨土經. Manuscripts include: P. no. 2003, reproduced in Tokushi Yūshō and Ogawa Kan'ichi, "*Jūō shōshichi kyō* santoken no kōzō"; manuscript held in the Nakamura Shodō Hakubutsukan, reproduced in Tokushi Yūshō and Ogawa Kan'ichi, "*Jūō shōshichi kyō* santoken no kōzō"; S. no. 3961, reproduced in THPT 32: 569–76; T. no. 3143, 92: 645–62; S. no. 4530, reproduced in THPT 36: 474–75; and S. no. 5544, reproduced in THPT 43: 361–63.

Yü-chu pao-tien 玉燭寶典. Tu T'ai-ch'ing 杜台卿 (ca. 581). Pai-pu ts'ung-shu chi-ch'eng, No. 75. Taipei: I-wen yin-shu-kuan, 1965.

Yü hai 玉海. Wang Ying-ling 王應麟 (1223–1296). 8 vols. Taipei: Hua-wen shu-chü, 1964.

Yü-lan-p'en [ching] chiang-ching-wen 盂蘭盆經講經文 (reconstructed title). Taiwan. Tun-huang MS. no. 32, reproduced in *Tun-huang chüan-tzu*, 2: 273–76.

Yü-li ch'ao-chuan ching-shih 玉歷鈔傳警世. Attributed to Tan Ch'ih-tsun 淡癡尊 (ca. 1030). Peking: Wen-yüan-chai, 1872.

Yün-ch'i fa-hui 雲棲法彙. Chu-hung 株宏 (1535–1615). Nanking: Ching-ling k'o-ching-ch'u, 1897.

Zoku gunsho ruijū 續辞書類從. Edited by Hanawa Hokiichi 塙保已一 and Ōta Tōshirō 太田藤四郎. Tokyo: Zoku gunsho ruijū kanseikai, 1923–28.

II. REFERENCE WORKS, SECONDARY SOURCES, AND TRANSLATIONS

Ahern, Emily M. *Chinese Ritual and Politics*. Cambridge Studies in Social Anthropology, No. 34. Cambridge: Cambridge University Press, 1981.

———. *The Cult of the Dead in a Chinese Village*. Stanford: Stanford University Press, 1973.

———. "The Power and Pollution of Chinese Women." In *Women in Chinese Society*, ed. Margery Wolf and Roxanne Witke. Stanford: Stanford University Press, 1975.

Aijmer, Göran. "A Structural Approach to Chinese Ancestor Worship." *Bijdragen tot de Taal-, Land-, en Volkenkunde* 124:1 (1968) : 91–98.

Ajia rekishi jiten アジア歴史辞典. 10 vols. Tokyo: Heibonsha, 1959–62.

Akanuma, Chizen 赤沼智善. *Indo bukkyō koyū meishi jiten* 印度佛教固有名詞辭典. 1931; reprint ed., Kyoto: Hōzōkan, 1967.

———. *Kan-Pa shibu shiagon goshōroku* 漢巴四部四阿含互照表. Nagoya: Hajinkaku shobō, 1929.

Akatsuka, Kiyoshi 赤塚忠. *Chūgoku kodai no shūkyō to bunka: In ōchō no saishi* 中國古代の宗教と文化殷王朝の祭祝. Tokyo: Kadokawa shoten, 1977.

Akiyama, Terukazu 秋山光和. "Tonkō ni okeru henbun to kaiga" 敦煌における変文と絵画. *Bijutsu kenkyū* 美術研究 No. 211 (July 1960): 1–28.

―――. "Tonkōbon gōmahen emaki ni tsuite" 敦煌本降魔変画巻について. *Bijutsu kenkyū* 美術研究 No. 187 (July 1956): 1–35.

Akizuki, Kan'ei 秋月觀英. "Dōkyō no sangen shisō ni tsuite" 道教の三元思想 について. *Shūkyō kenkyū* 宗教研究 34:3 (January 1961): 1.

―――. "Dōkyō to bukkyō no *Fubo onchō kyō*" 道教と佛教の父母恩重經. *Shūkyō kenkyū* 宗教研究 39:4 (March 1966): 23–44.

―――. "*Dōsō kō* no fukkyū ni tsuite" 道僧格の復舊について. *Tōhoku gakuin daigaku ronshū: rekishigaku, chirigaku* 東北學院大學論集歷史學地理學 No. 4 (1952).

―――. "Sangen shisō no keisei ni tsuite" 三元思想の形成について. *Tōhō gaku* 東方學 No. 22 (1961): 27–40.

Allan, Sarah. *The Heir and the Sage: Dynastic Legend in Early China*. Taipei: Chinese Materials Center, 1981.

Andersen, Poul. *The Method of Holding the Three Ones: A Taoist Manual of Meditation of the Fourth Century A.D.* Scandanavian Institute of Asian Studies, Studies on Asian Topics, No. 1. London and Malmö: Curzon Press, 1979.

Aoki, Masaru 青木正児. "Tonkō isho *Mokuren engi, Dai mokkenren meikan kyūbo henbun*, oyobi *Gōma ōzabun* ni tsuite" 敦煌遺書目連縁起大目乾連冥間救母變文及び降魔押坐文. *Shinagaku* 支那學 4:3 (May 1927): 123–30. Reprinted in *Shina bungaku geijutsu kō* 支那文學芸術考. Tokyo: Kōbundō, 1942, pp. 172–82.

Arai, Keiyo 新井慧譽. "On shisō kara mita *Urabon kyō* to *Fubo onchō kyō* no kankei" 恩思想から見た盂蘭盆經と父母恩重經の関係. In *On* 恩, Bukkyō shisō, Vol. 4. Edited by Nakamura Hajime 中材元. Kyoto: Heiryakuji shoten, 1979.

Ashikaga, Enshō. "Notes on Urabon (Yü Lan P'en, Ullambana)." JAOS 71:1 (January–March 1951): 71–75.

Aston, William G., trans. *Nihongi: Chronicles of Japan from the Earliest Times to A.D. 697.* 2 vols. Rutland: Charles E. Tuttle Co., 1972.

Baker, Hugh D.R. *Chinese Family and Kinship*. New York: Columbia University Press, 1979.

Bakhtin, Mikhail M. *Rabelais and His World*. Translated by Helene Iswolsky. Bloomington: Indiana University Press, 1984.

Barrett, T. H. "Taoism under the T'ang." Draft chapter for *The Cambridge History of China*, Vol. 3, Part 2. Edited by Denis C. Twitchett. Cambridge: Cambridge University Press; forthcoming.

Beal, Samuel, trans. *Si-yu-ki: Buddhist Records of the Western World*. 2 vols. Reprint ed., San Francisco: Chinese Materials Center, 1976.

Berling, Judith A. *The Syncretic Religion of Lin Chao-en*. New York: Columbia University Press, 1980.

Biot, Edouard, trans. *Le Tcheou-li ou Rites des Tcheou*. 2 vols. Paris: Imprimerie Nationale, 1851.

Birnbaum, Raoul. "Thoughts on T'ang Buddhist Mountain Traditions and Their Context." *T'ang Studies* 2 (Winter 1984): 5–23.

Bloch, Maurice, and Jonathan Parry. "Introduction: Death and the Regeneration of Life." In *Death and the Regeneration of Life*. Edited by Maurice Bloch and Jonathan Parry. Cambridge: Cambridge University Press, 1982.

Bloch, Maurice, and Jonathan Parry, eds. *Death and the Regeneration of Life*. Cambridge: Cambridge University Press, 1982.

Bodde, Derk. *Festivals in Classical China: New Year and Other Annual Observances during the Han Dynasty, 206 B.C.–A.D. 220*. Princeton: Princeton University Press, 1975.

———. "Myths of Ancient China." In *Mythologies of the Ancient World*, ed. Samuel Noah Kramer. Garden City: Anchor Books, 1961.

Boltz, Judith M. "Opening the Gates of Purgatory: A Twelfth-Century Taoist Meditation Technique for the Salvation of Lost Souls." In *Tantric and Taoist Studies in Honour of R. A. Stein*, Vol. 2. *Mélanges chinois et bouddhiques*, Vol. 21. Brussels: Institut Belge des Hautes Etudes Chinoises, 1983, pp. 487–511.

Boon, James A. "Incest Recaptured: Some Contraries of Karma in Balinese Symbology." In *Karma: An Anthropological Inquiry*. Edited by Charles F. Keyes and E. Valentine Daniel. Berkeley: University of California Press, 1983.

Bredon, Juliet, and Igor Mitrophanow. *The Moon Year: A Record of Chinese Customs and Festivals*. Shanghai: Kelly and Walsh, 1927.

Brown, Peter. *The Cult of the Saints: Its Rise and Function in Latin Christianity*. The Haskell Lectures on History of Religions, New Series, No. 2. Chicago: University of Chicago Press, 1981.

Burke, Peter. *Popular Culture in Early Modern Europe*. London: Temple Smith, 1978.

Burkhardt, Valentine R. *Chinese Creeds and Customs*. 2 vols. Hong Kong: South China Morning Post, 1953–55.

Bussho kaisetsu dai jiten 仏書解說大辭典. 13 vols. Edited by Ono Gemmyō 小野玄妙. Tokyo: Daitō shuppansha, 1933–36.

Catalogue des manuscrits chinois de Touen-Houang (Fonds Pelliot Chinois), Vol. 1 (Nos. 2001–2500), Vol. 2 (Nos. 3000–3500). Paris: Bibliothèque Nationale, 1970–.

Chang, Kun. *A Comparative Study of the Kaṭhinavastu*. Indo-Iranian Monographs, No. 1. Gravenhage: Mouton, 1957.

Chang, Kwang-chih. *Art, Myth, and Ritual: The Path to Political Authority in Ancient China*. Cambridge: Harvard University Press, 1983.

Chao, Ching-shen 趙景深. "Ch'üan-shan chin-k'o" 勸善金科. In *Ming ch'ing ch'ü-t'an* 明清曲談. Shanghai: Ku-tien wen-hsüeh ch'u-pan-she, 1957.

———. "Mu-lien chiu-mu te yen-pien" 目連救母的演變. (1946). Reprinted in

Chung-kuo min-chien ch'uan-shuo lun-chi 中國民間傳說論集, ed. Wang Ch'iu-kuei 王秋桂. Taipei: Lien-ching ch'u-pan shih-yeh kung-ssu, 1980.

Chavannes, Edouard. *Cinq Cents Contes et apologues: extraits du Tripitaka chinois.* 4 vols. Paris: Libraire Ernest Leroux, 1910–11, 1934.

———. *Dix Inscriptions chinoises de l'Asie Centrale d'après les éstampages de M. Ch.-E. Bonin.* Paris: Imprimerie Nationale, 1902.

———. *Le T'ai Chan: essai de monographie d'un culte chinois.* Annales du Musée Guimet, Vol. 21. Paris: Ernest Leroux, 1910.

Ch'en Fang-ying 陳芳英. *Mu-lien chiu-mu ku-shih chih yen-chin chi ch'i yu-kuan wen-hsüeh chih yen-chiu* 目連救母故事之演進及其有關文學之研究. History and Literature Series, No. 65. Taipei: Taiwan National University, 1983.

Ch'en, Kenneth K.S. *Buddhism in China: A Historical Survey.* Princeton: Princeton University Press, 1964.

———. *The Chinese Transformation of Buddhism.* Princeton: Princeton University Press, 1973.

———. "The Economic Background of the Hui-ch'ang Suppression of Buddhism." HJAS 19: 1–2 (June 1956): 67–105.

———. "Filial Piety in Chinese Buddhism." HJAS 28 (1968): 81–97.

———. "The Role of Buddhist Monasteries in T'ang Society." HR 15:3 (February 1976): 209–30.

Ch'en, Meng-chia 陳夢家. "Shang-tai te shen-hua yü wu-shu" 商代的神話與巫術. *Yen-ching hsüeh-pao* 燕京學報 No. 20 (December 1936): 485–576.

Ch'en, Yüan 陳垣. *Shih-shih i-nien lu* 釋氏疑年錄. Peking: Chung-hua shu-chü, 1964.

Cheng, Chen-to 鄭振鐸. *Chung-kuo su-wen-hsüeh shih* 中國俗文學史. 2 vols. Peking: Tzu-chia ch'u-pan-she, 1954.

Chiang, Li-hung 蔣禮鴻. *Tun-huang pien-wen tzu-i t'ung-shih* 敦煌變文字義通釋. Revised ed. Taipei: Ku-t'ing shu-ya, 1975.

Chiang, Wei-ch'iao 蔣維喬. *Chung-kuo fo-chiao shih* 中國佛教史. 1933; reprint ed., Taipei: Ting-wen shu-chü, 1974.

Ch'ien, Nan-yang 錢南楊. "Tu jih-pen Kuraishi Takeshirō te Mokuren kyūbo gyōkō gibun yen-chiu" 讀日本倉石武四郎的目連救母行孝戲文研究. *Min-su* 民俗 No. 72 (August 1929): 1–7.

Chikusa, Masaaki 竺沙雅章. *Chūgoku bukkyō shakai shi kenkyū* 中國佛教社會史研究. Tōyō shi kenkyū sōkan, No. 34. Kyoto: Dōhōsha, 1982.

Chou, I-liang. "Tantrism in China." HJAS 8:3, 4 (March 1945): 241–332.

Chou, Shao-liang, ed. 周紹良. *Tun-huang pien-wen hui-lu* 敦煌變文彙錄. Shanghai: Shang-hai ch'u-pan kung-ssu, 1955.

Chung-kuo fo-chiao ssu-hsiang tzu-liao hsüan-pien 中國佛教思想資料選編. Edited by Shih Chün 石峻. Peking: Chung-hua shu-chü, 1983.

Chung-kuo fo-hsüeh jen-ming tz'u-tien 中國佛學人名辭典. Edited by Ming Fu 明復. Taipei: Fang-chou ch'u-pan-she, 1974.

Chung-kuo jen-ming ta tz'u-tien 中國人名大辭典. Edited by Tsang Li-ho 藏勵龢. Shanghai: Commercial Press, 1921.

Chung-wai ti-ming ta tz'u-tien 中外地名大辭典. 9 vols. Edited by Tuan Mu-kan 段木干. T'ai-chung: Jen-wen ch'u-pan-she, 1981.

Chung-wen ta tz'u-tien 中文大辭典. Revised ed. 10 vols. Edited by Chang Ch'i-yün 張其昀. Taipei: Hua-kuang ch'u-pan yu-hsien kung-ssu, 1979. Abbreviated as CWTTT.

Clarke, G. W., trans. "The Yü-li, or Precious Records." *Journal of the Royal Asiatic Society of Great Britain and Ireland* 28:2 (1898): 233–400.

Cohen, Percy S. "Theories of Myth." *Man* 4:3 (September 1969): 337–53.

Collins, Steven. *Selfless Persons: Imagery and Thought in "Theravada" Buddhism.* Cambridge: Cambridge University Press, 1982.

Couvreur, F. S., S.J. *Dictionnaire classique de la langue chinoise.* 1890; reprint ed., T'ai-chung: Kuang-ch'i ch'u-pan-she, 1966.

Demiéville, Paul. "Le Bouddhisme chinois." *Encyclopédie de la Pléiade, histoire des religions*, Vol. 1. Paris: Gallimard, 1970. Reprinted in *Choix d'études bouddhiques.* Leiden: E. J. Brill, 1974.

———. "Les Débuts de la littérature en chinois vulgaire." *Académie des Inscriptions et Belles-Lettres, Comptes rendus* (1952). Reprinted in Demiéville, *Choix d'études sinologiques.* Leiden: E. J. Brill, 1973.

———. "Sur La Mémoire des existences antérieures." BEFEO 27 (1927): 283–98.

———. "Le Yogācārabhūmi de Sangharakṣa." BEFEO 44:2 (1954): 339–436.

Dewoskin, Kenneth J. *Doctors, Diviners, and Magicians of Ancient China: Biographies of "Fang-shih."* New York: Columbia University Press, 1983.

Doré, Henry, S.J. *Researches into Chinese Superstitions.* 10 vols. Translated by M. Kennelly, S.J. Shanghai: T'usewei Printing Press, 1914–33.

Dore, Ronald P. *Shinohata: A Portrait of a Japanese Village.* New York: Pantheon Books, 1978.

Douglas, Mary. *Purity and Danger: An Analysis of Concepts of Pollution and Taboo.* London: Routledge and Kegan Paul, 1966.

Dudbridge, Glen. *The Legend of Miao-shan.* Oxford Oriental Monographs, No. 1. London: Ithaca Press, 1978.

Dumont, Louis. "World Renunciation in Indian Religions." *Contributions to Indian Sociology* 4 (1960). Reprinted in *Homo Hierarchicus: The Caste System and Its Implications.* Revised ed. Translated by Mark Sainsbury et al. Chicago: University of Chicago Press, 1980.

Dutt, Sukumar. *Buddhist Monks and Monasteries in India: Their History and Their Contribution to Indian Culture.* London: George Allen and Unwin, 1962.

Duyvendak, J.J.L. "The Buddhistic Festival of All-Souls in China and Japan." *Acta Orientalia* 5:1 (1926): 39–48.

Dymond, F.J. "The Feast of the Seventh Moon." *The East of Asia Magazine* 2:4 (December 1903): 376–78.

244

Eberhard, Wolfram. *Chinese Festivals*. 1952; reprint ed., Taipei: Wen-hsing shu-tien, 1963.

———. *Guilt and Sin in Traditional China*. Berkeley: University of California Press, 1967.

———. *The Local Cultures of South and East China*. Translated by Alide Eberhard. Leiden: E. J. Brill, 1968.

Ebrey, Patricia Buckley. *The Aristocratic Families of Early Imperial China: A Case Study of the Po-ling Ts'ui Family*. Cambridge: Cambridge University Press, 1978.

Edkins, Joseph. *Chinese Buddhism: A Volume of Sketches, Historical, Descriptive, and Critical*. London: Trübner and Co., 1880.

Eitel, Ernest J. *Handbook of Chinese Buddhism, Being a Sanskrit-Chinese Dictionary with Vocabularies of Buddhist Terms in Pali, Singhalese, Siamese, Burmese, Tibetan, Mongolian, and Japanese*. Second ed. 1904; reprint ed., Peking: Wen-tien-ko, 1939.

Eliade, Mircea. *Birth and Rebirth: The Religious Meanings of Initiation in Human Culture*. Translated by Willard R. Trask. New York: Harper and Row, 1958.

———. "Mythologies of Death: An Introduction." In *Religious Encounters with Death*. Edited by Frank Reynolds and Earle Waugh. University Park: Pennsylvania State University Press, 1977.

———. *Shamanism: Archaic Techniques of Ecstasy*. Revised ed. Translated by Willard R. Trask. Bollingen Series, No. 74. Princeton: Princeton University Press, 1964.

———. *Yoga: Immortality and Freedom*. Revised ed. Translated by Willard R. Trask. Bollingen Series, No. 56. Princeton: Princeton University Press, 1969.

Elliott, Alan J.A. *Chinese Spirit-Medium Cults in Singapore*. Monographs on Social Anthropology, No. 14. Norwich: London School of Economics and Political Science, 1955.

Elvin, Mark. *The Pattern of the Chinese Past*. Stanford: Stanford University Press, 1973.

Feer, Léon, trans. *L'Avadāna-Cataka: cent légendes bouddhiques*. Annales du Musée Guimet, No. 18. Paris: Ernest Leroux, 1891.

Feuchtwang, Stephan D.R. "Investigating Religion." In *Marxist Analyses and Social Anthropology*. Edited by Maurice Bloch. London: Malaby Press, 1975.

Filliozat, Jean. "Sur Le Domaine sémantique du *puṇya*." In *Indianisme et Bouddhisme: mélanges offerts à Mgr. Etienne Lamotte*. Publications de l'Institut Orientaliste de Louvain, No. 23. Louvain: Institut Orientaliste, 1980.

Fo-tsang tzu-mu yin-te 佛藏子目引得. Harvard-Yenching Institute Index Series, No. 11. Taipei: Ch'eng-wen Publishing Co., 1966.

Forte, Antonino. *Political Propaganda and Ideology in China at the End of the Seventh Century: Inquiry into the Nature, Authors, and Function of the Tunhuang Document*

S. 6502, Followed by an Annotated Translation. Napoli: Instituto Universitario Orientale, Seminario di Studi Asiatici, 1976.

Freedman, Maurice. "Ancestor Worship: Two Facets of the Chinese Case." In *Social Organization: Essays Presented to Raymond Firth.* Edited by Maurice Freedman. Chicago: Aldine Publishing Co., 1967. Reprinted in *The Study of Chinese Society.* Edited by G. William Skinner. Stanford: Stanford University Press, 1979.

―――. "Ritual Aspects of Chinese Kinship and Marriage." In *Family and Kinship in Chinese Society.* Edited by Maurice Freedman. Stanford: Stanford University Press, 1970.

Fujino, Ryūnen 藤野立然. *"Urabon kyō dokugo"* 盂蘭盆經讀後. *Ryūkoku daigaku ronshū* 龍谷大學論集 No. 353 (1956): 340–45.

Fung, Yu-lan. *A History of Chinese Philosophy.* Second ed. 2 vols. Translated by Derk Bodde. Princeton: Princeton University Press, 1952–53.

Furuta, Shōkin 古田紹金. *"Keihō shūmitsu no kenkyū"* 圭峯宗密の研究. *Shina bukkyō shigaku* 支那佛教史學 2:2 (1983): 83–97.

Futaba, Kenkō 二葉憲番. *Kodai bukkyō shisō shi kenkyū: nihon kodai ni okeru ritsuryō bukkyō oyobi han-ritsuryō bukkyō no kenkyū* 古代佛教思想史研究日本古代における律令佛教及び反律令佛教の研究. Kyoto: Nagata bunshōdō, 1962.

Gates, Henry Louis, Jr. "Criticism in the Jungle." In *Black Literature and Literary Theory,* ed. Henry Louis Gates, Jr. New York: Methuen, 1984.

Geertz, Clifford. "Thick Description: Toward an Interpretive Theory of Culture." In *The Interpretation of Cultures.* New York: Basic Books, 1973.

Gennep, Arnold van. *The Rites of Passage.* Translated by Monika B. Vizedom and Gabrielle L. Caffee. Chicago: University of Chicago Press, 1960.

Gernet, Jacques. *Les Aspects économiques du bouddhisme dans la société chinoise du Ve au Xe siècle.* Saigon: Ecole Française d'Extrême-Orient, 1956.

―――. *Daily Life in China on the Eve of the Mongol Invasion,* trans. H.M. Wright. Stanford: Stanford University Press, 1970.

―――. *A History of Chinese Civilization.* Translated by J.R. Foster. Cambridge: Cambridge University Press, 1982.

Getty, Alice. *The Gods of Northern Buddhism: Their History, Iconography, and Progressive Evolution through the Northern Buddhist Countries.* Second ed. 1928; reprint ed., Rutland: Charles E. Tuttle Co., 1962.

Giles, Lionel. *Descriptive Catalogue of the Chinese Manuscripts from Tunhuang in the British Museum.* London: British Museum, 1957.

Gimello, Robert M. "Chih-yen (602–668) and the Foundations of Hua-yen Buddhism." Ph.D. dissertation, Columbia University, 1976.

Gjertson, Donald E. "The Early Chinese Buddhist Miracle Tale: A Preliminary Survey." JAOS 101:3 (July–September 1981): 287–301.

Gombrich, Richard F. "Merit Transference in Sinhalese Buddhism: A Case Study of the Interaction between Doctrine and Practice." HR 11:2 (November 1971): 203–19.

————. *Precept and Practice: Traditional Buddhism in the Rural Highlands of Ceylon*. Oxford: Clarendon Press, 1971.

Goody, Jack. *Death, Property, and the Ancestors*. Stanford: Stanford University Press, 1962.

Granet, Marcel. *Festivals and Songs of Ancient China*. Translated by E.D. Edwards. London: Routledge, 1932.

————. *La Pensée chinoise*. Paris: Albin Michel, 1968.

————. *The Religion of the Chinese People*. Translated by Maurice Freedmen. New York: Harper and Row, 1977.

Grapard, Alan G. "Japan's Ignored Cultural Revolution: The Separation of Shinto and Buddhist Divinities in Meiji *(shinbutsu bunri)* and a Case Study, Tōnomine." HR 23:3 (February 1984): 240–65.

Gregory, Peter N. "Chinese Buddhist Hermeneutics: The Case of Hua-yen." *Journal of the American Academy of Religion* 51:2 (June 1983): 231–49.

————. "The Teaching of Men and Gods: The Doctrinal and Social Basis of Lay Buddhist Practice in the Hua-yen Tradition." In *Studies in Ch'an and Hua-yen*. Edited by Robert M. Gimello and Peter N. Gregory. Studies in East Asian Buddhism, No. 1. Honolulu: University of Hawaii Press, 1983.

Griffiths, Paul J. "Notes towards a Critique of Buddhist Karmic Theory." *Religious Studies* 18:3 (September 1982): 277–91.

De Groot, Jan J.M. "Buddhist Masses for the Dead in Amoy." *Actes du sixième congrès international des orientalistes*, Part 4, Sec. 4. Leiden: E.J. Brill, 1885.

————. *Le Code du Mahāyāna en Chine: son influence sur la vie monacale et sur le monde laique*. Verhandelingen der Koninklijke Akademie von Wettenschappen te Amsterdam: Afdeeling Letterkunde N.S., 1:2. Amsterdam: Johannes Müller, 1893.

————. *Les Fêtes annuellement célébrées à Emoui*. 2 vols. Translated by C.G. Chavannes. Annales du Musée Guimet, No. 12. Paris: Ernest Leroux, 1886.

————. *The Religious System of China*. 6 vols. Leiden: E.J. Brill, 1892–1910.

Grube, Wilhelm. "Zur pekinger Volkskunde." *Veröffentlichungen aus dem Königlichen Museum für Völkerkunde* 7:4 (1901): 1–160.

Gumyō shū kenkyū 弘明集研究. 2 vols. Edited by Kyoto daigaku jinbun kagaku kenkyūjo chūsei shisō shi kenkyūhan 京都大學人文科學研究所中世思想史研究班. Kyoto: Kyoto daigaku jinbun kagaku kenkyūjo, 1973–75.

Hanan, Patrick. *The Chinese Vernacular Story*. Cambridge: Harvard University Press, 1981.

Hardacre, Helen. Review of Smith, *Ancestor Worship in Contemporary Japan*. HR 15:4 (May 1976): 388–92.

Hardacre, Helen, and Alan Sponberg, eds. *Maitreya, The Future Buddha*. Forthcoming.

Hardy, Robert Spence. *A Manual of Buddhism in Its Modern Development*. Second ed. London: Williams, 1880.

Harris, Olivia. "The Dead and the Devils among the Bolivian Laymi." In *Death and the Regeneration of Life.* Edited by Maurice Bloch and Jonathan Parry. Cambridge: Cambridge University Press, 1982.

Hayami, Tasuku 速水侑. *Jizō shinkō* 地藏信仰. Tokyo: Hanawa shobō, 1975.

Hertz, Robert. *Death and the Right Hand.* Translated by Rodney Needham and Claudia Needham. Glencoe: Free Press, 1960.

Hōbōgirin: dictionnaire encyclopédique du bouddhisme d'après les sources chinoises et japonaises. 6 vols. to date. Edited by Paul Demiéville and Jacques May. Tokyo: Maison Franco-Japonaise, 1929–.

Honda, Gi'ei 本田義英. *"Urabon kyō to jōdo urabon kyō"* 盂蘭盆經と浄土盂蘭盆經. In *Butten no naisō to gaisō* 佛典の内相と外相. Tokyo: Kōbundō, 1967.

Hopkins, L. C. "The Shaman or Chinese Wu: His Inspired Dancing and Versatile Character." *Journal of the Royal Asiatic Society of Great Britain and Ireland* (1945, Parts 1 and 2): 3–16.

Horner, Isaline B., trans. *The Book of the Discipline (Vinaya-Pitaka).* 6 vols. Sacred Books of the Buddhists, Vols. 10, 11, 13, 14, 20, 25. London: Luzac and Co., 1949–66.

Hou, Ching-lang. *Monnaies d'offrande et la notion de trésorie dans la religion chinoise.* Paris: College de France, Institut des Hautes Etudes Chinoises, 1975.

Hsiang, Ta 向達. "T'ang-tai ch'ang-an yü hsi-yü wen-ming" 唐代長安與西域文明. *Yen-ching hsüeh-pao* 燕京學報 Special issue, No. 2 (October 1933). Reprinted in *T'ang-tai ch'ang-an yü hsi-yü wen-ming* 唐代長安與西域文明. Peking: Sheng-huo tu-shu hsin-chih san-lien shu-tien ch'u-pan, 1957.

———. "T'ang-tai su-chiang k'ao" 唐代俗講考. *Kuo-hsüeh chi-k'an* 國學集刊 6:4 (January 1950): 1–42. Reprinted in *T'ang-tai ch'ang-an yü hsi-yü wen-ming.* Peking: Sheng-huo tu-shu hsin-chih san-lien shu-tien ch'u-pan, 1957.

Hsieh, Ch'un-p'in 謝春聘. *Tun-huang chiang-ching pien-wen chien* 敦煌講經變文箋. Taipei, 1975.

Hsu, Francis L.K. *Under the Ancestors' Shadow: Kinship, Personality, and Social Mobility in China.* Revised ed. Stanford: Stanford University Press, 1971.

Huang, Yu-mei. "China's Ghost Festival." *Free China Review* 32:11 (November 1982): 68–72.

Hulsewé, A.F.P. *Remnants of Han Law*, Vol. 1. Leiden: E.J. Brill, 1955.

Hurvitz, Leon, trans. *Scripture of the Lotus Blossom of the Fine Dharma (The Lotus Sūtra), Translated from the Chinese of Kumārajīva.* New York: Columbia University Press, 1976.

Hy, Van Luong. "'Brother' and 'Uncle': An Analysis of Rules, Stuctural Contradictions, and Meaning in Vietnamese Kinship." *American Anthropologist* 86:2 (June 1984): 290–315.

Ikeda, Chōtatsu 池田澄達. *"Urabon kyō ni tsuite"* 盂蘭盆經に就いて. *Shūkyō kenkyū* 宗教研究 N.S. 3:1 (January 1926): 59–64.

Imu, Doken [Im, Tong-gwŏn] 任東權. *Chōsen no minzoku* 朝鮮の民俗. Minzoku mingei sōsho, Vol. 45. Tokyo: Iwasaki bijutsusha, 1969.

Iriya, Yoshitaka 入矢義高. *"Tonkō henbun shū" kōgo goi sakuin* 敦煌變文集口語語彙索引. Kyoto, 1961 (mimeographed).

———, trans. "Dai Mokkenren meikan kyūbo henbun" 大目乾連冥間救母変文. In *Bukkyō bungaku shū* 仏教文学集. Edited by Iriya Yoshitaka. Chūgoku koten bungaku taikei. Tokyo: Heibonsha, 1975.

Ishida, Mizumaro 石田瑞麿. *Bommō kyō* 梵網經. Butten kōza, Vol. 14. Tokyo: Daizō shuppansha, 1971.

Ishida, Mosaku 石田茂作. *Shakyō yori mitaru nara-chō bukkyō no kenkyū* 寫經より見たる奈良朝佛教の研究. Tōyō bunko ronso, Vol. 11. Tokyo: Tōyō bunko, 1930.

Ishigami, Zennō 石上善應. "Mokuren setsuwa no keifu" 目連説話の系譜. *Taishō daigaku kenkyū kiyō* 大正大学研究集要 No. 54 (November 1968): 1–24.

Iwamoto, Yutaka 岩本裕. *Bukkyō setsuwa kenkyū* 佛教説話研究. 5 vols. Vol. 1: *Bukkyō setsuwa kenkyū jōsetsu* 佛教説話研究序説. Tokyo: Hōzōkan, 1962. Vol. 2: *Bukkyō setsuwa no genryū to tenkai* 佛教説話の源流と展開. Tokyo: Kaimei shoten, 1978. Vol. 4: *Jigoku meguri no bungaku* 地獄めぐりの文学 (includes *Mokuren densetsu to urabon* 目連伝説と盂蘭盆). Tokyo: Kaimei shoten, 1979.

Jan, Yün-hua. "Tsung-mi: His Analysis of Ch'an Buddhism." TP 58 (1972): 1–54.

———, trans. *A Chronicle of Buddhism in China, 581–906 A.D.: Translations from Monk Chih-p'an's "Fo-tsu t'ung-chi."* Santiniketan: Sri Gouranga Press private, 1966.

Janelli, Roger L., and Dawnhee Yim Janelli. *Ancestor Worship and Korean Society*. Stanford: Stanford University Press, 1982.

Jaworski, Jan. "L'Avalambana Sūtra de la terre pure." *Monumenta Serica* 1 (1935–36): 82–107.

Johnson, David. "Communication, Class, and Consciousness in Late Imperial China." In *Popular Culture in Late Imperial China*. Edited by David Johnson, Andrew Nathan, and Evelyn Rawski. Berkeley: University of California Press, 1985.

———. *The Medieval Chinese Oligarchy*. Boulder: Westview Press, 1977.

Johnson, David, Andrew Nathan, and Evelyn Rawski, eds. *Popular Culture in Late Imperial China*. Berkeley: University of California Press, 1985.

Johnson, Wallace, trans. *The T'ang Code*. Vol. 1: *General Principles*. Princeton: Princeton University Press, 1979.

Jonas, Hans. "The Nobility of Sight: A Study in the Phenomenology of the Senses." In *The Philosophy of the Body: Rejections of Cartesian Dualism*. Edited by Stuart F. Spicker. Chicago: Quadrangle Books, 1970.

Kamata, Shigeo 鎌田茂雄. *Shūmitsu kyōgaku no shisō shiteki kenkyū: chūgoku kegon shisō shi no kenkyū* 宗密教學の思想的研究中國華嚴思想史の研究. Tokyo: Tokyo daigaku shuppansha, 1975.

Kamekawa, Shōshin 龜川正信. "Kaishō no haibutsu ni tsuite" 會昌の廢佛に就いて. *Shina bukkyō shigaku* 支那佛教史學 6:1 (July 1942): 47–68.

Kan, Jie'on [Kang, Chae-ŏn] 姜在彦. *Chōsen saijiki* 朝鮮歳時記. Tōyō bunko, Vol. 193. Tokyo: Heibonsha, 1971.

Kanaoka, Shōkō 金岡照光. "Chūgoku minkan ni okeru mokuren setsuwa no seikaku" 中國民間における目連説話の性格. *Bukkyō shigaku* 佛教史學 No. 7 (1959): 224–45.

——. "Mokuren henbun" 目連変文. In *Chūgoku no meicho: Kuraishi hakushi kanreki kinen* 中国の名著倉石博士還暦記念. Edited by Tokyo daigaku chūgoku bungaku kenkyūshitsu 東京大學中國文學研究室. Tokyo: Keisō, 1961.

——. "Tonkō-bon jigoku bunken kanki awasete bakkōkutsu no seikaku o ronzu" 敦煌本地獄文献管窺併莫高窟の性格を論ず. *Komazawa daigaku bukkyō gakubu ronshū* 駒澤大學佛教教部論集 No. 13 (October 1982): 31–52.

——. "Tonkō bunken yori mitaru Miroku shinkō no ichi sokumen" 敦煌文獻より見たる彌勒信仰の一側面. *Tōhō shūkyō* 東方宗教 No. 53 (May 1979): 22–48.

——. *Tonkō no bungaku* 敦煌の文学. Tokyo: Daizō shuppansha, 1971.

——. *Tonkō no minshū: sono seikatsu to shisō* 敦煌の民衆その生活と思想. Tōyōjin no kōdō to shisō, Vol. 8. Tokyo: Hyōronsha, 1972.

Karlgren, Berhhard. *Grammata Serica Recensa. Bulletin of the Museum of Far Eastern Antiquities* 29 (1957).

——. "Some Fecundity Symbols in Ancient China." *Bulletin of the Museum of Far Eastern Antiquities* 2 (1930): 1–65.

Kaufman, Howard K. *Bangkhaud: A Community Study in Thailand.* Locust Valley: J.J. Augustin, 1960.

Kawaguchi, Hisao 川口久雄. "Tonkō henbun no sozai to nihon bungaku: Mokuren henbun, gōma henbun" 敦煌變文の素材と日本文學目連變文降魔變文. *Nihon chūgoku gakkai hō* 日本中國學會報 No. 8 (1957): 116–33.

Keightley, David N. "The Religious Commitment: Shang Theology and the Genesis of Chinese Political Culture." *HR* 17:3–4 (February–May 1978): 211–25.

Keyes, Charles F. "Introduction: The Study of Popular Ideas of Karma." In *Karma: An Anthropological Inquiry.* Edited by Charles F. Keyes and E. Valentine Daniel. Berkeley: University of California Press, 1983.

Keyes, Charles F., and E. Daniel Valentine, eds. *Karma: An Anthropological Inquiry.* Berkeley: University of California Press, 1983.

Kirfel, Willibald. *Die Kosmographie der Inder nach den Quellen dargestellt.* Bonn: Kurt Schroeder, 1920.

Kloetzli, Randy. *Buddhist Cosmology, From Single World System to Pure Land: Science and Theology in the Images of Motion and Light.* Delhi: Motilal Banarsidass, 1983.

Knipe, David M. "Sapiṇḍīkarana: The Hindu Rite of Entry into Heaven." In

Religious Encounters with Death. Edited by Frank Reynolds and Earle Waugh. University Park: Pennsylvania State University Press, 1977.

Kominami, Ichirō 小南一郎. *Chūgoku no shinwa to monogatari: ko shōsetsu shi no tenkai* 中國の神話と物語り古小説史の展開. Tokyo: Iwanami shoten, 1984.

Kuo, P'eng 郭朋. *Sung yüan fo-chiao* 宋元佛教. Fukien: Fu-chien jen-min ch'u-pan-she, 1981.

Kuraishi, Takeshirō 倉石武四郎. "Mokuren henbun shōkai no ato ni" 目連変文紹介の後に. *Shinagaku* 支那學 4:3 (October 1927): 130–38.

———. "Mokuren kyūbo gyōkō gibun ni tsuite" 目連救母行孝戲文に就いて. *Shinagaku* 支那學 3:10 (February 1925): 5–24.

LaFleur, William R. *The Karma of Words: Buddhism and the Literary Arts in Medieval Japan*. Berkeley: University of California Press, 1983.

Lamotte, Etienne. *Histoire du bouddhisme indien, des origines à l'ère Śaka*. Publications de l'Institut Orientaliste de Louvain, No. 14. 1958; reprint ed., Louvain-la-Neuve: Institut Orientaliste, 1976.

———, trans. *Le Traité de la grand vertu de sagesse de Nāgārjuna (Mahāprajñāpāramitā-śāstra)*. 5 vols. Louvain-la-Neuve: Institut Orientaliste, 1949–80.

Lao, Kan 榮幹. "Shang-ssu k'ao" 上巳考. *Chung-yang yen-chiu-yüan li-shih yü-yen yen-chiu-so chi-k'an* 中央研究院歷史語言研究所集刊 29:1 (1970): 243–62.

Lau, D.C., trans. *The Analects (Lun yü)*. Harmondsworth: Penguin Books, 1979.

———, trans. *Lao Tzu, Tao Te Ching*. Harmondsworth: Penguin Books, 1963.

———, trans. *Mencius*. Harmondsworth: Penguin Books, 1970.

La Vallée Poussin, Louis de, trans. *L'Abhidharmakośa de Vasubandhu*. 6 vols. Edited by Etienne Lamotte. *Mélanges chinois et bouddhiques*, Vol. 16. Brussels: Institut Belge des Haute Etudes Chinoises, 1971.

———. "Le Bouddha et les abhijñās." *Le Muséon* 44 (1931): 335–42.

———. "Cosmogony and Cosmology (Buddhist)." In *Encyclopaedia of Religion and Ethics*, Vol. 4. 13 vols. Edited by James Hastings, Edinburgh: T. and T. Clark, 1912.

Leach, Edmund. "Two Essays concerning the Symbolic Representation of Time." In *Rethinking Anthropology*. London School of Economics Monographs on Social Anthropology, No. 22. London: Athlone Press, 1961.

Legge, James, trans. *Li Chi: The Book of Rites*. 2 vols. Edited by Ch'u and Winberg Chai. Reprint ed., New York: University Books, 1967.

———, trans. *A Record of Buddhistic Kingdoms: Being an Account by the Chinese Monk Fa-hien of His Travels in India and Ceylon (A.D. 399–414)*. 1866; reprint ed., San Francisco: Chinese Materials Center, 1975.

Lessing, Ferdinand. "Skizze des Ritus: Die Spiesung der Hungergeister." In *Studia Sino-Altaica: Festschrift für Erich Haenisch zum 80. Geburtstag, in Auftrag der Deutschen Morgenländischen Gesellschaft*. Wiesbaden: Franz Steiner Verlag, 1961.

Lévi-Strauss, Claude. "The Story of Asdiwal." Translated by Nicholas Mann. In

The Structural Study of Myth and Totemism. Edited by Edmund Leach. ASA Monograph, No. 5. London: Tavistock Publications, 1967.

————. "The Structural Study of Myth." In *Structural Anthropology*, Vol. 1. Translated by Claire Jacobson and Brooke G. Schoepf. New York: Basic Books, 1963.

Lewis, Ioan M. *Ecstatic Religion: An Anthropological Study of Spirit Possession and Shamanism*. Revised ed. Harmondsworth: Penguin Books, 1978.

Li, Ch'ing-chih 李清志. *Kuo-li chung-yang t'u-shu-kuan so-tsang tun-huang chüan-tzu chiao-tu cha-chi* 國立中央圖書館所藏敦煌卷子校讀札記. 1973 (mimeographed).

Li Shih-yü 李世瑜. *Pao-chüan tsung-lu* 寶卷綜錄. Peking: Chung-hua shu-chü, 1961.

Liebenthal, Walter. "The Immortality of the Soul in Chinese Thought." *Monumenta Nipponica* 8: Semi-Annual No. 1/2 (1952): 327–97.

Lindquist, Carl Sigurd. *Siddhi und Abhiññā: Eine Studie über die klassischen Wunder des Yoga*. Uppsala: A.-B. Lundequistska Bokhandeln, 1935.

Link, Arthur. "Shih Seng-yu and His Writings." JAOS 80:1 (January–March 1960): 17–43.

Lo, Tsung-t'ao 羅宗濤. "Pien-ko, pien-hsiang, pien-wen" 變歌變相變文. *Chung-hua hsüeh-yüan* 中華學苑 No. 7 (March 1971): 73–99.

————. *Tun-huang chiang-ching pien-wen yen-chiu* 敦煌講經變文研究. Taipei: Wen shih che ch'u-pan-she, 1972.

————. *Tun-huang pien-wen she-hui feng-su shih-wu k'ao* 敦煌變文社會風俗事物考. Taipei: Wen shih che ch'u-pan-she, 1974.

Lombard-Salmon, Claudine. "Survivance d'un rite bouddhique à Java: la cérémonie du *pu-du (avalambana)*." BEFEO 62 (1975): 457–86.

Loon, Piet van der. "Les Origines rituelles du théâtre chinois." JA 265: 1–2 (1977): 141–68.

Lu, Hsün 魯迅. *Ku hsiao-shuo kou-ch'en* 古小說鉤沈. Peking: Jen-min wen-hsüeh ch'u-pan-she, 1951.

Maeno, Naoaki 前野直彬. "Meikai yūkō" 冥界遊行. *Chūgoku bungaku hō* 中國文學報 14 (April 1961): 38–57; 15 (October 1961): 33–48.

Magnin, Paul. *La Vie et l'oeuvre de Huisi (515–577): les origines de la secte bouddhique chinoise du Tiantai*. Paris: Ecole Française d'Extrême-Orient, 1979.

The Mahavastu. 3 vols. Translated by J.J. Jones. Sacred Books of the Buddhists, Vols. 17–19. London: Luzac and Co., 1949–56.

Mair, Victor H. "Lay Students and the Making of Written Vernacular Narrative: An Inventory of Tun-huang Manuscripts." *Chinoperl Papers* No. 10 (1981): 5–96.

————. "Notes on the Maudgalyāyana Legend in East Asia." Paper presented at the Mid-Atlantic Regional Meeting of the Association for Asian Studies, October 15, 1984.

252

———. *T'ang Transformation Texts*. Harvard-Yenching Monograph Series. Cambridge: Harvard University Press, forthcoming.

———. *Tun-huang Popular Narratives*. Cambridge: Cambridge University Press, 1983.

Makita, Tairyō 牧田諦亮. *Chūgoku kinsei bukkyō shi kenkyū* 中國今世佛教史研究. Kyoto: Heiryakuji shoten, 1957.

———. *Gikyō kenkyū* 疑經研究. Kyoto: Kyoto daigaku jinbun kagaku kenkyūjo, 1976.

———. "Hōshi oshō den kō" 寶誌和尚傳考. *Tōhō gakuhō* 東方學報 26 (March 1956): 64–89.

———. "Suirikue shōkō" 水陸會小考. *Tōhō shūkyō* 東方宗教 No. 12 (July 1957): 14–33.

Manabe, Kōsai 真鍋廣濟. *Jizō bosatsu no kenkyū* 地藏菩薩の研究. Kyoto: Sanmitsudō, 1960.

Marriott, McKim. "Little Communities in an Indigenous Civilization." In *Village India: Studies in the Little Community*. Edited by McKim Marriott. Comparative Studies of Cultures and Civilizations, No. 6. *The American Anthropological Association Memoir* 57:3 (June 1955), Part 2, No. 83.

Maspero, Henri. *China in Antiquity*. Revised ed. Edited by Paul Demiéville. Translated by Frank A. Kierman, Jr. Amherst: University of Massachusetts Press, 1978.

———. *Taoism and Chinese Religion*. Translated by Frank A. Kierman, Jr. Amherst: University of Massachusetts Press, 1979.

Mather, Richard B., trans. *Shih-shuo hsin-yü: A New Account of Tales of the World*. Minneapolis: University of Minnesota Press, 1976.

Matsumoto, Bunzaburō 松本文三郎. *Miroku jōdo ron* 彌勒淨土論. Tokyo: Heigo shuppansha, 1911.

Matsumoto Eiichi. 松本英一. *Tonkō-ga no kenkyū* 敦煌畫の研究. 2 vols. Tokyo: Tōhō bunka gakuin, 1937.

Matsunaga, Alicia. *The Buddhist Philosophy of Assimilation: The Historical Development of the Honji-Suijaku Theory*. Rutland: Tuttle and Co., 1969.

Matsunaga, Daigan and Alicia. *The Buddhist Concept of Hell*. New York: Philosophical Library, 1972.

Mauss, Marcel. *The Gift: Forms and Functions of Exchange in Archaic Societies*. Translated by Ian Cunnison. New York: W. W. Norton and Co., 1967.

McDermott, Joseph P. "Charting Blank Spaces and Disputed Regions: The Problem of Sung Land Tenure." JAS 44:1 (November 1984): 13–41.

Michihata, Ryōshū 道瑞良秀. *Bukkyō to jukyō* 仏教と儒教. Tokyo: Daisan bunmei sha, 1976.

———. *Bukkyō to jukyō rinri* 佛教と儒教倫理. Kyoto: Heirakyji shoten, 1968.

———. "Chūgoku bukkyō no minshūka" 中国佛教の民衆化. In *Chūgoku no*

bukkyō 中国の佛教. Kōza bukkyō, Vol. 4. Tokyo: Daizō shuppan kabushiki kaisha, 1957.

————. *Chūgoku bukkyō shi* 中国仏教史. Second ed. Kyoto: Hōzōkan, 1958.

————. *Chūgoku bukkyō shisō shi no kenkyū* 中国仏教思想史の研究. Kyoto: Heiryakuji shoten, 1979.

————. *Chūgoku bukkyō to shakai fukushi jigyō* 中国仏教と社会福祉事業. Kyoto: Hōzōkan, 1967.

————. *Tōdai bukkyō shi no kenkyū* 唐代仏教史の研究. Kyoto: Hōzōkan, 1957.

Migot, André. "Un Grand Disciple du Buddha, Śāriputra: son rôle dans l'histoire du bouddhisme et dans le développement de *l'Abhidharma*." BEFEO 46:2 (1954): 405–554.

Minn, Yong-gyu 閔泳珪. "*Wŏrin sŏkpo* che isip-sam chan'gwŏn" 月印釋譜第二十三殘卷. *Tongbang hakchi* 東方學志 6 (June 1963): 1–18.

Mitarai, Masaru 御手洗勝. *Kodai chūgoku no kamigami: kodai densetsu no kenkyū* 古代中国の神々古代傳説の研究. Tōyōgaku sōsho, No. 26. Tokyo: Sōbunsha, 1984.

Miya, Tsugio 宮次男. "Mokuren kyūbo setsuwa to sono kaiga: shutsugen ni yonde" 目連救母説話とその繪畫出現に因んで. *Bijutsu kenkyū* 美術研究 No. 255 (January 1968): 1–24.

Miyakawa, Hisayuki. "An Outline of the Naitō Hypothesis and Its Effects on Japanese Studies of China." *Far Eastern Quarterly* 14:4 (1955): 533–52.

———— 宮川尚志. "Rikuchō jidai no fuzoku" 六朝時代の巫俗. *Shirin* 史林 44:1 (January 1961): 74–97.

Mochizuki, Shinkō 望月信亨. *Bukkyō dai jiten* 佛教大辭典. Third ed. 10 vols. Kyoto: Sekai seiten kankō kyōkai, 1954–71. Abbreviated as MBDJ.

Moriya, Mitsuo 守屋美都雄. *Chūgoku ko saijiki no kenkyū* 中國古歳時記の研究. Tokyo: Teikoku shoin, 1963.

————. *Keiso saijiki* 荊楚歳時記. Tōyō bunko, Vol. 324. Tokyo: Heibonsha, 1978.

Morohashi, Tetsuji 諸橋轍次. *Dai kanwa jiten* 大漢和辭典. 13 vols. Tokyo: Taishūkan shoten, 1957–60. Abbreviated as MDKJ.

Murakami, Yoshimi 村上嘉實. "*Kōsō den* no shin'i ni tsuite" 高僧傳の神異について. *Tōhō shūkyō* 東方宗教 No. 17 (August 1961): 1–17.

Murase, Yukihiro 村瀬之熙. *Geien nisshō* 秋苑日渉. In Nihon zuihitsu zenshū 日本随筆全書, Vol. 1. Tokyo: Kokumin tosho kabushiki kaisha, 1927.

Mus, Paul. *La Lumière sur les six voies: tableau de la transmigration bouddhique.* Paris: Travaux et Mémoires de l'Institut d'Ethnologie, 1939.

Naba, Toshisada 那波利真. "Bukkyō shinkō ni motozukite soshiki seraretaru chūbantō godai ji no shayū ni tsuite" 佛教信仰に基きて組織せられたる中晩唐五代時の社邑に就きて. *Shirin* 史林 24: 3–4 (1939). Reprinted in *Tōdai shakai bunka shi kenkyū* 唐代社會文化史研究. Tokyo: Sōbunsha, 1974.

254

————. "Tō shōbon zashō kō" 唐鈔本雜抄考. (1942). Reprinted in *Tōdai shakai bunka shi kenkyū* 唐代社會文化史研究. Tokyo: Sōbunsha, 1974.

————. "Tōdai ni okeru kokugi gyōkō ni tsuite" 唐代に於ける國記行香につ いて (1955). Reprinted in *Tōdai shakai bunka shi kenkyū*. Tokyo: Sōbunsha, 1974.

————. "Tōdai no shayū ni tsukite" 唐代の社邑に就きて *Shirin* 史林 23: 2–4 (1938). Reprinted in *Tōdai shakai bunka shi kenkyū*. Tokyo: Sōbunsha, 1974.

Naitō, Konan 内藤湖南. *Shina kinsei shi* 支那近世史. In *Naitō konan zenshū* 内藤 湖南全書, Vol. 10. Tokyo: Iwanami shoten, 1969.

Ñāṇamoli, Bhikkhu, trans. *The Path of Purification*. Colombo: A. Semage, 1956.

Nanjio, Bunyiu. *A Catalogue of the Chinese Translation of the Buddhist Tripitaka*. 1883; reprint ed., San Francisco: Chinese Materials Center, 1975.

Needham, Joseph, with the assistance of Wang Ling et. al. *Science and Civilization in China*. 7 vols. Cambridge: Cambridge University Press, 1954–.

Ngo, Van Xuyet. *Divination, magie, et politique dans la Chine ancienne: essai suivi de la traduction des "Biographies des magiciens" tirées de "L'Histoire des Han postérieurs."* Bibliothèque de l'Ecole des Hautes Etudes, Section des Sciences Religieuses, Vol. 78. Paris: Presses Universitaires de France, 1976.

Niida, Noboru 仁井田陞. "Tonkō hakken *jūō kyō* token ni mietaru keihō shiryō" 敦煌發見十王經圖卷に見えたる形法. *Tōyō gakuhō* 東洋學報 25:3 (May 1938): 63–78.

Obeyesekere, Gananath. "Theodicy, Sin, and Salvation in a Sociology of Bud-dhism." In *Dialectic in Practical Religion*. Edited by Edmund Leach. Cam-bridge: Cambridge University Press, 1968.

Oda, Tokunō 織田得能. *Bukkyō dai jiten* 佛教大辭典. Reprint ed., Tokyo: Daizō shuppansha, 1969. Abbreviated as OBDJ.

O'Flaherty, Wendy Doniger. *Asceticism and Eroticism in the Mythology of Śiva*. London: Oxford University Press, 1973.

————, ed. *Karma and Rebirth in Classical Indian Traditions*. Berkeley: University of California Press, 1980.

Ogasawara, Senshū 小笠原宣秀. *Chūgoku jōdokyōka no kenkyū* 中國淨土教家の 研究. Kyoto: Heiryakuji shoten, 1951.

————. *Chūgoku kinsei jōdo kyō shi no kenkyū* 中國近世淨土教史の研究. Kyoto: Hyakkaen, 1963.

Ogawa, Kan'ichi 小川貫弌. *Bukkyō bunka shi kenkyū* 仏教文化史研究. Kyoto: Nagata bunshōdō, 1973.

Okabe, Kazuo 岡部和雄. "Shūmitsu ni okeru kōron no tenkai to sono hōhō" 宗密における孝論の展開とその方法. IBK 15:2 (March 1967): 574–78.

————. "Urabon kyōrui no yakkyō shiteki kenkyū" 盂蘭盆經類の譯經史的 研究. *Shūkyō kenkyū* 宗教研究 37:3 (March 1964): 59–78.

Ōmura, Seigai 大村西崖. *Shina bukkyō bijutsu shi: chōso hen* 支那佛教美術史彫 塑篇. 2 vols. Tokyo: Bussho kankōkai, 1915.

255

Ono, Katsutoshi 小野勝年. *Nittō guhō junrei gyōki no kenkyū* 入唐求法巡禮行記 の研究. 4 vols. Tokyo: Suzuki gakujutsu zaidan, 1964–69.

Ono, Shihei 小野四平. "Taisan kara hōto e" 泰山から豊都へ. *Bunka* 文化 27:2 (1963): 80–111.

Ortner, Sherry B. "Is Female to Male As Nature Is to Culture?" In *Woman, Culture, and Society*. Edited by Michelle Zimbalist Rosaldo and Louise Lamphere. Stanford: Stanford University Press, 1974.

Ōtani, Kōshō 大谷光照. *Tōdai no bukkyō girei* 唐代の佛教儀禮. 2 vols. Tokyo: Yūkōsha, 1937.

Overmyer, Daniel L. "China." In *Death and Eastern Thought: Understanding Death in Eastern Religions and Philosophies*. Edited by Frederick H. Holck. Nashville: Abingdon Press, 1974.

———. *Folk Buddhist Religion: Dissenting Sects in Late Traditional China*. Harvard East Asian Series, No. 83. Cambridge: Harvard University Press, 1976.

———. "The White Cloud Sect in Sung and Yüan China." HJAS 42:2 (December 1982): 615–42.

Pachow, Wayne. "A Study of the Dotted Record." JAOS 85:3 (September 1965). Reprinted in *Chinese Buddhism: Aspects of Interaction and Reinterpretation*. Lanham: University Press of America, 1980.

Pai, Hua-wen 白化文. "What is *Pien-wen*?" Translated by Victor H. Mair. HJAS 44:2 (December 1984): 493–514.

P'an, Ch'ung-kuei 潘重規. "Kuo-li chung-yang t'u-shu-kuan so-tsang tun-huang chüan-tzu t'i-chi" 國立中央圖書館所藏敦煌卷子題記. *Hsin-ya hsüeh-pao* 新亞學報 8:2 (August 1968): 321–73.

———. "Ts'ung tun-huang i-shu k'an fo-chiao t'i-ch'ang hsiao-tao" 從敦煌遺書 看佛教提唱孝道. *Hua-kang wen-k'o hsüeh-pao* 華岡文科學報 12 (March 1980): 197–267.

Pang, Duane. "The P'u-tu Ritual." In *Buddhist and Taoist Studies I*. Edited by Michael Saso and David W. Chappell. Asian Studies at Hawaii, No. 16. Honolulu: University Press of Hawaii, 1977.

Pas, Julian F., L.S.T. "Shan-tao's *Commentary on the Amitāyur-Buddhānusmrti-Sūtra*." Ph.D. dissertation, McMaster University, 1973.

P'ei-wen yün-fu 佩文韻府. 7 vols. Edited by Chang Yü-shu 張玉書. Taipei: Commercial Press, 1966. Abbreviated as PWYF.

Pelliot, Paul. "Meou-tseu, ou les doutes levées." TP 19 (1920): 255–433.

———. Review of Schlegel, "Les termes bouddhiques Yu-lan-p'en et Yu-lan-p'o." BEFEO 1 (1901): 277–78.

Peterson, Willard J. "Making Connections: Commentary on the Attached Verbalizations of the *Book of Change*." HJAS 42:2 (June 1982): 67–116.

Porée-Maspero, Eveline. *Etudes sur les rites agraires des cambodgiens*. 3 vols. Le Monde d'outre-mer passé et present, Series 1, Vol. 14. Paris: Mouton, 1962–69.

Potter, Jack M. "Cantonese Shamanism." In *Religion and Ritual in Chinese Society*. Edited by Arthur P. Wolf. Stanford: Stanford University Press, 1974.

Przyluski, Jean. "Les Rites d'Avalambana." *Mélanges chinois et bouddhiques* 1 (1931–32): 221–25.

Pulleyblank, Edwin G. *The Background of the Rebellion of An Lu-shan*. London: Oxford University Press, 1955.

———. *Middle Chinese: A Study in Historical Phonology*. Vancouver: University of British Columbia Press, 1984.

Rahula, Bhikkhu Telwatte. *A Critical Study of the Mahavastu*. Delhi: Motilal Banarsidass, 1978.

Redfield, Robert. *Peasant Society and Culture: An Anthropological Approach to Civilization*. Chicago: University of Chicago Press, 1956.

Reichelt, Karl Ludwig. *Truth and Tradition in Chinese Buddhism: A Study of Chinese Mahayana Buddhism*. Translated by Katharina van Wagenen Bugge. Shanghai: Commercial Press, 1927.

Reischauer, Edwin O. *Ennin's Travels in T'ang China*. New York: Ronald Press Co., 1955.

———, trans. *Ennin's Diary: The Record of a Pilgrimage to China in Search of the Law*. New York: Ronald Press Co., 1955.

Renou, Louis, and Jean Filliozat. *L'Inde classique: manuel des études indiennes*. 2 vols. Vol. 1, Paris: Payot, 1947; Vol. 2, Paris: Imprimerie Nationale, 1953.

Répertoire du canon bouddhique sino-japonais. Revised ed. Supplementary fascicle to *Hōbōgirin*. Edited by Paul Demiéville. Tokyo: Maison Franco-Japonaise, 1978.

Reynolds, Frank E. "The Two Wheels of Dhamma: A Study of Early Buddhism." In *The Two Wheels of Dhamma: Essays on the Theravada Tradition in India and Ceylon*. Edited by Bardwell L. Smith. AAR Studies in Religion, No. 3. Chambersburg: American Academy of Religion, 1972.

Reynolds, Frank E., and Mani B. Reynolds. *Three Worlds According to King Ruang: A Thai Buddhist Cosmology*. Berkeley Buddhist Studies Series 4. Berkeley: Asian Humanities Press, 1982.

Rhys Davids, Caroline A.F., and F.L. Woodward, trans. *The Book of Kindred Sayings (Sanyutta-Nikaya) or Grouped Suttas*. 5 vols. Pali Text Society Translation Series, Nos. 7, 10, 13, 14, 16. London: Oxford University Press, 1917–30.

Rhys-Davids, T.W., and Hermann Oldenberg, trans. *Vinaya Texts*. 3 vols. Sacred Books of the East, Vols. 13, 17, 20. Oxford: Clarendon Press, 1881, 1882, 1885.

Robinet, Isabelle. *Les Commentaires du Tao tö king jusqu'au VIIe siècle*. Mémoires de l'Institut des Hautes Etudes Chinoises, Vol. 5. Paris: Presses Universitaires de France, 1977.

———. "Metamorphosis and Deliverance from the Corpse in Taoism." HR 19:1 (August 1979): 37–70.

Rotours, Robert des. "Le T'ang lieou-tien décrit-il exactement les institutions en usage sous la dynastie des T'ang?" JA 263: 1–2 (1975): 183–201.

———, trans. *Traité des fonctionnaires et Traité de l'armée, traduits de la Nouvelle histoire des T'ang (chap. XLVI–L).* 2 vols. Bibliothèque de l'Institut des Hautes Etudes Chinoises, Vol. 6. Leiden: E.J. Brill, 1948.

Ryū, Shiman [Liu, Chih-wan] 劉枝萬. *Chūgoku dōkyō no matsuri to shinkō.* 中国道教の祭と信仰. 2 vols. Tokyo: Ōfusha, 1983–84.

Sadakata, Akira 定方晟. *Shumisen to gokuraku: bukkyō no uchūkan* 須弥山と極楽仏教の宇宙観. Tokyo: Kōdansha, 1973.

Said, Edward W. *Orientalism.* New York: Random House, 1978.

Sakai, Tadao 酒井忠夫. *Chūgoku zensho no kenkyū* 中国善書の研究. Tokyo: Kōbundō, 1960.

———. "Taisan shinkō no kenkyū" 太山信仰の研究. *Shichō* 史潮 7:2 (1937): 70–118.

Sakurai, Tokutarō, ed. 桜井徳太郎. *Jizō shinkō* 地蔵信仰. Minshū shūkyōshi sōsho, Vol. 10. Tokyo: Yūzankaku shuppan, 1983.

Sawada, Mizuho 沢田瑞穂. *Hōkan no kenkyū* 寶卷の研究. Revised ed. Tokyo: Kokusho kankōkai, 1975.

———. *Jigoku hen: chūgoku no meikai setsu* 地獄変中国の冥界説. Kyoto: Hōzōkan, 1968.

Schafer, Edward H. *Pacing the Void: T'ang Approaches to the Stars.* Berkeley: University of California Press, 1977.

———. "Ritual Exposure in Ancient China." HJAS 14: 1–2 (June 1951): 130–84.

Schipper, Kristofer. *Le Corps taoïste: corps physique—corps social.* L'Espace intérieur, 25. Paris: Fayard, 1982.

———. "Vernacular and Classical Ritual in Taoism." JAS 45:1 (November 1985): 21–57.

Schopen, Gregory. "Filial Piety and the Monk in the Practice of Indian Buddhism: A Question of 'Sinicization' Viewed from the Other Side." TP 70: 1–3 (1984): 110–26.

Seidel, Anna K. *Le Divinisation de Lao tseu dans le Taoïsme des Han.* Publications de l'Ecole Française d'Extrême-Orient, Vol. 68. Paris: Ecole Française d'Extrême-Orient, 1969.

Shimaji, Taitō 島地大等. *Tendai kyōgaku shi* 天台教学史. 1933; reprint ed., Tokyo: Nakayama shobō, 1978.

Soothill, William Edward, and Lewis Hodous. *A Dictionary of Chinese Buddhist Terms with Sanskrit and English Equivalents and a Sanskrit-Pali Index.* 1937; reprint ed., Taipei: Ch'eng-wen Publishing Co., 1976.

Soper, Alexander C. *Literary Evidence for Early Buddhist Art in China.* Ascona: Artibus Asiae Publishers, 1959.

Soymié, Michel. "*Ketsubon kyō no shiryōteki kenkyū*" 血盆經の資料的研究. *Dōkyō kenkyū* 道教研究 1 (December 1965): 109–66.

Speyer, J.S., ed. *Avadāna çataka: A Century of Edifying Tales Belonging to the Hīnayāna.* 1909; reprint ed., The Hague: Mouton and Co., 1958.

Spiro, Melford E. *Buddhism and Society: A Great Tradition and Its Burmese Vicissitudes.* Second ed. Berkeley: University of California Press, 1982.

Ssu-k'u ch'üan-shu tsung-mu t'i-yao 四庫全書總目提要. 4 vols. Edited by Chi Yün 紀昀. Shanghai: Commercial Press, 1931.

Ssu-shih-erh chang ching yü Mou-tzu li-huo lun 四十二章經與牟子理惑論. Edited by Chang Man-t'ao 張曼濤. Hsien-tai fo-chiao hsüeh-shu ts'ung-k'an, Vol. 11. Taipei: Ta-sheng wen-hua ch'u-pan-she, 1978.

Stein, Rolf A. "Religious Taoism and Popular Religion from the Second to the Seventh Centuries." In *Facets of Taoism.* Edited by Holmes Welch and Anna K. Seidel. New Haven: Yale University Press, 1979.

Strong, John. *The Legend of King Aśoka: A Study and Translation of the "Aśokāvadāna."* Princeton: Princeton University Press, 1983.

————. "The Transforming Gift: An Analysis of Devotional Acts of Offering in Buddhist *Avadāna* Literature." HR 18:3 (February 1979): 221–37.

Sundararajan, Kuen-wei Lu. "Chinese Stories of Karma and Transmigration." Ph.D. dissertation, Harvard University, 1979.

Suzuki, Chūsei 鈴木中正. "Sōdai bukkyō kessha no kenkyū" 宋代佛教結社の研究. *Shigaku zasshi* 史學雜志 52 (1941): 65–98, 205–42, 303–33.

Suzuki, Mitsuo 鈴木満男. "Bon ni kuru rei" 盆にくる霊. *Minzokugaku kenkyū* 民族学研究 37:3 (1972): 167–85.

Taishō shinshū daizōkyō sakuin 大正新修大藏經所引. 30 vols. to date. Tokyo: Taishō shinshū daizōkyō kankōkai, 1940–.

Takamine, Ryōshū 高峯了洲. *Kegon shisō shi* 華嚴思想史. Second ed. Tokyo: Hyakkaen, 1963.

Takenaka, Nobutsune 竹中信常. "Sōsō no gireiteki ichi" 葬送の儀禮的位置. In *Bukkyō to girei: Katō Shōichi sensei koki kinen ronbunshū* 佛教と儀禮加藤章一先生古稀記念論文集. Edited by Bukkyō minzoku gakkai. Tokyo: Kokusho kankōkai, 1977.

Tambiah, Stanley J. *Buddhism and the Spirit Cults in North-east Thailand.* Cambridge Studies in Social Anthropology, No. 2. Cambridge: Cambridge University Press, 1970.

————. "Buddhism and This-Worldly Activity." *Modern Asian Studies* 7:1 (January 1973): 1–20.

————. *The Buddhist Saints of the Forest and the Cult of Amulets: A Study in Charisma, Hagiography, Sectarianism, and Millennial Buddhism.* Cambridge Studies in Social Anthropology, No. 49. Cambridge: Cambridge University Press, 1984.

Tanaka, Issei 田仲一成. *Chūgoku saishi engeki kenkyū* 中国祭祀演劇研究. Tokyo: Tokyo daigaku shuppankai, 1981.

T'ang-shih tzu-liao cheng-li chi-k'an 唐史資料整理集刊. Edited by Yang Chia-lo

楊家駱. Yang-ming shan: Chung-hua hsüeh-shu-yüan chung-kuo hsüeh-shu shih yen-chiu-so, 1971.

T'ang wu-tai jen-wu chuan-chi tzu-liao tsung-ho so-yin 唐五代人物傳記資料綜合所引. Peking: Chung-hua shu-chü, 1982.

T'ang, Yung-t'ung 湯用彤. *Han wei liang-chin nan-pei-ch'ao fo-chiao shih* 漢魏兩晉南北朝佛教史. Reprint ed., Taipei: Ting-wen shu-chü, 1976.

Tanigawa, Michio. *Medieval Chinese Society and the Local "Community."* Translated by Joshua A. Fogel. Berkeley: University of California Press, 1985.

Tao-tsang tzu-mu yin-te 道藏子目引得. Harvard-Yenching Institute Sinological Index Series, Index No. 25. Taipei: Chinese Materials and Research Aids Service Center, 1966.

Teiser, Stephen F. "Ghosts and Ancestors in Medieval Chinese Religion: The Yü-lan-p'en Festival as Mortuary Ritual." HR 26:1 (August 1986): 47–67.

———. "Mother, Son, and Hungry Ghost: Gender and Salvation in the Mythology of Mu-lien." Paper presented at the Annual Meeting of the American Academy of Religion in Atlanta, November 1986.

———. "T'ang Buddhist Encyclopedias: A Bibliographical Introduction to *Fa-yüan chu-lin* and *Chu-ching yao-chi*." *T'ang Studies* No. 3 (Winter 1985): 109–28.

———. "The Yü-lan-p'en Festival in Medieval Chinese Religion." Ph.D. dissertation, Princeton University, 1986.

Teng, Ssu-yü, trans. *Family Instructions for the Yen Clan: "Yen-shih chia-hsün" by Yen Chih-t'ui*. T'oung Pao Monograph No. 4. Leiden: E.J. Brill, 1968.

Thiel, P. Joseph. "Schamanismus im alten China." *Sinologica* 10: 2–3 (1968): 149–204.

Thomas, Edward J. *The History of Buddhist Thought*. Second ed. London: Routledge and Kegan Paul, 1953.

Ting, Fu-pao 丁福保. *Fo-hsüeh ta tz'u-tien* 佛學大辭典. 4 vols. 1921; reprint ed., Taipei: Hsin-wen-feng ch'u-pan kung-ssu, 1978. Abbreviated as TFTT.

Tokiwa, Daijō 常盤大乗. *Go-kan yori sō-sei ni itaru yakkyō sōroku* 後漢より宋齊に致る譯經總錄. 1938; reprint ed., Tokyo: Kokusho kankōkai, 1973.

———. *Shina bukkyō no kenkyū* 支那佛教の研究. 3 vols. Tokyo: Shunjūsha, 1938–43.

Tokushi, Yūshō 禿氏祐祥. "*Fubo onchō kyō* no ibun ni tsuite" 父母恩重經の異本に就いて. *Shūkyō kenkyū* 宗教研究. N.S. 5:4 (July 1932): 116–23.

Tokushi, Yūshō, and Ogawa, Kan'ichi 小川貫弌. "*Jūō shōshichi kyō* santoken no kōzō" 十王生七經讃圖卷の構造. In *Seiiki bunka kenkyū* 西域文化研究. 6 vols. Edited by Seiiki bunka kenkyūkai. Tokyo: Hōzōkan, 1958–63. Reprinted in Ogawa, *Bukkyō bunka shi kenkyū*.

Tsuda, Sōkichi 津田左右吉. *Shina bukkyō no kenkyū* シナ佛教の研究. Tokyo: Iwanami shoten, 1957.

Tsukamoto, Zenryū 塚本善隆. *Shina bukkyō shi kenkyū: Hokugi hen* 支那佛教史研究北魏篇. Tokyo: Kōbundō, 1942.

———. *Tō chūki no jōdokyō* 唐中期の淨土教. 1933; reprint ed., Kyoto: Hōzōkan, 1975.

Tun-huang i-shu tsung-mu so-yin 敦煌遺書總目所引. Peking: Commercial Press, 1962.

Tun, Li-ch'en. *Annual Customs and Festivals in Peking.* Second ed. Translated by Derk Bodde. Hong Kong: Hong Kong University Press, 1965.

Tung, Tso-pin 董作賓. *Chung-kuo nien-li tsung-p'u* 中國年歷總譜. 2 vols. Hong Kong: Hong Kong University Press, 1960.

Twitchett, Denis C. "The Composition of the T'ang Ruling Class: New Evidence from Tun-huang." In *Perspectives on the T'ang.* Edited by Arthur F. Wright and Denis C. Twitchett. New Haven: Yale University Press, 1973.

———. "The Fan Clan's Charitable Estate." In *Confucianism in Action.* Edited by David Nivison and Arthur F. Wright. Stanford: Stanford University Press, 1959.

———. "Hsüan-tsung." Chapter 7 of *Sui and T'ang China, 589–906,* Vol. 3, Part 1 of *The Cambridge History of China.* Edited by Denis C. Twichett. Cambridge: Cambridge University Press, 1979.

———. "Introduction." In *Sui and T'ang China, 589–906,* Vol. 3, Part 1 of *The Cambridge History of China.* Edited by Denis C. Twitchett. Cambridge: Cambridge University Press, 1979.

———. "Monastic Estates in T'ang China." *Asia Major* 5:2 (1956): 123–46.

Ui, Hakuju 宇井伯壽. *"Onshitsu gyōsho"* 温室經疏. In *Seiiki butten no kenkyū: Tonkō isho kanyaku.* 西域佛典の研究敦煌遺書簡譯 Tokyo: Iwanami shoten, 1970.

Vajirañāna, Paravahera. *Buddhist Meditation in Theory and Practice: A General Exposition According to the Pāli Canon of the Theravāda School.* Colombo: M.J. Gunasena and Co., 1962.

De Visser, Marinus Willem. *Ancient Buddhism in Japan.* 2 vols. Leiden: E.J. Brill, 1935.

———. *The Dragon in China and Japan.* 1913; reprint ed., New York: Philosophical Library, 1972.

Vogel, Jean Phillipe. *Indian Serpent Lore, or the Nāgas in Hindu Legend and Art.* London: Arthur Probsthain, 1926.

Waley, Arthur. *Chiu Ko—The Nine Songs: A Study of Shamanism in Ancient China.* London: Allen and Unwin, 1955.

———. *The Life and Times of Po Chü-i, 772–846 A.D.* London: George Allen and Unwin, 1949.

———, trans. *Ballads and Stories from Tun-huang: An Anthology.* London: George Allen and Unwin, 1960.

Wan, Man 萬曼. *T'ang-chi hsü-lu* 唐集叙錄. Peking: Chung-hua shu-chü, 1980.

Watson, James L. "Of Flesh and Bones: The Management of Death Pollution in Cantonese Society." In *Death and the Regeneration of Life*. Edited by Maurice Bloch and Jonathan Parry. Cambridge: Cambridge University Press, 1982.

Weber, Max. *Economy and Society*. 3 vols. Edited by Guenther Roth and Claus Wittich. New York: Bedminster Press, 1968.

———. *From Max Weber: Essays in Sociology*. Translated and edited by Hans. H. Gerth and C. Wright Mills. New York: Oxford University Press, 1946.

———. *The Religion of China: Confucianism and Taoism*. Translated by Hans H. Gerth. New York: Free Press, 1958.

———. *The Religion of India: The Sociology of Hinduism and Buddhism*. Translated by Hans H. Gerth and Don Martindale. New York: Free Press, 1958.

Wechsler, Howard J. *Offerings of Jade and Silk: Ritual and Symbol in the Legitimation of the T'ang Dynasty*. New Haven: Yale University Press, 1985.

Weinstein, Stanley. *Buddhism under the T'ang*. Cambridge: Cambridge University Press, 1987.

———. "Imperial Patronage in the Formation of T'ang Buddhism." In *Perspectives on the T'ang*. Edited by Arthur F. Wright and Denis C. Twitchett. New Haven: Yale University Press, 1973.

Welch, Holmes. *The Practice of Chinese Buddhism, 1900–1950*. Cambridge: Harvard University Press, 1967.

Whitfield, Roderick. *The Art of Central Asia: The Stein Collection in the British Museum*. 3 vols. Photographs by Takahashi Bin. Tokyo: Kōdansha Ltd., 1982–.

Wilhelm, Richard, trans. *The I Ching or Book of Changes*. Third ed. Translated by Cary F. Baynes. Bollingen Series, No. 19. Princeton: Princeton University Press, 1967.

Winternitz, Maurice. *Geschichte der indischen Litteratur*. 2 vols. Leipzig: Amelangs Verlag, 1912–20.

Wolf, Arthur P. "Gods, Ghosts, and Ancestors." In *Religion and Ritual in Chinese Society*. Edited by Arthur P. Wolf. Stanford: Stanford University Press, 1974.

Wolf, Margery. *Women and the Family in Rural Taiwan*. Stanford: Stanford University Press, 1972.

Wright, Arthur F. *Buddhism in Chinese History*. Stanford: Stanford University Press, 1959.

———. "Fo-t'u-teng: A Biography." HJAS 11: 3–4 (December 1948): 322–70.

Yabuki, Keiki 矢吹慶輝. *Sangaikyō no kenkyū* 三階教の研究. Tokyo: Iwanami shoten, 1927.

Yamazaki, Hiroshi 山崎宏. *Shina chūsei bukkyō no tenkai* 支那中世佛教の展開. Second ed. Tokyo: Kiyomizu shoten, 1947.

———. *Zui tō bukkyō shi no kenkyū* 隋唐佛教の研究. Kyoto: Hōzōkan, 1967.

Yampolsky, Philip B. *The Platform Sutra of the Sixth Patriarch*. New York: Columbia University Press, 1967.

Yanagita, Kunio 柳田国男. "Senzo no hanashi" 先祖の話. In *Yanagita kunio shū* 柳田国男集. Kindai nihon shisō taikei, Vol. 14. Tokyo: Tsukuma shobō, 1975.

Yang, C.K. *Religion in Chinese Society: A Study of Contemporary Social Functions of Religion and Some of Their Historical Factors*. Berkeley: University of California Press, 1961.

Yang, Ch'eng-tsu 楊承祖. "Yang Chiung nien-p'u" 楊炯年譜. *Tung-fang wen-hua* 東方文化 (*Journal of Oriental Studies*, Hong Kong) 13:1 (January 1975): 57–72.

Yang, Lien-sheng. "The Concept of 'Pao' as a Basis for Social Relations in China." In *Chinese Thought and Institutions*. Edited by John K. Fairbank. Chicago: University of Chicago Press, 1957.

Yoshikawa, Tadao 吉川忠夫. "Butsu wa kokoro ni ari: *Hakkoku ron* kara yōshō no *irei* made" 佛は心に在り白黒論から姚崇の遺令まで. In *Chūgoku chūsei no shūkyō to bunka* 中國中世の宗教と文化. Edited by Fukunaga Mitsuji 福永光司. Kyoto: Kyoto daigaku jinbun kagaku kenkyūjo, 1982.

Yoshioka, Yoshitoyo 吉岡義豊. "Chūgoku minkan no jigoku jūō shinkō ni tsuite" 中国民間の地獄十王信仰について. In *Bukkyō bunka ronshū* 佛教文化論集. Edited by Kawasaki daishi kyōgaku kenkyūjo. Tokyo: Kawasaki daishi heikanji, 1975.

———. *Dōkyō to bukkyō* 道教と佛教. Vol. 1, Tokyo: Nihon gakujutsu shinkōkai, 1959; Vol. 2, Tokyo: Toshima shobō, 1970.

Yü, Anthony C., trans. *The Journey to the West*. 4 vols. Chicago: University of Chicago Press, 1977–83.

Yü, Chün-fang. *The Renewal of Buddhism in China: Chu-hung and the Late Ming Synthesis*. New York: Columbia University Press, 1981.

Zürcher, Erik, *The Buddhist Conquest of China: The Spread and Adaptation of Buddhism in Early Medieval China*. Revised ed. Leiden: E.J. Brill, 1972.

———. "Buddhist Influence on Early Taoism: A Survey of Scriptural Evidence." TP 66: 1–3 (1980): 84–147.

Index